THE ORIGINS
AND DEVELOPMENT
OF FEDERAL
CRIME CONTROL POLICY

THE ORIGINS
AND DEVELOPMENT
OF FEDERAL
CRIME CONTROL POLICY

HERBERT HOOVER'S INITIATIVES

James D. Calder
Foreword by George H. Nash

Westport, Connecticut
London

Library of Congress Cataloging-in-Publication Data

Calder, James D.
    The origins and development of federal crime control policy :
Herbert Hoover's initiatives / James D. Calder ; foreword by George
H. Nash.
      p. cm.
    Includes bibliographical references and index.
    ISBN 0-275-94284-8 (alk. paper)
    1. Criminal justice, Administration of—United States—
History—20th century. 2. Hoover, Herbert, 1874–1964. 3. United
States—Politics and government—1929–1933. I. Title.
HV9950.C34 1993
363.2′0973—dc20   93–20298

British Library Cataloguing in Publication Data is available

Library of Congress Catalog Card Number: 93–20298
ISBN: 0-275-94284-8

First published in 1993

Praeger Publishers, 88 Post Road West, Westport, Connecticut 06881
An imprint of Greenwood Publishing Group, Inc.

Printed in the United States of America

∞™

The paper used in this book complies with the
Permanent Paper Standard issued by the National
Information Standards Organization (Z39.48—1984).

10 9 8 7 6 5 4 3 2 1

To

Monika Wolff Calder

Shannon S. Calder

William D. and Margaret O. Calder

All my sisters (Margaret, Katherine and Carol)

and their families

"Reform, reorganization, and strengthening of our whole judicial and enforcement system, both in civil and criminal sides, have been advocated for years by statesmen, judges, and bar associations. First steps toward that end should not longer be delayed. Rigid and expeditious justice is the first safeguard of freedom, the basis of all ordered liberty, the vital force of progress."
—Herbert Hoover, March 4, 1929

Contents

Foreword

Americans have short memories which are becoming ever shorter in our media-saturated Information Age. Consider crime and the now prevalent expectation that the federal government should take the lead in combating it. Whence did this expectation arise? Many older Americans, if asked this question, would probably mention the growth of the Federal Bureau of Investigation under J. Edgar Hoover. Somewhat younger Americans would probably cite the role of national law enforcement agencies in implementing the civil rights laws of the 1960s. A few citizens might recall public concern about labor racketeering and organized crime dating back to the Kefauver hearing of the 1950s.

It is one of the merits of James D. Calder's book that he takes us on a journey deeper into our past and thereby provides fresh perspective on the frenetic present. While all complicated social policies and institutional arrangements have many roots, he contends that the decisive moment in the development of comprehensive federal crime control was the period between 1929 and 1933, the presidency of Herbert Hoover.

For those conditioned to think of the Hoover era as a time of economic adversity and political stagnation, Professor Calder's findings will come as a surprise. But, he argues persuasively, these very years witnessed a confluence of three factors that combined to produce a break with the past. The first was the proliferating stress on the judicial system, stress associated mostly with the enforcement (and non-enforcement) of Prohibition. The second was the emergence of new perspectives in law, sociology, and criminology, and the rise of academically-trained social scientists eager to apply their knowledge to reform of the legal system. The third (and necessary) catalyst was the election in 1928 of a president committed to reform and receptive to the approaches of the activist social scientists.

In examining this interplay of circumstances, theory, and political behavior, Professor Calder introduces us not only to the sensational events of Hoover's term of office—the Al Capone trial and the Lindbergh kidnapping—but to subjects that for most readers will be unfamiliar: prison reform (itself a multifaceted subject), reorganization of the federal court system, and the inner workings of the once-famous Wickersham Commission. Despite President Hoover's personal interest in these matters, and his often successful efforts to achieve constructive results, federal crime fighting at the administrative level was not generally front-page news during his presidency. As Calder notes, Hoover's initiatives in this field did not attract "high political acclaim." Nor, for the most part, have they attracted much attention from historians and students of criminal justice. The book before us at last eliminates this lacuna.

In doing so, it illuminates not only the genesis of a reorientation in social policy, but also the long-neglected contributions of an unpopular and still-misunderstood president. For many Americans today (although less so for historians), the tendency to identify Herbert Hoover solely with the Great Depression is almost Pavlovian. One of the strengths of Professor Calder's book is that it emancipates Hoover from this straitjacket. In contradiction to the once dominant stereotype of Hoover as an unimaginative, "do-nothing" chief executive, Calder reveals a strong-minded and energetic idealist. Hoover, he reports, was the first president to initiate a comprehensive national investigation of the administration of justice in the United States. He was the first president to "personally lead an organized crime investigation." His was the first administration "to give formal policy attention to federal prisons and prisoners."

Calder also demonstrates that Hoover in his way was a Progressive who believed in social amelioration through the application of expertise to public policy. He had faith in the scientific study of social problems and in the utility of statistics. He believed in the efficacy of government reorganization—a conviction that persisted through his leadership of two commissions many years after he left the White House. By emphasizing the rationalistic, melioristic, and idealistic elements in Hoover's approach to governance, Calder has reinforced a deepening perception among historians of the modernity of this complex man.

On the day Hoover left the White House in 1933, a famous contemporary asked of him: Was he the last of the old presidents or the first

of the new? On the evidence of this book, Hoover belongs in the latter
category.

Professor Calder's impressively researched volume, then, enhances
our understanding of the origins of modern federal crime control
policy and of Herbert Hoover, the man who catalyzed so much of it.
On both counts, scholars and students can be grateful.

George H. Nash

Acknowledgments

Historical authorship demands single-minded dedication to archival evidence and sensible interpretations of the past. Archival repositories and dusty collections of papers and books become, indeed, jealous lovers. The pursuit of morsels of information and the arrangement of the puzzle are not enterprises that many would not accept as useful work. But this is the historian's craft. To all those who have stood by and who have attempted to understand, both in deeds and words, I express my admiration, gratitude and respect.

My academic mentors deserve the highest admiration for their examples of intellectual achievement and collegial encouragement. The seeds of this work germinated in the patience expressed and time taken by Professors George S. Blair (deceased), Gerald I. Jordan, John P. Kenney, and Peter P. Lejins. George H. Nash, official biographer of Herbert Hoover and friend in historical inquiry, inspired completion of this project by examples of dedication and belief in his subject.

In the main, this book was a labor of love and personal funding. A seed grant was given by the board of directors of the Herbert Hoover Presidential Library Association and its former executive director, R. Lawrence Angove. Additional travel support to visit collections was provided by the University of Texas at San Antonio. To each of these organizations and the persons who signed the checks, I express my sincere appreciation.

The stalwarts of research and publication are the archivists, librarians, computer wizards, and production editors. Space does not permit a complete list of the professionals who assisted in this research

effort. In most cases I must therefore name their organizations and
hope they will understand how important they were to the outcome:
National Archives and Records Administration, Washington, D.C.,
and Suitland, Maryland; federal libraries and records branches of
the Bureau of Prisons, FBI, Internal Revenue Service, Congress, and
Parole Board; the University of Maryland libraries; the Georgetown
University library; the Stanford University library; the Honnold
Library of the Claremont Colleges; the University of California at
Los Angeles library; the University of Texas at Austin libraries; the
University of Texas at San Antonio library; the Trinity University
library; the St. Mary's University law library; the Sam Houston State
University library; the historical societies of Chicago and the State
of Illinois; and the Herbert Hoover and Franklin Roosevelt presidential libraries. To all the staff and directors who assisted my
efforts, I am indebted. Final editing and computer problems could
not have been resolved without the able assistance of my former
student and friend, Robert Behrens, and of the editors at Greenwood.

A special note of thanks goes to family, colleagues, and friends
who offered accommodations and encouragement. In particular, I
thank my loving wife Moni for her special inner strength and her
belief in me. All my family deserve a medal of valor for enthusiasm
and tolerance during my many trips to Washington. My daughter
Shannon deserves a special hug for her faith in her dad and her ever-
patient manner.

Chapter 1

Hoover's Mark on Federal Justice Policy

My own duty and that of all executive officials is clear—to enforce the law with all the means at our disposal without equivocation or reservation.[1]

Reform of federal law enforcement, court, and corrections agencies from 1929 to 1933 is a piece of crime policy history largely unrecognized by criminologists, criminal justicians, and social historians. The administration of Herbert Clark Hoover, thirty-first president of the United States, marks the origins of federal crime control policy. Hoover's crime policy initiatives merit revisitation for their larger relevance to crime and justice administration in the twentieth century. They have received neither definitive study nor formal credit, perhaps attributable to perceptions of Hoover, constricted by memories only of failed economic policies of the Depression.[2] This book explores the corners and depths of Hoover's record on crime control initiatives, thereby correcting a deficiency in the criminological record.

Rich and discoverable archives of the Hoover administration's work on crime and federal justice administration are essentially unorganized and untapped. Letters, reports, directives, memoirs, and secondary accounts are located in many branches of the federal government, including several investigative agencies, and in the federal and private libraries. The corpus of these records reflects diversity of the Hoover initiatives, and they bond the evolution of crime policy initiatives with twentieth-century advances in behavioral and social sciences. Drawing on scattered archival records of the Hoover's initiatives permits a deeper appreciation of Hoover's work to raise public confidence in, and performance of, federal justice administration.

From George Washington to Calvin Coolidge, insignificant interest had been taken in comprehensive organization of federal justice administration. Incrementally, of course, units of federal organization, such as United States marshals, federal appeals and district courts, the Department of Justice, and federal prisons were introduced to accommodate an expanding and geographically dispersed nation in which crime slowly but persistently emerged as a major social concern. Between 1870 and 1929, in particular, presidents Grant, Hayes, Garfield, Arthur, Cleveland, Harrison, McKinley, Roosevelt, Taft, Wilson, Harding, and Coolidge bypassed opportunities to introduce a complementary relationship between police, court, and prison organizations and the Department of Justice. Their incrementalist policies on justice administration reflected no malice. But the fact remains that on March 4, 1929, federal policing attracted low popular respect, federal court dockets were jammed with civil and criminal cases, federal prisons were filled beyond capacities, and the impact of new forms of crime called for new administrative organizations and new legislation. Moreover, federal agencies hardly imagined they were related to each other in a common mission.

The Hoover administration introduced a comprehensive approach to federal criminal justice administration. Hoover's managerial approach to administrative functions led to a demand for an analysis of the crime problem and its impact on federal organizations and processes. The focus on crime and justice during the Hoover presidency, supported by a Congress amenable to inquiries and facility improvements, suggested that these issues were no longer mere local matters. Economic, demographic, legal, political, and social changes had considerably altered American culture in the previous sixty years, and these alterations carried new implications for managing civil and criminal justice agencies, most especially at the federal level. Increasingly, a nation deeply invested in the notion of local government's virtues expected the federal government to provide resources to overcome transjurisdictional problems. The Hoover initiatives on crime and justice administration were the first to conceive of a range of interrelated problems requiring solutions through governmental leadership organized to communicate the best available thinking and innovative strategies for action. Indirectly, the intention was to send messages to the society that the efficiency and integrity of the criminal justice system was the first order of business and that previous negligence regarding the health of federal justice administration could be replaced by an appropriate commitment to change.

Previous administrations had introduced individual reforms, but no administration after 1870 considered formal study of the elements of improved federal justice administration, nor did they consider federal justice as a system of interactive elements. Hoover was the first president to assemble a team of practitioners and scholars to comprehensively investigate the conditions under which federal, state, and local governments administered justice. Completion of that study by the Wickersham Law Observance Commission was never intended as a definitive statement of problems associated with criminal administration. It was, however, the first preliminary attempt to introduce a way of thinking about both the complexity of crime as a social problem and the limited potential of federal authorities to encourage state and local initiatives.

Hoover's unwavering personal and political commitment to progressive reforms put experts in place to offer federal government the best available insights in the direction of this new way of thinking. His affirmative steps institutionalized thought and planning as essential prerequisites to a first-rate system of federal justice administration. He employed both in his cabinet and in key departments of federal administration the kinds of thinkers and doers who could investigate conditions requiring reform, who would draw upon leading scholars and scientific methods, who would encourage creative strategies of law enforcement and prison management, and who would remain committed to reform objectives in years after his presidency. By March 3, 1933, most of Hoover's criminal justice reforms had been achieved or staged for implementation. Legacies of the Hoover reforms have survived succeeding administrations, and some have been models for recent presidents.

I have mined archival records of the Hoover administration in numerous locations, some private files, and many public documents. In the course of twelve years of research, I have developed a favorable impression of the scope and depth of Hoover's crime control initiatives. This perspective is set before the reader. I discuss Hoover's contributions in terms of his forthright intentions to begin his presidency with an agenda for changing federal criminal justice administration and to leave office with his agenda completed. Between the two points in time, he ordered systematic investigation of specific problems of justice administration, he employed professional administrators to lead reforms and to pursue congressional support for implementation of his recommendations, and he occasionally gave personal attention to details of federal crime control operations. Hoover wasted no time drafting and announcing his appeals to the public and the Congress to give priority to his justice reform initiatives. He was fortunate, of course, to have been president at a time when popular interest lay in system reforms, but his measures were aimed at action and results at a time when they were most obviously needed. The archival records sustain this viewpoint.

This book examines only the work of the Hoover administration from March 4, 1929, to March 4, 1933, with particular emphasis on how Hoover energized action for results in terms of both scientific study and program implementation. Historical research is, of course, dependent not only upon primary records but also on experiences an author cannot truly know several generations removed. It tends to limit judgment about contemporary policy relevance. At the end of this work, however, I offer brief comments on the implications of Hoover's initiatives for future presidents who chose to engage in a close analysis of all branches of federal justice. The majority of this account is devoted to setting forth the evidence that the Hoover initiatives are important, if ignored, artifacts of crime control history. They transformed federal justice administration at a time when it was necessary to do so, and their effects, ignored perhaps for ideological reasons, have found their way into modern criminal justice policies.

Two tests of the evidence are offered in this study. First, Hoover's perspective and actions to move federal justice administration forward by measurable degrees are compared throughout with conditions and legacies of previous administrations. In this sense, Hoover is conceived as a president unhappy with the status quo of the justice system, indeed greatly disturbed by it. Second, Hoover pursued a policy of reform that reached for a comprehensive organization of the unorganized federal justice system by reform measures designed to recognize trends, rearrange agency responses to match the trends, and improve the overall quality of performance. By 1929, the electorate had been well prepared for leadership in the domain of justice administration, and in some respects it was willing to permit expansion of federal intervention in traditionally local crime matters. Hoover's policy initiatives were timely in this regard, but "the great engineer" insisted upon fulfilling the popular expectations by intellectually considered advice from those most respected in the academic and practitioner worlds of crime. Hoover's commitment to criminal justice reforms was manifested on his first day in office and sustained for the entire term. In brief, the author intends to show that no comprehensive sense of federal justice administration existed before Hoover's presidency and that what Hoover put in place in a four-year period was intelligently addressed, practically guided, diligently pursued, and demonstrably enduring.

HOOVER'S OPENING WORDS

Hoover took office on a cold, rainy, and windy day in Washington, March 4, 1929. Wiping the rain from his face, he spoke to a gathering of fifty thousand wet and ambivalent onlookers. It was the first inaugural address to be given by worldwide radio hookup.[3] The most profound feature of the address is its first substantive order of business, "The Failure of Our System of Criminal Justice." Crime and justice were unlikely topics for a worldwide audience, but the order of their invocation suggested volumes about Hoover's administrative priorities. One quarter of the address was devoted to their significance in the social order. He warned of the need to attend to the "constant dangers from which self-government must be safeguarded," referring in the second order of discussion to "Enforcement of the Eighteenth Amendment." Crime had increased, he said, and confidence in the system of criminal justice had decreased. Compensating for the independent role of government, he acknowledged that the fiber of Americans had not decreased; rather, federal justice administration could be put in better order to more efficiently enforce the law. By decrying the popular view that Prohibition had been responsible for crime and the disarray of federal justice, he urged a "redistribution of [federal justice] functions, the simplification of its procedure, the provision of additional special tribunals, the better selection of juries, and the more effective organization of our agencies of investigation and prosecution."

Reorganization of federal agencies of justice administration would be aimed at the objectives of swift and certain justice. New performance standards would be introduced at the federal level so that states and local governments could emulate federal strategies. Pointing to the intricacies of the federal courts, he complained that in some ways court rules had "become the refuge of both big and little criminals, [and] those who can pay the cost" are the people who thwart the ends of justice. The civil and criminal sides of federal justice should be revamped in order to counter "the indifference of the citizens, . . . exploitation of the delays and entanglements of the law, [and in obvious reference to organized crime] combinations of criminals." He would not allow justice to fail because of delinquency or inefficiency of the law enforcers. Remedies had to be found for "the most sore necessity of our times."

Hoover was especially clear in reminding his audience of his constitutional duty to enforce the Eighteenth Amendment. The failures of law, he recognized, could be blamed on the maladies of federal administration and a general unwillingness of state and local authorities "to accept the obligation under their oath of office." The result, further referring to organized crime, had been the development of "a dangerous expansion in the criminal elements who have enlarged opportunities in dealing in illegal liquor." A finger of guilt for the failures of Prohibition was pointed at citizens as well as governments, but he vowed to stop "those of criminal mind [by use of] vigorous enforcement of law." Correspondingly, he said he would appoint "a national commission for a searching investigation of the whole structure of our Federal system of jurisprudence," including, but not limited to, the enforcement of the Eighteenth Amendment. Transfer of Prohibition enforcement activities from the Treasury Department to the Justice Department was announced as a plan of action for improving the organization of federal efforts, but clearly a plan not open to broad consideration on the merits. Hoover concluded the address with a reminder that his election was partly a mandate to uphold "the perfection of justice whether in economic or in social fields; the maintenance of ordered liberty; [and] absolute integrity in public affairs." This mandate would be accomplished by investments in "thought, . . . conscience, [and] responsibility."[4]

The inaugural address sharpened the focus on a social problem most Americans had come to know much about in the 1920s: crime and the administration of justice. The popular belief was that crime had increased and governments at all levels had become less able to control its growth. Hoover's opinion varied from the popular view. Crime had shown signs of increase, but the magnitude of the increase required scientific determination. Furthermore, local and state enforcement of federal and state laws had deteriorated, partly because of inconsistent support for the Eighteenth Amendment and widespread violation of the Volstead Act, which had implemented Prohibition. Law observance, a recurrent but benign theme in Calvin Coolidge's public speeches, had by 1929 fallen on deaf ears. It was generally believed that a growing number of people were challenging the value of laws that could not be enforced without considerable cost both to the public treasury and to the integrity of the Constitution. Hoover understood the public hypocrisy concerning law observance and the call for reforms, but he wanted to proceed with courses of action to enlarge popular support for all laws and for redesigning governmental systems for "rigid and speedy justice."[5]

INDICATORS OF HOOVER'S INTEREST IN
THE ADMINISTRATION OF JUSTICE

It is impossible to trace with absolute certainty the motivational ingredients in a president's interest in a policy preference. In Hoover's case, the indicators of interest in crime and federal justice administration are subtle but detectable. The earliest traces appear in the years of private entrepreneurship as a mining engineer, increasing with public service after World War I. During the years as commerce secretary, 1921–1928, signs of applied interest in police and prison concerns are more pronounced, the result mainly of personal associations in the position and interests in administrative efficiencies and technologies. Naturally, no single association or event transformed Hoover's consideration of the inadequacies of federal criminal justice. Fragments of earlier lessons in crime and justice administration provided awareness of problems to be addressed. Such lessons were given by the administrative limitations of associates, peers, and political superiors; by rising expectations of the role of the government in crime control; and by demands upon his personal performance in public service. Personal views on life and responsibility blended with attitudes about law observance. A retrospective on these fragments provides some limited understanding of Hoover's sustained interest in crime and justice.

Hoover's mining career took him to projects in Asia and Australia in the 1890s.[6] After marrying Lou Henry on February 10, 1899, Hoover and his wife traveled to China. Chinese bureaucracy, he soon learned, taxed the limits of his patience. The workforce was undeveloped; basic skills and business acumen were lacking. By his Western standards of business negotiation, reinforced by his own family values and religious orientation, corruption was a dimension of business transactions to which he would require adaptation. Systemic corruption, he believed, seriously affected the ability of the Chinese to make progress in mine productivity; but it was hardly his place to alter conditions well beyond his control. He had some minor successes, however, in improving accounting and operational practices; and his two years in residence in China, 1899 to 1901, were reflected in later published articles. His pieces were replete with organization, efficiency, and the need for professional mining management. Efficiency became Hoover's main concern in professional life, and it was the key to his faith in constructing prosperity.[7]

More direct experience with corporate crime and the rigors of internal investigation resulted from Hoover's discovery of fraud in a business partner's handling of company securities. The partner had gambled company funds in the British stock market after altering company books and forging hundreds of internal documents. When Hoover discovered the collusion of at least one other company director, he was asked to take charge of cleaning up the mess and consoling victims of the fraud. Numerous legal actions followed, requiring Hoover to account for the losses and to reflect upon the security of his personal finances in the hands of unscrupulous partners. The public scandal arising from the affair caused Hoover to insist upon sophisticated accounting systems in future business ventures.[8] When the dust settled, Hoover's personal assets remained fairly well secured, but he had become keenly aware of the need to control information given to the press and to share control of decisions with those who worked alongside him and immediately in his service. He was not to be free of unethical and illegal business operators in the mining industry, and it was only through tough-minded determination to improve the operational features of mining that he managed to overcome troubles in the years between 1901 and 1908.

In 1908, finding himself free of corporate partnership and economically independent, Hoover formed a mining valuation company in San Francisco. Trudging over mountains in Burma, developing mining operations in Russia, and assisting in petroleum investments kept Hoover tied to the intrigues of corporate life in the years before 1914. There can be little question that he associated with, either directly or at some distance, men whose driving interests in fortune involved activities bordering on illegalities. Entrepreneurial adventures included occasions involving the control of corruption and requiring fair negotiations between parties to contracts. He came to expect an improvement in the professional integrity of reasonable men drawn together by engineering, science, or business interests.[9]

The years of public life began in 1914 when World War I broke out in Europe. Hoover's enrollment in the American Citizens Committee, an effort he helped organize to repatriate displaced Americans caught in Europe at the opening of hostilities, brought him in contact with both incompetent government bureaucrats and sniveling and unappreciative benefactors of the committee's work. Turning his attentions to American efforts to relieve starving Belgian refugees and using the press to stir public support, he worked around constraints imposed by bureaucratic inertia. Through stubborn refusal to seek approval for actions, he made decisions that were opposed by virtually no one.[10] His personal contributions gained worldwide attention.

Hoover's successes in administrative organization and diplomacy in the food relief program could not insure against corruption. While millions of tons of food were processed through hostile lines, some food found its way into the hands of the enemy, which opposed Hoover's relief program. Early in 1916, the system Hoover had installed for controlling corruption in food distribution was breached, attracting controversy and a measure of the inventor's wrath. More than a million tons of rice passed illegitimately into German hands. Hoover was irate. He blamed the failure on a weak Belgian system of internal regulation. His reaction, highly consistent with previous experiences in mining, was to reorganize the distribution system and impose new controls.[11] The circumstances gave indication of Hoover's impatience with the inadequate administrative systems that contributed to corruption.

Hoover's association with crime and federal justice administration expanded greatly after the war. Following an unsuccessful bid for the presidency, he was named secretary of commerce by President Warren G. Harding in 1920. Upon Harding's death in 1923, Coolidge retained him. Hoover formed hundreds of new associations, including new relationships with federal bureau chiefs and state and local officials in agencies of justice administration. In commercial matters, he set a course toward the "collectivizing of free individual initiative, a light but efficient ordering of the nation's private and local energies to national purposes."[12] He organized study commissions to bring business and government into agreement about the directions of international trade. Fundamentally, he recognized that the marketplace behavior of private corporations often resulted in monopolistic patterns, thus requiring the firm hand of government regulation. Emergence of monopolistic cartels, especially in the international arena, violated national economic interests.[13]

Hoover stood firmly against cartels created to fix prices.[14] Earlier, as food administrator, he opposed pricing fraud, employing former Secret Service agent Lawrence Richey to conduct investigations.[15] In a speech in 1924, he said, "when legislation penetrates the business world it is because there is abuse somewhere. . . . In the main . . . the public acts only when it has lost confidence in the ability or willingness of business to correct its own abuses."[16] Conspiracies of greed and power in business or government, including complicity in the Department of Justice, were flatly opposed by Hoover. His worst nightmare in this regard was played out in the massive oil lease scandal of Teapot Dome. Recognizing Attorney General Harry M. Daugherty's complicity in fraudulent schemes and malfeasances of office, Hoover urged President Coolidge to fire Daugherty to recapture integrity in the Justice Department.[17] The magnitude of corruption in the Teapot Dome affair was never forgotten by Hoover.

Included among positive experiences in the years at the Department of Commerce were his interests in organizing commercial enterprises, including the public–private interests in airwave regulation. In this area of interest he contributed to the emergence of police radio bands.[18] From 1922 to 1927, Hoover addressed the problem of how to regulate the new radio industry, a concern that culminated in the Radio Act of 1927. The industry, he argued, should retain much of the self-regulatory initiative, but order and fair division of the radio waves would ultimately be enforced by government.[19] Allocation and use of the airwaves was a necessary function of government. Dedication of a portion of the radio spectrum to police was a necessary "public benefit" strongly endorsed in police circles. August Vollmer, the leading authority on police administration, commented late in 1930 that police radio was an "invaluable means of communicating with patrolmen," although few departments had yet installed the new equipment.[20]

Hoover's interest in crime control was also influenced by his associations with key members of the federal and local law enforcement, including distant associations with Bureau of Investigation director J. Edgar Hoover and with Coolidge's second attorney general, Harlan F. Stone. Stone, requiring a new bureau director when he fired William Burns in May 1924, named J. Edgar Hoover to the position.[21] The recommendation came from Lawrence Richey, Herbert Hoover's confidential assistant, and Mabel Willebrandt, head of Justice's Prohibition enforcement and tax division.[22] Stone was well known to Hoover, both men having urged Coolidge to clean out corruption in the Justice Department.[23] Described by Hoover as an unusually superior public servant, Stone was named attorney general on Dwight Morrow's recommendation in 1924.[24] Before leaving his Justice Department post for a seat on the U.S. Supreme Court in 1925, Stone ordered broad reforms to the practices of the Bureau of Investigation. These included limiting agent investigations to violations of law, firing hangers-on and scoundrels, and instituting new standards of agent professionalism.[25] Stone's characteristics of "independence, stubbornness, honesty, and fidelity to conviction"[26] comported with Hoover's personal and professional views.

Herbert Hoover and J. Edgar Hoover, related by surname only, established a lifelong relationship beginning in 1924. J. Edgar Hoover had worked for the Library of Congress prior to becoming a young investigator with the Bureau of Investigation. His experience there was useful in his work as head of the general intelligence division, a position to which he was appointed by director William J. Flynn in 1919. In this assignment, J. Edgar gathered names and other information on thousands of alleged political dissidents and ordered publication of pamphlets warning of the so-called "Red menace." Of course, this was a time of weak presidential leadership and fear of the importation of communist conspiracy, much of it trumped up by President Wilson's attorney general, A. Mitchell Palmer.[27] Unscathed by the extremes of Palmer's raids to round up radicals in 1920, Hoover lay low, working diligently on intelligence matters of value to his bosses and to the White House.[28]

Appointment as assistant director of the bureau in the Harding administration, then director in the Coolidge years, were his last two promotions. He would die in the latter office in 1972. From all historical accounts, J. Edgar cleaned out the bureau's hacks, nuts, and incompetents in the years between 1924 and 1929, finding approval and fame in the public's insistence upon a highly limited and clean government investigative organization. J. Edgar learned early that Coolidge would not tolerate vestiges of the Harding scandals and that the greatest rewards would come from reinstating the integrity of the bureau.[29] In the early days of the Herbert Hoover administration, solicited by Lawrence Richey, J. Edgar passed information to the president concerning various organizations and individuals.[30] A reasonable cloud hovers over who, exactly, ordered the information, similar to the cloud over President Hoover's unproven involvement in a Naval Intelligence break-in of the Democratic headquarters in 1930.[31] Perhaps the most direct source of influence on Hoover's ability to get reforms organized and to maintain their forward motion was his personal secretary, Lawrence Richey. As a teenager, Richey had spied on counterfeiters for the Secret Service, and he was subsequently used as a private agent to perform illegal acts that agents were prohibited from doing. When he was sixteen, he joined the service and later served as a bodyguard for Theodore Roosevelt, himself a former New York City police commissioner. Richey met Herbert Hoover when Hoover served as food administrator; Richey and J. Edgar Hoover held memberships in some of the same social organizations.[32]

Richey has been characterized as a "sinister" man, working for Hoover behind the scenes.[33] A more reasonable view notes simply that he was devoted to Hoover's success both as secretary of commerce and as president. No evidence of illegalities or improprieties has ever been produced. Richey's background role included supplying Hoover with names and records of people recommended for cabinet or other positions; serving, although unsuccessfully, as the go-between to persuade White House Secret Service agent, Colonel Edmund W. Starling, to become superintendent of the Washington, D.C., police department;[34] and persuading a reluctant William J. Donovan (later director of the O.S.S. in World War II) to travel by train from New Mexico to Washington to meet Hoover regarding appointment as governor general of the Phillipines.[35] During the 1928 campaign, Richey traveled to England in search of documentation that Hoover had been convicted in 1902 of robbing a Chinaman.[36] As a member of the "medicine ball cabinet," Richey was nearly always present in Hoover's professional and social affairs, which included planning the summer retreat location at Rapidan, Virginia.[37] Hoover's *Memoirs* list Richey as one of several men who met his test of public service dedication: "If all men in public service were of their caliber and character, representative government would be perfect."[38]

Hoover's other strong link with law enforcement was Arthur Woods, a New York City police commissioner.[39] Retiring as commissioner in 1917, Woods worked for Hoover in the food relief program in Europe then served in the Commerce Department in 1921 to coordinate state and local actions to relieve unemployment.[40] Woods coordinated information from hundreds of cities pertaining to job opportunities for war veterans and others. According to David Burner, his work "partially restrained the traditional practice of government and business retrenchment during depression."[41] Although Hoover used him in the fall of 1930 as chairman of the President's Emergency Committee on Employment to conduct investigations of unemployment matters, Woods, described as "conscientious and sensitive," is not mentioned in Hoover's *Memoirs*. Woods, Stone, J. Edgar Hoover, and Richey were all men of intelligence, men of good education, men of criminal justice experience, and men whose reputations for hard work and efficiency had earned Hoover's attention and respect.

POLICY IMPLEMENTERS

Attorney General William DeWitt Mitchell was, perhaps, the most centrally important staff selection made for purposes of speeding along the Hoover reforms for federal justice administration. A seasoned Minnesota lawyer and "Hoover Democrat," he had served as President Coolidge's solicitor general from 1925 to 1929. He had been recognized for his astute legal mind and flair for administrative efficiency, qualities Hoover valued. Hoover met Mitchell in the course of their work in the Coolidge years, and Hoover recognized Mitchell's support for the Republican tickets in 1920 and 1924. Approval of Mitchell by Chief Justice William Howard Taft convinced Hoover that he had selected the kind of attorney general who could manage the numerous reforms he had in mind. Mitchell, argues William Swindler, like his predecessor John G. Sargent, had not "displayed great initiative in the enforcement of Federal law—although it could be said in their defense that the impossible task of seeking to make prohibition a viable constitutional principle was a thoroughly unnerving assignment."[42] In contrast, Mitchell was well regarded by Hoover: "There never was an Attorney General more able or more devoted to the uplift of the judiciary or more diligent in his primary tasks of law enforcement."[43] World War I hero and prominent New York attorney, William J. Donovan was rejected for the positions of attorney general and secretary of war on grounds of his lack of support for the Eighteenth Amendment, lack of experience, and insufficient mental capacities.[44]

Secretary of the Treasury Andrew W. Mellon had also served in the Coolidge administration. His relevance in Hoover's federal justice reforms lay mainly in supervision of the tax investigations of gangsters like Capone. Mellon, a wealthy Pennsylvania financier, had been President Harding's second choice for treasury secretary. Oddly, Hoover's selection as commerce secretary was linked to Harding's selection of Mellon, a decision in which Harding valued Hoover's administrative skills over Mellon's ability to manipulate the grand finances of the nation.[45] Hoover and Mellon did not seek each other's company, but neither escalated his ambivalences to public disagreement. Mellon, the archetypical financial snob, and Hoover, the energetic and inveterate insider, did not often communicate with each other; but each served his purpose in the Harding and Coolidge administrations.[46]

Hoover's prison reforms could not have succeeded without the appointment of Sanford Bates as superintendent of the Bureau of Prisons. Bates, said Hoover, "had made a distinguished reputation by his reform of the Massachusetts penal system."[47] Hoover asked Mabel Willebrandt for names of qualified candidates for the prison superintendency.[48] Her suggestions were favorably received, a testimony to a small pocket of residual credibility she held in her last few days as assistant attorney general in 1929.[49] Bates graduated in law from Northeastern University in 1906 and was later elected to the Massachusetts Senate. In 1917 and 1918, he was appointed as a distinguished member of the state constitutional convention, leaving state office to become Boston's street commissioner. In 1919, newly elected Governor Calvin Coolidge appointed him commissioner of corrections. His numerous and progressive accomplishments in this post included a wage bill for prisoners, the first crime prevention bureau in the United States affiliated with a corrections department, and the first special camps for male and female delinquents. He overcame political resistance to consolidate all Massachusetts jails and county houses of correction into a single agency. His rise to national recognition as a prison administrator, professional association leader, and spokesman for correctional reforms appealed to Mitchell and Wickersham.

Hoover's campaign promise to conduct a scientific study of crime and law enforcement was fulfilled by George W. Wickersham, Hoover's third choice for chairman of the Commission on Law Observance and Enforcement after both Harlan Stone and Charles Evans Hughes, the former progressive governor of New York, had declined. Wickersham had served as President Taft's attorney general, and the latter recommended him. He was a lawyer of high professional reputation who fit Hoover's need for someone with "ability, understanding, youth, energy, imagination, and established position of confidence in the country."[50]

Wickersham and Hoover held similar views on the use of the Sherman Anti-Trust Act, the former having brought suit in the Taft administration against the United States Steel Corporation and several other giant corporations. Wickersham was a man of culture who found pleasure in using government authority to regulate corporate monopolies.[51] As attorney general in 1909, he ordered the formal creation of the Bureau of Investigation to serve as the investigative arm of the Justice Department.[52] As chairman of Hoover's commission, Wickersham was not entirely trusted by the "drys," who viewed the commission's work as a way to confirm the logic of the Prohibition enforcement strategies. In public pronouncements, he had taken positions on the need for state-level enforcement of interstate traffic in alcohol, thus feeding the extreme view that federal action was futile. Throughout the course of its work, Wickersham wrote to Hoover on many occasions concerning the commission's progress, an indicator of his access on matters of reforms to federal justice practices.

STARTING UP

Hoover's inaugural address left no question about his determination to advance the development of a long-neglected federal system of justice administration. System inadequacies, worsened by contradictions of Prohibition enforcement, permeated both Hoover's campaign rhetoric and his addresses upon taking office. In a campaign speech in October 1928, he declared that the "abolition of the liquor traffic has become a part of our fundamental law and great problems of enforcement and obedience to law have risen from it."[53] Other pledges defined objectives to protect the American home, the need for revising court procedure, the importance of swift justice, and the attribution of American progress to "education, prohibition, invention, scientific discovery, [and] increase in skill in managers and employees."[54] He regularly mentioned his commitment to a probing search for facts upon which to improve federal justice. Leading his concerns were rampant nullification of the Eighteenth Amendment and lax enforcement of the congressionally generated Volstead Act.[55]

Prohibition was the unavoidable issue of 1928, "forced into the campaign by Governor Smith,"[56] but by no means more than a catalyst to broader issues of federal justice competency and efficiency.[57]

The first announcements of Hoover's crime and justice agenda emphasized appointment of a crime study commission and plans to reorganize certain federal justice agencies. A study commission would draw on intellectuals and practitioners and employ new social science information from the fields of criminology, law, political science, psychology, public administration, and sociology. Advice from all corners poured into the White House recommending topics of inquiry. Committees were formed immediately to address the central topics of investigation, including police practices and abuses of police authority, prosecution and court administration, penal institutions, probation and parole, Prohibition, the cost of crime, the causes of crime and juvenile delinquency, criminal justice and the foreign born, and criminal statistics. Hoover was convinced that the heart of the commission's potential lay in the collection of statistics on crime and the administration of justice. At the opening of the commission's work in May 1929, Hoover wrote to Wickersham: "It may be desirable to set up a statistical unit for general purposes of the Commission."[58] Wickersham took Hoover's message, and at the kickoff luncheon on May 28, he commented, "we understand there is a vast accumulation of records, including statistics, reports and other material bearing upon the administration of justice, assembled in departments of the national government and state governments, which should be examined, analyzed, classified and studied as bearing upon the matters before us."[59]

Among all the topics selected for deep investigation by the commission, Hoover was most interested in the costs of crime to the business community. He asked secretary of commerce Robert P. Lamont to make a presentation to him on how the "criminal situation" affected American industry and commerce and to provide "some comparative figures of twenty years ago." Hoover suggested to Lamont, "credit mens' associations have a pretty clear idea of what the total costs are of various crimes of misrepresentation and arson in their field, the burglary, robbery, insurance losses paid, and some estimate of the cost to banks and industries of their own police and armored cars and watchmen."[60] He followed with a letter to Wickersham telling him that Lamont could "work up a very telling presentation" concerning the costs of crime to business. He concluded that "even though it be a preliminary estimate and approximately divided into various categories, it would be an impressive thing to the country as a whole and would seem to me to be a help in aligning psychology to the general problem."[61] This final remark was indication of Hoover's need to bring the business community, so often ambivalent to progressive measures of crime control, into the dialogue.

OVERHAULING FEDERAL COPS AND COURTS

Hoover knew that a major overhaul of federal law enforcement and court administration was a long overdue advancement. Politically, of course, he could not promote such widely recognized objectives without invoking vigorous enforcement of the Eighteenth Amendment. Federal police agencies had been allowed to develop as independent bureaucracies isolated from the other functions of criminal justice. The federal judiciary was entirely understaffed for the volume of cases presented to it after passage of the Volstead Act. With the "wets" reading every line of his speeches on prohibiton, Hoover faced a dilemma in limiting the costs of government while providing police and courts with personnel in adequate supply to carry out legal and political mandates.

Caseloads in active litigation at the time Hoover came to office rendered a nightmarish quality to the tasks ahead. While pending cases remained reasonably stable in the years immediately preceding 1929, cases commenced in the first six months of 1929 rose 23 percent over the entire 1928 caseload. Moreover, new cases had increased steadily from 1926 to 1929, suggesting pressure from the Justice Department to raise the odds of convictions. Federal prison populations for June 1928, an indicator of prosecutorial and judicial activism, showed 10,068 prisoners housed in federal institutions, an increase of 20 percent over 1927.[62] Arrests for all types of federal violations rose from 65,000 in 1927 to 75,300 in 1928, declining again to 66,900 in 1929.[63] A survey of federal court activity in late March 1929 revealed 147,142 civil and criminal litigations pending in federal courts on December 31, 1928. Without question, the caseloads handled by federal prosecutors and judges had exploded at the end of the decade, in large part because of more active enforcement of Prohibition and drug control laws.[64]

Hoover acted quickly to resolve problems of prosecutorial incompetence and case delay. The Justice Department launched a screening campaign to clean out inefficient prosecutors, a relatively bloodless bath that resulted in only minor resistance from recalcitrants. Traditionally, appointments of federal prosecutors had been upon executive discretion, thus Hoover had authority to remove corrupt or incompetent prosecutors. Performance on matters involving Prohibition violations was more carefully watched, especially in the large urban districts.[65] Competent U.S. attorneys would be needed to compete with experienced gangster trial lawyers. Eighteen federal prosecutors were dismissed, mainly for failure to perform official duties, corruption, or legal ineptitude. Hoover sought quick investment return on statements he made to the press on March 8: "The first step in law enforcement is adequate organization of our judicial and enforcement system."[66] "Laxness" in prosecutorial work would not be tolerated.[67] Assistant Attorney General for Prohibition and Prisons Mabel Willebrandt was asked to submit lists of United States attorneys who should be made to toe the line.[68] Hoover and all members of the Wickersham Commission agreed unanimously "that one of the most serious defects in the administration of justice was the hampering of judges by legislation, constitutions or custom and the inefficiency of most prosecutors—as a result of selection for political reasons only."[69] On March 29, Hoover ordered investigative inquiries of several offices of United States attorneys.

New scrutiny of appointments of federal judges was also implemented. Court procedural reforms required congressional authorization, and the United States Supreme Court needed legislative authority to impose new rules in lower courts. Implementation of new controls on judicial selection and provision of new rules, argued Hoover and Mitchell, would speed the process of justice and thereby strengthen crime prevention. Experience in the Teapot Dome period had taught Hoover that clean and hard-fought investigations had little force if government lawyers were not free of taint. He also knew not only that corrupt and inefficient courts could bring embarrassment but also that their failure to advance more expeditious processing of heavy caseloads would yield an even larger docket.

THE FIGHT AGAINST ORGANIZED CRIME: CAPONE AS MODEL CASE

Herbert Hoover had low tolerance for criminal conspiracies and economic monopolies. Alphonse Capone, notorious Chicago racketeer, was the 1920s role model for organized crime and criminal cartels. Hoover entered office determined to advance efforts begun in 1928 to attack Capone's economic resources. In late 1930, he was equally determined to pursue congressional approval to strengthen antitrust laws for use against corporate corruption. "The prevention of monopolies [he said] is of the most vital public importance. Competition is not only the basis of protection to the consumer but is the incentive to progress."[70] Hoover made no distinction between Capone's power and the monopolistic behavior of corporations.

Hoover regarded Capone as a common street thug, modified slightly by a remark that "he apparently was kind to the poor."[71] Henry Pringle, a writer for the *New Yorker,* once quoted Hoover as saying, "there ought to be a law allowing the President to hang two men a year, and without being required to give any reason."[72] A facetious remark, Hoover made it at a sensitive turning point in the government's investigation and prosecution of Capone. Hoover took active and ongoing interest in the Capone investigation, and there never was any hesitation that Capone's power would eventually be checked by superior federal investigative and prosecutorial talents.

Capone, a cunning and popular racketeer, was a bane of democratic government in Chicago. He was an idol of some impressionable young minds, a master of public relations.[73] The press often billed Capone as a man of stature and photographed him with all-American football players and renowned boxers. Newsreel coverage of Capone's staged appearances with people of cultural, political, or social standing gave undue attention and preferential treatment to a man whose only aspiration was to dominate control of organized crime.[74] Hoover could do nothing about these tools of power, but Capone was vulnerable in the ways he displayed wealth and the crude techniques he used to intimidate his competition. Previous federal efforts to secure his conviction lacked political will and competent, unintimidated investigators and prosecutors. Hoover's *Memoirs* provide only a small sketch of his initiative to apply concentrated federal attention to Capone's crime group, but a trail of evidence in several government files suggests that Hoover guided the investigation from the Oval Office. Hoover said that Treasury Secretary Mellon and Attorney General Mitchell had been ordered to commence formal investigations of Capone's organization. He wrote, "a committee of prominent Chicago citizens, under the leadership of Walter Strong, the publisher of the [Chicago] *Daily News,* and Judge Frank Loesch, president of the Chicago Crime Commission, called upon me to reveal the situation in that city. They gave chapter and verse for their statement that Chicago was in the hands of the gangsters, that the police and magistrates were completely under their control, that the governor of the state was futile, that the Federal government was the only force by which the city's ability to govern itself could be restored. At once, I directed that all the Federal agencies concentrate upon Mr. Capone and his allies. Our authority was limited to violations of income-tax and prohibition laws. It was ironic that a man guilty of inciting hundreds of murders, in some of which he took a personal hand, had to be punished merely for failure to pay taxes on the money he made by murder."[75] The date of this meeting was unspecified, but Hoover's only meeting with Mr. Strong in March 1929 took place on the afternoon of the nineteenth with Claudius H. Huston, Republican party chairman.[76] Hoover's recollection also leaves out his instructions that all publicity of the multiagency attack on Capone and others was to be barred and that no expense was too great.

With appropriate strategic modifications to personnel and methods, Hoover believed, the fundamental strength of the federal investigative and prosecutorial regimes as tools of innovation against entrenched criminal organizations would prevail. He did not want to allow the kind of abuse of government authority he had witnessed during the Red Scare. Strategies against the Capone organization and other gangs were developed locally in Chicago and at the Department of Justice building in Washington.[77] On September 20, 1929, a conference was held in Washington to reach an understanding of methods and agency jurisdictions. Attendees included Howard T. Jones, acting head of the Prohibition-tax division; C. M. Charest, general counsel to the Internal Revenue Bureau; several IRB staff investigators and lawyers, and three attorneys or investigators from the Department of Justice. J. Edgar Hoover was absent, and the United States attorney for the Northern District of Illinois, George E. Q. Johnson, remained in Chicago at work on numerous criminal matters. Much of the meeting dealt with internal revenue cases launched by the Justice Department in the Chicago area against both the Capone organization and several public officials.

Agreement was reached by Justice and Treasury that Justice would seek grand jury review of cases believed to warrant prosecution but that "the Treasury Department would recommend prosecution only in strong cases in which, at the time of reference, there were no indications of grounds for compromise."[78] George Johnson, considerably surprised by the meeting's results, wrote immediately to Mitchell to demand whatever information the conferees had on hand with respect to crimes committed by those named in the meeting.[79]

FEDERAL PRISON REFORMS

So little had been accomplished by any previous administration to address the role of federal prisons in the overall equation of criminal justice or to take responsibility for a growing population of offenders of federal laws. In 1910, the federal prison population was 2,075; in 1928, it was 8,401. Throughout this period, the population was housed in the same three institutions, although there was every reasonable expectation that law enforcement in the late 1920s, including Hoover's, would produce even larger populations.[80] From the beginning, the objective had been to use prisons to change the lives of offenders. Public disregard of the isolated federal prison system, insufficient funds, and overcrowded conditions undermined this objective. Federal criminal laws passed between 1910 and 1920 added interstate prostitution ring leaders, drug traffickers and users, interstate automobile thieves, and Prohibition violators to the prison population.

Hoover, Mitchell, Bates, and the staff of prison administrators confronted two critical problems. First, it was necessary to relieve overcrowding and to provide decent and safe housing facilities. Second, existing and proposed facilities required sufficient trained personnel and program diversification to carry out a rehabilitation program. As secretary of commerce, Hoover sat on the department's prison labor committee, thereby maintaining an arm's-length awareness of conditions in the federal prison system. A combination of Quaker upbringing, fundamental acceptance of humanitarian and progressive ideals, an outline of the federal prison system dilemma, and an engineering orientation to problems most reasonably contributed to his desire to change conditions. An insistence upon the best leadership and operational management led him to accept Mabel Willebrandt's resignation and select Sanford Bates as his prison superintendent. Bates's administrative skills and knowledge of legislative politics were necessary adjuncts to compiling the reform proposals for congressional action. A new organizational structure was needed to bring centralized control over historically fragmented prison operations, and a new parole system was needed to handle the sheer volume of parole cases and relieve the superintendent of the tedium of case review. In essence, Hoover wanted federal prisons to improve in organization, physical space, and diversity of programs. By 1933, all three objectives had been achieved.

POLICY MARGINS

Presidents from Washington to Coolidge were distracted by conditions or events at the margins of their policy initiatives. Distractions from principal concerns cannot be avoided, but the test of a president's conception of the larger framework of his policy is the emphasis he gives to marginal concerns. In the main, the problem is one of time management, and concerns that sink to the bottom of his priorities are not explosive or even potentially embarrassing. Some marginal matters, however, can have major negative impact on policy objectives if not properly regarded for their timely relevance. Hoover was distracted by five marginal criminal justice issues, each of which distracted attention to or perception of criminal justice reforms: lynchings of blacks (1929–1931), the Massie murder case (1931–1932), the Lindbergh baby kidnapping and murder case (1932), Teapot Dome pardons (1929–1931), and the Bonus Army march (1932). Two of the five issues, lynchings of blacks and the bonus situation, affected the overall image of the criminal justice reform efforts.

By 1929, lynchings had become significantly less frequent than in previous decades, but social and political pressures to increase federal involvement persisted. The National Association of Colored People (NAACP), formed in 1909 on an antilynching platform, had been given passive support by several presidents, even Theodore Roosevelt whose quietly contradictory belief in Negro inferiority led many to question his sincerity in matters of racial violence. Roosevelt nevertheless angrily protested vigilante justice in 1911.[81] Wilson, hesitant to take a position early in his presidency, provided a more comprehensive statement of opposition to lynching in 1918, largely a response to Republican Congressman Leonidas Dyer's statements linking the war effort with federal antilynching policy.[82] Except for Harding's support for the Dyer antilynching law, the two administrations preceding Hoover's had not included particular attention to lynchings.[83] Racial hatred and white supremacy remained widespread and politically influential, although outside the South racial attitudes were openly discussed by candidates for office. A letter from Charles E. Swartz to Herbert Hoover in June 1929 suggested the crudity of racism: "The thing will never work down south here when the testing time comes for real action. Fren-instance [sic] a mob Hung a young Buck nigger the other night for insulting and punishing a white woman. They will hang one to every telegraph pole or tree in the country."[84]

Related in concept to lynchings and a distraction for the Hoover administration, the assault and alleged rape of Thalia Massie took place in Honolulu, Territory of Hawaii, near midnight on September 12, 1931. Thalia Massie, the young wife of Navy Lieutenant Thomas H. Massie, set out walking toward home from a club party that she and her husband had attended near the beach. She had been bored and upset at the party; her marriage was under strain. Later she claimed to police that on the way home several men abducted her, then beat and raped her. After the men dumped her on a roadside, she flagged a ride home, telling the people who picked her up that she had been assaulted. Meanwhile, Lieutenant Massie and friends searched for Thalia. He learned that she had arrived safe at home, but severely traumatized. Information she gave police combined with other allegations and events led to the arrests of Horace Ida and David Takai, American born Japanese, Benny Ahakuelo and Joseph Kahahawai, native Hawaiians, and Henry Chang, American born Chinese. Ethnicities played a significant role in the unfolding of succeeding events and in the manner in which the Navy and the press characterized the interpersonal dynamics of the situation.

Until December, events and conditions surrounding the case drew no special attention in Washington. The accused were well defended by legal counsel in a trial that began on November 21. Evidence linking them to the crime was weak. Mrs. Massie's testimony contained numerous inconsistencies. On December 6, the court freed the defendants due to a hung jury. Prosecutors announced, of course, that they would pursue a second trial, an event that never took place. Throughout this period, despite the expanding implications of the case for interracial hostility between Navy personnel and a racially mixed local population, Hoover was preoccupied with pressing problems of economic disorder. He knew he had less than one year to prove to the public that the Depression would not deepen. Hawaii was, he believed, in good hands. He had appointed Lawrence M. Judd, a business leader whose family had a long history of public service on the islands, as territorial governor in July 1929. Crime connected with discord in Hawaii had not come to his attention during his earlier years of public service.[85]

Following the release of the defendants, ensuing complications and increasing racial disharmony suggested deeper concern in Washington. Anger and racial prejudice spread among Navy personnel who believed that an injustice had been done by a jury comprised of no whites or women. High Navy officials in Honolulu and Washington fanned the flames of discord by public charges of police and prosecutorial incompetence. The local commandant and the Chief of Naval Operations instantly became the sources of press information that local officials were unconcerned with rape victims. To support their allegations, they offered the national press their renditions of more than forty criminal assaults against women which they claimed had occurred in the previous year. The obvious intention was to stir public outrage on the mainland.[86] Later, these incidents were generally refuted, but they reinforced the Navy's impressions of inefficiency in the local justice system. Further aggravating the situation were plans stated by navy men to commit retaliatory crimes against natives. A retaliation took place on December 12 when a group of sailors, including Albert Jones (a name that would reappear), abducted and severely beat Horace Ida, a crime that was intended to extract an admission of guilt. The totality of the civil unrest caused Hoover to conduct a cabinet meeting aimed at defining the elements of the situation and placing the Marines on standby alert in mid-December.

A third crisis to be faced was the kidnapping of the son of Hoover's close personal friends, Anne and Charles Lindbergh. When Anne Morrow Lindbergh gave birth to Charles Augustus Lindbergh, Jr., on June 22, 1930, the event drew national attention.[87] Hoover sent his congratulations to the new parents with whom he had formed a friendship growing out of their mutual interest in commercial air travel in the mid-1920s.[88] The kidnapping of their twenty-month-old son on the evening of March 1, 1932, shocked the nation and deepened sentiment that crime and the criminal justice system remained impotent against determined, vicious gangsters. The crime, once reported to local and state police, was immediately aired on the radio, portrayed as a bold act of organized criminals. Dozens of reporters, photographers, broadcasters, and newsreel men descended upon the Lindbergh home, each pursuing a lead that would tell the human interest story and boost audience interest.[89] New Jersey State Police director, Colonel H. Norman Schwarzkopf, took command of the case; and as Anne Lindbergh recalled, "it is impossible to describe the confusion we are living in—a police station downstairs by day—detectives, police, secret service men swarming in and out—mattresses all over the dining room and other rooms at night. At any time I may be routed out of my bed so that a group of detectives may have a conference in the room. It is so terribly unreal that I do not feel anything."[90]

Federal, state, and local investigations proceeded in earnest. Every form of technology then available was employed in the search, and even a primitive television was used to transmit the baby's picture across the State of New York.[91] The kidnapping menace had become a national crime issue. Political and media pressures were imposed upon police agencies as newspapers and radio reported record numbers of cases. By late February 1932, citizens groups across the country were contending that ransom kidnappings were no longer mere local matters and that federal aid was necessary. According to Robert Isham Randolph, head of Chicago's "Secret Six" organization, the crime was increasingly committed by organized criminals, some of whom were former bank robbers who had discovered that banks often contained less cash than they had in previous years.[92] Hoover, however, had retained his opinion that kidnapping remained a state crime requiring state initiative and cooperation. Federal policy in this regard was of marginal concern.

In the spring of 1932, on the heels of the Lindbergh case, Hoover was confronted with protests from World War I veterans. In the spring and summer of 1932, veterans streamed into Washington, delivering an untimely ultimatum for executive action. It was an election year, and Hoover wanted to avoid further restatements of his disapproval of the bonus. His need to dispense with the issue in favor of other, more pressing issues triggered a perception of unconcern. His many informal initiatives to help the most needy veterans were insufficient to appease their progressively hardening leadership. Encampments of tents and shacks sprang up in several locations in Washington on both sides of the Potomac River. A persistent barrage of demonstrations became increasingly difficult to ignore.

Military forces and police spied on the camps, building files on leaders and followers alike. Hundreds of veterans returned home with funds supplied by Hoover, but the remaining demonstrators, including wives and children, escalated the potential for riot and the spread of disease. Ultimately, Hoover's instructions to employ military and civilian police to clear the marchers from their encampments in Washington, D.C., whether or not they were carried out in the gentle spirit he intended, contradicted the spirit of his law observance reforms.[93]

The final marginal concern was generated by pardon requests from the imprisoned offenders in the Teapot Dome oil-lease scandal of 1923. Coming from people like the wealthy Harry Sinclair and the impoverished Albert Fall, they became public relations tests of Hoover's evenhandedness in pardon administration. Actually, these requests were little more than bothersome to a president committed to the highest possible standard of ethical and legal conduct in government service.

THE DIRECTION OF THIS STUDY

In the following chapters, discussion will focus on the discrete elements of President Hoover's crime control initiatives. Chapter 2 outlines Hoover's experiences during the 1928 campaign and the first year of his presidency. Chapter 3 considers the intellectual resources available to promote advancement of federal crime initiatives. Chapter 4 discusses Hoover's objective to study crime and justice administration scientifically via the President's Commission on Law Observance and Enforcement (the Wickersham Commission). Chapter 5 recounts reorganization and cleanup of federal law enforcement and initiatives to provide federal courts with competent personnel and procedural reforms. In Chapter 6, Hoover's initiatives to reduce organized crime are discussed in the context of his direct actions to secure the conviction of Alphonse Capone. Chapter 7 summarizes federal prison reforms proposed and implemented between 1929 and 1933. Marginal policy issues are discussed in Chapter 8 as distractions to Hoover's central criminal justice objectives. In Chapter 9, I evaluate Hoover's successes as the first president to give special priority to the adequacy of the federal criminal justice system.

Chapter 2

From Campaign to Crash: The Honeymoon

The Presidential campaign is a time of education of the people upon the issues of the day.[1]

The 1928 presidential campaign marked a new day in federal crime policy. Neither crime nor the failure of criminal justice had been raised to national issues in previous campaigns. The first eight months of the Hoover presidency could be characterized as a honeymoon of popular support. This period ended with the stock market crash in late October 1929. Between March 4 and the crash, however, Hoover's enthusiasm for reform and progress was endless. Expressing mild concern about inflated popular expectations,[2] Hoover forthrightly articulated positions and moved with high energy to complete his objectives. Despite later absorbing involvement in economic recovery initiatives, Hoover tenaciously pursued achievements in federal justice administration. He was convinced that social progress could proceed only under conditions of efficient and fair justice.

From Hoover's first days on the campaign trail in August 1928 through December 1929, first as candidate then as president, Hoover laid out the direction and shape of his crime and justice plans. Premises were openly revealed, although not always in explicit terms. First, social reforms—including education, child health, and housing—were linked to reforms in justice administration. Second, moderate federal leadership could engender new cooperation between individuals, communities, and professionals. Third, reforms in justice administration could spring from a plentiful supply of intellectual and practitioner advice. Finally, organizational and procedural changes would introduce efficiencies and strengthen law observance.

This chapter narrates the continuity of Hoover's criminal justice reform objectives from the campaign to December 1929. Between March and August 1929, several fortuitous events added and deepened commitment to his original plans. With the exception of the Wickersham Commission work, the annual message to Congress in December marked the end of significant public interest in Hoover's crime policies. But within Hoover's administrative team, and with the eventual cooperation of the Congress, the sustained adherence to original policies resulted in a remarkable record of achievement. At most, the honeymoon never truly ended for criminal justice reforms. At least, he succeeded in accomplishing nearly all his discrete policy objectives.

HOOVER, RATIONAL SOCIAL ENGINEER

Hoover's approach to policy formation conformed fundamentally to the theory of rational choice, which suggests that decisionmakers contemplate goals and objectives, alternatives and consequences, ultimately deciding upon that which yields the best results.[3] Most favorable outcomes are achieved when the values underlying a policy objective are clearly stated and when the policy leader clarifies the intended outcomes, the types of information needed, and the direction and phases of the initiatives.

Hoover's life to 1917 contained clear evidence of rational choice approaches to leadership and to situations posed during his years of career development. First as a young engineer, later in positions of management and partnership, Hoover was the consummate "professional" with "a more expansive sense of mission";[4] the "man of force" who had made his way by plans and self-direction;[5] and "the master of efficiency" who consistently calculated the nature of the problem before him and gathered the resources for solutions.[6] Arguably, rational choice theory cannot describe all the corners of Hoover's approaches to every problem. He surely was not an insensitive machine, and on numerous occasions, he demonstrated an ordinary level of vulnerability to bad information, a capacity to manipulate the direction of outcomes, and an awareness of fundamental unfairness.

In the long run, Hoover's systematic approach to economic policies was considered misguided and ineffective,[7] but it proved successful in shaping a new rational order to crime control policy. Solutions to this social problem of great importance to Hoover could be derived from careful analysis and the appropriate allocation of resources, an approval not unlike the solution of engineering problems. As commerce secretary, Hoover promoted government as a major source of commercial and social information. Federal government, he believed, could serve as a warehouse of information useful to particular segments of the economy and society. Hoover, says Richard Smith, "expanded the Census Bureau into an informational trove for business planners, and undertook at [President] Harding's request a study of national petroleum reserves."[8] Added to this were personal values of the socially responsible engineer, humanitarian principles, belief in social reform as a net good, and an operating methodology employing a plan of action. Each contributed to a commitment to achieving enlightened cooperation on economic and social conditions.[9] He was, indeed, "a new kind of president" with firm ideas about respect for law and personal integrity of the law enforcers.[10]

He was familiar with, although not an expert in, popular problems of alcohol and drug addiction, crime rates and crime commissions, miscegenation, poverty, theft, pornography, prostitution, organized crime, and other social blights. His early years overlapped the period of the realist chroniclers of social blight, such as Mark Twain, Frank Norris, Theodore Dreiser, Upton Sinclair, and Sinclair Lewis. These novelists introduced the intellectual middle class to forces of economics, morality, biology, race, and other conditions of life in America. Hoover's mining period and later experiences as European food administrator and as commerce secretary spanned the peak years of emerging national concern for crime and criminal justice administration, corresponding also to popular acceptance of progressive and scientific solutions. Hoover was consistently a man of action more comfortable with solutions than with mere acknowledgments of organizational and social concerns.

Hoover accepted the orderly methods of his respected engineering peers, men like Frederick W. Taylor and Henry L. Gantt, believing that most problems could be resolved by the balance of "capitalists, workers and a public represented by its national government."[11] He was tempered, however, by the humanitarian perspectives of thinkers like Mary Parker Follett, Elton Mayo, and Kurt Lewin. This was an era of progressive application of knowledge to commercial and social problems. For the first time, scientific thought had a major role in social action. Hoover's private and government service spanned the era of Taylor's 'scientific management' and the early years of the behaviorist and social science movement. By the time he had participated in the Belgian relief, by the time he had observed the excesses of counterradicalism during the Red Scare, by the time he had contemplated corporate narrowness in postwar labor-management relations, and by the time he had served as commerce secretary, Hoover held reinforced faith in the methods of engineering, information, organization, science, and technology. He aligned himself with the new wave of social progressivism that regarded as beneficial the employment of planning, organization, and information to solve human problems.[12] Government was an agent of organization to encourage individual and group actions.

Hoover, therefore, was possessed with experience in and philosophical orientation to complexities, such as those presented by crime control and justice administration. In fact, he was more prepared in this regard than any previous president. He was also determined to transform an inept, partially corrupt, disorganized, inefficient, and unprofessional collection of federal anticrime organizations. His commitment to the political "progressive center" had been clear as early as 1917,[13] and his run for the presidency in 1920 was an attempt to represent the interests of a new, socially conscious group of engineers and social thinkers.[14] His philosophical development instructed not only that individuals, business, and government were mutually responsible for developing cooperative associations to alleviate social problems but also that government held special responsibility for leadership.[15] As commerce secretary, he adhered to principles of partnership between corporate initiative and the role of government in regulating private tendencies toward monopolies.[16]

CRIME AND JUSTICE IN THE CAMPAIGN OF 1928

In Chapter 3 it is argued that the informational and scientific resources for Hoover's crime control initiatives were abundantly available in 1928–1929. These resources included theories, experiments, surveys, and willing policy implementers. The only missing element was federal leadership and political will, both of which Hoover offered the electorate. The Coolidge administration had been unwilling to expand public dialogue on crime beyond preachments about law observance. No connection was envisioned between law observance and social factors or between law observance and the structural integrity of criminal justice administration. A community of scholars and a small library of information were overlooked elements in the law observance equation. University researchers, mainly sociologists interested in crime and other social problems, as well as lawyers and police practitioners, were eager to contribute to national policies.

Coolidge did not bless Hoover's candidacy in 1927, but this failed to frustrate Hoover's bid. Consistent with the policies of his commerce secretaryship, he worked around those with limited vision and gained a reputation for expanding government's role in areas that many Republicans feared were fraught with political repercussions.[17] His strategy was to retain a low profile, awaiting encouragement and looking for someone to nominate him at the convention. By holding party standing as the most reasonable nominee, by currying favor with blacks and the National Urban League, and by favoring Prohibition, Hoover constructed a winning strategy. His name was placed in nomination by sweeping majority.[18] With promises to live up to the party platform and "to advance the moral and material welfare of all our people," Hoover launched a campaign much ignored by political historians.[19]

Campaign speeches attempted to demonstrate Hoover's renewed commitment to social progress. Ideas and applied theoretical approaches to crime and justice administration had appealed to Hoover. More significant, he believed that a combination of political persuasion, a limited but achievable social policy, and a firm stand in favor of Prohibition could defeat his opponent, Governor Alfred E. Smith. Smith was an outsider to economic control switches, and he favored revision of the Eighteenth Amendment to permit states to decide on Prohibition enforcement.[20] In 1928, crime was associated more with mismanagement of Prohibition enforcement than with the underlying futility of morals legislation. Continued experimentation through symbolic adherence to 'law observance' was favored over outright elimination of the concept. This, of course, would change in time.

Crime control issues could be slipped into Hoover's speeches with full personal sincerity and without anyone to oppose his mildly stated plans for overcoming the objections of his "wet" opponent. Furthermore, with far greater credibility than Smith, Hoover could promise to ride the tide of support for employing experts, ideas, and information in the reform of federal justice administration. Drawing on insider experience, he could promise to pull together the requisite political leadership to bridge executive and legislative functions, and he could appoint from a long list of competent experts of high integrity those with the intellectual and managerial resources to implement his plans.

Hoover acted purposefully to construct a platform for crime control innovations, and he made good use of information offered by the new social scientists. Smith could declare that he was "unwilling to accept the old order of things";[21] but it was difficult to steal from Hoover the firm, righteous commitments to uphold the Constitution and to organize a body of experts who would look into causes of crime and administrative implications of law violations. Among voters who sought continuity with the Coolidge administration but also believed in progress in federal administration, Hoover secured the high ground. In 1928, crime control reforms could be presented as achievable policy outcomes by promising an eager electorate that the best available minds would be put to the task. Moreover, federal government owed a duty to determine the best ways to improve justice administration.

Hoover's program intended a vigorous effort to reform the conditions under which federal authority had become more a part of the problem of crime than a part of the solution. Mere slogans and political exigencies were not part of the campaign strategy. He said that he would bring to his administration the best resources, portraying the experts on crime and justice as valued commodities in search of policy enhancement. It would be difficult for skeptics to challenge these methods when the core concepts had already been reflected both in the thinking and in the published works of influential theorists and practitioners.[22]

Law enforcement was ranked among other policy priorities, such as agriculture and tariffs.[23] Both candidates were expected to assert firm positions and to advocate curatives. Hoover's real advantage lay in his support for Prohibition enforcement, knowing that the enforcement regime required executive reshaping. Hoover recognized the advantage of associating 'law observance' with efficient justice administration. He articulated this position in a way that appealed to popular sentiments about the social correctness of law observance. Also, he accepted and took seriously Al Smith's claim that Prohibition's constitutional mandate could not legitimate injustices and inefficiencies in the administration of federal justice.[24]

The formal party nomination took place early in August 1928. His letter of acceptance laid out a concern for the moral role of government in the pursuit of economic imperatives. He asked, "shall honesty and righteousness in government and in business confirm the confidence of the people in their institutions and their laws?"[25] His sense was that "government must contribute to leadership in answer to these questions."[26] On August 11, his acceptance speech at Stanford University stressed economic achievements and asserted positions on crime and justice, opposing in particular repeal of the Eighteenth Amendment.

The speech included his most frequently quoted and misinterpreted remarks regarding Prohibition: a "social and economic experiment, noble in motive and far-reaching in purpose." He vowed that Prohibition could be worked out "constructively," while never making clear what he meant. He promised to follow his expectations for "efficient enforcement of the laws." He called attention to the "grave abuses" that had been carried out in the name of the Eighteenth Amendment and asserted that a solution necessitated "an organized and searching investigation of fact and causes" of such abuses, and presumably of the total picture of "crime and disobedience of law." He implied that improvements in federal law enforcement had become the keys to understanding how to preclude "nullification" of the Constitution, through either nonenforcement or mal-enforcement. Regarding the perception that the constitutional mandate for Prohibition required rethinking, he suggested that if there was sufficient support to change the law by "straightforward methods," this was preferable to the destruction of the "purposes of the Constitution by indirection."[27] Hoover's ability to frame Prohibition in the larger issue of law observance by citizens and government alike undercut Smith's ability to portray Hoover as a narrow moralist.[28]

The speech also addressed government's role in regulating some aspects of economic life and in controlling the damaging impact of business crime on free enterprise. Hoover stressed the delicate balance of cooperation and power between government and business: "It is the duty of business to conduct itself so that government regulation or government competition is unnecessary." With regard to ethics and professionalism in business, he said, "when business cures its own abuses it is true self-government, which comprises more than political institutions."[29] The proper balance in the relationship is aided, he suggested, by reorganization of agency responsibilities and authority. He made special reference to "individual officials and members of both political parties in national, state, and municipal affairs" as he emphasized a belief that corruption had often been treated with indifference "by a great number of our people."[30] Furthermore, he said, "dishonesty in government . . . is a double wrong. It is treason to the state. It is destructive of self-government."[31] The remarkable feature of these concepts was their candor. They represented Hoover's recognition of the commercial excesses of the decade, but they also served as methods for distancing himself from the greed of high officials of the Harding administration whom he knew and disliked.[32] Indeed, his public philosophy differed little from those of Theodore Roosevelt and William Taft.

Returning to crime issues on September 28 in Newark, New Jersey, Hoover argued that Prohibition, along with education, invention, scientific discovery, and employee and managerial skills, had contributed to the prosperity. Furthermore, the increased role of government in Prohibition enforcement had contributed to the rate of employment and the corresponding decline in joblessness.[33] Realistically, however, he acknowledged on October 6 in Elizabethton, Tennessee that "abolition of the liquor traffic has become a part of our fundamental law and great problems of enforcement and obedience to law have arisen from it. From the violence of the war we have inherited increases in crime. Technicalities of court procedure have been used to defeat justice and to aid law violators."[34] Hoover was unwilling to relinquish an association between alleged contributions of prohibition and more efficient administration of justice. He outlined "important national projects" and directly stated that, "the purpose of the Eighteenth Amendment is to protect the American home. A sacred obligation is imposed on the President to secure its honest enforcement and to eliminate the abuses which have grown up around it; I wish it to succeed."[35] Revised court procedures, he said, would produce swifter and surer justice.[36]

Alluding to enforcement against forms of corporate or gangster corruption, Hoover urged a balance between regulatory enforcement and suffocating bureaucracy: "Violations of public interest by individuals or corporations should be followed by the condemnation and punishment they deserve, but this should not induce us to abandon progressive principles and substitute in their place deadly and destructive doctrines."[37] He reinforced the chief executive's role in law enforcement: "The President . . . has the responsibility of co-operating with Congress in the enactment of laws and securing their enforcement."[38] Catering to a Southern audience, he concluded with the observation that "history shows that crowded cities too often breed injustices and crimes, misery and suffering."[39] He restated that the continuation of Republican policies of prosperity would "hold the hope of the final abolition of poverty."[40] Crime and other social problems were thus linked.

On October 22, Hoover's address in New York City interpreted the idea of the sale of liquor in state-licensed stores, a Smith proposal, as a form of state socialism. The idea was philosophically abhorrent to him. However, in the same speech he defended government's role in policing anticompetitive tactics of large corporations against small business.[41] Naturally, the New York vote was important. Here, Hoover avoided remarks about Prohibition enforcement or concerns for crime in major cities, saving these for the November 2 speech in St. Louis: "Shall there be secured that obedience to law which is the essential assurance of the life of our institutions? Shall honesty and righteousness in government and in business confirm the confidence of the people in their institutions and in their laws? Government must contribute to leadership in answer to these questions. The government is more than administration; it is power for leadership and co-operation with the forces of business and cultural life in city, town, and countryside. The Presidency is more than executive responsibility. It is the inspiring symbol of all that is highest in America's purposes and ideals."[42] His final speech, on November 5, 1928, delivered by nationwide radio, summarized without particulars his proposition that government was obligated to address matters of "moral and spiritual welfare."[43]

The campaign mandates imposed a new order of federal justice reforms, followed by thematic objectives. Hoover intended quantum leaps in the way government contributed to the broadest ideals of law enforcement, in the way government was expected to investigate the causes of crime, and in the obligations of federal government to achieve substantive improvements in police, court, and prison organizations. Hoover understood the limitations imposed on a president in expanding federal jurisdiction in social policy and in meddling in staunchly advocated states rights concerns for local enforcement of laws.[44] The vagaries of Prohibition enforcement made this crystal clear, but Hoover remained philosophically comfortable with widening federal law enforcement power. The federal executive's role, he believed, encompassed investigation of social problems like crime, followed by implementation of model programs for state-level replication. A corollary was government's capacity to construct a reservoir of information from which state and local governments could learn new scientific methods.

THE MAJOR SPEECHES ON CRIME AND JUSTICE OF 1929

Following his election, Hoover traveled to several countries in Latin America, taking up medicine ball on shipboard and giving speeches along the way. The "good will tour" was intended to demonstrate that American foreign policy in the next four years would be one of assistance and cooperation.[45] No speeches on crime and justice were delivered, only the occasional mention of the "purposes of government": to maintain justice, to provide for ordered liberty, to guarantee individual security, the security of the home, and the security in individual achievements.[46]

Upon taking office, Hoover demonstrated a pressing commitment to fulfilling his campaign promises, in terms both of administrative changes apart from congressional approval and of lobbying for funds and reorganizational authority. Between March and December 1929, he delivered three major addresses and one lengthy statement to the press on crime and the administration of justice. The inaugural address stressed priorities and the urgency of action he hoped the Congress would recognize: "The most malign of all these dangers today is disregard and disobedience of law. Crime is increasing. Confidence in rigid and speedy justice is decreasing." He would move speedily to enforce the Eighteenth Amendment, he would launch a national investigation into the structure of federal administration of justice, and he would transfer certain law enforcement functions to the Justice Department to bolster the enforcement objective.[47]

The second speech was delivered at the Associated Press meeting in New York on April 22, 1929. Hoover had accepted the offer to speak to the press to give "a frank statement of what I consider the dominant issue before the American people." The enforcement of and obedience to law were held out as matters "vital to the preservation of our institutions." Connecting the overall importance of law with the importance of universal support for law, he said, "A surprising number of our people, otherwise of responsibility in the community, have drifted into the extraordinary notion that laws are made for those who choose to obey them." Law, he stressed, was the key element in civilization's achievements, yet in the United States it was being selectively upheld by the citizenry while its justice system remained mired in "infirmities arising out of its technicalities, its circumlocutions, its involved procedures, and too often . . . from inefficient and delinquent officials."[48]

Joining together the concepts of a delinquent citizenry and a defective justice system, Hoover offered evidence of their impact: murder in more than nine thousand cases per year resulted in arrests of only half the perpetrators, only one sixth "of these slayers are convicted, and but a scandalously small percentage are adequately punished." Robbery, murder, burglary, embezzlement, and forgery were far more common in the United States than in Great Britain, a nation where he had lived for several years. The Eighteenth Amendment had little to do with the overall crime rate, and individuals had an obligation to enforce the law until "by the proper processes of our democracy" it was changed. His concern was to establish the standards of law enforcement, reminding his audience of newspaper reporters that "the processes of criminal-law enforcement are simply methods of instilling respect and fear into the minds of those who have not the intelligence and moral instinct to obey the law as a matter of conscience." One of Hoover's objectives would be to awaken the moral consciousness of the many, and "if necessary to segregate such degenerate minds where they can do no future harm." In essence, law enforcement held both general and special deterrent value.

The remainder of the speech set forth the missions of government: "to investigate our existing agencies of enforcement and to reorganize our system of enforcement" to eliminate weaknesses. Steady administrative pressure would be applied, he suggested, to eliminate from government service "all incapable and negligent officials no matter what their status" and by putting in office the competence necessary to build up the system. He would proceed with a reorganization of executive-branch functions and offer legislative changes in judicial procedures, reminding his audience once again that he would acquire facts from a hand-picked national commission. Conforming to the views of many professionals and academics, Hoover claimed that imbalances of the justice system favored the criminal. Clearly hoping that his tough law enforcement policy would reach publication, he underscored the view that "in our desire to be merciful the pendulum has swung in favor of the prisoner and far away from the protection of society. The sympathetic mind of the American people in its over-concern about those who are in difficulties has swung too far from the family of the murdered to the family of the murderer." He concluded with an appeal to the press to encourage values of law observance: "If, instead of the glamor of romance and heroism which our American imaginative minds too frequently throw around those who break the law, we would invest with a little romance and heroism those thousands of our officers who are endeavoring to enforce the law, it would itself decrease crime."[49]

From March to December 1929, Hoover spent a significant amount of time on matters of crime and justice administration. He was skillful in selecting his attorney general and other key staff members who would redirect the administrative endeavor within the various federal police, court, and prison functions. Under the president's executive authority, those believed to resist his desires for immediacy, efficiency, and incorruptibility were removed from office. As promised in the campaign, the Law Observance Commission was named, with all the appropriate public relations fanfare. Reorganization plans were constructed in the bureaus and departments. Regular announcements of forthcoming plans and progress reports attracted consistent press interest. Indeed, Hoover was in charge of the transformation agenda in criminal justice reform, and with the aid of certain fortuitous events beyond his control, the Congress was reminded of the need to come round to legislative action.

In fact, the major obstacle to rapid progress was congressional sluggishness. Hoover's final major address of 1929 was delivered on December 3, the annual message to Congress. He made three lengthy references to criminal justice reforms, each a reminder of congressional inaction. A section on federal prisons addressed overcrowded conditions he had warned about four months earlier. It was impossible to reconstruct the lives of prisoners to permit return to normal citizenship, he argued, under conditions of inadequate prison, parole, and probation facilities. He announced that his executive authority would be used to open temporary facilities on Army posts, but the Congress was urged to act to create a bureau of prisons in the Justice Department and to construct new institutions. Another section was devoted to Prohibition, emphasizing that proper enforcement depended upon proper organization. Shrewdly, he reminded Congress that he had suggested that it create a joint committee to collaborate in the crafting of legislation and coordination with the White House on Prohibition enforcement. He wanted immediate authority to transfer the Prohibition Bureau to the Justice Department, to simplify federal court procedures to deal with the large volume of petty cases, to codify more than twenty-five federal statutes relating to Prohibition, to reorganize border patrol functions under the Coast Guard to attack smuggling, and to grant new powers to the District of Columbia commissioners and the police to enforce the Prohibition laws in Washington, D.C.

Much like the opening words of his inaugural address, Hoover's final section lectured the Congress on the need to give equal priority to law enforcement and observance: "No one will look with satisfaction upon the volume of crime of all kinds and the growth of organized crime in our country. . . . We need to reestablish faith that the highest interests of our country are served by insistence upon the swift and even-handed administration of justice to all offenders, whether they be rich or poor." The Wickersham Commission had proceeded under congressional authority, he said; but further legislation was needed to increase appropriations for the Justice Department in order to relieve conditions that "tend to clog the machinery of justice." Encouraged by what he viewed as a new sense of responsibility, a refutation of cynicism, and a "moral awakening" to the rule of law, Hoover closed his address with an instruction he hoped would inspire action: "We can no longer gloss over the unpleasant reality which should be made vital in the consciousness of every citizen, that he who condones or traffics with crime, who is indifferent to it and to the punishment of the criminal, or to lax performance of official duty, is himself the most effective agency for the breakdown of society."[50]

In earlier months, Hoover's news conferences, called to address issues including criminal justice, reported only briefly upon actions or recommendations. His final news conference of 1929 varied greatly from the others, however. He took the opportunity to give considerable reinforcement to his annual message and to push even harder to gain congressional support. "For some 25 years or more," he said, "the Government has been steadily falling down in its criminal work." The failures of the court system, population expansion, and the broadening of the federal government's obligations in crime control were to blame. The breakdown in Washington, D.C., where the court docket was eighteen months behind in its workload, was particularly noticeable: "One effect of this enormous piling up of criminal activities of the courts has been the tendency of district attorneys to try to get relief by wholesale confessions, and the net result of that is the establishing of a sort of a licensing system by which the various offenders can go and confess and be assured of a small fine, and that puts them in a position of considerable safety."

From here, Hoover launched into an education of the press concerning the buck-passing that resulted from inadequate organization between enforcement, prosecution, and court functions. Federal detectives blamed prosecutors for failures, prosecutors blamed police, federal authorities blamed state inaction, states blamed federal inefficiencies, and everywhere was the tendency "to forego responsibility by passing it off on some agency of the government." Much of the burden in all jurisdictions of the federal government developed from minor cases that could be addressed by enlarging the authority of federal court commissioners. The Wickersham Commission would give "exhaustive consideration" to the problems it had identified in all areas of federal authority, and he hoped the Congress would codify its own committee structure to more effectively coordinate with the efforts of the commission. The list of proposals he had laid out in the previous nine months was again offered in brief form, with an added recommendation that salaries be improved. He closed with an admonition that his administration would not proceed to build up law enforcement agencies by "dramatics and sudden onslaught and fire of one kind or another." Rather, he would proceed only "step by step in the spirit of the men who have the problem in their hands . . . in the spirit of the people [and] with an adequate consideration of a century and a half of background of constitutional authority."[51]

Messages to Congress and the press were intended to muster public support in the direction of quick congressional resolution. Popular enthusiasm for his objectives had greeted his arrival. Public and official expectations were raised out of faith in rationally planned actions and enlightened ideas to guide change. Headlines and editorials raised hopes for modernizing federal law enforcement, the courts, and prison facilities. Often, of course, Prohibition was the key stimulus to justice system reforms, but the occasional wellspring of informed professional opinion served to level out the more extreme demands to focus only on the alcohol problem. After all, broad ideas for changing and improving federal justice agencies had been propounded for more than ten years before Hoover's presidency.

A third factor, less orderly in nature, was a series of fortuitous events that served as reminders to action. Beginning with the sinking of the *I'm Alone* schooner, Hoover was strengthened in his position that conditions of justice administration required improvement in the ways he had already outlined. But he also recognized that it would be necessary to address the main body of his initiatives before too many challenges came from a Prohibition-fixated Congress and before the sheer passage of time increased diversionary marginal issues.

Hoover could not control all social events affecting the pace of policy advancement. The Coast Guard's willful sinking of the Canadian schooner *I'm Alone* on March 22, 1929, heightened the tension of Prohibition enforcement. Firings of corrupt or incompetent staff in the executive branch was expected, but it was unexpected that at least one vocal U.S. attorney would refuse to leave his office without Hoover's direct action. Gangster Al Capone was arrested in Philadelphia on May 17, 1929, thus giving federal agents a ten-month breather to build cases against the Capone empire Hoover wanted destroyed. Finally, Hoover's prison reform policy, which languished through the summer of 1929, was given a boost by riots at state and federal prisons in July and August. Each of these events cast no negative shadows on Hoover's administrative management during the honeymoon period. Quite the opposite, each stirred reminders of proposals already offered in good administrative faith.

THE SINKING OF THE *I'M ALONE* SCHOONER, MARCH 1929

The international implications of actions taken by federal law enforcers came under considerable examination in the *I'm Alone* incident. Hardly any time had been available for the new administration to delve into practices of federal policing agencies before the incident. The vessel, sailing under British markings, was a known transport for booze smugglers operating between ports in Honduras, Bermuda, and other islands in the Caribbean. In fact, it was later discovered that the boat had been constructed in 1924 specifically for booze shipments; it was owned by a New York bootlegger and operated by an American speed boat expert.[52] The Coast Guard caught up to her on March 20 about eleven miles off the coast of Louisiana and ordered the captain to permit inspection. This schooner, like others used to smuggle liquor into the United States, employed sophisticated communication and coding systems that had forced the Coast Guard to install interception and decipherment machines to translate messages transmitted ship to shore.[53] When *I'm Alone* refused to stop for search, the patrol boat fired cannon shots across her bow and through her sails. Two days later, with the assistance of a second patrol boat, the vessel was sunk by repeated firings into her sails and hull, resulting in the death of one crew member. Never before had a foreign vessel been sunk in the course of Prohibition enforcement. The untimely event and its aftermath contrasted with the notions of gradual organizational improvement in the law enforcement branches.

An investigation was begun immediately between representatives of the State Department, the Customs Service, the Coast Guard, and the British Consul General. After the crew had been questioned, the U.S. position was announced: the United States had invoked the international legal principle of "hot pursuit" and provisions of the Tariff Act of 1922 to board the ship and seize illegal cargo within its announced twelve-mile territorial limits. Canada gave heated protest, arguing that hot pursuit was unwarranted beyond the three-mile limit, especially since the vessel was destroyed two hundred miles from shore. Moreover, the Canadians pointed out, the violence used to sink the ship was unnecessary.[54]

Hoover was kept apprised of negotiations, but Secretary of State Henry L. Stimson believed the United States held all the cards. Neither the British nor the Canadians were comfortable in defending a ship's crew whose activities were recognized by all parties to have been criminal in nature under U.S. law. The press in all three countries maintained a generally dispassionate tone about the incident, perhaps a wry commentary on smugglers who took chances and sometimes lost.[55] Harsh action to enforce the law, argued administration officials, had been justified by the ship captain's refusal to heave to.[56] When the press offered speculations about possible war with Canada, Hoover countered with calm firmness that an investigating commission had been appointed to look into the matter. Hoover's negotiating skills in the international setting, it has been argued, yielded formal agreements with Canada that ultimately pared back, but never completely sealed off, illegal smuggling into the United States.[57]

U.S. ATTORNEY REFUSES TO LEAVE OFFICE, APRIL 1929

One William De Groot, U.S. attorney for Brooklyn, New York, had presented problems for the Justice Department and the federal district court since 1927. De Groot, it seems, had regularly defended his staff attorneys and investigators against a barrage of complaints about defective bribery indictments, mishandling of arrest warrants, and allegations of petty graft and bribery of suspects to obtain confessions. No direct evidence of corruption was mustered against De Groot, but a detailed file alleging incompetent management had expanded from 1928 into the first months of 1929. U.S. attorney C. E. Stewart, reporting to Solicitor General William D. Mitchell in March 1928, said, "It is quite apparent that Mr. De Groot's administration

of the office has been seriously lacking both in the proper conception
of his duties and ability to see what is quite apparent to the Court and
to others—inefficiency, lack of application of their duties, and gross
and flagrant irregularities on the part of members of his staff."[58]
John B. Reynolds, another U.S. attorney on the staff of Assistant Attorney General John Marshall, also concluded that De Groot was
aware of the poor condition of his office and made no efforts to fix
it: "He looks at the morning mail, but outside of that he spends very
little time with the problems before the office."[59] He proposed that
an immediate change be made, one year before Hoover took office.

The Bureau of Investigation had opened several inquiries into De
Groot's office, and its repetitive reporting of incompetencies to Assistant Attorney General Mabel Willebrandt and several other officials in the Justice Department finally reached a level of magnitude
that Hoover was unwilling to overlook. De Groot, the bureau reported, was a rather boisterous and unthinking person who gave
misleading statements to the press. He often took credit for grand
activities of his office, claiming achievements in sharp contrast to
the observations of the federal court and the Justice Department.
Mitchell's awareness of the problems in the Brooklyn office encouraged him to take aggressive action to unseat De Groot within a month
of becoming attorney general. Preoccupied by a month of honeymoon
press releases and initiatives normally attending the first days of
any high energy president, both Mitchell and Hoover recognized the
ground that could be gained by making an example of De Groot's
misdeeds and mismanagement. The effectiveness of U.S. attorneys
was, in contrast to that of federal court judges, a matter that could
be controlled by the president and the attorney general.

On April 3, Mitchell wrote to De Groot requesting his immediate
resignation. By April 24, De Groot remained seated in his office,
determined to stay and claiming that he never received Mitchell's
notice. Mitchell fired off a specially delivered letter to De Groot, re-
newing his demand. Another week went by before De Groot wired
Mitchell saying that he did not intend to resign and demanding a
hearing on charges he believed Mitchell had in file.[60] The stalemate
would not long await Hoover's attention. After reading the Justice
Department report and learning of press interest in the outcome,
mainly from questioning during his April 30 press conference,
Hoover signed a notice terminating De Groot's employment May 1.
Shrewdly, Hoover handed his notice to the press, guaranteeing national publicity. De Groot's final desperate retort was that even the
president's notice had not been received. United States marshals
were ordered to physically eject De Groot, an end applauded in
Brooklyn.

On May 2, H. V. Kaltenborn's column in the *Brooklyn Daily Eagle* supported Hoover's persistence: "His case is significant from two points of view. In the first place, it is comforting to know that a public official can actually be removed without having committed an offense for which he ought to go to jail. This rarely happens. Too often mere incompetence in public servants is taken as a matter of course. . . . In the second place it looks as though the Hoover Administration intended to establish generally higher standards in the Federal service. Minor offices that have been filled by political hangers-on are to be administered by more competent individuals. The United States District Attorney's office in Brooklyn is called the worst in the country. No doubt it was in bad shape. But if other offices received the same detailed examination there might be some keen competition for the booby prize."[61] From the De Groot engagement, Hoover's administrative authority was never distant from the attorney general's efforts to remove unwanted and recalcitrant officials. For example, in early 1930 he wrote to Mitchell, "I understand that in the attack that will be launched on the district attorneys, the District Attorney for North Carolina and the one for Detroit will be the test."[62]

AL CAPONE ARRESTED AND JAILED, MAY 1929

The main source of Al Capone's power was brute force. His strategies employed a mix of covert intimidation of government officials and overt appeals to popular morality. The former was used during times of low attention by police; the latter found more application when street wars turned deadly or local government officials challenged his public relations. His power had been sufficient to stall legal actions by local or federal authorities and to muscle his marketplace enemies. He was remarkably capable of avoiding major tactical mistakes, particularly in view of the size of his organization and the complexity of its illegal enterprises. But on May 17, 1929, a tactical mistake bordering on stupidity put the most notorious American gangster in jail. He was arrested by Philadephia detectives inside a movie theatre on a charge of carrying a concealed pistol. Arrested with Capone on the same charge was Frank Cline (alias Frank Rio). Both were booked, arraigned, tried, and sentenced to jail within twenty hours.[63]

The efficiency of Philadelphia justice in this case remains a curiosity, especially since this was the territory of nefarious local gangsters, Max "Boo Boo" Hoff, Sam Lazar, and Charles Schwartz and since gun toting in the city where the Constitution was framed was commonplace. Capone's plea of guilty to the gun charge gave rise to a theory that he wanted a respite from racket activities because he sensed that his competitors intended to kill him and that police investigations were beginning to close in. This theory carries little credibility if one accepts the view that the St. Valentine's Day murders solidified his power and that he had just come from a meeting in Atlantic City with major mafia leaders where his turf was secured by agreement.[64]

A more reasonable view was that Capone believed he was untouchable; he could tote a gun with impunity anywhere he traveled. Even federal authorities had been unable to secure his appearance before a grand jury in Chicago. The facts and statements surrounding Capone's arrest and conviction are entirely unclear. No records have been retained. On July 1, the *New York Times* reported that Capone, housed in the Holmesburg County Prison, had appealed his conviction. The Philadelphia district attorney reported in August that he received a bribe offer of $50,000 to free Capone from jail, speculating that the gang believed it could not be refused.[65]

Capone spent ten months of a twelve-month sentence, first in the Philadelphia County Prison and thereafter in the Eastern State Penitentiary. During this period, on Hoover's orders, federal investigators organized their attack, developed leads, and installed undercover agents in the Capone organization.[66] According to Capone's early biographer, however, "Al's stay in Eastern Penitentiary, whether or not he realized it, was the happiest period of his career. In the circumscribed world of its stone walls, in his convict's garb, he won the freedom he had so long desired—freedom from fear of 'the lights going suddenly out.' He had peace of mind. He could sleep nights."[67] In light of later developments, this observation seems romantically contrived.

MABEL WILLEBRANDT RESIGNED, JUNE 1929

Amidst a whirlwind of crime control policy statements in the days following the March 1929 inaugural address, Hoover selected key personnel to fill his crime study commission and to head the Prisons Bureau and the Parole Board. Competent agency leaders and administrative staff were needed in all branches of the Justice Department and among the various commissions and committees he marked for employment of scientific methods of reform.[68] William Mitchell's selection as attorney general, a progressive Minnesota Democrat, signaled an activist legal department. The aggressive crime fighter J. Edgar Hoover was already in place at the Bureau of Investigation, having been recommended for the position of director by Herbert Hoover in 1924. Assistant Attorney General Mabel W. Willebrandt headed the Prisons, Prohibition and Tax Division of the Justice Department. The president expected major reorganization in the department's prison component, and he insisted upon a competent, recognized leader as a replacement for Superintendent of Prisons Albert H. Conner.

Willebrandt's resignation was an untidy affair. Reporters had been familiar with her stridency, and they believed that she presented the Hoover administration with political liabilities. Her reappointment under a plan to reorganize the Justice Department, they speculated, was uncertain. Through inuendo and speculation of her administrative demise, Willebrandt carried on until early April. In the meantime, she recommended Sanford Bates, the distinguished commissioner of corrections in Massachusetts, for the superintendency of the Prisons Bureau. As April passed, press articles implied only a slim chance of her survival in the Hoover administration.

Willebrandt, for all good intentions, had allowed her prohibitionist attitudes to dominate the methods she chose to enforce the Volstead Act and to manage the prison population. Her respected track record in both areas of responsibility earned an appropriate press label, "generalissimo." Opportunities to identify, pursue, and prosecute bootleggers were rarely overlooked,[69] but her initiatives had become irritants for the new Hoover administration. Hoover decided that prison reforms would be less palatable in Congress if administrative embarrassments and outright abusive actions by prison administrators or federal agents were the focus of press exposure. She was already on Hoover's list for removal for unauthorized campaign remarks, having become a political liability in the 1928 campaign.[70] She had given speeches on behalf of Hoover, both as candidate and as newly elected president, about the lengths to which the federal government ought to go to enforce the Volstead Act. Some remarks included criticisms of Democratic candidate Al Smith, associating his Catholicism with his antiprohibitionist stand.

Willebrandt's statements added the wrong message to a philosophy of law observance that had become more difficult to sustain. Moreover, Hoover had agreed with Al Smith that religion and Prohibition would not be joined in campaign exchanges. Hoover's commitment to a fundamental policy of firm and honest enforcement, adjudication, and punishment was based on a popular faith in the fairness of the justice process as a rockbed foundation of law observance. Mabel Willebrandt, perhaps too embittered by years of chasing bootleggers in cities where Democrats tended to hold political power, retained little faith in the popular view. For her, administrative expediency and aggressive undercover activities were the methods of choice to overcome criminal organizations profiting from Prohibition.

On May 6, while traveling in Chicago, she sent a stinging telegram to President Hoover's secretary, Lawrence Richey, in response to an editorial concerning a Hoover–Mitchell plan to separate the Prison Bureau from the Prohibition Bureau. Her message marked the gap in policy priorities between the Coolidge and Hoover administrations. It also offered a defense of practices that were now out of style. Pointedly, she demanded that Richey urge the attorney general to prepare a rejoinder to the editorial: "I think you owe it to me to make a statement of facts in reply that Bates was my friend appointed on my recommendation; that it is due solely to my labor and vision that the prison bureau is reclassified into a scientific major bureau. That for eight years I have made prison betterment along the best scientific lines a study and as a monument to my hard work a young man's first offender's reformatory has been established at Chillicothe, Ohio where first offenders may be segregated from hardened criminals. . . . That I have also handled the legal end of prohibition. Has nothing to do with my competency in other lines. That in prison work I was awarded the international gold medal in 1924. The same as given to President Coolidge this year and have had the approbation and support of such penologists as Hastings Hart, Sanford Bates, Burdette Lewis, Calvin Derrick, Dwight Morrow and that you as attorney general could do nothing worse for prisons than to remove from it my active support and interest and put it with one unfamiliar and uninterested in the problem. That you are glad [for the editor's] active support of Mr. Bates and prison betterment. . . . I hate to ask you for self serving statements but I cannot longer endure the belittling of my part in every accomplishment resulting from years of devoted labor in other than prohibition lines. . . . It is unjust to give you, a newcomer to the whole problem, sole credit and picture me as a danger to prisons and I think your sense of fair play will make you willing to break silence for I am convinced we can be passive in face of actual misrepresentation no longer."[71]

A week later, Willebrandt wrote again to Richey concerning a *New York World* article on her reappointment. She was moved to express her anxieties about recent events: "The only time my name was under consideration that I know of was when you and Mark Requa [a Hoover confidant] and I talked about it. Who is this Robert Barry [the article's author] anyway, and who leaks such rumours?"[72] On May 26 Willebrandt resigned. An attorney by training, she turned to private law practice in the emerging field of commercial airways law.[73] Her resignation letter was handed to President Hoover. It read, in part, "The solution [to] the problem of lawlessness is sure in your hands, and I relinquish the Prisons work with a sense of achievement in having had the Bureau made a major scientific one and having secured my friend, Sanford Bates, as its chief."[74] Hoover accepted her resignation two days later, praising her work and acknowledging its many challenges: "The position you held has been one of the most difficult in the government and one which could not have been conducted with such distinguished success by one of less ability and moral courage."[75]

On May 31 in a letter to Congressman John Richardson, Hoover put an entirely different cast on Willebrandt's contributions and the underlying tension surrounding her possible reappointment: "I think there are reasons why she should not be appointed, but she is pretty active. I don't want her stirring up a lot of people on this."[76] Hoover knew that Richardson had supported Willebrandt's attempts to stay on. Hoover, however, would not have her in his administration, and on June 3 he made a clear private statement of his complete frustration with the whole matter and his future intentions: "It is not proposed to again put a woman in the position of having to deal with criminal elements, their supporters and the wet press throughout the United States. A woman may be appointed in the Department of Justice, but some entirely different position."[77] Hoover did not oppose women in government service; but Willebrandt's style convinced him that he could not afford a woman of her verbally aggressive nature in the Justice Department, where change depended upon quiet persistence in a narrow political terrain between vigorous law enforcement and enlightened punitive sanctions.

Willebrandt had retained her position for nearly eight years. Her responsibilities were both weighty and controversial. The enforcement task, despite statistical representations, offered few opportunities for administrative closure. Successes were rare. While she did not shrink from duties she believed important, she was embittered by popular ambivalence and nullification of Prohibition. On May 28, a *New York Evening Post* editorial captured the essence of what Hoover could have been thinking: Could Willebrandt serve any longer in a cabinet department in which the image and practice of impartial justice were fundamental? She had acquired too much official power, and she had demonstrated religious zealotry. Indeed, the editorial screamed, "she lost all sense of proportion. . . . She was a symbol and inciter of political passion, and such a person, whether man or woman, cannot make a good enforcing chief."

RIOT AT LEAVENWORTH, AUGUST 1929

The last fortuitous event of Hoover's first year were riots in July and August at New York's Dannemora and Auburn prisons and at the federal penitentiary at Leavenworth, Kansas. Naturally, Hoover could do nothing about the New York situations, but the riot at Leavenworth was politically useful. Legislative proposals for additional prison facilities were stalled in the Senate and House judiciary committees, and Bates had lobbied for weeks to gain the necessary commitments for a vote on new appropriations. Recognizing that the Congress could easily bypass prison reforms for more politically appealing matters, Hoover wasted no time in reminding the Congress of needed actions. The riots had resulted from poor food, crowded conditions, idleness, mass treatment, and low-grade personnel.[78] Hoover's proposals called for elimination of these conditions. Aided by press conferences and public statements, he had the best opportunity since the inaugural address to win public favor on prison expansion. This was a fleeting chance to enlighten the public on the impact of so much law enforcement success on federal prison populations. Virtually no concern was given to the logistical implications of warehousing law enforcement's products.

Throughout the summer of 1929, while Coolidge rocked on his front porch and Al Smith busied himself on the board of directors at Metropolitan Life, Hoover was preoccupied with administrative appointments to agencies, committees, and commissions. In April and May, Mitchell and Bates worked tirelessly to complete the prison plan for congressional approval. Bates wrote to Frank Loveland, Jr., "I may say that we have set up a very ambitious and extended organization here in the office, and that is has received the unofficial approval of the Attorney General. If we can get the money to carry it out, I think you will agree that it will be a long step in advance."[79] Mitchell urged the secretary of agriculture, Arthur M. Hyde, to do what he could to set up work programs to absorb part of what he called the "intolerable conditions of over-crowding in the federal penitentiaries."[80] Meanwhile, Hoover continued negotiations with congressional leaders called to special session to address farm legislation and import tariffs.[81]

On August 1, 1929, Bates sat down to write Chicago criminologist Sheldon Glueck an upbeat note about progress toward fulfillment of his progressive ideas, noting that "things are opening up very auspiciously." The budget requests he had presented to Mitchell were large, but he believed they would be supported and that a separate organization of the Bureau of Prisons could be achieved. He praised the selections of Austin H. MacCormick and James V. Bennett as assistant superintendents, commenting that MacCormick could spend most of his time on education and prisoner welfare programs while Bennett could develop the prison industries program. He told Glueck that legislation was likely to revise the parole system, consolidate the working capital fund for prison industries, provide for a new prison, and alter the prison commitment laws. He was also hopeful that the new commission he was selected to sit on would pick the sites for two new federal narcotics rehabilitation farms and arrange for use of prison labor to build national park roads and trails.

Just five days later, after the riot at Leavenworth penitentiary, Glueck put an entirely different light on Bates's cheery report: "I was sorry to hear of the Leavenworth situation, but nobody can possibl[y] blame you for that condition. All these riots will probably result in some drastic measures for improvement at least of the housing and employment problems in penal institutions generally; and with the sympathetic attitude of the President's Commission you ought to be in a strategic position to put across many of your ideas and plans."[82]

The Leavenworth penitentiary had a designed space for approximately two thousand prisoners. It housed nearly twice that number in August 1929, and the atmosphere was tense. As the toughest of the federal penitentiaries, it housed the most difficult prisoners, including those serving sentences for narcotics, robbery, and murder convictions. The front page of the *New York Times* for August 2 read "3,700 Convicts Riot At Leavenworth; One Dead, Many Hurt." Early reports suggested that bad food and harsh discipline were the causes of major property destruction and the shooting death of one inmate. News of the riot's imminence, said the *Times*, had not leaked from the prison because of a Justice Department blackout on communications with the press. The disturbance began during the noon meal, when prisoners banged food trays, overpowered guards, and eventually brought a standoff in nearly all internal locations. Soldiers were summoned from the nearby Army post, and gunfire from the guards was random and uncontrolled. Within hours, the inmates were back in their cells, and the cleanup had begun. Attorney General Mitchell reported to Hoover on the circumstances of the riot, emphasizing the deplorable conditions requiring immediate congressional action.

On August 2, J. Edgar Hoover dispatched a bureau agent out of the Kansas City office to investigate the situation. That same day, warden Thomas B. White reported to Bates that during the noon meal several prisoners began banging their food trays and demanding something better to eat. White said that the prisoners had disliked the spanish rice, potatoes, and bread. After leaving the meal hall, some went to their cells while others went to the shoe factory where they pulled out wire fixtures and threw them out the windows. A general revolt began around 2:30 P.M. in the laundry and dining areas. White went down among approximately five hundred prisoners assembled in the exercise yard to listen to complaints. Riot guns were at the ready. When word spread that the power plant would be burned, some guards opened fire, killing inmate Mike Martinez and wounding inmates Harold McLaughlin, John Jones, and Fred Connor. White complimented the guards on their overall restraint and their work to restore order within two hours. Only $750 in property damage had occurred. White wrote, "The source of the trouble is our extremely crowded condition and lack of work and the excessively hot weather. We are so crowded that we cannot give them the proper recreation, it is true, and they don't have enough work to anywhere near work up the right kind of appetite, and food in the Harvey House would go stale under these conditions."[83]

Upon reading White's report, Attorney General Mitchell issued a press release in which he announced that order had been restored. He was disturbed by the overcrowded conditions: "It has been impossible under the present laws to provide work sufficient to take up the attention of the majority of the inmates. This situation, combined with the intense heat and the knowledge which was undoubtedly borne in upon some of these men as to prison riots in other parts of the country, are the only causes that can now be assigned for this demonstration." No mention was made of bad food, but Mitchell called for immediate congressional approval of appropriations requests to relieve congestion and to extend prison industries.

Austin MacCormick was dispatched to Leavenworth to inquire of the conditions reported, and as Bates ordered, to investigate "whether the chef is competent or careless, and whether improvements can be undertaken in the quality and character of serving" the food.[84] MacCormick picked out the real problem from among the many issues related to overcrowding and idleness, a lack of any measure of individuation: "To the prisoner his own personal affairs are naturally even more important than general conditions. When nobody has time to look into his troubles, real or fancied, you get a man who is ready for trouble and joins in like a sheep when some bolder man starts it."

Bates was impressed with MacCormick's observations regarding lack of individuation. Immediately, he wrote to all wardens urging implementation of private mailboxes to be used for prisoner communications with staff, possible use of the Army's disciplinary barracks for prisoners, increasing guard personnel to achieve a ratio of one guard for every thirty prisoners, and establishment of a position of "supervising steward" to travel between institutions to check on food preparation. Regarding the last matter, he asked MacCormick to consider "the question as to whether this person could be a woman or whether it would be necessary to have a man to properly undertake this work." The president, Bates advised, "has put his seal of approval on our expansion program. I think our work is cut out for us for the next five to ten years." MacCormick was pleased to learn that progress was in the offing, and he hoped to make better use of the disciplinary barracks at Leavenworth rather than to set up at the newly acquired Alcatraz property.[85]

After reviewing conditions at Atlanta and Leavenworth, Bates notified Mitchell that three problems required rapid attention: overcrowding, food, and paroles. Acquisition of the disciplinary barracks at Leavenworth would resolve some overcrowding, but only in the short run. The steward at Leavenworth had turned in his resignation, but it was necessary to hire a "competent steward and dietician" to ensure that there would be no skimping on the wholesomeness of the food. The kitchen was to be extended and the food supply was to be audited on a more regular basis.[86] Paroles were to be handled more efficiently to preclude processing delay and to allow inmates to appear before the parole board to get feedback on their cases. The mailboxes would permit direct communications between inmates and either Bates or the attorney general. Mitchell was pleased with Bates's recommendations and the professional manner of handling the Leavenwoth incident.

A CRIME POLICY IN MOTION

Few could argue in December 1929 that the previous nine months had not been filled with energy, the language of reform, and purposeful actions to bring ideas to action. In particular, Hoover insisted upon readjusting the way the public thought about its responsibilities for law observance and pointing out repeatedly how the federal government could be transformed from reactionary ingredient in the problem of crime to a limited but efficient element in the solution. His early plans for studying crime and improving the federal justice system were neither thoroughly articulated nor eloquently arranged for public consumption. His campaign speeches reflected neither particular special insights into the richness of social and behavioral study nor of awareness of the diversity of thinking about crime and justice throughout the 1920s.

During the campaign, it would have been politically unwise for Hoover to give a more refined delineation of the approaches he intended to take toward crime and justice system reforms. He faced an electorate in 1928 that was not at all aware of the complexity of the justice system and of the massive, rapidly expanding studies of criminality. In general, the electorate contemplated crime in quite shallow terms, but with slow progress in the new social science community reform proposals. Moreover, the degree to which the people appreciated the collection of ideas and proposals of the social science community was problematic. No real basis of understanding had been provided by previous office seekers. Indeed, presidents, police, and judicial and correctional officials had never undertaken the responsibility for educating the public or in mobilizing support for reforms. Hoover's actions in this regard were therefore innovative.

In 1928, Hoover was probably unclear about the role he would play in bringing public attention to crime and justice reforms. The one clear fact is that once in office in 1929 he wasted little time in constructing general policies of reform relevant to all aspects of the federal justice system, and he insisted upon the acquisition of knowledge from the best minds—mainly in the fields of law, sociology, political science, and psychology—and from a diverse cadre of current and past practitioners in justice administration. A sophisticated body of knowledge and group of experts were in place at precisely the time political leadership was needed to push a comprehensive reform agenda.

Chapter 3

Intellectual Resources for New Policy Initiatives

Criminology . . . draws information, to be sure, from a great variety of specialized investigations—physiological, psychological, legal, chemical, economic, statistical, educational, and sociological.[1]

Herbert Hoover was not a criminologist. Neither was he an expert in federal justice administration. Public service in the Belgian Relief Program and his years as commerce secretary, however, had introduced him to Newton Baker, Lawrence Richey, George Wickersham, William Mitchell, Mabel Willebrandt, Max Lowenthal, Arthur Woods, each becoming a key insider in his presidency. In turn, insiders introduced Hoover to distant but respected experts in the new behavioral and social sciences. By 1929, Hoover's affiliations with intellectual and practitioner resources ranged across law, criminology, penology, public administration, judicial procedure, and police administration. A trained appreciation of scientific method deepened his respect for the social sciences and belief in the possibilities for scientific inquiry into social problems.

This chapter discusses the legacy of neglect in federal justice administration that, by 1929, had been subjected to probings by academic and justice system experts. Thinkers and doers had aimed criticisms at police organizations, the courts and prisons, juvenile delinquency, and organized crime. They could be found at leading universities and research organizations in departments of criminology, law, political science, psychiatry, government, psychology, and sociology and in police and welfare departments, courthouses, and prisons. Each gave special attention to inadequacies in criminal justice administration, and many published research findings in professional journals and books. Each was enthusiastically committed to reforms in justice administration, and their accumulation of scholarship was becoming popularly acknowledged. Linked by personal appreciation and association to the richness of these resources, Hoover was presented in 1929 with an opportunity to make substantial progress in criminal justice by tapping these resources for scientific inquiry and policy formulation.

FEDERAL JUSTICE AND LEGACIES OF NEGLECT

Hoover and his key insiders, Attorney General William Mitchell and Law Observance Commission chairman George Wickersham, were prepared to set a new tone for federal criminal justice reform. Hoover's plans to accomplish what no previous administration had contemplated, however, could not overlook legacies of neglect in the area of federal justice administration. These were legacies imposed by the policies of earlier administrations and congresses; laws covering federal crimes; agency performance histories; and entrenched bureaucratic practices among police, courts, and prison agencies. Hoover's intentions were to transform agency performance and administrative procedures and to apply new intellectual and practitioner resources to overcome these legacies of neglect. Unquestionably, federal justice was in disarray on March 4, 1929, and the new president set a course of marked improvement.

The Constitution's Framers had not installed a comprehensive system of criminal justice, including multiple law enforcement agencies, specialized courts, and prisons. The Framers sketched only a faint outline of federal justice administration on European models, but definitions of crimes, laws, and judicial processes and administrative and jurisdictional structures remained unclear and uncodified.[2] The times were comparatively simple in terms of population size, density, and rural–urban mix. Travel was slow, technology was primitive, and commercial relations operated by basic methods of exchange. Heinousness of offenses varied from ordinary theft to violence and civil disorder to conspiracies, but frequency of occurrence and territorial dispersion posed no burden to a modestly constructed federal government. Federal crimes and their associated punishments were defined in the 1789 Crimes Act, but no detailed provisions were made for prosecutorial, sentencing, or prison functions.[3] This resulted from the general philosophy that state courts could handle most litigations of a federal nature, leaving the federal courts more as political entitities than as triers of fact or appellate reviewers of state court actions.[4]

Criminal acts against the mail system—including burglary, robbery, theft, and use of the mails in fraud conspiracies—were frequent enough for Congress to create a postal inspection service in 1836. New protection for the mails served mainly the interests of the middle and upper classes who could afford mail service.[5] The postal investigative force was almost immediately overtaxed by the creativitiy of criminals and gangs, especially after the expansion of railroad transportation of mail.

A market for phony currency had developed early in the nation's history, but counterfeiting became a high art by the opening of the Civil War. The impact of phony money on banking interests and the U.S. Treasury combined with Lincoln's need to maintain the integrity of the currency system. Added to this was fraud by war implements companies. Lincoln's assassination advanced development of a secret service function, formally developed in 1865. The service was partly an intelligence agency and partly a law enforcement body that depended upon inept and often shady efforts of private investigators to infiltrate counterfeiting rings and to identify potential assassins.[6] With exception of the Postal Service and the Secret Service, however, the Union objective of sustaining the federal structure did not contemplate a unified federal police agency.

After the Civil War, however, the relaxed nature of crime and federal justice administration changed markedly, demanding discrete organizations of federal police, court circuits, and prisons. The Department of Justice, created in 1870, also did not contemplate a federal investigative staff. It was installed as a cabinet department to litigate cases in the federal circuit courts, many of them brought by southern blacks seeking to enforce the Civil Rights Act of 1866.[7] The Ku Klux Klan's criminal acts, including all forms of terrorism and lynchings against southern black empowerments, were squelched mainly by federal troops, not by investigative national police authorities.[8] The Secret Service was charged with infiltrating and repressing the klan, mainly in 1871, but with the sharp decline of federal prosecutions and the loss of political will to sustain the intent of the enforcement acts, service chief Herman C. Whitley followed the tenor of the times and offered recommendations to pardon numerous klansmen.[9] As late as 1881 and the assassination of President James Garfield, the Secret Service worked mainly against counterfeiters except during inauguration periods. Not until threats had been made against President Grover Cleveland in 1894 and the later assassination of President William McKinley in 1901 was serious political attention given to the president's security and to identification of people bent on killing the chief executive.[10]

From 1789 to the late nineteenth century, the United States Marshals Service was the major federal police authority, placed mainly at the disposal of the federal courts. U.S. marshals did not attract respect, and disrespect centered on the fee system for paying deputies and on internal corruption and freewheeling abuse of authority. A negative image, garnered from government officials and the Congress, did not affect the marshals' successes against outlaws in the unorganized territories.[11] Their work had always been limited to law enforcement at the edges of civilization and, until 1900, in Indian country and along federal borders. Their reputation among participants in the labor movement worsened with their role in suppressing union activity during the railroad strikes of the late nineteenth century.[12] The creation of the Bureau of Investigation in 1908 and the separation of the investigative function from ordinary law enforcement froze development of the Marshals Service and stymied popular respect in the quest for exclusive identity.[13] As Calhoun has observed, "At their best, the marshals comprised a loose confederation of independent judicial districts. At their worst, they were a collection of private fiefdoms concerned only with affairs in their own area."[14]

The dawn of the twentieth century witnessed new aggravations of the federal law enforcement situation. Criminals were increasingly adept at using transportation systems, the mails, the automobile, the telephone, and various techniques for defrauding the money system. In response, new laws on drugs, interstate transportation of women for illicit purposes, tax law violations, stolen automobiles, espionage, and alcoholic beverages were handed to the few federal law enforcers for action. New levels of law enforcement involvement were employed against illegal immigration, public land fraud, and antitrust violations from Theodore Roosevelt's administration forward. Congress constructed the Bureau of Investigation and the Intelligence Division of the Internal Revenue Service in recognition of the limited abilities of the Secret Service, the postal inspectors, and the U.S. marshals to curb criminal inventiveness and mobility. Correspondingly, it became increasingly necessary to introduce branches of existing law enforcement agencies specializing in criminal intelligence information as weapons against the highly secretive nature of many criminal conspiracies, such as tax fraud, organized crime, and internal subversion.[15] There were many grades of respect for new law enforcement organizations, and the bottom rung was occupied by the Justice Department's customs mounted guard (known as the border patrol after 1924). Chinese laborer smuggling to the railroad construction camps was among the customs service's difficult tasks. This agency gained respect when liquor smuggling on the Mexican and Canadian borders increased.[16]

Prohibition's stresses on federal law enforcement, courts, and prisons gradually overpowered their resources and compromised their original missions. The larger the economic stakes to criminal conspirators, the greater the pressures on agents to overlook violations or to use violent enforcement methods. Money and criminal power brokerage in major urban areas brought federal cops to ordinary street police work. As administrative and political pressures bore down on agencies to produce enforcement results, liquor law violators and citizen bystanders were killed or injured with greater frequency. Occasionally, a hail of gunfire injured prominent or respected citizens, including a U.S. senator.[17] Escalation of violence deepened academic and professional concerns for abusive police practices and the competence of the men hired as federal agents. Reforms introduced into large local departments, for example New York City's police department,[18] implied that citizens had developed a new interest in political initiatives to control police. Federal law enforcement remained relatively free of popular criticisms but no less culpable. As the 1920s neared closure, political concern focused more directly on issues of abuse of force and corruption among federal law enforcement personnel.

Apart from Prohibition, other stresses that threatened the integrity and performance of federal law enforcement and courts included automobile theft, international smuggling, and organized crime. Drug trafficking and interstate transportation of stolen vehicles necessitated improved record-keeping systems, special training, and overseas personnel deployment. Racketeering created special problems for federal police weakly prepared to confront large and sophisticated criminal cartels. Adaptation and new skill development were slow to emerge. By 1928, organized crime had become a federal and urban political issue.[19] Federal agencies, limited in their authority to act in local matters, were targets of disdain, having failed to effectively enforce Prohibition and other federal laws. Ideological commitment to local jurisdictional crime control and the rhetoric of cross-blaming for enforcement failures further stalled advancement among federal agencies.

Federal courts and prisons also filled up with a diverse collection of criminals. Parole and probation systems retained small staffs, and budget resources for these pressure-release functions were not balanced with caseloads. Furthermore, little detailed information on the scope of federal criminal justice agency operations appeared in the press. Law observance was polite cover for a seething failure of social institutions and a symbolic platitude for Prohibition enforcement. Public knowledge of the dynamics of crime's impact on federal jurisdiction and the limits of law, police, and judicial functions was rarely considered. On Prohibition law enforcement, urban politicos verbalized support for the law while ignoring gross violations. Arrests were made, stills were busted, politicians gave speeches, and the consumption of alcohol continued. Oddly, federal police and courts, ill prepared in all departments, were considered popularly as the enforcement agents of final hope, particularly among moralists and local political pessimists.

The new mandates for federal involvement in crime control reflected three major developments. First, criminal techniques had advanced from earlier periods when bank robbers, counterfeiters, and cattle rustlers occupied the time of law enforcers. Second, geographic distribution of crime, aided by the emergence of new criminal organizations in all regions of the country, made state boundaries largely irrelevant. And third, the automobile, the truck, and eventually the airplane gave mobility to criminals, thus encouraging new law enforcement communications links between states, as well as other new technologies for countering distance and time. From 1870 to 1920, federal law to aid local authorities was slow in responding to these developments, justified mainly in terms of strengthening morality and observance of the law. With snail-like speed, a small bureaucratic framework grew up around the laws. Expansion of restricted interstate authority virtually guaranteed institutional conflict and disorganization. Standards of personnel selection tended not to follow civil service themes, thereby allowing employment of people who were less intelligent or more corrupt than their criminal targets. Indeed, not until the end of World War I, did any call for greater coherence in the federal system of justice appear to be taken seriously. The catalyst for greater coherence turned out to be not rational planning but reaction to the stresses of Prohibition.

AN EMERGENT FEDERAL CRIMINAL JUSTICE AGENDA

Although local police departments became operational fifteen years before the Civil War, the federal government saw no need to introduce centralized investigative force. Secret services and advanced military and civilian undercover investigative techniques followed developments in criminal geography and sophistication.[20] Internal threats associated with new bank and train robbers, money counterfeiters, gun smugglers, thieves, and labor organizers became sources of entrepreneurship for persons who had worked for Union or Confederate military intelligence or who opened companies of private detectives.[21] Industrialists opposed to worker unions employed detectives and uniformed forces to undercut organizing movements, particularly in areas where local police were few in number.[22] Private detectives, local police, military intelligence agencies, and newly formed federal investigative branches maintained loose networks of communication in the late nineteenth century, often exchanging information about criminals and spies.[23] By 1918, a "flying squadron" intelligence unit had been formed in the

Department of the Treasury to determine the sources of moonshine whiskey production. It was composed of former military men.[24] Developments in undercover work, including the use of new technologies of detection, resulted in new case law to legitimate the expansion of secret law enforcement work.[25]

The Volstead Act, for all its spirited intentions, speeded recognition of enforcement absurdities when the constitutional mandate contradicted street level popular support. How might state and local governments be expected to provide uniform, fair, and humane enforcement of a law that was, at best, unevenly accepted? Moreover, how could federal authorities expect to achieve the objectives of a law that required close attention to all border entry points, to thousands of towns and villages, and to millions of potential manufacturing or distribution locations. Presidents Harding and Coolidge gave little official attention to the gradual weakening of political commitment to Prohibition, and neither was willing to persuade Congress of the need to radically increase the number and size of agencies engaged in policing the manufacture, transportation, and sale of alcohol products. Shouldering the burdens of an unclear political atmosphere, enforcement personnel frequently crossed agency jurisdictions to serve priorities placed on Prohibition enforcement, thereby draining respective agency resources. Until 1927, Prohibition Bureau agents were not governed by civil service rules, thus permitting acceptance into service of many incompetent, patronage-seeking men with little interest in career or professional duty.[26]

Progressively, accommodation of the geographic spread of duties weakened any sense of uniform administrative command and control. Fresh opportunities for corruption were also presented to hundreds of new, untrained, poorly paid agents in the Border Patrol, the Customs Service, the Prohibition Bureau, and the Coast Guard. Abuses of authority, emanating from agent greed or crude authoritarianism, increased in frequency and consequences. Federal men with badges and guns broke down doors, searched and seized private property, beat up and shot suspects, and continued to justify their proper and improper burdens through a law of questionable social value. Violent use of authority in arresting and questioning suspects was, of course, not new to police organizations at any jurisdictional level. Increases in reported incidents of innocent bystander shootings and "third degree" investigative practices during the 1920s were indicative of agency hunger for enforcement results and seething frustration with the overall problem. Since Hoover was elected partly for his stand in favor of Prohibition enforcement, the only option for saving the law's intent was to introduce practices of administrative control, consistency of organizational purpose, and methods of discipline across federal service.

Four major factors influenced demands to change these conditions. First, disarray in most federal justice bureaus at the end of the 1920s was clear evidence of low administrative standing and policy neglect. Second, few measures were proposed to address problems of federal justice, and there was no comprehensive plan for linking constitutional prescriptions concerning individual rights with police practices, prosecutorial behavior, and keepers of punishment facilities. Third, no intellectual resources had been invested in the evaluation of federal justice organizations. Finally, between 1900 and 1928, presidents failed to acknowledge the emergence of new forms crime, especially organized crime, and applications of new technologies and strategies to counter criminal invention and entrepreneurship. Indeed, federal law enforcement and criminal procedure had not advanced very far beyond its status at the end of the Civil War.

Burdens upon federal justice administration demanded new political resolve to accommodate the weight of social change. Only glimmers of recognition of the expanded burdens upon federal justice agencies appeared in the dialogues between Congress and the presidents after 1870. Naturally, federal political processes could reasonably have been expected to ignore some conditions of social change in the post–Civil War years. The nation, after all, remained ambivalent about federal structure. The pace of domestic development clearly outstripped political will, most evident from the slow administrative response to new forms of crime, such as human and drug smuggling, auto theft, and organized crime.

Intellectual investment in federal justice administration had rarely been contemplated since 1789. Multiplication of crime problems after the Civil War and a barely recognized need to coordinate federal criminal justice agencies resulted in the creation of the Department of Justice in 1870. In the 1890s during congressional investigations of private detective organizations employed as federal law enforcers, some slight concern was expressed for a need to centralize investigative authority. Other indicators of interest appeared in congressional discussions attendant upon construction of federal prisons at Atlanta, Leavenworth, and McNeil Island; in congressional concerns about the role of the Bureau of Investigation; and upon creation of the Division of Prohibition, Prisons and Tax in the Justice Department. In the main, however, presidents had not interpreted their duties to include contemplating the future of federal justice institutions or plans for agency expansion. None considered that the growth of the population would demand new resources, including new agencies, more personnel, and modernized procedures. Systematic study of such possibilities was not even a remote idea, thereby assuring that federal justice would remain merely reactive.

INFLUENTIAL THINKERS AND DOERS

By the mid-1920s, however, the situation had changed. The demands of federal justice administration had closed in on presidents, especially the frequency with which they were required to consider expanded budgets for the Justice Department and pressures to add other investigative agencies. Influential scholars of crime and justice studies, including Harry E. Barnes, Robert H. Gault, Edwin H. Sutherland, Frank Tannenbaum, Roscoe Pound, Zechariah Chafee, and Sam B. Warner, had published their inquiries into inadequacies at all levels of justice administration. Practitioners such as August Vollmer and Sanford Bates were leading their respective professions in police and prison administration, also occasionally publishing ideas and trends.

When beckoned by the Hoover administration to participate in the formulation of federal justice reforms, some like Roscoe Pound became influential insiders, while most others served only as consultants to Hoover's Law Observance Commission. Professors of political science and sociology, such as Charles E. Merriam of the University of Chicago, Raymond C. Moley of Columbia University, and Edwin H. Sutherland of the University of Illinois (later Chicago), and several law professors and practitioners — most known to one another — comprised an information network for locating other scholars and studies. Their backgrounds were as diverse as their approaches to crime and justice topics, but their net influence was measurable and enduring. Some, like Moley and Raymond B. Fosdick, became philosophically committed to New York's Governor Franklin Roosevelt, thus drawing away from direct input to the Hoover policies as time passed from 1929 to 1932. Some, like Harry Barnes, chose to remain distant from inside participation for ideological or professional reasons.

First among influential scholars was Harvard Law School's Dean Roscoe Pound.[27] From 1906, as a young dean of the University of Nebraska Law School, Pound goaded the American Bar Association with his description of the "sporting theory of justice," a game in which lawyers give priority to beating the law over pursuing truth.[28] For the next twenty years, Pound spent much of his time calling attention to the procedural nightmare of the criminal justice sytem. In 1921, Pound and law colleague Felix Frankfurter, conducted a systematic study of criminal justice in Cleveland, offering a year later the first urban crime commission treatise on the legal aspects of criminal procedure and their influence on justice system efficiency. The incremental processes of justice were, for the first time, recognized as interrelated phenomena. Particular attention was given to system leakage, principally through frequent plea bargaining.[29] This was also the first occasion in which statistical evidence was used to demonstrate that the law had not been administered fairly.

In 1924, Pound published *Criminal Justice in America,* a collection of three Colver lectures he had given the year before.[30] The single most important characteristic of these lectures is their multidisciplinary nature, giving particular recognition to the social sciences as academic activities worthy of equal standing to the legal profession in the study of crime's impact on society. Pound referred to "criminal justice" within the larger framework of "social control." Criminal law was treated as a vehicle for "securing interests." Ineffectiveness of the justice system stemmed, he argued, from a variety of cultural, economic, historical, and institutional factors; and specific obstacles to improvement could be found in "democratic ideas," "attitude of the press," "disinclination of rural communities to heed the difficulties of the cities," and the "propensity to needless regimentation of conduct." The last difficulty was a reminder of his long-term view that procedural aspects had become far too complex. In succeeding years, Pound and Frankfurter emphasized the weakened condition of justice delivery, particularly in urban areas. They attributed poor administration of justice to procedural entanglements, political influence, unqualified personnel, and inefficient court organization.[31] The Cleveland Crime Commission was one of several such commissions which provided models for organized studies of crime on the part of governments seeking policy applications. Scholars and practitioners who served on them were, by 1929, seasoned researchers available for the rigors of investigating federal criminal justice problems.

Pound offered three improvements: the "development of preventive justice" (i.e., "the fullest team play between legal and other social agencies, between jurisprudence and the other social sciences, between lawyers and social workers"); "systematized individualization" (i.e., the systematic study of crime causation through the "cooperation of social scientist, psychologist, physician, and lawyer"); and "a balance between the general security and the individual life" (i.e., a focus upon civilization instead of individual personality or political organization as the goal of the politically ordered society). Perhaps the most appealing idea for the Hoover administration's consumption came in the last sentence of the lectures. Following reference to the ideal of contribution by both "spontaneous free individual action and collective organized effort," Pound wrote, "As this mode of thinking becomes general, the paths of criminal justice will be made straight."[32]

Less well known, but no less influential was Edwin H. Sutherland, assistant professor of sociology at the University of Illinois in 1924, the year his classic work titled *Criminology* first appeared in print. Sutherland began his crime studies three years earlier at the suggestion of a senior colleague in sociology. He moved to the University of Minnesota in 1925 where he stayed until 1929, then to the University of Chicago as a full professor. Each move among major departments of sociology in the Midwest contributed to Sutherland's recognition as one of America's leading criminologists. Chicago's president greeted his appointment in August 1930 as a forward move "to strengthen the university's crime-study program."[33] In 1929, Sutherland was at work on a new theory of crime and social conflict.[34]

Crime and its prevention and control were, perhaps, the most frequently discussed social issues of the decade. Academics were, quite naturally, attracted to these issues since they implicated deeper and wider social problems. Industrialism and urban corruption had already created natural research laboratories in inner-city areas in Boston, Chicago, Cleveland, Detroit, New York, and Philadelphia. Social blight, including crime and maladies of the justice system, was readily available for investigation and policy application, especially in cities where urban universities were located.[35] Work dealing with these problems was appearing in the leading journals of scholarship in political science, psychology, social work, and sociology throughout the decade. Departments of social and behavioral sciences, and of a new field of public administration, contained both young faculty and those who had already reached their prime years of intellectual achievement.

Professors like Harry Elmer Barnes and Frank Tannenbaum provided rich sources of information about diverse considerations in crime causation and problems of American criminal justice. Barnes was professor of historical sociology at Smith College from 1923 to 1930 and professor of economics and sociology at Amherst College from 1923 to 1925. Throughout the 1920s, his reputation as a dynamic teacher and scholar secured many short lectureships at the New School for Social Research, University of Oregon, University of California, University of Wisconsin, and Cornell University. Before 1929, he had published nearly a shelf full of books.[36] Without question, Barnes was a major contributor to popular knowledge about crime; and in his published work he insisted upon incorporating history, social studies, and economics. The collection of his published articles, the range of his professional associations, and his many travels to foreign countries provided an impression of a man with limitless energy, yet one who held sincere commitment to the spread of sociological thinking about social problems.[37] He was not unlike Frank Tannenbaum in eclecticism. In 1920, Tannenbaum drove from New York to San Francisco to carry on research at state prisons, producing in 1922 in a book titled *Wall Shadows: A Study of American Prisons.* When it was completed, he traveled to Mexico to survey land and economic conditions.[38] Neither Barnes nor Tannenbaum served as an active participant in the Hoover research agenda, but their progressive ideas were additional sources of influence upon others.

Behavioral science, social psychology, public administration, and specializations in political science were all new fields of scholarship. They were represented by scholars like Sheldon Glueck, who led the school of theory aimed at constitutional defects, mainly applied to juvenile delinquents; W. F. Willoughby, Brookings Institution director of government research; William E. Mosher, professor and chair of Syracuse University's School of Citizenship and Public Affairs; Frederic A. Ogg, professor of political science at the University of Wisconsin; Howard W. Odum, director of the Institute for Research in Social Science at the University of North Carolina; Lent D. Upson, secretary of the Detroit Bureau of Governmental Research; Samuel C. May, professor of political science at the University of California at Berkeley; Luther Gulick, director of the National Institute of Public Administration;[39] Herman Adler, state criminologist of Illinois; Alfred Bettman, attorney and former consultant on the Boston and Cleveland crime studies; Hastings Hart, director of the Russell Sage Foundation; Bernard Glueck, Sing Sing Prison psychiatrist; William Healy, director of the Judge Baker Foundation; and Robert H. Gault, associate professor of psychology at Northwestern University.[40] And Charles E. Merriam was professor and chairman of the political science at the University of Chicago, one of few from his discipline who took an early interest in studies of organized crime. As a former Chicago alderman, Merriam was familiar with Chicago's vice activities, somewhat disappointed in the mid-1920s that other academic disciplines had been given the credit for discovering its impact on city government.[41]

Besides Roscoe Pound, who by 1929 was under fire for his brand of sociological jurisprudence,[42] legal authorities interested in the linkages between justice administration, crime and the law were plentiful. Diversity of philosophical approach and research methods introduced a spirit of controversy in the late 1920s that helped to bring criminal justice issues to the foreground of juriprudential consideration. Some thinkers, like Felix Frankfurter, had been persistently activist in their views that the law must consider judicial behavior and that lawyers had a professional duty to point out injustices in the name of law. From his law faculty position at Harvard, Frankfurter put his signature on a report opposing Attorney General A. Mitchell Palmer's tyrannical behavior against radicals in 1920.[43]

Zechariah Chafee had also signed the report criticizing Palmer. Most of the lawyers had already achieved formal recognition as litigators, academicians, or jurists. Chafee had published a pathbreaking but greatly criticized work in 1920, *Freedom of Speech*, in which he argued for free speech both as a safety valve against conspiracies and violence and as a representative of the balance of social and individual interests.[44] Chafee was both academically and professionally experienced, becoming professor of law at Harvard in 1919 after working for his family's profitable founderies, as a practicing attorney, and as chairman of the Commission on Coal and Civil Liberties. Ray Moley at the Columbia University government department, participated with Pound and Frankfurter in research on prosecutorial practices, warning in 1930 that "it is not the power of discretion that should be the concern of students of criminal justice but the manner in which it is exercised."[45]

Sam Bass Warner played an important role in the application of statistics to crime analysis.[46] Warner was professor of law at Syracuse University and took leave in 1930 to the Harvard Law School where he worked on the Wickersham Commission study. He had practiced law in San Francisco and held several other teaching jobs from 1915 to 1929, including professor of law at the University of Oregon, Thayer teaching fellow at Harvard, and visiting professor of law at Northwestern University. He served as an aerial observer during World War I. From 1922 to 1926 he was director of research of the American Institute of Criminal Law and Criminology, and he later became a staff member of the Harvard Crime Survey. Warner had developed an excellent reputation in the field of statistics and crime research during the 1920s. In addition to his activities with the American Institute, he served as chairman of the committee on criminal law statistics of the American Prison Association; and with Sanford Bates he organized schedules for use by the U.S. Census Bureau to collect penal institution data. The work of Bates and Warner eventually served as the American Prison Association model for compiling statistics for reformatories, penitentiaries, and state prisons.[47]

Influential doers included Arthur Woods, August Vollmer, and Sanford Bates, all progressive agency heads with ideas about the organizational factor in crime control. Progressive police reform appeared in the writing of Arthur Woods, former New York police commissioner and author in 1918 of *Policeman and Public*. August Vollmer, the Berkeley, California, chief of police, ranks among the most memorable proselitizers of police reform. Between 1917 and his election in 1921 as president of the International Association of Chiefs of Police (IACP), Vollmer was internationally recognized for his innovations and organizational leadership, influencing police department reorganizations in San Diego, Los Angeles, Kansas City, Detroit, and even Havana, Cuba.[48] In particular, one cannot refer to the history of California police agencies in the twentieth century without consideration of the contributions of Vollmer.[49] By 1929, August Vollmer was generally considered the leading authority on the scientific selection and training of police officers and on methods for reorganizing and improving police departments. His published articles reflected progressive innovations planned and implemented in his tenure as the Berkeley, California, police chief.[50] Each piece expressed Vollmer's passion for adding police reforms to the other reforms in the new 'good government' movement, and each was founded on principles of professionalism, scientific detection, and organizational design.[51] Other innovations included new crime reporting procedures; regularized and proactive community contacts; criminal characteristics or 'M.O.' system; procedures for fingerprinting arrestees; handwriting and chemical analyses for documentary evidence; the Berkeley Police School; police officer mobilization by means of bicycles, motorcycles, and automobiles; and assistance in development of the polygraph machine.[52] His IACP acceptance speech detailed a list of remarkably innovative initiatives, some of which did not have universal acceptance among his colleagues. For example, he argued for expanded employment of policewomen; wider use of all available technologies and training techniques to "meet the criminal with better tools and better brains than he possesses";[53] comprehension of the causes of crime; uniform crime classifications; simplified and efficient court procedures; and solicitation of universities to offer "training of practical criminologists, jurists, prosecutors, policemen, and policewomen."[54] As David Johnson summarized, "Knowledge, technique, and bureaucratic centralization were fast becoming the hallmarks of Vollmer's drive for police professionalism."[55]

Sanford "Sandy" Bates was trained in law, graduating cum laude from Northeastern School of Law in Boston. In 1915 he became a Massachusetts state senator, serving with distinction as a member of the Massachusetts Constitutional Convention from 1917 to 1918. He was then asked by Governor Calvin Coolidge to serve as Boston street commissioner and in 1919 to become Coolidge's commissioner of corrections for Massachusetts. As commissioner, Bates urged state legislation to achieve wages for prisoners, to establish the first official crime prevention bureau connected with a prison, and to establish the first facilities for male and female "defectives."[56] He worked diligently to consolidate the jails and houses of correction in Massachusetts, a task that attracted hard political resistence from county groups with vested interests in perpetuating inefficient rules and practices for the housing of offenders. Throughout the 1920s, Bates was extraordinarily active in the American Prison Association, and he was elected to the presidency of the organization in 1926.

Bates's theoretical views of penology sought outlets through leadership in professional organizations and publication in academic circles. These factors aided his recognition in both academic and professional worlds. By 1925 Bates had achieved national recognition in penology, indeed become a major spokesman for penological reform. He had served on numerous committees of the American Prison Association (later the American Correctional Association). In 1925, he was elected vice president of the American Institute of Criminal Law and Criminology, appointed to the convention of the International Prison Congress, and served on the executive committee of the American Crime Study Commission. After his election as APA president in 1926, his opening address at the annual convention called for the development of a "protective penology."

The application of this concept required (1) the collection and analysis of prison, probation, and parole statistics; (2) the pursuit of new knowledge about crime through cooperative and sensitive efforts of all officials in the administration of justice, "prosecutors, police officials, psychiatrists, newspaper men, business men, social workers"; and (3) an emphasis on crime prevention aimed at repairing the "social structure" and "community conditions which conduce toward crime."[57] With all his formal credentials in the community of penologists, plus knowing Hoover from his service on Commerce Secretary Hoover's Committee on Prison Labor, no other candidate for federal prison director had Bates's advantages. That his writings received narrow attention was due mainly to the pace of his professional schedule. During service in Massachusetts, however, he found time to commit some of his thoughts to paper for publication in the pages of the American Prison (later Correctional) Association *Proceedings*. Prisons and emerging themes in correctional reform were not topics of wide popular reading in the 1920s; but within the circle of influential prison scholars and practitioners, Bates' found a place to make significant contributions.

Bates's professional philosophies ranged far and wide, but there was a consistency to their perspectives on correctional objectives. He believed that construction of the criminal law was "not due solely to the prevalence of crime but is simply one manifestation of a general social tendency." The society, he argued, was not more criminally inclined than earlier generations; and no crime wave had been encountered during the 1920s, a view not shared by several members of the Wickersham Commission.[58] Consistently, Bates argued that more could be done to improve crime prevention methods and that such efforts were more economical in the long run than the construction of prisons and the employment of police.[59] He believed that prison treatment programs were not complete answers to correcting criminal behavior: "With the large majority of the inmates of adult prisons the irreparable damage has been done and as to this proportion of those inmates the great opportunity of any prison is to pass on to future generations the lessons learned from the failures of its predecessors."[60]

The prison, Bates believed, was a place of short-term "protective penology" from which the public cannot reasonably expect protection if the criminal comes out worse than he went in: "The temporary protection to the community is more than offset by the subsequent danger from an individual who has become more lawless and more of a menace." Change in the individual character could occur only by "removing physical handicaps to success," teaching a trade to minimize economic pressures, individuating offender classification, releasing the most qualified prisoners under supervised parole, and permanently segregating defective or incorrigible criminals.[61] A combination of professional service and written communications, therefore, raised Bates' profile among those likely to be called on for formal study of specific proposals. Correctional reforms implemented in Massachusetts brought national recognition from the prison management community. The key measure of his influence lay in the responses he got to urging formal links between politicians and prison administrators.[62]

IDEAS AND EXPERTS IN SEARCH
OF A NATIONAL AGENDA

The most prominent mandates of crime studies in the 1920s were the development of theoretical foundations and the acquisition of accurate and representative statistics. Crime studies aimed at developing a new theory of social causation to replace nineteenth-century biological theory. Theory development expanded in several directions. Crime statistics was a relatively new field of study, and systematic collection and analyses had only begun in academic institutions and agencies of government. Advances in crime theory paralleled the gradual growth of statistical collections. The meandering progress of criminological theory, however, and expanded applications of statistical tools, concurrent with demand for new action plans, were key factors in the potential for misguided social science. This development, of course, was not contemplated by the spirited new intellectuals of crime research.

Unlike current concerns for applying tests of statistical adequacy to questions of policy evaluation, the demand for theory and statistics in the 1920s was an effort to enlarge the credibility of an emerging subscientific endeavor.[63] Intended uses were mainly the measurement of public agency performance and the provision of marginal outlines of social problems.[64]Indeed, the observation was made that "statistical measurement of crime and the administration of criminal justice [were then] where the statistics of health and mortality were a generation ago."[65] Little progress had been made to improve criminal statistics between L. N. Robinson's groundbreaking work in 1911[66] and 1927 when IACP adopted resolutions favoring police statistics.[67]

Edwin Sutherland's first edition of *Criminology* was, perhaps, the single most important contribution to crime theory in the 1920s. Sutherland was heavily influenced by the work of Gabriel Tarde, one of the early analytical sociologists whose theory of social imitation suggested that criminal behavior may result from a human need to copy a model of action believed to be acceptable to others.[68] The social environment, said Robert Gault in his interpretation of Tarde, "impresses itself upon the features of the criminal, but most of all upon his disposition."[69] Sutherland asserted an associational dimension of crime as a "personal and group phenomenon," thus fundamentally "sociological" in its method. Analytically, the study of crime was rooted in the origin and enforcement of laws.[70]

Sutherland's text was applauded by Harry Barnes as "the most important . . . one-volume manual which has yet been prepared on the joint and related subjects of criminology and penology."[71] Perhaps somewhat overstated, the text at very least was the first significant attempt to craft sociological explanations of crime. Sutherland, said Barnes, was "candid and courageous in criticizing the anachronisms and abuses of our criminal procedure and prison administration without lapsing into cynicism or being disheartened. . . . The clue to the crime problem and its solution is in careful study of the causes of crime and the methods of their elimination. Prevention and reformation are the only positive fields of action which can enlist the interest or secure the respect of the enlightened student of criminology."[72] Befitting the era, Sutherland sidestepped economic explanations, despite the fact that his graduate training had included a heavy dose of political economy.[73]

Edwin Sutherland's work at Minnesota and at Chicago reflected clear social and political contexts. There was no question of his philosophical attachment to reform, in terms of both the individual and the administration of justice. Chapter 24 of *Criminology*, "Methods of Reformation," assumes the existence of two types of criminals: "those who can be reformed by known methods and those who cannot be reformed by known methods."[74] He had little patience for the latter class, while emphasizing that a "salvaging" of the first class would result from "increasing our knowledge of the methods of reformation" and through a social decision that "those who have a good prospect of reformation should be dealt with in a different manner."[75] In the remainder of the chapter he pointed out "conventional criminal policy" and contrasted it with a collection of "new system" characteristics designed to individualize punishment and treatment of offenders.

Included among proposals for justice system reforms were court organization and unification; "clearing-houses and psychopathic laboratories"; indeterminate sentences; parole and probation; prisoner classification; prisoner self-government; prison education and training; and state farms for misdemeanants.[76] In essence, although not new, Sutherland aimed at the obsolescence of the old ways of punishing prisoners that were not comprehended in terms of economic or social purposes. His final chapter, "Prevention of Crime," argued that "punishment is, at best, a method of defense; prevention is a method of offense." The larger context of prevention was stated crisply: "If we deal with that whole set of social relations, we shall be working to prevent crime."[77] Sutherland was recognized also for contesting the "conventional method of prevention" by harsh punishments thought to have no connection with individual deterrence.

A professional colleague of Sutherland's, Thorsten Sellin, assistant professor of sociology at the University of Pennsylvania, was one of several scholars to stress the need for refining statistics for measuring crime's impact on society. Sellin was introduced to criminological studies by accident, having finished graduate school in 1921 in labor economics.[78] Through teaching experiences and a growing interest in crime research, he acquired a grant to visit Europe for one year to study legal concepts in Paris and the records of the early criminologists. The May 1926 issue of *Annals of the American Academy of Political and Social Sciences* carried an article of Sellin's, "Is Murder Increasing in Europe?" His stated objective was to provide an answer to the question of whether or not the violence in the United States was unique in comparison with similar cultures with similar legal systems. This carefully qualified piece reflected his extensive work to gather and report statistical data on murder in a systematic manner. Appearing in the same issue was an entirely different kind of report, "A New Phase of Criminal Anthropology," in which he discussed the work of endocrinologists to renew interest in some of

Cesare Lombroso's biological explanations of crime. He was reserved and neutral in his commentary about limitations of endocrinological findings, but he closed the piece diplomatically with: "It is . . . fitting that this new orientation of the study of the relationship between organic structure and criminal conduct should come from the land of Lombroso."[79]

Other scholars, such as sociologist Fred Haynes and John Gillen wrote extensively about the social context of crime. Haynes also published a text titled *Criminology* which opened with a chapter titled "Social Responsibility for Crime." His strident views on social causation were evident: "Lack of provision of opportunities for suitable recreation produces juvenile delinquency. Our prisons probably train more criminals than they deter or reform."[80] His crisply stated solution echoed the work of so many others of his generation: "Unless we are going to kill all of our criminals, or keep them shut up for life, there is only one way to protect society from crime. That is to discover why the individual commits crime and cure him of his impulse to do so. This calls for remedial measures and for the resources of all the sciences bearing on human conduct. In such a program punishment will play only a minor part. With this must go a program that will keep people from acquiring the states of mind that end in crime."[81] Two sentences near the end of the final chapter, "Prevention," capture Haynes's central theme: "Unless we provide for the social needs of our people, we shall be confronted with the problems of crime, vice, vagabondage, and abnormality due to bad environment. To paraphrase Wells' statement—that the preservation of modern civilization is a race between education and catastrophe— we may say that the prevention of crime, or its measurable reduction, is dependent upon a race between social research and a growing social disorganization, resulting from the infinite complexities and confusions of our modern industrial world."[82]

John Lewis Gillen was professor of sociology at the University of Wisconsin when he published the first edition of *Criminology and Penology* in 1926. His perspective on social causation was made explicit in the final chapter, "A Program of Treatment and Prevention." Pointing to a discriminatory aspect of the justice system, Gillen concluded that the punishment and treatment aspects of penology have "disregarded the welfare of the individual and sacrificed large numbers in the supposed interest of the state, at the same time allowing others to escape."[83] Furthermore, he warned of the paucity of involvement of psychology and sociology "in the campaign against crime," leveling his deepest criticism of crime research—that it had depended on "antiquated methods founded upon an unscientific basis."[84]

Gillen's views urged that attention be given evaluating what the society hoped to achieve by imprisoning people in institutions where the criminal's outcome may be worse than was expected by the intended punishment. Prisons, Gillen acknowledged, were abnormally difficult places for the keepers and the kept. He wrote that across the country physical facilities were rapidly degenerating. Prison food was of such low quality that mental and nutritional problems had increased. The "irregular life" of prisoners encouraged immorality. Institutional labor systems were "ill-organized and inefficient." Repression of normal human communications produced monotony in the daily routine, and official use of spy or informer systems encouraged mistrust at the expense of prisoner reform.[85] The net outcome, he concluded, was a society that could not be proud of its prison system and could not make productive lives for criminals. He urged substantially more individualization of treatment by enlightened prison staff and management trained in prison psychology and social psychology.[86] Legendary trial attorney Clarence Darrow contributed to educating the public about conditions producing injustice in American prisons. Long recognized for his defenses of unpopular people and causes, Darrow published articles and books on his first-hand observations of prison conditions and the need for a reevaluation of American popular commitment to justice. In *Crime: Its Causes and Treatment,* Darrow argued that penal institutions were not equipped to carry out remedies or individualize prisoner reeducation.[87] He insisted that a prisoner's ability to overcome a ravaging combination of "heredity and environment" demanded individual care.[88] Institutional effectiveness, he concluded, depended upon recognizing the mix of environmental and genetic factors that produced criminal behavior without subscribing to any particular view as to the percentage of either that might have induced any one individual's criminality. Darrow was convinced that society and the justice system had failed to recognize the inutility of punitive institutions. Institutions, he argued, must nurture in criminals and society a fundamental sense of "human responsibility." Punitive prisons sent the wrong message.

Numerous inputs came from the University of Chicago's department of sociology where the greatest single density of theoreticians and practitioner-academics were housed. The publication in 1928 of *The City: The Ecological Approach to the Study of the Human Community* by sociologists Robert Park, Ernest Burgess, and Roderick McKenzie established the leaps and directions in the new field of geography and crime. Burgess and Park carved the City of Chicago into five concentric circles, each of which represented a stage in a continuous process of invasion, dominance, and succession as customs and values about community move from the inner (central business district) zone to the outer zone of "commuters." As an early theory of the social and criminal evolution of communities, it considered such factors as community, ethnic succession, and crime mobility. The work of Clifford Shaw in *Delinquent Areas* followed on the heels of the Park, Burgess, and McKenzie studies, setting in motion the idea that environment and juvenile delinquency were related in important ways.

Beginning in 1923, Walter Reckless organized studies in the Chicago area dealing with the impact of commercialized vice. Publishing *Vice in Chicago* in 1931, Reckless summarized his several research investigations as "part of several correlated studies of urban community life in Chicago."[89] The research was ecological in its orientation, arguing that vice enterprises resulted from "the underlying forces which determined the growth of urban community life."[90] Chapter 10, "Remedial Possibilities," acknowledged the proposition that law enforcement, even "in its most effective form can only reduce to a minimum the evils of commercialized vice."[91] Here, Reckless stressed that vice followed the pace of urban social changes (e.g., mobility, leisure time, population, neighborhood life, freedom of women, and the breakdown in the "caste of the prostitute"), tended to locate in "disorganized neighborhoods" where police activities were low, and outpaced suppression tactics because of an inability of "political heritages which lag behind modern exigencies."[92] His concluding thoughts called for a stronger working relationship between the police, private citizen groups, and the state attorney's office to build better administrative records of vice activities and to guide injunction and abatement law enforcement. Ultimately, however, Reckless argued that community rehabilitation efforts, which had made some progress under the direction of social work thinking, required more study as a way of ensuring that "a program of community reorganization [was] suited to the particular area. . . . Perhaps instead of making their programs fit the area, they are trying to make the area fit their programs."[93]

Juvenile delinquency had become a focus of concern in the 1920s as it appeared that increasing numbers of urban youth were seeking paths to crime by way of criminal gangs. Frederick M. Thrasher's study *The Gang* was published in 1927, one of several books in the University of Chicago Press's sociological series devoted to research intended to uncover new social findings and new methods of social science discovery. Thrasher, professor of educational sociology at New York University and member of the advisory committee on criminal justice for the American Institute, studied 1,313 gangs in Chicago in multidisciplinary fashion but never specified his methodology for the study, presumably relying on police reports, public and private crime commissions, social welfare agencies, and street observations. The study attracted attention largely because of the paucity of insight into this new social concern, the fact that it attempted a confluence between the social psychology of group behavior and the ecological studies of Burgess and Park, and its firm conclusions about the potential for redirecting gang behavior into socially acceptable behavior.

Thrasher's chapter titled "Attacking the Problem" suggested that the key to understanding gang behavior lay in the breakdown of the family in large, urban areas mainly populated by immigrants. The redirection of youth away from the "care-free activities of the gang [required] a high degree of intelligence and understanding on the part of any leader or agency." He urged the development of police workers trained in redirection of gang members toward "substitute activities," such as boys clubs and scout groups, instead of the normal preoccupation of police with gang suppression. He insisted that gang members should be dealt with as persons with particular social needs that form the basis of their gang affiliations, instead of merely as social outcasts. He recommended a total reform of institutions for delinquents, specifically the removal of corporal punishment and the development of a total treatment atmosphere, the promotion of boys' work organizations (e.g., Boy Scouts; social settlements; urban boys' clubs; Young Men's Christian Association; Boys Brotherhood Republic) to steer gang members and leaders away from their original loyalties, and finally to "give life meaning for the boy" by stimulating imagination, giving ambitions, and realigning interests. Essentially, the latter objectives were to be reached via vocational training, hiking and competitive sports, civic duties, cooptation as property protectors for the police, and even the development of boys militias.[94]

Psychology and social psychology of criminal behavior were also persistently emergent areas of theory construction. The collection of inquiries into the role of the mental state in crime causation had exploded by the mid-1920s.[95] Robert Gault, editor of the *Journal of the American Institute of Criminal Law and Criminology* from 1911, insisted that criminology, while mainly correct in attending to sociological and legalistic interpretations, required explanation of the "hair trigger" in the individual organism, chiefly the "emotional life." He called for more study of the "acquisition of undesirable social habits and attitudes and to emotional states."[96]

Raymond Moley and Sam Warner each insisted that the justice system lacked statistics to inform all phases of decision making. Moley, writing for the *Columbia Law Review* in May 1928, outlined statistical needs in terms of crime complaints (reported crime), facts concerning arrested persons (criminal characteristics), judicial statistics (criminal process), and penal statistics (convicted persons and institutional characteristics). Regarding reported crime, Moley suggested that police departments had made significant progress in gathering information about arrestees but that such statistics were "marred by inaccuracies emanating from unsatisfactory methods of collection or by deliberate manipulation or both."[97] Noting the inadequacy of police data outside the largest cities, Moley urged IACP to broaden its collection and analytical capabilities to include "statewide non-urban crime complaint statistics" and to work on the problem of the "inter-relations between a study of crime complaint records and other types of criminal statistics."[98] Here, Moley referred to, for example, the association between police statistics and the characteristics of "the persons who are included in the daily grist of arrests in our great cities."[99] Moley reasoned that judicial statistics aided state legislatures in evaluating "the operation of the rules they propose to amend," to measure court administrative efficiency, and to redistribute judicial personnel according to prosecutorial case loads.[100] Penal statistics, with the exception of probation and parole statistics, had already achieved respectability through the joint efforts of the Bureau of the Census and the American Institute of Criminal Law and Criminology.[101]

Moley identified three major obstacles to improving criminal statistics: standardization; collection and publication; and, record-keeping. Standardization was difficult because of the variations among offense definitions between state laws. Collection and publication were problems of agreement upon the sending and receiving agencies, that is, which agency at the state level would collect and arrange data for transmission to the Census Bureau or the Department of Justice. Records orderliness, argued Moley, could be achieved if the state attorneys general were granted power to prescribe local accounting systems for records submitted by police, court, or penal agencies. Moley completed his outline for progress with a call for a complete study of criminal statistics. The progressive agenda he set forth included recognition of the links between police and court records in certain cities, the careful classification of crimes according to simplified legal definitions, the location of the collection units in the offices of the attorneys general, and the employment of existing experts in public records for the study of criminal statistics.[102] His concluding remarks acknowledged the diversity of input needed for any new study of statistics, and he seemed encouraged that the task would be likely to yield the elimination of "useless statistics, which [have] so characterized statistical compilations in the past."[103] Sam

Warner challenged some of Moley's ideas about the manner of collecting and reporting of federal statistics.

By the late 1920s, the work by Harry Elmer Barnes on prison conditions was well recognized in the community of criminologists.[104] *The Repression of Crime: Studies in Historical Penology* was, in essence, a summary of all the investigations so far undertaken to change prison conditions, organized according to research application: "Failure of Prisons," "Science and the Criminal," and "Necessity of Progress in Criminal Jurisprudence." Aside from Barnes's careful scholarship in showing the gradual erosion of the original intentions of prisons as reform organizations, his work argued for immediate implementation of specific reform measures and a new ideological commitment to prisoner reform. He saw these objectives as the only logical value of institutional punishment: "If we can make the penal and correctional institutions ever more efficient instruments of reformation or permanent segregation, we shall cut off one of the most important sources of the production of criminals, and render socially effective any improved type of criminal jurisprudence and criminal procedure."[105]

EMERGING FEDERAL INTEREST IN IDEAS, THINKERS, AND DOERS

Beneath the calm veneer of economic prosperity in the 1920s were a concern for social problems and, in particular, a perception that crime and the administration of justice merited greater political and scientific attention. Early in the decade, crime commissions peppered the urban landscape. At a minimum, their results peeled back layers of superficialities about ordinary crimes, the condition of local criminal justice systems, and modest proposals for action. Newspapers heralded the results: sharply increased rates of crime and impressions that criminal incidents had become increasingly violent. Popular myth blamed gangsters and immigrants for much of the so-called crime wave; justice systems were incapable of controlling criminal groups or ward bosses believed to have subsidized street thugs. Popular culture produced novels and movies aimed at crime and justice themes.[106] Law journals published more articles than ever before on criminal law and procedural matters. By the end of the decade, the established *Journal of Criminal Law and Criminology* carried articles associating justice system failures with social problems and inadequate resources.

By 1928, neither Democrats nor Republicans could set aside an emerging belief that "law observance" had failed in practical application, lacking any programmatic role for government. Ambivalence toward broader and more sophisticated explanations of crime was attributable mainly to moralistic support for Prohibition. Law enforcement was capable of upholding the sanctity of the law, according to the common view, quietly horrified by the magnitude of the problem. The cover of Prohibition, however, was nearly a decade old and vulnerable to contradictions and alternative explanations. It was increasingly difficult to blame every robbery, passion murder, store theft, delinquent youth, or stolen car on the influences of failed support for Prohibition. New awareness of the complexities of the crime problem, limited even to federal crimes, virtually assured a call for new insights and new proposals.

Hoover came to office at a time when ideas for criminal justice reforms, although limited mainly to institutional reorganization, were plentiful. His affinity for the use of science, including the new field of administrative science, was naturally suited for a public airing of new ideas through a formal process of investigation. Leaving aside Hoover's personal views on crime causation, most reasonably replete with notions of individual responsibility, the thirty-first president declared a social and governmental duty to explore what the best minds had determined were the most practical government responses.

Quite literally, a small library of criminological thought had been developed containing the wisdom and research results of respected authorities on policing, the judiciary, and penology. The experts waited in the wings; and their universities, research centers, and progressive agencies were already bringing along new students of criminology and criminal justice. Some centers, such as Harvard Law School, were willing to pay the salaries of experts like Roscoe Pound to work full time on governmental investigations.[107] The results of the 1928 campaign suggested a public willingness to invest in expert counsel and formal study. Experts in criminology and related behavioral and social sciences spoke publicly of needed changes, and many were experienced in the role of advising governments on policy redirection. The literature of the nineteenth-century criminological philosophies had been replaced by a new criminology, a new social science of measurable causation and action prospects. Measurability depended upon the gathering of statistics and the application of scientific analysis. Institutional problems of police, courts, and corrections could best be spotted by the experts. Reform was in the air, lacking only commitment, direction, and financial support for scientific inquiry. Hoover's appointment of the Wickersham Commission was formal recognition of a federal role in the scientific inquiry into crime and justice administration.

Chapter 4

Scientific Investigation:
The Wickersham Commission

I have an incorrigible belief in reason, provided reason is made manifest by impressive evidence.[1]

Presidents learn much about domestic and foreign policy after they take office.[2] From the first days at the pinnacle of executive power, they begin to close the "separation between brain and state."[3] Commissions are tools for closing the separation by distributing the burdens of information management and for establishing priorities among equally demanding issues. The complexity of criminal justice administration demands a commission comprising representatives from many academic disciplines and operating agencies. At minimum, a federal crime commission is obligated to determine the impact of crime on federal justice administration and to suggest innovations to state and localities.

Appointed in May 1929, Hoover's congressionally funded eleven-member Commission on Law Observance and Enforcement (hereafter called the Wickersham Commission after its chairman, George W. Wickersham) was the first occasion in thirty administrations on which a federal commission was formed to examine comprehensively federal criminal justice. This chapter outlines some of the key topics and policy concerns of the commission. Extensive archival records of the commission cannot be fully reflected here, but an attempt can be made to offer perspective on major elements of the commission's work.[4]

Hoover handed the commission a difficult task. But he was convinced that federal justice administration could not advance without a systematic audit of crime conditions and system responses. To accomplish this audit, he retained at little cost to the government the best available intellectual resources, some of them widely known in American criminology and social scientific thought. The Wickersham Commission was, indeed, a monument to intellectual and practical reforms in federal crime control policy, instituted with sincere intent to narrow the gap between brain and state.

GETTING STARTED: MANDATE, STAFF, AND BUDGET

Hoover met with all eleven members of the commission at 2:30 P.M. on May 28, 1929.[5] His remarks were warm, firm, and direct, setting forth a commitment to scientific investigation and to meaningful recommendations for reforming federal justice administration. He had already publicly stated his views on the commission's purpose, and he expected the investigations to formulate "constructive, courageous conclusions which will bring public understanding and command public support of its solutions."[6]

There would be no compromise on objectives to improve justice system practices and to reinstate law's role in civilized governance. The American people, Hoover said, "are deeply concerned over the alarming disobedience of law, the abuses in law enforcement and the growth of organized crime, which has spread in every field of evil-doing in every part of our country. A nation does not fail from its growth of wealth or power. But no nation can for long survive the failure of its citizens to respect and obey the laws which they themselves make. Nor can it survive a decadence of the moral and spiritual concepts that are the basis of respect for law nor from neglect to organize itself to defeat crime and the corruption that flows from it. Nor is this a problem confined to the enforcement and obedience of one law or the laws of the Federal or State Governments separately. The problem is partly the attitude toward all law."[7] His introduction reached well beyond Prohibition concerns.

Hoover was careful not to ask the commission to engage in the operational aspects of organizing federal enforcement and judicial functions. On June 6, he addressed a special message to Congress announcing his support for a congressional joint committee to examine questions of Prohibition enforcement. He wanted to appoint an additional coordinative cabinet-level committee comprising agency or department representatives to work with a comparable committee in Congress. Also, he asked the Wickersham Commission to exchange information with the Congress, thereby ensuring that all parties to the decision processes would share equally in the results of the legislatively authorized work. Extending his March 19 press statement, "I am not looking for dramatics. I am looking for substantial, permanent advance of the country to a realization of the necessity of enforcing the laws of the United States as they are on the books."[8] While he would not leave reorganization and consolidation to the commission, he wisely sought input from Congress through a proposed joint committee.[9] To link the commission's work with independent congressional actions on other initiatives, Hoover appointed John L. McNab, a prominent San Francisco lawyer, to plan for administrative reorganizations.[10] Congress, however, failed to act on Hoover's suggestion to create a joint committee.[11]

Chairman George W. Wickersham, who had served as attorney general under President Taft, and Attorney General William D. Mitchell also gave welcoming remarks to the commission. The Justice Department, they said, was fully supportive of the commission's work and would assist in any ways it could. Pleasantries concluded, Hoover, Mitchell, and Wickersham returned to their offices to let the commission formulate the research agenda. Dialogues took off in several directions. Paul J. McCormick, a federal district judge in the southern district of California, urged that priority be assigned to law enforcement criminal procedure, in particular to ways to speed up the process of criminal justice, including a proposed new level of lower federal courts for criminal justice matters only. "The basic evil," McCormick announced without hesitation, "lay in the professional criminal lawyers," police "third degree" tactics, and "marketed injustice."

Ada L. Comstock, a sociologist and president of Radcliffe College, recommended that the state of mind of lawbreakers was worthy of research as to lawbreakers' perceptions that beating the law was a "meritorious game." Monte M. Lemann, distinguished New Orleans trial attorney and president of the Louisiana Bar Association, wondered whether Prohibition was the basis for general disrespect of the law. Frank J. Loesch, judge, citizen leader in Chicago's antigangster efforts, prominent member of the Chicago Bar Association, and vice president of the Chicago Crime Commission, zeroed in on more specific issues of bail practices, jury challenges, judicial waivers of felony cases to misdemeanors, and jury instructions. Judge William S. Kenyon, former senator from Iowa and sitting judge on the United States Circuit Court of Appeals, said that most criminals "of the gangster type bore foreign names," and that criminal defense lawyers were "the greatest obstacle in the way of the administration of justice."[12] A Prohibition supporter who insisted upon an objective study of the question, Kenyon showed some objectivity late in the commission's work when he said he was "appalled at the venom and malice of the people whom we term the 'wets,' and . . . the stupidity of the 'ultra drys.'"[13]

William I. Grubb, a federal district judge from the northern district of Alabama, blamed the unwillingness of some juries to convict offenders. A more contemplative approach was taken by Kenneth R. Mackintosh, a prominent Seattle lawyer and a former chief justice of the supreme court of the State of Washington, who suggested the need for more scientifically derived statistics and measures of court efficiency that could be used to reduce docket congestion. Finally, Henry W. Anderson, former colleague of Hoover's in the World War famine relief, prominent Virginia lawyer, president of the Virginia Bar Association, and twice-defeated candidate for governor of Virginia, reinforced the suggestion of needed statistics by proclaiming that far too many remedies had been proposed without more precise data.[14] Anderson's unique claim was that the main offenders in society were in the "highest class" and the "lowest class" while the great middle was comparatively law abiding. Government, he said, was the law breaker, thus calling for its cleanup before expecting new respect for the law.[15]

The core of the commission's leadership consisted of men with lengthy and sometimes controversial histories. Each member was well known to Hoover. Newton D. Baker, Roscoe Pound, and George Wickersham were the most prominent practitioners and legal scholars. With these exceptions, the commission consisted mainly of distinguished practitioners of no academic recognition but nonetheless competent representatives of the topical fields of study under consideration. Baker had been President Wilson's embattled secretary of war, an acclaimed architect of World War planning, author, and later a partner in the Cleveland law firm of Baker, Hostetler & Sidlo.[16] Pound was one of America's most towering legal scholars, dean of the Harvard Law School, author of several books and articles on criminal justice, and a famous name in legal theory.[17] Wickersham had been attorney general in the Taft administration, acclaimed for vigorous prosecution of corporate trusts. He had opposed without hesitation federal incorporation of the Rockefeller Foundation, a special-interest organization he viewed as a slick method of empowering John D. Rockefeller's Standard Oil Company.[18] Wickersham, suggests Swindler, held a particular vision of the attorney general's job that was not far different from Hoover's point of view on corporate power: "He was aware . . . of the difference between efficiency and monopoly. The answer to him was a form of government surveillance to promote efficiency and to control monopolies." He feared that the legal system lacked the capacity to keep watch over a growing threat, thus "he seized upon the only (though imperfect) weapon at his command, the Sherman Act, and set out to slay giants."[19] In 1927, after he returned to private law practice with William Howard Taft's brother, Wickersham also represented Hoover's eligibility to the presidency on the issue of residency in the United States.[20] The bonds between these men and Hoover were strong.

Pound was clearly the central intellectual giant on the commission. With years of legal scholarship behind him and experience in leading the earlier Cleveland crime commission, he was best suited to the role of harmonizer of contentious internal factions.[21] Perpetually in pursuit of the best minds and credentials, Pound was not uncomfortable expressing opinions about the quality of scholarship represented on the commission. When asked for his views on the proposed appointment of Judge Joseph C. Hutcheson, Jr., to the commission, Pound wrote to commission secretary Max Lowenthal that he was not familiar with the judge's competency to investigate questions of judicial organization: "What I do know is that very few people in this country have any adequate notion of the problem of judicial organization. I have been studying that since 1906, and know that it is a very big problem. . . . I have not talked with a federal judge yet who had any conception whatever of judicial organization beyond that of his own state." To reinforce his point, Pound said that he had recently talked with two district judges "who denied that they had the power to comment on the evidence in a charge to the jury. It is that sort of thing which we are up against in any attempt to do something for judicial organization and procedure in this country."[22] Hutcheson was appointed to chair the commission inquiry into the federal courts.[23] Something of a more favorable contrast in opinion is found in Pound's assessment of other scholars, such as Sheldon Glueck: "Glueck's work is absolutely first class."[24] Regarding Edith Abbott, dean of the Graduate School of Social Service at Chicago, Pound was equally complimentary: "I am rejoiced that [she] is to undertake criminal justice and the foreign born. No one could be bet[t]er. She is the sort of "expert" who can be of use to you."[25]

The advisors and consultants to the commission represented, indeed, a who's who of mid–twentieth-century criminologists, lawyers, and social and behavioral scientists. Every academic discipline demonstrating a published concern for crime and justice administration was included in some fashion within the main body of the commission or in a consultative capacity. Research support staffs included dozens of prominent academics of either rising or established prestige. Independent investigations, published reports, and policy recommendations originated with such luminaries in criminology, law, and public administration as Edwin H. Sutherland,

Thorsten Sellin, Sheldon Glueck, Felix Frankfurter, Raymond Moley, Francis Sayre, Samuel C. May, Frederic A. Ogg, W. F. Willoughby, Howard W. Odum, William E. Mosher, Luther Gulick, Raymond B. Fosdick, and Charles E. Merriam.

Most research products were aimed directly at fulfilling the main objectives of the commission's liberally crafted topical plan, but relevant peripheral interests were also given air. For some consultants, such as Edwin Sutherland and political scientist Charles Merriam, consultation provided an opportunity to introduce fledgling theories and new data on crime and justice administration to a nationwide audience. Writing to Jerome Michael at Columbia University in August 1929, Wickersham said of his research staff, "We have found it difficult to secure the services of the best experts in the country, but we have thought it wiser to employ none but the very best rather than to seek more rapid progress with others who are not of the first order."[26]

Equally prestigious practitioners and university administrators were asked to serve as experts and consultants.[27] August Vollmer, perhaps the best recognized police chief in the United States, had retired as Berkeley's chief and was teaching in both California and Chicago.[28] In June 1929, he was asked to set his calendar for trips to Washington to assist the law enforcement research committee. Wickersham needed the most knowledgeable and reputable police official in the nation to lead the investigation of police organizations and activities. This proved somewhat difficult, however. Wickersham wrote to Vollmer on June 12, invoking Hoover's name and the importance of the commission's work. He offered to write to city and university officials to secure approval for a leave of absence so that he could begin at once the tasks of organizing and directing the police studies.[29] Three days later, Vollmer responded that his doctor said "it would be positively unwise for me to leave here at the present time and has as his able ally my good wife, who refuses under any consideration to give her consent. Having been a soldier, your request was accepted as a command and there would have been no question about my responding to the call at this particular time were it not for the physical impairments." Vollmer, in fact, told the chairman that interceding with either city officials or the university would be unnecessary, and that a personal meeting with him was simply not possible.[30]

An old friend from his early days as marshal of the Berkeley Police Department, Henry E. Curzon, wrote in September to congratulate him on his assignment to President Hoover's crime commission. Vollmer replied, "Friendships [referring to Curzon] formed on the battle fields are not easily broken. I am delighted to have heard from you, old man, and what I need more than anything else is sympathy, and not congratulations." Vollmer left Berkeley on September 29 on leave for six months to teach political science and police administration courses at the University of Chicago. Thereafter, he was consulted privately on numerous occasions to contribute to the commission report on Lawlessness in Law Enforcement.[31]

Max Lowenthal filled the most important administrative position on the commission. As secretary to the commission, he coordinated the diverse fields of interests and specializations, and he frequently moderated personality differences between strong egos among members, staff, and consultants. Lowenthal was central to the progress and stability of the commission's work. As a former Bureau of Investigation agent and as counsel to congressional committees, he was equipped with invaluable knowledge of networks of information on police operations and influential leaders, statistical compilations, personnel backgrounds, and other essentials useful to commissioners. Lowenthal's aims were to attract the appropriate kinds of participants in the research tasks and to avoid "selection of any persons who are not absolutely first-rate."[32] He remained as secretary to the commission until July, 1930, quitting in disgust over "antics in the realm of political expediency."[33]

Broad and prestigious representation on the commission did not extend to blacks or other racial and ethnic minorities. Several commissioners and numerous citizens, however, wrote to Hoover expressing hope that blacks and others would receive appointments. Black leaders argued that blacks had endured more than a century of police abuse, rigged court rooms, and harsh prison treatment and that they were overrepresented in crime statistics for reasons that demanded inquiry. After consideration of possible black membership, Hoover decided that such an appointment would violate his principle of having no special interests represented. Appointment of Ada L. Comstock to the commission and of consultants Edith Abbott and Mary van Kleeck, former organizer and first director of the Labor Department's women's bureau, would, presumably, ensure that the interests of blacks and other minorities were represented.[34] Harvard law professor Zachariah Chafee wrote to Wickersham, "My indebtedness to some members of that race has been so great that I should be very sorry indeed not to have the Commission pay adequate attention to their problems and the injustices which they have suffered in connection with the enforcment of the law."[35]

Carl Murphy, editor of *The Afro-American* newsweekly, wrote to Hoover on April 20, 1929, urging appointment of Negro members from among W. E. B. Dubois, a Harvard graduate and caustic social critic; Charles Wesley, teacher and historian; Dr. Robert R. Moton, president of the Tuskegee Institute; or Warner T. McGuinn, Baltimore city councilman. Murphy advised Hoover that an appointment from this list "would be regarded by Negroes as evidence of the nation's sincerity in correcting existing lawlessness."[36] Murphy no doubt had in mind serious attention to lynchings and police brutality. Perhaps more subtly, he intended to raise the possibility of hypocrisy in the commission's endeavors: was it possible to examine law's violation in white society, mainly white urban society, when it was white urban society that condoned or gave only fleeting attention to murder by lynching.[37] Federal judge Joseph C. Hutcheson, Jr., of Houston, Texas, believed that a study of crime, criminal justice, and conditions of blacks in the South could be conducted without serious negative political implications for the commission.[38] Hoover was interested in the impact of crime on racial and ethnic groups, but his stated reasons for not appointing at least one black member or consultant stemmed from his opposition to any form of special representation.[39]

The commission conducted several substantive meetings in June 1929 to clarify the research agenda, to contrive data collection and dissemination strategies, and to affix the division of labor. Alfred Bettman addressed the June 18 gathering to summarize the findings of the earlier Cleveland and Boston crime surveys.[40] Commissioner Loesch discussed his conversations with Walter A. Strong, editor of the Chicago *Daily News*. Strong had offered to arrange a "successful educational campaign" regarding the commission's work, most probably resulting in Hoover's politically correct note of congratulation to Strong on July 5.[41] Loesch suggested that corruption and lawlessness among government law enforcers should rank high among topics of investigation.[42]

Beginning on June 19, commissioners talked about budget allocations for research projects, the lessons of local crime commissions, police and Prohibition matters, and criminal procedure. Resolutions were reached on ten major research topics, each with a budget allocation: causes of crime ($15,700); costs of crime ($7,500); courts ($6,000); crime and the foreign born ($7,500); official lawlessness ($12,500); police ($5,000); penal institutions, probation, and parole ($6,500); Prohibition ($50,000); prosecution ($7,500); and statistics ($1,000). Congress had authorized $250,000 for its operating budget.

Hoover was frequently asked by the press to defend his use of commissions as devices for educating him and the nation on public issues. Fearing no serious opposition to commission appointments, he told the press on July 19, "I am just taking [the appointment of many commissions] as a right—as many as I like."[43] Later, as the Depression deepened, Hoover defended his commission record, reporting that he had appointed only twenty commissions by comparison with President Wilson's seventy-five and President Coolidge's forty-four.[44]

The Wickersham Commission intended scientific investigation, using the most recent and methodologically sound approaches. As Lowenthal wrote in August 1929 to the acting dean of the faculties at the University of Chicago, "We are endeavoring in the fields of our study to proceed in a spirit of scientific inquiry, to put before the country only data which has been arrived at scientifically and impartially, so that the country may have a real foundation of facts on which to consider each aspect of what the President in appointing this Commission called 'the dominant issue before the American people.'"[45]

The commission employed state-of-the-art survey research designs to acquire data pertaining to banks of questions from authorities at all levels of government and from influential organizations and individuals. For example, one lengthy survey of police manpower distributions found that six American cities had substantially higher ratios of police to population than did six European cities, which suggested that crime was a function of police presence.[46] Consultants from the field of psychology developed several attitude studies pertaining to crime, Prohibition enforcement, and criminal court practices. Economists, law professors, political scientists, and sociologists were responsible for the development of most survey instruments.

PROHIBITION ALBATROSS

The most contentious issue addressed by the commission was Prohibition. On one extreme, testimony given in June 1929 by assistant secretary of the treasury Seymour Lowman offered astounding optimism: "I want to say to you of the Commission that in my opinion the amount of liquor coming into this country by smuggling has now been reduced to a minimum." He claimed that since the Mexicans were not interested in whiskey and since the border was well protected, the amount of liquor coming from Mexico was minimal. The Prohibition department was limited to internal enforcement, but the Customs Bureau's "elaborate intelligence unit all over the world" was furnishing sufficient tariff and smuggler information to trace liquor shipments. Even more astounding was his report that smuggling from Cuba was hardly a problem, "because we have a close agreement with the Cuban Government. The Cuban Government is cooperating with the American Government in a wonderful way so far as smuggling . . . is concerned, and our special service over there is in very close touch with theirs. While there may occasionally be a little rum that gets into this country from Cuba, the amount is small." Without much question, a high official of Prohibition enforcement told the commission that things were well in hand, and by implication, the illegal production and distribution of alcohol was essentially an internal problem that more judges and convictions could cure faster than more Prohibition agents.[47] Commissioner Frank Loesch found such testimony unsettling, particularly in light of his own experiences in Chicago. He asked, "Will you give me an explanation that I have not been able to get from anyone else, how such men as Capone, D[r]uggan, Lake, Moran and others could operate on the extensive scale on which they are operating, and run great quantities of liquor into that section supposedly from Canada?" Loesch pointed out that the Canadian authorities considered Volstead Act enforcement against liquor smuggling a U.S. internal problem for which they accepted no responsibility. This position was pointed out by Prohibition bureau commissioner James M. Doran who testified on June 6 that Canada's only concern in the exportation of liquor was that "an honest export paper" was completed reflecting the true destination. Doran told Loesch, "One of the things that aids them is the corruption at key spots" in the United States. Twenty-five agents, he reported, were devoted to internal corruption detection, yet the vast majority of the cases they investigated were unfounded.[48] Loesch and the other commissioners were left scratching their heads. How could the Prohibition bureau report that success was just around the corner when liquor shipments continued to flow freely into the country. The commission's task was to make sense out of the confusion. The mandate called for study of a broad spectrum of crime justice administration well beyond Prohibition.

While the commission worked to sort out the point of balance, Hoover continued vigorous enforcement. He was interested primarily in stopping major shipments of booze into the United States, but over time even he recognized that managing every last incident of nullification would achieve nothing. For example, in June 1929, he wrote to Mitchell: "Have I the right to assign either the Army or the Marines to patrol of the border at Detroit and thereabouts. This situation seems to represent a complete breakdown in Government."[49] And in February 1932, he again wrote to Mitchell: "I am receiving many complaints that the breweries in Newark are running full blast and shipping their product all over New Jersey. The complaint is that the breweries in Camden have been put out of action while the Newark concerns are allowed to supply the state. I think the matter should be looked into."[50] In contrast, he asked Mitchell in October 1929 to look into "a rather pathetic presentation of an Oklahoma

[Prohibition] conviction." By 1932, he took a somewhat more reserved position: "The repeal (or modification?) of the 18th Amendment should be submitted to conventions to be called by the various states during the year 1933."[51]

Wickersham and Hoover hoped that some firm evidence that Prohibition was successful could be found, although both recognized that enforcement had been only marginally productive. Turning to the social value of the law, Wickersham wrote to Bethlehem Steel's president Eugene G. Grace to learn whether "the experience of the managers of the various steel plants as to the influence of prohibition upon their operators, particularly as to whether during the last two or three years there has been any improvement or retrogression in the sobriety and absence of alcoholism among them." Grace responded that "the economic and social status of our workers has shown a decided and continual betterment. . . . Prohibition, even in spite of any weaknesses in its enforcement has had a very definite beneficial effect in our industrial life."[52]

But the problem of widespread nullification could not be overlooked. Newton Baker, for example, believed that the public could analogize active nullification with passive disregard for police authority. He cited as "harmless nullification" a hotel that had ignored a police ordinance prohibiting bed sheets less than seven feet long and twin beds less than two feet apart. Such violations had no further consequences. But nullification of the Volstead Act, he contrasted, manufactured an industry in law breaking while it also "expose[d] law enforcing officers not merely to social discipline for failing to enforce but to corruption, so that however much we might acquiesce in a disregard of the Volstead Act, there is alway[s] a powerful temptation upon those entrusted with public authority at least sporadically to enforce in the interest of being corrupted into acquiescence."[53] Cornelius Bliss, director of the Association for Improvement of Conditions of the Poor, agreed with Baker: "In fact, I am looking to your Commission and hoping that you may be able to wave the magic wand and settle the problem once and for all."[54]

At the end of the commission's work, half the commissioners wanted a magic wand while the others voted to sustain the albatross. No new solutions were found in the final report of the Prohibition research committee. Perhaps Felix Frankfurter's warning in July 1929 was most prescient. He urged Wickersham and the commission to heed George Washington's advice to the Constitutional Convention: "It is probable that no plan we propose will be adopted. . . . Let us raise a standard to which the wise and honest can repair. The event is in the hand of God."[55]

CRIME STATISTICS: MOST CRITICAL, MOST CONTENTIOUS

In 1871, Attorney General A. T. Akerman included in his annual report the first federal crime statistics. For nearly sixty years thereafter, no formal system of crime statistics was implemented, with the minor exception of Census Bureau efforts in the mid-1920s. Statistics on crime occasioned persistent internal disagreement and factionalism within the commission's work. Accurate statistics reflecting a comprehensive activity report of federal, state, or local criminal justice systems were simply not available to commissioners. New data, therefore, would require development. Felix Frankfurter observed: "One cannot withhold expression of the feeling that every contact one has with American criminal statistics discloses how seriously lacking we are even in the most primitive instruments of knowledge."[56] George Wickersham responded: "I suppose that in a rapidly developing civilization, reliable records note the last stages of progress. Assuredly that seems to be the case in these United States."[57] The path to developing crime statistics from criminal records divided along the edges of two stridently argued points of view, each based on experience and scholarship. The outcome determined the approach to crime statistics for the next twenty-five years.

Harvard law professor Sam Bass Warner argued that the Census Bureau should become the central repository for crime statistics. Early in commission deliberations, Warner urged a study aimed at establishing a "unified system of criminal statistics,"[58] in which police, prosecution, and penal statistics would be uniformly collected and published. He had been instrumental in introducing prosecutorial and prisoner statistics in the Census Bureau, and he was held in high regard by Max Lowenthal. Warner's objective was to standardize the reporting of all agency statistics on crime, including data from police, court, prison, parole, jail, and probation agencies.[59] Alfred Bettman of Cincinatti, an associate of Roscoe Pound's through the Boston and Cleveland crime studies and an expert on the operations of district attorneys, agreed to complete research on prosecution statistics.[60] Warner opposed federal collection and publication of police-supplied crime data for four reasons. First, he believed that police data were collected and published for an insignificant part of the country. Second, local police data were, by definition, unreliable indicators of the crime picture. Third, federal law enforcement statistics were not included, and to include them would require lengthy development. Finally, Warner argued that state statistical bureaus should serve as receiving points for police statistics before they were passed to the Bureau of Census. The latter proposal suggested that police statistics should have been treated no differently from judicial statistics, with parallel collection remaining at the state level.

Warner ran headlong into opposition from the newly formed International Association of Chiefs of Police (IACP) Committee on Uniform Crime Records and the Bureau of Municipal Research. IACP had the support of major state and local crime commissions. The competing faction contended that the IACP should direct national collection and interpretation of police statistics, ultimately turning that task over to the Department of Justice. The opposition included the membership of the IACP's Advisory Committee on the Uniform Crime Reports, including Bruce Smith, police consultant; William Rutledge, commissioner of police in Detroit; August Vollmer, chief of police in Berkeley, California; and advisory committee members Leonard V. Harrison, New York City police department; and J. Edgar Hoover, director of the Bureau of Investigation.[61] Author and attorney Raymond B. Fosdick also entered the fray. In blunt terms, Smith summarized the IACP's perspective. Beginning in 1927, IACP had organized a "complete scheme for national crime accounting, comprising manuals for the use of police departments and a national bureau of criminal statistics, record forms, and a detailed procedure" that had already received the approval of numerous police departments.

During the summer of 1929, Warner became the unyielding opponent of the IACP system. Wickersham asked Warner to report on crime statistics following the first commission meeting, a task that was completed with a report submitted to Max Lowenthal on June 14.[62] Warner offered an extensive critique of available crime statistics and statistical gathering techniques of police agencies. In essence, he argued, statistical rigor was lacking in the police evaluations of the extent of crime in the United States. Moreover, he posited that overall respect for criminal statistics would improve greatly if data collection and analysis were performed by the Department of Commerce's Census Bureau.[63] After all, he questioned, what agency of the federal government had more experience with statistical matters than census. Study of the options proceeded while the interpersonal hostilities of those holding each view increased.

Writing to Newton Baker, Wickersham said that he preferred to wait for Warner's study results "in order that the whole subject may be studied as one, and that this particular phase of it [police statistics] should not be jammed through, perhaps to the detriment of a comprehensive system which we would feel convinced should be advocated."[64] Wickersham had no particular objection to legislation promoted by IACP, but he clearly objected to the methods used by IACP to obtain the commission's blessing.

The statistics issue seemed to divide along practitioner–scholar lines. Experts like Raymond B. Fosdick, president of the Rockefeller Foundation, Smith, and Rutledge[65] remained convinced that police statistics were adequate indicators of the crime problem and that other statistics would only confuse matters. Wickersham, Roscoe Pound, and Sam Warner were equally strident in their opposition to police statistics as the only significant measure of crime. The only common ground was an intellectual agreement among the adversaries that criminal justice policy could not advance without improved statistical collections. Reporting to the full commission on March 12, 1930, chairman Wickersham concluded, "The more the work in the various branches of the Commission's inquiry continues, and particularly the work with respect to activities of the Federal Government, the more it becomes obvious that a thorough survey and over-hauling of the statistics of the Federal administration of criminal justice is necessary."[66]

The commission had every intention of compiling model statistics for later use by the state agencies. Correspondingly, it also desired to cultivate both political support for state statistics units and a codified and systematic arrangement of data to blend with federally collected information. Naturally, the latter objective was an uphill climb. Commissioners could not always agree on which statistics should enter the model and which statistics were likely to be available from state or local governments.[67] The Department of Commerce had observed in June 1929 that authoritative and reliable statistics were available in only a few jurisdictions. By retaining Maurice Ploscowe to give particular attention to federal criminal statistics, the commission believed that "the subject of statistics lies at the very threshold of any consideration of the problem of crime in the United States [and that] it is of the utmost importance that every state as well as the national government should adopt the best, the most thorough, the most informative scientific basis of keeping statistical records pertaining to crime."[68]

The police faction promoted legislation to create in the Justice Department a bureau specifically organized to collect "uniform crime reports." Smith was convinced that it was "rather doubtful whether the support of the police chiefs for any other system could be secured; and I am sure that without such support from individual police departments, no system of police statistics can even get under way." The police chiefs stood firmly against Warner's proposal. Linking the interests of the IACP to the Justice Department's Bureau of Identification and Information, Smith claimed that the bureau had been "originally established through the almost unaided efforts of the [IACP]. It follows that the Association has a very special and intimate interest in that Bureau and desires to make the monthly and annual returns [i.e., crime reports] to it." Bruce Smith had drawn the battle lines over centralized police statistics, and he was unwilling to concede any portion of Warner's opposition.[69] The beneficiary of centralized Justice Department statistics was a crony, J. Edgar Hoover.

In early July 1929, Warner outlined his objections to Smith's position. On July 9, Smith fired back. Reacting to Warner's acceptance of the task of setting up a "unified system," he expressed concerns that the Wickersham Commission might find itself with no statistics if the IACP's approach to statistical gathering were not adopted.[70] Smith reported that his IACP committee on uniform crime records was "not a mere project nor even a plan for a system. Rather, it is a complete scheme for national crime accounting." He warned that he was "rather doubtful whether the support of the police chiefs for any other system could be secured; and . . . without such support from individual police departments, no system of police statistics can even get under way." Adding further heat to an already apparent confusion of objectives, Smith said that Warner had served on the IACP committee and had been consulted for his suggestions. In the end, Smith said, Warner had congratulated him for the work of the committee, thus putting Smith at "a loss to understand the reason" for an alternative "unified system." On July 24, Smith took aim at Warner's concern that the Census Bureau and the Justice Department would develop entirely different statistics if the latter agency were permitted to take charge: "At the most it appears to be a contingency which would not arise for some years, and which might possibly be offset by conference committees representing the two interested federal agencies."[71]

Fosdick wrote to Wickersham on July 10, restating the need for some form of uniform system of crime statistics never before achieved in federal justice administration. He endorsed wholeheartedly the work of Rutledge and Smith, and could not resist mention that "the necessary funds were supplied . . . with considerable liberality by the Rockefeller interests, and the work has been carried on under the general auspices of the Bureau of Social Hygiene." Fosdick stressed that input had been encouraged from Census Bureau through the committee's advisory committee member William M. Steuart. Several people in the nation could develop an adequate crime reporting system, including Sam Warner, Fosdick concluded, but to introduce another system at that point "would be a most unfortunate backward step." Moreover, Fosdick warned Wickersham, "would it be proper for your Commission to consider what effect such action would have on the chiefs of police of a very large number of American cities on whose assistance and cooperation your Commission must, of course, to a very considerable degree depend?"[72]

By early August, the impending showdown had become clear to both Max Lowenthal and Wickersham. Sensing great tension between equally strident viewpoints, Lowenthal asked Pound to chat with Sam Warner concerning relations with both Bruce Smith and the entire statistics debate. Lowenthal had met with Warner and had encouraged him "to seek to avoid anything which will, however unintentionally on his part, promote feeling and make a solution of the difficulty less simple." Hoping Pound would agree, Lowenthal said, "I assume that sooner or later all parties will agree on the best method of handling statistics, and I hope it will be possible to look to you in straightening things out as early as this can be done effectively."[73]

By early September, Smith appeared to be in a conciliatory mood, hoping for an accommodation between the Census Bureau and the Justice Department's Bureau of Identification and Information. Smith proposed that the two agencies share participation in the reporting of crime statistics but that the Justice Department retain the central repository for data collected from police departments. In a lengthy letter to Vollmer on September 7, Smith indicated that he had met with the key funding representative of the Rockefeller Memorial Foundation and with Roscoe Pound to promote the commission's official recognition of the overall IACP plan. With firm conviction, Smith wrote that the IACP committee wanted "legislation empowering Edgar Hoover's bureau to collect, compile and distribute criminal statistics." Simply put, Smith's logic was that the police chiefs were already sending their fingerprints to Hoover, so why not merely extend the power of an existing organization that was both familiar with the ways of police organizations and, by implication, favorably disposed to Edgar Hoover's views on law enforcement.[74]

Warner, it appeared, had not changed his mind. Vollmer had supplied him with a copy of Smith's letter of September 7. Warner took exception on two points, saying that he hoped Vollmer "will be more successful in talking with Mr. Smith than I was." First, Warner said that he and Pound stood firmly on the notion of a centralized statistics organization for related but different reasons. Without setting forth specific reasons, which would appear later in a formal report, Warner understood Pound's view to stress the importance of statistics gathered by an agency other than Justice so that those statistics could serve "as a check upon the Department of Justice." Pound, Warner reported, had surveyed reports of at least six major European criminal statistics organizations, finding none of the organizations working for their respective offices of the attorney general.

Second, Warner told Vollmer, a compromise system in which the Department of Justice collected statistics for the Census Bureau would not serve a useful purpose. Census researchers, he said, preferred to collect their information "direct rather than through a third agency."[75]

All of this was taxing for Vollmer who had just arrived at the University of Chicago to teach a new police science course.[76] Vollmer stood ready to find the middle ground between the Warner and Smith positions, even though he preferred not to take the time to do so. He wrote to Bruce Smith: "It has occurred to me that the differences between Warner's program and your program might be easily reconciled, if both sides approach the matter with the hope that a compromise might be effected. . . . Hence, it is my suggestion, that if not too inconvenient, you visit Warner and show him that the committee has no desire to force him to accept all of their views."[77] In the same tone, he wrote to Sam Warner urging Warner and Smith to meet in order to iron out their differences "diplomatically." Vollmer suggested that the value of such a formal meeting would be "to adjust the difference before it reaches that point where it could not be settled unless by a fight."[78]

It was virtually impossible for Vollmer to take a position favoring any of the Warner–Pound proposal. Therefore, there was no middle ground to be found. Since 1917, Vollmer had looked favorably upon the California model, a centralized organization known as the Bureau of Identification and Investigation which served as a clearinghouse for all the state's criminal history information, including crime statistics. He had been president of the IACP in 1922, and he had promoted J. Edgar Hoover's directorship in the Bureau of Investigation from 1924 onward, believing perhaps that Hoover would avoid captivation by political interests.[79] For all its credibility in law enforcement matters, the fight between Warner and Smith was not entirely a matter of the merits of each position. It concerned aggrandizement of Justice Department power at a time when law enforcement nationwide was gaining stature.

Newton Baker found himself in the middle of the flap. Baker wanted Raymond Moley, a New York Democrat who had conducted a study group on crime statistics in 1926 and 1927 under the auspices of the private National Crime Commission,[80] to clarify the police association position and iron out all differences. Moley, however, was already in the police camp, having urged that police statistics become the central measure of crime in the United States. Moley remarked to Baker: "It would be unfortunate to withhold very active and warm support for the work that the chiefs of police have done because their plan represents a practical immediate possibility while the other is still in a rather vague and indefinite state."[81] Moley believed that the police officials had sponsored and promoted greater sophistication in statistical compilations of crime than had any other group.[82]

In an earlier letter, Moley had also laid out the political flavor of the issue: "It ought to be occasion for rejoicing that the police officials have themselves recognized the problem and energetically attack it. The co-operation of these officials will be absolutely necessary to any such comprehensive compilation. How much better an informed, willing, even ardent co-operation, than a sullen, half-hearted one."[83] In this context, Moley seemed to suggest that without a Wickersham Commission endorsement of the IACP plan, future statistics from police organizations would be difficult to acquire. Such an endorsement could not have been expected, since Moley had been quoted in a September 26, 1929 newspaper article as saying, "The commission will merely attempt to get the Republican administration out from under in the embarrassing question of prohibition enforcement." Adding insult to injury, Moley said, "Criminal justice . . . is best administered in Milwaukee and Baltimore, two 'dripping wet cities.' This . . . is due to the effort to catch real criminals and bring them to bar instead of directing practically all of the police activity against bootleggers."[84]

Baker cut through the fog of personality differences, petty jealousies, and internal politics. Writing to Moley in late October, he concluded that the differences of view did not "involve the principles upon which the collection of statistics should be based, but rather the appropriate agency through which those principles [of statistics collection] should be applied."[85] Moley had drawn far more vitriolic responses from Pound, mainly because Pound had revealed Moley's scheme to politicize the statistics issue, and he believed that the 'Rockefeller people' wanted to use statistics as a publicity stunt to embarass Hoover. Pound asserted that most of the statistics put forth by special interest groups "will not be missed if they are left out," thus implying that only scientifically derived data would be used.[86] Pound refused to read the manual on crime statistics prepared by an internal committee of the IACP, while Wickersham was completely opposed, because of Moley's New York political affiliations, to Moley serving the commission.[87] Moley was angered by this: "It is a piece of behavior that is somewhat hard to understand or condone. . . . The attitude of Dean Pound in this matter, if continued, and if permitted to determine the official attitude of the National Commission on Law Enforcement, is likely to provoke widespread censure."[88] Baker wanted the matter resolved, telling Moley, "I can not . . . imagine that the difference is either very fundamental or very important. . . . You will be interested to know that I am getting letters from all over the United States on this subject, which rather mystifies me, since such casual knowledge as I have of the matter would hardly seem to justify the summoning of so many forces."[89] Lowenthal had hoped he could be present at the bargaining session between the competitors: "I thought maybe you [Sam Warner] mightn't mind my sitting in for a few minutes to see how science works and truth and wisdom are arrived at."[90]

No bargaining was to occur. Bruce Smith registered the *fait accompli:* "The police for the first time have come to see the necessity for a system of national crime statistics, but they realize their power to grant or withhold, and feeling that they are entitled to consideration in this matter, are inclined to insist upon it." It was, most constructively, Smith's hope that future systems of statistics collection would take different forms from those the committee had constructed; but the opportunity was presented in the fall of 1929 to have legislation to begin the process of centralization in Edgar Hoover's Bureau of Identification and Information.[91] Warner and Pound had come up against a deepening tradition of police professionalism which had strong roots in the links between several young, aggressive thinkers and police chiefs who were part of the new wave of municipal reform.[92] In short, Warner and Pound lost the argument. The Bureau of Investigation received statutory authority on June 11, 1930, to collect and report police statistics only. Clair Wilcox, the commission's director of research, tended to align himself with Warner's concerns, but as a realist he recognized that the Department of Justice held a strong position of credibility with police departments. For all his work to introduce the early stages of comprehensive, multiagency statistics, Warner was left to publish a lonely but spirited retort to his victorious adversaries in the *Harvard Law Review.*[93]

A DIVERSITY OF TOPICS

The commission sponsored several inquiries never before accomplished at a national level. Some attracted public controversy. Public hearings sought to acquire information from knowledgeable persons, but hearings were not used "merely to satisfy the desires of various individuals to air their views."[94] A sampling of the results of hearings and research studies provides evidence of the diversity of the commission's interests.

Crime among the foreign-born was a topic of special concern. Interest in the topic arose from post–World War I nativist beliefs that immigrant populations were more criminal than other groups. The commission's objective was to take up "the question whether or not there was an undue proportion of crime coming into the mill of justice from the foreign born."[95] Carl Kelsey, for example, wrote in 1926, "we have sought evidence to justify our emotional reaction against strangers. It is discovered that criminals have entered the country as well as missionaries and we have sought to understand, unconsciously hoping that our study would show that the later arrivals were more likely to be criminals than were their predecessors."[96] In the three years after Kelsey's observations, several studies failed to show a link between immigrants and crime. Commission consultant Edith Abbott wrote, "For more than a century there has been continuously in this country a clamorous group who have tended to emphasize only the difficulties connected with immigration and to lose sight of all its beneficial effects. Unfortunately these attacks on the alien have frequently laid stress on the popularly supposed relation between immigration and crime. Statistics have never justified their assumptions."[97] Her analyses in 1915 for the Chicago Crime Commission had concluded, in fact, that the native born, not the alien, had contributed a substantially larger percentage of crime.[98] In contrast to nativist views, Abbott concluded that "we should be seriously disturbed that in the enforcement of the law the alien does not at all times meet with the even handed justice that America demands."[99] With patience and tact, Abbott's final report in January 1931 offered no evidence of any extraordinary representation of the so-called foreign-born in crime statistics. A trail of unanswered questions seemed longer than the list of what had been discovered.[100]

The study of official lawlessness was primarily an inquiry into police "third-degree" tactics and other abusive justice system practices. The work was assigned to professor Zachariah Chafee, Walter H. Pollak, and Carl Stern. Pound and Loesch were the prime initiators of the study, favoring a thorough consideration of the controversy. Some on the commission rejected it for ideological reasons while others believed that authentication of facts would be difficult. A preliminary paper on the subject was written in July 1929; but within one year, Wickersham had restricted the research effort, mainly out of consideration that congressional funding decisions for the entire effort might be jeopardized by a very seriously controversial topic.[101] Wickersham did want the commission to uncover any evidence of police abuse. Chafee and his team developed leads on hundreds of cases throughout the federal court system, many involving Prohibition officers who violated search warrant requirements and used brutality in arrests, as well as numerous acts of abuse that occurred in enforcing immigration statutes.[102] In particular, he wrote to Leopold Friedman with a request that "the film of the police 'rough-housing the Communists'" and Friedman's suggestions on police abuse should be presented to the full Commission.[103]

One of the most contentious special investigations undertaken by consultants Chafee, Pollak, and Stern was the report on "Unfairness in Prosecutions." The consultants insisted upon studies of the Mooney–Billings, Sacco–Vanzetti, and Centralia cases, but the commission rejected a budget allocation for them. The strategy was to continue with the studies and incorporate the results in the larger study of "Lawlessness of Government Enforcing Agencies." In June 1931, nearly six months after the commission had finished its formal work, George Wickersham reported that he had just been notified of Pollak's work on the investigation and, more important, that the commission had in November 1930 rejected a motion to spend funds on individual cases.[104] Wickersham, disturbed by his late discovery of Pollak's use of commission funds for the law enforcement lawlessness inquiry, urged Baker to avoid formal recognition of the report because of lack of time available to the whole commission. Apparently the research director knew of the study since many requests were sent to Chafee to get the report completed no later than June 1. When the draft was finally received, several commissioners rejected its contents flatly and their animosity ensured refusal to publish the final product.[105]

During early meetings, commissioners took up the costs of crime to the private sector, principally private protection of life and property. Goldthwaite H. Dorr, assistant director of munitions during World War I and special assistant to the attorney general, chaired the research committee, reporting to commissioner Monte Lemann. Hoover had recognized, as had many in the business community, that private police and security devices had become commonplace additions to law enforcement methods. Businesses were encountering not only the costs of such crimes as burglary, larceny, and shoplifting, but also the costs of private detectives and insurance. Research included a Commerce Department study commissioned by Hoover in June 1929 and a longer commission study on the total costs of crime. The commission effort received only a small budget to carry out the innovative work of the subcommittee. Some corporate heads, such as Henry S. Dennison of Dennison Manufacturing, agreed to perform research inside their plants if secrecy could be maintained.[106] Dennison and other business leaders had other interests in agreeing to study internal crime costs, namely they wished to have a pretext to evaluate the positive impact of Prohibition on their workers.[107]

Roscoe Pound suggested that they ought to compare the cost of private protection, the economic costs of violations of law, and the amount of money spent unnecessarily by the machinery of law enforcement with what ought to be spent.[108] The commission team devoted to this investigation was expected to evaluate expenditures for burglar alarms, armored cars, and security watchmen and to determine the cost of administering criminal justice at federal, state, and local levels. Among the difficult tasks of the research team was the design of an accounting method to distinguish precisely civil costs from criminal costs and to screen information. Regarding the latter problem, Lowenthal wrote to Lemann, "I do know that a great deal of unreliable information is floating round and I hope that you will feel that with you on the Committee you will be able to make at least one important contribution—preventing a lot of people from palming off on us material which is worse than pitch."[109] While the work of estimating federal costs proceeded during the next year, on June 12, 1930, the innovative segment on private costs was postponed.

Juvenile crime also interested the commission. Clifford Shaw's work with delinquents had been sufficiently publicized and useful as a primary source of information. Commenting on Shaw's work, Clair Wilcox, the commission's director of research, observed the methodological bias of several previous studies, "Most of our inquiries have related primarily to urban areas because it is there that material is most readily to be collected and it is there that the problem of organized crime makes its appearance."[110] The difficulty was in securing the services of Miriam Van Waters, a juvenile court referee in Los Angeles. Van Waters was caught between a boss who would not release her and George Wickersham's insistence that he could use appropriate pressure through Hoover to get her a release to work for the commission. She remained in Los Angeles until clearance for her to leave for Washington was granted in late 1929, although she turned in a confidential preliminary report in late October.[111] The final report was the first formal reflection on federal juvenile crime. Its many sections summarized the number of children violating federal laws, methods used in children's cases by federal authorities, and possibilities for more adequate treatment of juvenile offenders. Hoover used the report to enlighten his proposals to change federal criminal actions against juvenile offenders.

AVOIDANCE OF POLITICAL COMPROMISE

The administration's trick was to sustain the research objectives of the commission while avoiding congressional alienation. Hoover's insistence on a multifaceted crime investigation heightened the risk of political condemnation and funding cuts. George Wickersham observed, "The fact is that whatever this Commission or one of its members says is sure to be pounced upon by representatives of some school of thought (perhaps that is over-dignifying it), and the heathen rage and disquiet themselves in vain over it."[112] Hoover seemed, however, to undertake the venture with knowledge that political apathy and outright rejection might result.

On May 1, 1930, Hoover submitted to Congress a supplemental appropriation bill for fiscal 1931 to secure an additional $250,000 to allow the commission's work to continue. Congressional reaction from those favoring Prohibition was hostile. Harkening back to Hoover's broad interpretation of the use of funds to study far more than the Prohibition problems, aging Senator Carter Glass announced that he would seek to cut off the commission's funds.[113] Hoover, greatly angered by the narrowness of Glass's perspective, proposed to fund the commission with private finances, immediately running headlong into a question of whether or not this was constitutional. On May 27, the day Hoover signed the law transferring the Prohibition Bureau to the Justice Department and other legislation to create two additional prisons, Wickersham told Newton Baker that Senator Glass's resolution had passed. Appropriations for the work of the commission, according to Senate approval, would be limited to studies of Prohibition enforcement. Wickersham said, however, that the president had ordered the commission to continue its work on all planned fronts and that Hoover was searching for the necessary funds. Commissioners agreed to continue.[114] Baker was somewhat relieved that Hoover had ordered continuation in spite of the Senate action to cut off funds: "I think that [Glass] and his associates will be amazed at the thrift with which our expenditures have been made."[115]

Indeed, Hoover stood his ground and on June 27 issued a public statement in which he acknowledged congressional resistance to the new appropriations for the commission's work. He pointed out that the enforcement of any particular law must contemplate the enforcement of other laws: "Seventy percent of [federal prisoners] are for other crimes than those arising out of prohibition. Our State prisons show about the same story." He drew support for the view that the whole system of federal justice required study from the recommendations "of every bar association and public body," thereby insisting adamantly that he would not "abandon the question for one moment or allow the work of this Commission to cease." Pushing his insistence one step further and reminding the Congress that commissioners were "volunteers serving solely out of regard to public interest," he announced that he would "secure from private sources the $100,000 necessary to carry this work forward to completion." Astutely, the statement included a suggestion that the commission establish a separate committee on Prohibition.[116]

On June 30, Commissioner Anderson wrote to Wickersham questioning whether commissioners could receive compensation from private sources, since they had been appointed under federal law. There was also the question of whether or not the public servants on the commission (i.e., Anderson, Grubb, Kenyon, and McCormick) could legally accept funds from private sources. Anderson tended toward opposing Hoover's insistence that private funds should be used to continue: "I wonder if it would not be better both for the President and for the work in which we are engaged and its ultimate usefulness if we suspended all work on subjects other than prohibition until the next session of Congress when the President can undoubtedly secure an appropriation for the completion of the work." Anderson's conclusion was that all other members of the commission favored the earliest disposal of the president's private funding notion and that with a staff cut the residual funds of the first appropriation could easily be used to complete the work on the Prohibition subject.[117] He proposed a staff cut and use of the remaining $138,000 of commission budget for the Prohibition investigation, a clear sign of his support for Prohibition's continuation.

REPORTING THE FINDINGS

The commission's preliminary report was completed in late October 1929. It was sent over to the White House in confidence on October 28, the day before the stock market crash. The commission had worked round the clock to provide the president with an outline of its progress, and with exceptions of internal squabbles over crime statistics and Prohibition, commissioners appear to have been satisfied with the effort. Judge Kenyon was bothered that Wickersham had refused to hold public hearings on Prohibition, but he was pleased that the president had proceeded with plans to reorganize the Justice Department to handle prohibition enforcement more effectively.[118] Ada Comstock hoped the report would "be clear to his engineering eye [and] that a solid foundation is being laid."[119] The preliminary report struck at the problems confronted by the research teams in public hearings and in main commission meetings. On commencing the commission work, "it was at once evident that on the subjects of crime and criminal justice almost everyone has opinions and few have any facts. The Commission decided that while it wanted informed opinions on desirable lines of inquiry, it must just have facts." There had been few scientific studies to draw upon in any topic, and what had been initiated was not more than seven or eight years old, among them "a handful of competent, but localized, crime surveys."[120]

Hoover's need to review the preliminary report of the commission was a reaction to congressional pressure on economic and social fronts. Senator William Borah kept his eye on the commission's Prohibition inquiries too. Hoover knew that at least with respect to Prohibition matters, he should be fully informed. Wickersham wired Newton Baker that the "President is anxious [to] have Commission's present recommendations concerning Prohibition for use [in] connection with his annual message." On November 19, Wickersham also wrote to Ada Comstock: "The President has expressed a desire to have an interim report from us on the subject of Prohibition, and after a discussion between him and Judge Kenyon, Dean Pound, Judge Mackintosh and myself, we have prepared a report." Comstock was to review the work and get it back to Wickersham as soon as possible "as the President's secretary is clamoring for it, in order that the President may use it in connection with the preparation of his [annual] Message."[121] Despite thinness of content, the draft was sent over to the White House on November 21, 1929 and later printed by the House of Representatives.[122]

Hoover released the preliminary report of the commission on January 13, 1930, appending it to a brief special message to Congress on law enforcement organizational changes. The message emphasized that the federal courts and other organizations in the federal system had been unable to keep up with criminal law violations. Federal criminal laws had expanded greatly in the previous twenty years. Prohibition violations accounted for more than one-half of all arrests and prosecutions. In essence, the system was jammed with cases, and the impact was being felt on the civil side as well. "The development of the facts," Hoover reported, "shows the necessity of certain important and evident administrative reforms in the enforcement and judicial machinery." Hoover asked the Congress to examine the commission's proposals to speed up court handling of minor criminal cases, mentioning carefully that such proposals were both workable and constitutional according to "the eminent jurist upon the commission and others whose advice they have sought." In closing, he reminded the Congress that more study was intended beyond the "immediate questions [such as] causes of crime, the character of criminal laws, the benefits and liabilities that flow from them, the abuses which arise from them, the method by which enforcement and judicial personnel is secured, the judicial procedure, [and] the respective responsibility of the Federal and State Governments to these problems." More time was needed to study these problems, and more time would be taken.[123]

The commission continued its work for more than a year longer, releasing its fourteen volumes in July 1931. It had begun with a sincere concern, as suggested in the preliminary report of October 1929: "We found that with huge investments in plant and personnel and with great operating costs, the country has been proceeding largely in a haphazard manner, without any inventory of the available facts, without commensurate research for checking a great social evil, without the application of the principles that have been so successful in some of the professions, in many businesses and in the social sciences." Completion meant that Hoover became the first president to convene a national study of crime's impact on federal law enforcement, courts, and prisons. He hoped that the outcome would guide and influence similar state and local initiatives. Perhaps aiming unreasonably high, he also expected the commission's results to find ways to "defeat crime and the corruption that flows from it" and to reinstitute moral and spiritual respect for law. Despite distractions of economic chaos and prohibition politics, the commission achieved its overall objectives. Neither internal disagreements nor congressional intrigues stalled publication of research by the most distinguished intellects of crime and criminal justice.

Chapter 5

Reforming Federal Cops
and Courts

*The strong man must at all times be alert to the attack of insidious
disease.*[1]

The Framers of the Constitution intended that the chief executive
supervise federal law enforcement and judicial nominations. The
administrative structure for carrying out this intention, however,
was not well defined. Criminal jurisdiction of the federal courts required special acts of the First Congress.[2] Following the Civil War,
federal police, court, and prison functions expanded in number and
procedural intricacy. Over the next sixty years, the federal government employed a small force of marshals, investigators, intelligence
agents, judges, and prison guards. Federal jurisdiction in civil and
criminal matters had indeed expanded. Along the way, presidents
and congresses failed to plan a cohesive justice system. States jealously guarded authority over internal criminal affairs. By 1870,
criminal legislation stressed federal policing over judicial or prison
functions, reflecting new social forces, such as urbanization, criminal markets, criminal inventiveness, and population mobility.
  Expanded federal intervention in crime control obligated presidents from Grant to Coolidge to enlarge law enforcement agencies,
clarify agency jurisdiction and tasks, hire personnel, relocate centers of operation, and install formal procedures. By contrast with
earlier presidents, Herbert Hoover used his inaugural address to
acknowledge executive responsibility to reorganize and improve

federal criminal justice. Hoover regarded this as a major policy priority, referring to the repairs as "the most sore necessity of our times." Domestic and international progress was, he believed, inherently linked to the performance of justice organizations. He was responsible for managing more than five thousand police, administrative, clerical, parole, probation, and prison personnel. Apart from normal duties of appointments and department supervision, Hoover considered department reorganization an intergral part of the chief executive's duties.

In the first year of Hoover's presidency, special attention was aimed at raising the stature of federal law enforcement and revising federal criminal procedures. The former was accomplished by expanding, reorganizing, and professionalizing federal law enforcement. The latter required legislation and persistence with the Congress. This chapter explores the Hoover administration's initiatives to make federal government more directly responsible for promoting fundamental change in law enforcement and the courts.

PROHIBITION'S NEGATIVE IMPACT ON FEDERAL POLICING

All presidents inherit legacies of earlier administrations, congresses, and courts. Hoover inherited declining law enforcement agencies and obsolete court practices. Separating all other enforcement obligations imposed upon federal police before 1914, no other duties presented the corrupting influences, statistical nightmares, and organizational degradation introduced by the Harrison Act of 1914, which dealt with drugs other than alcohol, and the Volstead Act of 1920, which dealt with alcohol. Enforcement actions imposed by these laws added street-police tactics to a small and underdeveloped force of investigators, all of whom held limited authority to investigate mail fraud, interstate prostitution, tax violations, assassination plots, counterfeiting, and illegal immigration. Drug and alcohol enforcement, mainly responses to moral crusades, altered the size and scope of federal police operations. In fifteen years, alcohol and drug laws transformed elite investigative organizations into decentralized and poorly functioning departments more closely analogous to local police departments. By 1929, federal law enforcement in these areas languished in arrested professional development and ineffectiveness leading to widespread popular disrespect. Two competing futures were possible: continued decline and further negative labeling of all investigative branches or new operational controls on performance and reorganization to meet objectives. Hoover chose the latter course.

Local and state police organizations had displayed signs of significant qualitative improvement after 1900. The 'good government' movement of the late nineteenth century had implicated local police in harsh practices and systematic corruption, thereby encouraging the emergence of citizen campaigns for change.[3] Terms such as 'professional' and 'police role in crime prevention' appeared in the language of law enforcement.[4] Widespread experimentation with state-controlled city law enforcement departments yielded to local movements to control metropolitan police forces.[5] A literature reflecting rising expectations of the role of police in democratic government appeared in autobiographies of politicians and police officials.[6] Qualitative improvements in uniformed and detective forces had become commonplace by 1920, and chroniclers of police advancements, such as August Vollmer, Bruce Smith, and Raymond B. Fosdick were optimistic about a profession of policing.[7] Crime commission reports published in the early 1920s by citizen and public investigating bodies recounted clean up campaigns and police reforms.[8] Newspaper exposure of abusive, corrupt, and illegal practices of local police assisted the efforts of business leaders and citizen action groups to demand change and professionalization.

Local publics were not well informed, however, of developments in federal law enforcement, mainly because of their relatively obscure activities and because of low interest in federal organizations on the part of the press. Passage of the controversial income tax of 1913 and the Prohibition law of 1920 increased significantly the accounts of federal police raids, agent corruption, and incompetence.[9] No literature reflecting advances in federal law enforcement developed with any degree of comparability to that which traced local police development. With few exceptions, federal law enforcement was hardly acknowledged by congressional or executive politicians. No professors of criminology or other social studies in the 1920s devoted entire books to an examination of federal policing organizations. Yet, by 1929, federal investigative services employed several thousands of people.[10]

From the turn of the century through the 1920s, effective and professional work of federal enforcement agencies was largely ignored, overshadowed by the negative impact of Prohibition enforcement.[11] Reports of incompetence, corruption, and abusive exercise of authority eroded confidence in fair and efficient federal law enforcement. Mabel Willebrandt, assistant attorney general responsible for Prohibition enforcement agents, was plagued by reports of failed policing opportunities and corrupt agents. Other federal departments employing investigative arms suffered similar charges, but Prohibition agents bore the brunt of the criticism.[12] The worst cases involved bystander shootings in federal or combined federal–local raids. Innovations in investigative practices had already been checked in the Bureau of Investigation and the Internal Revenue's intelligence unit.[13] The Prohibition Bureau, however, remained the "unwanted enforcers,"[14] comparatively understaffed, underpaid, and unregulated by civil service practices.[15]

Publicly, Hoover stood by his duty to enforce the Eighteenth Amendment and the Volstead Act. He offered no apology for his view that "obedience to the law should be taught as the first lesson in self-government."[16] Congressional and general audiences were reminded, "My own duty and that of all executive officials is clear — to enforce the law with all the means at our disposal without equivocation or reservation."[17] Constitutionally granted authority would be used to promote the philosophical ends of Prohibition, most of which he regarded as economically and socially sound, and to exercise administrative authority to carry out the law. On a more pragmatic level, however, he told the Associated Press in April 1929, "If a law is wrong, its rigid enforcement is the surest guaranty of its repeal. If it is right, its enforcement is the quickest method of compelling respect for it."

Privately, however, Hoover recognized problems inherent in enforcing laws against social vices, particularly when an unsupportive public shifted the burden of responsibility to government alone.[18] As he reflected upon occasional abusive governmental actions to secure compliance, he approached the balance as fundamentally a task of reorganization and elimination of corruption. His rejection of repeal of the laws was unacceptable, the only course to constructive results was well-organized, consistently firm, and legally endorsed police methods. New organizational arrangements, competent and enlightened leadership, and increased pressure on state authorities, were therefore his choices of action.

Such a course posed a new dilemma for Hoover. By his refusal to continue the policies of previous administrations, he would be expected to add enforcement personnel and to clean out corrupt and incompetent personnel. By doing so, however, he would send an unintended message to the states that federal enforcement was increasing its responsibility for the problem. Therefore, when he spoke about expanded and reorganized federal enforcement services, he chose his words carefully. For example, in May 1929 he told the National Congress of Parents and Teachers: "Obedience to law is thus the first duty of the citizen of a self-governing State." On September 17, 1929, he wrote to the president of the National Women's

Christian Temperance Union that "too many people have come to rely wholly upon the strong arm of law to enforce abstinence, forgetting that the cause of temperance has its strong foundations in the conviction of the individual of the personal value to himself of temperance in all things."[19] Responding to a Des Moines citizen who wrote to ask that he put a stop to shipboard bars on the high seas, Hoover replied that "it has always seemed to me that standards outside the law are matters for individual determination. The government must not go outside of its legal authority. Government officials or private concerns may set examples in matters beyond the law, but the government must not force such action."[20] His frustration with the inadequacies of a purely enforcement strategy brought him eventually to consider trading off new forms of economic enforcement to sustain the overall principle of self-imposed restraint.[21] Intuitively and practically, Hoover was fully aware that degradation of citizen attitudes toward police and other justice agencies would ultimately impair overall obedience to law. Purely federal initiative could not change this situation.

ENFORCEMENT ABUSES AND POLICY RESPONSES

Organizational performance of Internal Revenue agents, Postal Inspectors, or agents of the Bureau of Investigation rarely concerned President Hoover or Attorney General Mitchell. Agents in these organizations operated under established standards of professionalism, and they were managed by men of high integrity.[22] Thus, when Hoover referred to improving federal law enforcement, he was talking about new controls over organizations most closely associated with the corrupting elements of ordinary city police work: Treasury's Prohibition Bureau, Treasury's Narcotics Bureau, and the Labor Department's Immigration Border Patrol. These organizations had experienced nearly uncontrollable growth by comparison with other agencies. Organization size and the overwhelming enforcement tasks degraded executive command and made control difficult.

At operational levels, these factors often led to the employment of unruly, often mean-spirited and unprofessional men.[23] The Prohibition Bureau relied on state directors of enforcement and a skeleton crew of agents who were not uniformly committed to gaining ground in the war to eliminate unregulated alcohol.[24] Perpetual enforcement failures intensified pressures to invade privacy, destroy private property, and use "third-degree" interrogation tactics against entrenched liquor and drug conspiracies.[25] Furthermore, it was not uncommon for state directors to employ thugs and private detectives to assist. By invoking new procedural controls over these agencies and by realigning organizational reporting within the executive branch, Hoover expected that new levels of control, efficiency, and professionalism among prohibition and narcotics agents would improve citizen respect. The successful implementation of these changes came with the appointment of Amos W. W. Woodcock as director of Prohibition enforcement upon reassignment of the bureau to the Justice Department.[26]

The federal policing of Prohibition was mainly a nightmare of understaffing and maladministration. On June 30, 1927, for example, the Bureau of Prohibition had 4,261 employees to cover the United States, including clerks, headquarters personnel, and field forces, of whom 2,423 were Prohibition administrators, deputy administrators, assistant administrators, special agents, investigators, and agents.[27] In the Customs Bureau, the problems were the result of imbalances in the assignment of agents and the authority of customs agents to destroy property seized during liquor raids. Over 700 customs personnel worked on the U.S.–Canadian border, while only 174 were assigned to the Mexican border. Border personnel were equipped only with service revolvers, rifles, a few aircraft, horses, and sawed-off shotguns. Staffing complaints persisted from all twenty-seven Prohibition enforcement districts. Poor enforcement was compounded by inability to get cases into court. U.S. attorneys frequently complained that backlogs in their departments arose from "an unduly large number of cases made by agents who are either new or incompetent. . . . In many instances search warrants are defective and will not stand when attacked."[28]

Deadly force was an accepted tool of Prohibition and drug enforcement. Booze entered the country by ship, automobile, and truck, transported by ordinary thugs and former legitimate businessmen who expanded and introduced methods for shipping bulk quantities.[29] International incidents with Canada and Mexico persisted during Hoover's presidency, but none became war-threatening. Foreign vessels were seized, and cargoes were forfeited to the Treasury. Foreign service officers filed regular reports on known or suspected cargoes of booze or drugs destined for U.S. ports. Occasionally, overly aggressive enforcement agents thought that deadly force was justified to stop transgressors, foreign or domestic.[30]

The border with Canada in the Great Lakes region was an endless source of international tension.[31] The sinking of the *I'm Alone* strained U.S.–Canadian relations in the first days of Hoover's new administration. In later months, several other vessels were seized by force, and crew members were sometimes injured or killed in shootouts with Customs Service patrol boats or the Coast Guard. The State Department concluded in 1933 that had the Hoover administration failed to keep open lines of communication between England, Canada, and other European countries regarding enforcement practices, any of the individual incidents of violent force "might have led to war in former days."[32]

Guns blazed, cannons fired, doors were smashed, and moving vehicles were targets. On April 5, 1929, the Treasury Department issued a report claiming that 190 people had been killed by state and federal authorities enforcing the federal Prohibition law, 55 of them federal agents, the remainder citizens or local police. Data did not include hundreds of citizens and local police who had been killed in strictly state Prohibition enforcement operations. Publication of the limited federal information was calculated to counter criticism arising from the *I'm Alone* case and the unfortunate killing by state authorities of a woman from Aurora, Illinois.[33] Distancing himself from the Aurora incident, Hoover told reporters, "I have no right to pass any judgment on that question, the facts of which have not been thoroughly sifted by any public tribunal, but I might say that this is entirely a case of local authorities, and was not participated in any shape by the Federal authorities, right or wrong. Federal visitation and search of private dwellings, as you know, is strictly limited by the laws, and directions have been given to the Federal service [some months ago] that are of the most stringent order on that whole question, and I know of no cases since this administration is where there has been anything which could even be called an excessive zeal by any agents."[34]

An assistant secretary of the treasury, Seymour Lowman, a verbal heavy-hitter for the administration's law enforcement policy, told the press that in all cases wherein federal officers had been charged by local grand juries or coroners' juries with abuse of authority or other crimes, they had been exonerated by trial juries. Admitting that several cases were pending in various widely scattered courts, Lowman insisted that in each case his officers had acted according to procedure. Hoover's intolerance for lawlessness in enforcing the Volstead Act was often publicly announced,[35] but his orders to remove shotguns as enforcement weapons were not entirely explicit.[36]

Neither enforcement controversies nor international incidents altered Hoover's encouragement to treasury and other departments to continue vigorous policing efforts. "It seems obvious," he wrote to Treasury Secretary Andrew Mellon on April 8, "that there are large operations in illicit liquor current in the country. Otherwise the general distribution of liquor in large supplies which appears in retail would not take place. It seems obvious also that the most important area for enforcement of the 18th Amendment should be directed toward these larger rings and conspiracies." He suggested that Mellon work with Mitchell to organize special teams of Justice Department attorneys and hand-picked Prohibition Bureau investigators to make cases against the large liquor organizations. Elite squads, such as Eliot Ness's nine-man unit established in Chicago, served to taunt big organizations, but Hoover and others became progressively convinced that indirect methods using tax and drug laws would net faster, less dangerous results.[37] Mellon was asked to consider the wisdom of the proposal.[38]

Mellon, perpetually indifferent to Prohibition enforcement,[39] approved Hoover's proposal and went further to suggest that the innovation "might well, pending the enactment of legislation, constitute a preliminary and logical step looking to the ultimate transfer of the Bureau of Prohibition to the Department of Justice."[40] Mellon, long an advocate of ridding the Treasury Department of the enforcement responsibility, hoped that a transfer of the Prohibition Bureau to Justice would take no more than one year to accomplish. Even after this had been achieved in 1930, Hoover retained his attachment to the idea that teams of investigators and U.S. attorneys could have significant impact upon conspiracy crimes.[41]

But Prohibition enforcement could not be micromanaged from the White House or from any other office in Washington. Enforcement officers had a difficult task, and heavy-handedness often went unsupervised. In June 1929, Prohibition enforcers stirred one of many international incidents on land analagous to the sea incident involving the *I'm Alone* schooner. The Border Patrol shot and killed a Minnesota resident, Henry Virkkula, under circumstances that received national press attention.[42] Virkkula, characterized by the press as one of "Enforcement's Innocent Victims," was shot in the neck and heart while attempting to stop his car at a Border Patrol checkpoint on a darkened road near International Falls, Minnesota. The incident happened on June 8 as he was driving home from vacation with his family; his wife was seated in the passenger seat, and two children were asleep in the rear seat. Patrolman Emmet J. White was ordered by his supervisor to fire his sawed-off shotgun at the rear of the Virkkula's car, claiming later that he had properly instructed the driver to stop. According to procedure, Border Patrol officers were armed with pistols and shotguns, and they were authorized to use deadly force against people they determined were fleeing, including Prohibition law violators.[43]

Investigators were dispatched from Washington to review the situation and report to Assistant Secretary Lowman. On the way to Minnesota by train, inspector Henry A. Roberts told the press that "the shooting was wholly unjustified and unwarranted." Washington officials, including Lowman, were necessarily rankled by Roberts's remarks, but an order was issued immediately removing use of sawed-off shotguns by Border Patrol officers.[44] Lowman's defensive reactions to press inquiries reflected embarrassment both over the incident and about leaked information in general. Consistent with earlier statements, Lowman accepted patrolman White's account of the incident; White, he believed, had acted within his authority.[45] Behind the scenes, it was later learned, Lowman had uncovered a tidbit of evidence that Virkkula had once been convicted of a Prohibition violation. This provided him with a cover story for White's actions and enabled him to justify the behavior of other allegedly besieged federal officers. Reporter Abraham I. Harris pointed out the absurdity of Lowman's challenge to Virkkula's integrity in the July 24 issue of *The Nation:* The Treasury Department "will make the most of that fact and is already making the most of it, even though it has nothing to do with the case, since Wirkkula was not hauling liquor . . . and the patrolmen in any case did not know who he was."

On June 18, Hoover was asked in a news conference if he had taken steps to investigate the incident. His response suggested that Lowman's investigation of Virkkula's background had influenced his outlook: "I deeply deplore the killing of any person. The Treasury Department is making an effort to prevent the misuse of arms. Any case of misuse will be determined by the orderly proceedings of the Department and the courts. I hope that the communities along the border will do their best to help the Treasury and the systematic way that is being carried on by international criminals against the laws of the United States. It is these activities that are at the root of all of our difficulties." The Virkkula shooting caused the International Falls city council to send Hoover a resolution asking him "to end the terrorism inflicted upon our citizens and neighbors by Federal customs patrolmen, engaged in prohibition enforcement." The resolution made reference to "the vicious and unlawful conduct of . . . Government agents." In an indirectly conciliatory tone, Hoover wrote to the council on June 21: "You may rest assured that there is no intention on the part of the Federal Government in any way to transgress the limits of the law."[46]

Lowman was not at all conciliatory, charging the press with inaccurate and incomplete reporting. Testifying before the Wickersham Commission on the day that Hoover sent his letter to the city council, Lowman held out harsh accusations of misplaced press sensibilities for Virkkula: "Well, I get a picture every morning of Virkulla [his spelling] and his wife sitting by his coffin. That is on my table every morning. And then sometimes they have pictures of little children, and so forth. But Virkulla was a well-known bootlegger up in that country. He ran a little confectionary store in front and he had a speakeasy in the rear. He plead guilty in March and was fined in the District Court." Lowman also charged that Virkkula had willfully passed by the large customs stop sign, causing officer White to shoot at the tires. With questionable veracity, he also claimed that two empty liquor bottles were found in the car.[47] It seemed important to him to conclude that the press were in error in reporting the matter as a Prohibition Bureau case rather than a Customs case. Equally defensive were Lowman's remarks regarding a May 1928 situation in which Coast Guard officers accidentally shot to death a man named Jacob D. Hanson:[48] "I would not have shot him, and probably you would not, but you want to recollect that the men engaged as Coast Guardsmen there are not college professors or lawyers; they get $36 a month and their food." In contrast, Customs Bureau agents, he reported, were paid $2100 per year.[49] Increasingly, Lowman appeared to be the administration's voice for tough law enforcement.

Prohibition Bureau and Border Patrol shootings related to liquor enforcement drew fire from newspaper editors, members of Congress, and even leading citizens. Editors asserted that political pressures on these agencies had induced overactive trigger fingers among law enforcement personnel.[50] Some congressmen feared that citizens might revolt in some areas by defending themselves against federal and local police believed to be abusing authority.[51] Henry Ford believed that published concerns for shootings merely served propaganda interests of the "wets": "There is more discussion over one shot fired in attempting to enforce prohibition than there was over 50,000 shots fired in the last war. If our government cannot take care of the enforcement of the prohibition laws, what is to become of the government."[52] Even the head of the Methodist Board of Temperance wanted increased penalties for buying and selling booze, and he insisted that Hoover should use the Army and Navy.[53] Increasingly, newspapers suggested that Hoover had lost faith in Andrew Mellon's management of the Treasury Department's Prohibition Bureau, and in theory this caused Hoover to urge the Congress to transfer the enforcement functions to the Justice Department.[54] Clearly, Hoover was pressured from several quarters to bring immediate control over Prohibition enforcement practices. Mellon remained in the wings applauding organizational realignments.

Along the Mexican border, U.S. Prohibition enforcement practices were not significantly better. A month before Hoover took office, the Border Patrol was again implicated in unauthorized use of deadly force. An officer shot a Mexican national believed to be carrying il-legal booze into Arizona. On August 6, 1929, Robe White, assistant secretary of labor, handed Attorney General Mitchell a report of the facts concerning the incident. Apparently, surveillance of smuggling and illegal alien activities had been set up at Silverbell, Arizona, in February 1929. U.S. authorities were accustomed to capturing bands of smugglers, the ultimate purpose of this practice was to find and destroy contraband, mainly alcohol or drugs.

Two men passed through a surveillance zone on the night of Feb-ruary 5. They were confronted by three border agents, including an inspector named Mathis E. Cleveland. When the smugglers tried to escape, the agents fired their shotguns. A coroner's inquest announced that the death of one Ernesto Lopez had been caused by the agents. Two agents were arrested but released on bail while Cleveland was charged with murder. The United States attorney's office in Tucson dispatched John Gung'l to temporarily represent Cleveland in the state criminal case. Mitchell and Oscar R. Luhring, assistant attorney general, conferred on the proper and sensitive course of action.[55]

With the earlier border cases still fresh in their minds, Arizona authorities proceeded against Mathis Cleveland; but within days of his arrest, the U.S. district court took jurisdiction. The ensuing in-vestigation raised questions about law enforcement practices along the Mexican border, in particular matters of jurisdictional authority between Prohibition, border patrol, and immigration agents. On August 10, Luhring advised Mitchell: "This is another border patrol shooting case, in which a Border Patrol Inspector is charged with murder by the state authorities in Arizona. . . . This seems to be another case in which an investigating officer of the Government is given a gun and a badge and without instruction as to his rights and duties in the enforcement of the law he proceeds to fire indiscrimi-nately upon persons traversing the highways, under the mistaken belief that his position with the Government authorizes him to go to any length in the supposed enforcement of the law without regard to the facts actually at hand." Luhring's lengthy summary ended with a cautionary note regarding illegal use of authority, hoping that fed-eral officers would avoid almost certain recurrences and "consequent embarrassment and loss of public confidence."[56]

Drug smuggling had also come to require a major federal enforce-ment effort. Opium importation and domestic heroin use had shown no significant decline since the implementation of the Harrison Act in 1914.[57] Adding cocaine and heroin efforts worsened the overall burdens on law enforcement agencies. Treasury's narcotics unit had complained that it employed far too few agents to stop the flow of drugs to the alleged 110,000 addicts. Druggists, physicians, and border check points were among the key concerns of federal narcotics enforcers; but with only three hundred narcotics agents and a budget of less than $2 million, the task remained impossible to accomplish. Bribery and lax enforcement at state and federal levels were not uncommon.[58] By 1929, violators of the Harrison Act comprised one-third of the federal prison population at Atlanta and Leavenworth, while Volstead Act violators contributed only 14 percent.[59] Hoover reported this statistic to a public he believed was convinced the prisons held mostly Prohibition criminals.

In June 1929, Seymour Lowman told the Wickersham Commission that although raw opium smuggling had been nearly wiped out the main increases in drug importations were attributable to illegally manufactured drugs and cocaine. In both cases, "we frequently find quantities of drugs from Europe in the center of a great box of merchandise, and it is very difficult to detect, and practically the only way we can detect it is through information that our agents get abroad."[60] According to Lowman, the drug problem was creeping up in national social significance.[61] Hoover knew better, having understood from his foreign travels in Asia the nature of the Chinese and Japanese opium problem.[62]

U.S. law enforcement policy on illegal drug importation had depended upon agreements with countries that engaged in raw drug harvesting or manufactured cocaine, morphine, or heroin.[63] D. W. MacCormack, director of the Internal Revenue, testified before the Wickersham Commission on the international aspects of narcotics control, suggesting that the policy was appealing in theory but ineffective as a device for eliminating drug trafficking. MacCormack had discovered in a study he made for the Persian government that raw material production controls would have no impact on trafficking in heroin and morphine, "which is the vital problem insofar as the United States and the countries of Europe are concerned. There are probably not less that ten thousand tons of raw opium produced annually. Not more than three hundred tons are required to meet the medicinal and scientific requirements of the world. Under the most favorable political and economic conditions many years must elapse before this excess production can be suppressed."

MacCormack told the commission that drug manufacturing was the most easily accomplished task. Manufacturing countries, he said, "are for the most part numbered among the great nations of the world [and] once their own hands are clean they will be in a much better position to bring pressure to bear on the small producing countries." The suppression of opium growing, MacCormack reported, could only be accomplished in places like Persia and India by substitution of new crops, since opium was a significant factor in the economies of several countries. Strict controls over domestic distribution, MacCormack concluded, were essential to the overall drug enforcement program, but law enforcement efforts would fail in succeeding generations if education on "the war on narcotics" and international cooperation on raw and manufactured drugs were not also undertaken.[64]

REORGANIZATION RESPONSE TO
ENFORCEMENT PROBLEMS

Hoover accepted and understood his enforcement obligations. Neither personal values nor experience allowed him to ignore his constitutional duty or fail to remind the states of their responsibilities. He was determined to carry on with enforcement priorities, but he had no intention of usurping state functions. "Our proposals," he told the press in January 1930, "are merely to correct the deficits in our administrative machinery, and are purely Federal. We have no notion of relieving the States of responsibilities or extending the Federal activities beyond their proper relationships with the States."[65] Later that year, after the Capone tax-evasion investigation was announced, he corrected a false report that he intended new criminal laws on racketeering: "Every single State has ample laws covering such criminality. What is needed is enforcement of the laws, not more laws. Any suggestion of increasing the Federal criminal laws is a reflection upon the sovereignty and stamina of State government."[66] Hoover announced intentions to reorganize and expand enforcement agencies. The inaugural address associated reorganization with sure and swift justice and its influence upon state justice systems.[67] Hoover told the Associated Press on April 22 that it was necessary to scrutinize the records and attitudes of people qualified to participate in the reorganization task, ultimately placing the major burden on the Justice Department. Mere executive authority was insufficient to achieve the organizational realignment. Congressional approval, preceded perhaps by committee inquiries into the implications of the transfer, would be needed to move the Prohibition Bureau from Treasury to Justice.[68]

Hoover did not wait, however, to impose new performance expectations upon federal law enforcement agents: "It is the purpose of the Federal administration systematically to strengthen its law enforcement agencies week by week, month by month, year by year, not by dramatic displays and violent attacks in order to make headlines, not by violating the law itself through misuse of the law in its enforcement, but by steady pressure, steady weeding out of all incapable and negligent officials no matter what their status; by encouragement, promotion, and recognition for those who do their duty; and by the most rigid scrutiny of the records and attitudes of all persons suggested for appointment to official posts in our entire law enforcement machinery."[69]

A priority of both Hoover and the attorney general was codification of federal law enforcement activities. In furtherance of Hoover's objective, Mitchell convened conferences attended by the heads of the various federal law enforcement branches. On May 7, 1929, in the office of the secretary of labor, James J. Davis, a plan was constructed to merge all the border patrol functions with the other Justice Department functions in Prohibition and narcotics enforcement.[70] Agency representatives were not in agreement, finding policy contradictions that presented particular problems for law enforcement, especially on the Mexican border. The Agriculture Department had supported a policy of allowing illegal aliens to cross the border to work on farms, while the Labor Department was in business to prevent illegal entrants to the United States. The meeting served, however, to halt temporarily the hostility between affected agencies. Participants agreed on the common objective of promoting legislation to allow codification of a border patrol function.

Hoover and Mitchell could find no significant difference between the objectives of the Coast Guard, the Agriculture Department, the Labor Department, and the Treasury Department.[71] The Coast Guard supported a unified border patrol in the Treasury Department, even though it would be expected to give up some functions, personnel, and equipment.[72] The meetings, as well as the new policy of requesting broad input to proposed reorganization plans, stirred expected administrative controversy, but the major leaders of change remained in fundamental agreement. Mitchell, upon reviewing the notes and minutes of the meeting wrote, "We have sure got some action."[73]

Overlapping enforcement actions had caused abdication of responsibility and interagency conflict. Prohibition's political volatility ensured a constant stream of blame for border smuggling, while the immigration situation remained comparitively benign after the spy scares of World War I ended. Interagency rivalries, as well as implications they held for incidents on both northern and southern borders, intensified Hoover's interests in a unified border patrol service. Competing interests in Congress, however, developed separate lines of reorganization proposals: to reorganize the border patrol under the Treasury Department's Coast Guard or to absorb all border patrol enforcement functions into the Justice Department.[74]

J. Edgar Hoover, who had been asked to offer his views on the plans, later wrote to Mabel Willebrandt, "I might state that several years ago I made a rather comprehensive study and prepared a plan

for the operation of Border Patrol but became discouraged somewhat in view of the notorious jealousy that seems to permeate the
majority of Governmental investigative agencies. I think all agree
that the Border Patrol is a very desirable thing to have established
but each agency that is interested in it seems to adhere to only the
view that it is desirable provided that the individual agency had control of it. However, in view of this attitude of the President upon
reorganization of Government Departments, it may be possible that
efficiency will gain the ascendency over petty bureaucratic policies."[75]

Mabel Willebrandt's resignation in May 1929 eliminated an obstacle to Hoover's reorganization plans. Few tears were shed at her
departure, as Hoover's letter to Willebrandt accepting her resignation,
although expressing "deep regret," indicated that after her lengthy
service as assistant attorney general for Prohibition, tax, and prisons,
"I do not feel that I am justified in again asking you to reconsider."
Hoover denied reports that there had been friction between Mitchell, Willebrant, and himself over Prohibition reorganization.[76]
Calling her respectfully a "very estimable lady," Hoover and Mitchell
were anxious to get on with appointing a new assistant attorney
general who would be more responsive to Mitchell's direction.[77] G.
Aaron Youngquist, a hesitant candidate for Willebrandt's position,
took charge of Prohibition and tax matters late in 1929.

Attorney General Mitchell drafted and laid before congressional
committees Hoover's reorganization plans. Testimony was heard of
the horrors and inefficiencies of the Treasury Department and of
the difficulties in coordinating with U.S. attorneys and the Justice
Department. Three presidents before Hoover had heard these complaints, and all three had wanted Prohibition enforcement moved to
Justice.[78] Congressional action was slow, causing Hoover to publicly
reemphasize the need to concentrate and strengthen law enforcement. More verbal pounding would be necessary. In his news conference on December 27, his special message to Congress on January
13, 1930, his news conference the following day, and a second special
message on April 28, he repeated his initiatives. Finally, in the spring
of 1930, Congress passed the Prohibition Reorganization Act, and
Hoover signed it on May 27. The long awaited transfer of the Prohibition Bureau to the Justice Department was completed.

Hoover was less noticeably vigorous about, but no less interested
in, a new, separate agency to handle narcotics investigations. Harry
J. Anslinger, an unknown but hard-working assistant commissioner
of Prohibition, had laid the groundwork for a new Narcotics Bureau
in the Justice Department.[79] The prominence of Prohibition, however,
suggested to Hoover that, while he could link booze and drug violations in the occasional speech, he must also proceed cautiously to

avoid confusing Congress on his priorities. Anslinger was another of the many department heads in Treasury's enforcement branches on whom Andrew Mellon had relied to police a law he regarded with ambivalence.[80] To help surpass possible congressional and public resistence to a new agency, the proposal to create a special narcotics force was characterized as an effort to attack the foreign invasion of drugs. Hoover quietly signed the bill approving the new organization on June 14, 1930.

A two-front attack on drug smuggling was proffered by Anslinger to achieve agreements with selected drug-producing nations—especially those suspected of doing little to deter the exportation of opium, heroin, and marihuana to the United States—and to begin significantly increased domestic enforcement. Anslinger's personal observations of Russian smuggling of narcotics into the United States seemed to combine nicely with forces in the Congress determined to pass punitive enforcement legislation. He was appropriately credentialed and experienced for the directorship of Hoover's proposed Narcotics Division, and on September 23, 1930, Hoover announced the appointment.[81] New congressional funding for narcotics enforcement comported with popular sentiments about drugs, mainly those whipped up in the press by Richmond Hobson and belabored by members of Congress who feared communist influence.[82] Hoover quietly urged the Congress to increase funding for narcotics enforcement on June 18, 1930; and with few exceptions, the enforcement work of the new division was reclusive and without significant press attention in late 1930, 1931, and 1932.[83]

Agreements with foreign countries to control manufacturing and exportation of narcotics greatly interested Hoover. In February 1930, he endorsed the International (or World) Narcotics Association and the World Conference on Narcotic Education: "I earnestly commend [these organizations] for [their] recognition of the menace to society in the excessive manufacture of narcotic drugs and for their use of scientific methods and surveys to establish the facts concerning the evils and extent of the traffic in these drugs. The consistent leadership of Americans in the effort to control this traffic is a world-wide service to the health, morals and public safety of the race."[84] Hoover's endorsement continued in 1931 with a call for the organization to "energize the police power of the several states of this Union to destroy illicit traffic in narcotics," and in 1932 to aspire "to yet more effective measures to destroy this fearful menace to the well-being of the race."[85]

Beyond words of encouragement, Hoover appointed and funded four U.S. representatives to the May 1931 meeting of the League of Nations Conference on the Limitation of the Manufacture of Narcotic Drugs: John K. Caldwell, foreign service officer; Harry J. Anslinger, commissioner of narcotics; Dr. Walter L. Treadway, chief of the Public Health Service's Bureau of Mental Hygiene; and Sanborn Young, chairman of the California State Narcotic Commission. Clearly, these appointments carried on Hoover's quiet commitment to both international conventions and domestic state legislation to control the use of illegal narcotics.[86]

The general secretary of the World Narcotics Defense Association, another name for the International Narcotics Association, was Richmond P. Hobson, a former navy officer, Spanish–American War hero and Alabama congressman. Hobson's post–World War I crusades to promote vigorous enforcement of Prohibition and drug laws had gained national media attention. Hobson had been the first member of Congress to pursue passage in 1913 of the first national Prohibition law. Unquestionably, he was a force to be contended with. Hoover's plans for rational domestic and international narcotics enforcement, however, would not permit Hobson to control their direction and content through maneuvers to gain the president's official recognition.[87] Edgar Rickard, Hoover's long-time associate and confidant, had instructed the president in January 1930: "Our reports here on Hobson and his activities are not any too good, and my suggestion is to go slow in cooperating with him or lending him too large encouragement."[88] Nine months later, the State Department reinforced its opinions of Hobson, "a man who makes all sorts of trouble for us and makes it very difficult to accomplish anything particular. He is, as you probably know, a fanatic, who works for his own glory."[89] Wisely Hoover instructed his secretary, George Akerson, to ask the State Department to meet with Hobson.

DEAD WOOD IN THE FEDERAL COURTS

Hoover's first objective in court reform was the removal of incompetent or corrupt government attorneys. This occurred on eighteen occasions during his term. Despite gradual strengthening of the attorney general's administrative controls over federal court operations, Mitchell was not vested with the power to remove U.S. attorneys.[90] Unquestionably, Hoover would have preferred to delegate firings to Mitchell, but commencing with William De Groot, he was obliged to send letters with simple direct language to administer the *coup de grâce* to unacceptable federal prosecutors. In twenty words written on May 1, 1929, Hoover solved the problem of William De Groot, "Sir: You are hereby removed from the Office of the United States Attorney, eastern district of New York, effective immediately." Terminations were required to introduce efficiencies or new respect for agencies of law enforcement. Hoover retained the high ground in such matters, insisting that cases of incompetence undergo thorough review by Mitchell. De Groot was documented as a case of gross incompetence, detracting from public confidence in the justice system.[91] In keeping with this spirit, the De Groot firing and resignation of Mabel Willebrandt were followed by the appointment of Solicitor General Charles Evans Hughes, later Justice Hughes of the Supreme Court.

Added to prosecutor incompetence were infrequent allegations of federal judge bias against government Prohibition cases. Some U.S. commissioners, especially in larger districts, grew accustomed to requiring U.S. attorneys to produce evidence well beyond probable cause standards applied in other offenses. They also forced hearings on probable cause issues and full trials on case merits. Repeated case failures intimidated U.S. attorneys, thus causing some Hoover supporters to argue for selected judicial impeachments for favoritism toward Prohibition defendants. Neither Hoover nor Mitchell wanted to suffer the antipathy and constitutional headaches that would result from impeachments. Both, in fact, had sufficient faith in the overall integrity of the federal courts to avoid interference with judicial discretion.

Where executive monitoring of the judiciary was required, discrete investigations of improprieties or illegalities were conducted. In the main, however, Hoover maintained a positive relationship with the federal courts and made every effort to add judges where criminal and civil dockets contradicted law enforcement objectives. Only the worsening of the Depression after 1930 forced him to apply to the federal courts his conservative fiscal policies to reduce federal court budgets.[92]

All efforts taken to clean house in the judicial branch were carefully administered by Attorney General Mitchell. A case in point was an investigation of a sitting federal judge begun in 1925 by the Bureau of Investigation. Then assistant attorney general John Marshall looked into allegations that Harry B. Anderson, under consideration for a federal judgeship, had demonstrated favoritism in his previous administration of Prohibition cases as a U.S. attorney in Tennessee. President Coolidge appointed Anderson to the federal trial bench in Memphis, later raising him to the appellate court. In May 1929, the U.S. attorney in Memphis gave Mitchell a detailed report of the background pertaining to allegations against Anderson, concluding that grounds for impeaching could not be found. After reading the report, Mitchell sent Mabel Willebrandt a terse handwritten note: "We can't do anything about a Federal judge. Nothing here justifying any activity about impeachment. The U.S. Atty. had better be careful or he will get into serious trouble with the court."[93] A year later, Judge Anderson, now firmly seated on the appellate court, came under investigation by the Senate and House Judiciary committees. Senate chairman Kenneth McKellar insisted upon learning the origins and reasoning behind any other inquiries the Bureau of Investigation may have conducted in 1929.

Mitchell turned to J. Edgar Hoover to explain to McKellar the contents of the bureau's files on Anderson. On May 6, Edgar Hoover told assistant attorney general Charles P. Sisson that the bureau's investigations in the earlier Prohibition matter were entirely separate from a 1929 inquiry into allegations that Anderson's court administration, not Anderson per se, had come under investigation for violations of the federal bankruptcy law.[94] On June 11, Mitchell notified McKellar that there had been no investigation based on a pretext of impeachment. He reminded the senator of the attorney general's legal authority to investigate matters, such as those involving alleged bankruptcy-law violations, under United States Code Title 5, Section 301. Of more important concern, however, Mitchell reported that the bureau's inquiry had not been aimed specifically at Anderson. The file, Mitchell said, contained only information given to bureau agents which alluded to, but did not confirm, any involvement by Anderson in improprieties.[95] Edgar Hoover's trip to McKellar's hearings was, under these circumstances, uncomfortable but necessary.

Unable to convince McKellar that the bureau's interest had been limited to bankruptcy-law violations, Edgar Hoover was called back for further testimony in January 1931. McKellar ordered Hoover to turn over to the committee all the files on Judge Anderson, a matter that Hoover said should be taken up with the attorney general. On June 14, Mitchell asked Sisson to find the source of the bureau's investigation: "I have consistently taken the position that it is not the business of this Department to investigate Federal Judges with a view to impeachment. I have understood, without any definite information on the subject, that our inquiry at Memphis had something to do with bankruptcy matters and that the other things developed incidentally. For my own information, I would like to know in detail how we came to make an investigation at Memphis; who ordered it, and what it was directed to and how it happened that we gathered information reflecting on the Judge. Is it true that recently agents of the Dept. have been sent to Memphis to get further information against the Judge?"[96] Privately, Mitchell had always considered Anderson a "poor" choice by Coolidge for the appellate court in Tennessee.[97]

On the matter of restoring integrity, Hoover would not fail to voice his principles on every reasonable occasion. Repeatedly, he argued that citizen support for law was the fundamental ingredient in enforcement. For example, when a man wrote to him complaining that Army aviators had been regularly violating the Prohibition law, Hoover wrote back: "The Army regulations on the matter which you mention are of the most stringent order. The great difficulty is that persons who may see violations of such orders refuse to come forward and give evidence to the Army authorities. If there is any way you could furnish information on the subject to the Secretary of War, it would be most helpful."[98] He also applied his high standards of integrity to investigating a company in which his brother Theodore was a member of the board of directors,[99] and to an investigation of Robert H. Lucas, executive director of the Republican National Committee and former collector of the Internal Revenue.[100]

Mitchell and Hoover believed that the ideas and energy for improving the levels of integrity and performance could be found among agents of the federal judiciary, administrative officers, and law enforcement chiefs. Hoover relied consistently upon the careful advice of his key justice system advisors, including Mitchell, Bates, and Wickersham, sometimes calling on them to draft their methods for altering conditions within their areas of expertise. He asked Wickersham in November 1929 to provide him with a definitive plan for reorganizing the federal court system. The massive court congestion, especially in the District of Columbia, was particularly bothersome, indeed an obtrusive example of failure in the federal court system.[101]

Mitchell, in fact, was Hoover's right arm in making appointments to the federal bench. He was trusted implicitly by the president for his judgment in sorting out the nominations from the very best legal minds available for district and appellate levels. Exchanges of letters between Hoover and Mitchell offer some insights into this bond of trust. For example, Hoover attempted to estimate the number of appointments he would be expected to make by calculating the ages of the sitting trial and appellate judges. Writing to Mitchell in September 1929, Hoover said that he had discovered that a number of judges on the New York Customs Court were over seventy years old, many were no longer performing the work of the court but were unwilling to retire. He asked Mitchell to look into the nature of their appointments and whether or not they would receive a pension. More bluntly, he asked, "have I the power to suggest their resignations, etc?"[102] Mitchell advised the president not to try to fire two of five judges on this court who were suffering health problems, reasoning that their low performance posed no great difficulty.[103]

In a similar vein, Mitchell opposed vigorously the appointment of Ernest A. Michel to a Minnesota district court, noting for the press that Michel's law firm had been guilty of "ambulance chasing" in personal injury cases. Mitchell administered the coup de grâce: "when every lawyer in Minnesota knows that what the methods of this firm have been, I cannot make myself believe that it would be anything less than a reproach upon the administration of justice to select for the high position of federal judge a lawyer coming from such an atmosphere." No administration would be well served, Mitchell argued, by making appointments to the federal bench "by bartering judicial offices to pay political debts, or by making objectionable judicial appointments for political reasons."[104]

Hoover wrote to the obstinate Senator Thomas D. Schall, pointing out that he was fully aware of the "implications which have been made of reprisals against this administration if I fail to agree with this appointment." He refused the appointment of Michel, stating that "no question of corporate influence or personal popularity does or should enter into this question."[105] On February 6, 1931, Hoover reminded Schall that the Constitution gave him the power and, by implication, the "independent obligation" to make judicial nominations. "No question of corporate influence or personal popularity does or should enter into this question," Hoover said.[106] This was his way of indicating that he would not be bullied into accepting the nomination of a judge plainly rejected for causes known to both Mitchell and Justice Department investigators. Later in the month, Hoover wrote once again to ask Schall for a list of possible nominees, instructing that any candidates "shall not only have judicial experience, but shall be entirely free from any private connections which might be challenged."[107] Mitchell relied on the U.S. attorneys as the most appropriate initiators of changes that would most directly impact the operations of the prosecutorial and judicial functions. On June 8, 1929, Mitchell mailed to all such offices a request for "any suggestions you may desire to submit for the improvement of the service; such as, condition of the docket, personnel, compensation, office space, causes of delay and congestion, and any other matters which, in your opinion, should be considered."[108] The initiative was historic, and reports flowed into the Justice Department a month later with volumes of suggestions for improvements. Complaints included low salaries for attorneys, case load demands and the need for additional attorneys, an excessive number of Prohibition cases, judicial peculiarities, and lack of sufficient office facilities.

From the Southern District of Illinois, Walter Provine wrote: "There is an unduly large number of cases made by agents who are either new or incompetent. This makes a very difficult situation for this office to handle. In many instances search warrants are defective and will not stand when attacked."[109] George E. Q. Johnson in Chicago was greatly discouraged by the lack of leadership in the Prohibition

Bureau to pursue violations of the Volstead Act. His report set forth six major proposals for improvements: a federal law to enable the courts to hear cases on jury waivers; investigative oversight of the Prohibition Bureau by either the Treasury's Intelligence Unit or the Bureau of Investigation; improvement of investigative talents in the Prohibition Bureau up to the standards of the Post Office Inspectors, the Secret Service, and the Intelligence Unit; assignment of specially trained agents to work on larger criminal conspiracies directly for attorneys; authorization by law to U.S. attorneys to furnish witnesses with special protection when death or violence was threatened; and assignment to the U.S. attorney of two or three investigators to situations in which the attorney believes he has been mislead by information acquired from other government agencies on whose support he depended.[110] All eighty-five districts responded and the files bulged with suggestions.

The concern expressed most frequently was the backlog of cases in the federal courts and among the staff attorneys. George Johnson reported that as of June 30, 1929, some 363 criminal cases were pending action in his office without any action in over a year. In response, Charles Sisson urged him to dispose of old cases by prosecution or dismissal, Johnson retorted that the courts were not handling well the cases that could be processed more speedily, and that only one judge, with occasional help from other jurisdictions, had been hearing the overcrowded criminal calendar.[111] By August 1929, there were more than 2000 pending civil litigations in the federal courts with $2 billion at issue.

IMPROVING FEDERAL COURT PROCEDURES

By the middle of 1930, imbalances between the increasing proficiency of federal law enforcement agents and the courts were acute. Observing this imbalance in the Southern Illinois district court, John W. Gardner, general agent, informed assistant attorney general Charles P. Sisson that a balance should be drawn between the investigative force, the prosecuting force, and the judicial force. "The failure on the part of any one of these branches," he argued, "results in either a clogging of criminal dockets or lax law enforcement." Gardner called attention to the fact that the Prohibition force in the district had been weak, thus yielding only minor cases. But substantial improvements in their performance had imposed new case burdens on the U.S. attorney and federal judges, each of whom was operating without added staff.[112]

The controversy with Senator Schall extended into 1931. In January, Mitchell reminded the press of the president's absolute authority to nominate federal judges and the function of the Senate to approve or disapprove of his nominations. Qualifications for federal judges would be screened carefully by him and by the president, and no selection would be made on the basis of political debt: "I have been told that I might help President Hoover politically in Minnesota if I should recommend this appointment. President Hoover has raised a standard of Judicial appointment in which 'usefullness' does not enter. He has refused repeatedly to be bent by such motives. [He] want[s] men about whose qualifications there is no room for difference of opinion."[113] For the remainder of 1931, a particularly difficult year for economic policy, Hoover made several court appointments and awaited congressional action on his court procedural initiatives. In a news conference on February 26, 1932, Hoover complained to the Congress that although federal prosecutors and judges had kept pace with the increase in criminal and civil cases through efficiencies they administered, court congestion had not been eliminated.[114]

One method proposed for processing minor cases, particularly those involving the Volstead Act, was to empower the courts to eliminate jury trials where they believed offenses were petty in nature. The proposal to accomplish this was favored by the House Judiciary Committee and the Wickersham Commission. Nugent Dodds at Justice was asked by the White House to give his opinion on the efficacy and legality of a law to provide for elimination of juries in petty cases. He wrote to Mitchell on December 9, 1930, that he opposed the measure because it would "tend to raise legal difficulties regarding the right to prosecute by information in cases where the sentence may be more than six months, but not exceeding a year." He urged, by contrast to members of Congress and even the eminent Roscoe Pound, that Hoover not approve the bill. Pound believed the innovation would be legal and practical, arguing that as long as the petty offenses for which it applied were clearly defined, prosecution for such offenses could proceed on complaints rather than informations.[115] Hoover avoided the measure.

The time of the federal courts had been consumed for several years by indictments based on grand jury proceedings. Commenting on the deterioration of the indictment phase, Wickersham observed, "In some of the states a simplified form of indictment has been adopted, but the federal courts and those of several of the states still follow the ancient r[o]domontade with which offenders were charged of crime in the days of Sir Matthew Hale."[116] Hoover was persuaded that federal court efficiency could be enhanced without injury to defendant rights by eliminating grand juries where defendants wished to admit guilt and go immediately to sentencing. This practice would allow U.S. attorneys to file information documents. He was also persuaded by Mitchell that adding a large number of new federal judges to handle the caseload was a dangerous course of action. Instead, Mitchell proposed experimentation with a system of prosecution before U.S. commissioners, thus if the process failed to achieve results in the future it would be relatively easy to retreat, unlike a condition in which new federal judges would become entrenched or a new court level difficult to eliminate.[117]

An innovation originally proposed in the Coolidge administration would have permitted U.S. attorneys to compel testimony and production of evidence from witnesses without requiring them to appear before grand juries. Attorney General Mitchell supported this plan, but the timing of its proposed submittal to Congress late in 1931 caused him to doubt that it would be passed. The criminal courts had been jammed with thousands of Prohibition cases, many of which could have been resolved through legally proper private sessions with defendants and witnesses. Prosecutors could then file information documents with the court and thus secure comparatively quick resolutions. Mitchell hesitated to press the issue with the Congress in 1931, however, because he believed that congressional opponents to Prohibition judged "all legislation affecting criminal procedure from the standpoint of prohibition prosecutions." With more pressing matters before the Congress, Mitchell was convinced that the administration could expect "violent opposition" to granting prosecutors power that key congressmen might view as oppressive. The strategy, he instructed Nugent Dodds, was to limit initiatives for change in the forthcoming 1932 session of Congress to those that would pass "without serious controversy." Hoover, of course, faced a tough election year, and Mitchell recognized that the Congress might be slow to act on noneconomic measures: "We are just wasting our time by recommending legislation which will meet with substantial opposition."[118]

An initiative was put to the Congress to stop the practice of defendant challenges to the qualifications of grand jurors after a hearing and vote had been taken to indict. The practice had been particularly noticeable in Washington, D.C.; and Hoover's consistent objective was to make the court system in the capital a model for state replication. The Prohibition law was frequently violated in Washington, where enforcement was compounded by the fact that all cases of law violation were technically federal offenses. Hoover's proposal was to stop the hemoraging of indictments by precluding challenges when at least twelve eligible grand jurors had voted for indictment.[119]

Hoover held particular interest in child welfare issues and promotion of constructive pursuits for young offenders. In an address to his White House Conference on Child Health and Protection on November 19, 1930, Hoover spoke of many afflictions, both medical and emotional, that affected children and youth: "And if we do not perform our duty to these children, we leave them dependent, or we provide from them the major recruiting ground for the army of ne'er-do-wells and criminals." His interest was raised by reports of the increased number of juveniles arrested in the course of interstate law enforcement actions and subsequently prosecuted in federal courts. Boys were often agents of bootleggers, car thieves, or pimps; and when they crossed state lines in their involvement with crimes, they were picked up and charged by federal authorities. Hoping that state governments would assert more interest in reform measures aimed at child protection, Hoover said, "We need to turn the methods of inquiry from the punishment of delinquency to the causes of delinquency. It is not the delinquent child that is at the bar of judgment, but society itself."[120]

The federal courts were entirely inadequate places for most juvenile offenders, Hoover believed. Such persons should be dealt with by state agencies and juvenile courts. Hoover offered a proposal that federal law should be changed to empower the attorney general to divert juveniles to state authorities. On recommendation of the Wickersham Commission and state social workers, Hoover signed a bill to accomplish this objective on June 11, 1932: "This measure is an important step forward in that it sets an example through its recognition by the Federal Government of the principle that even the relatively small number of juveniles in the Federal system should be handled on a modern scientific basis. It is also a recognition . . . of the Juvenile Court as the proper place for the handling of the case of all juveniles, and is an acceptance of the principle that juvenile offenders are the product of and the responsibility of their home communities."

Just before he left office, the Congress delivered a bill to Hoover that brought him personal satisfaction that his insistence upon court procedural reforms had been merited. Hoover had formally requested action in a special message to Congress on February 29, 1932, calling for the Supreme Court to install uniform rules of practice such that cases at the district court level would be handled expeditiously and criminal appeals would be reduced.[121] Attorney General Mitchell, the Wickersham Commission, and many U.S. attorneys had expressed dissatisfaction with the ability of wealthy defendants to tie up the appellate court process after verdicts of guilty had been rendered by trial courts. Having conferred with Charles Evans Hughes on the adequacy of the Hoover–Mitchell proposals to Congress, Mitchell was particularly angered by delays that were caused by matters internal to court management, such as "delays in procuring transcripts of the record, in preparing bills of exception, in making motions for new trial, in perfecting appeals, and in bringing the appeals on for argument." He blamed prosecutors and the courts, stressing that convicted criminals, such as persons who had bilked people out of their savings through the fraudulent use of the mails, remained free on bail, sometimes for years, while the appellate courts muddled through procedural nightmares. Mitchell was as proud as Hoover the day the bill was signed allowing the Supreme Court to prescribe new rules for the lower courts. Hoover said the bill "should prevent well endowed criminals, who have been convicted by juries, from delaying punishment by years of resort to sharp technicalities of judicial procedure. It will increase the respect for law."[122]

Chapter 6

Al Capone and the Campaign
against Organized Crime

*"You don't need to be ordering fancy duds. You're going to prison;
why don't you have a suit made with stripes on it?" "The hell I am,"
replied Capone, "I'm going to Florida for a nice long rest, and I
need some new clothes before I go."*[1]

The life and times of Alphonse Capone, America's most memorable
gangster, have been recounted many times.[2] Ordinarily, Herbert
Hoover has only a minor role in such accounts. With few exceptions,
Capone is larger than life itself and seemingly more powerful than
community forces or federal agents. Actually, Capone's power was
weakly organized and shallow, vulnerable to the efforts of ordinary
people of high integrity and leadership.

The Hoover administration gave priority to convicting Capone,
thereby enlarging and transforming federal intervention in organized
crime. Hoover was the first president to personally lead an organized
crime investigation. On taking office, he ordered Attorney General
William Mitchell and Secretary of the Treasury Andrew Mellon to
cooperate in strategies designed to insure Capone's conviction. This
chapter discusses the administrative pattern of instructions from
the White House to field investigators, establishing a clear sense of
determined purpose and competent leadership.

CAPONE'S DOWNFALL BEGINS: DUMB GANGSTER,
SHREWD COPS

The Internal Revenue Service opened the first investigations of Al
Capone in the final months of the Coolidge administration.[3] Perceived

inequities in personal income tax enforcement attracted public interest, developed from a decade of white collar scandals and visible gangster fortunes. Tax records of King Vidor, movie director for Metro-Goldwyn-Mayer, and actor Tom Mix were scrutinized by the Internal Revenue Bureau.[4] Even presidential candidate Herbert Hoover was accused of failing to file tax returns after 1913. In Hoover's case, Andrew Mellon treated the charge seriously, ordering a search of tax records.[5] Had the allegations against Mr. Hoover been correct, such news would have brightened an otherwise bad year for Capone and Al Smith.[6]

The government's opening actions have remained unclear. But by early 1929, the revenue bureau was experienced in tax evasion cases, acquiring new investigative tools from a 1927 tax case, *United States v. Manly S. Sullivan,*[7] and a 1928 wiretapping decision, *Olmstead v. United States.*[8] Coolidge increased resources for income tax enforcement. Vice President Charles Dawes was asked by Frank Loesch, chairman of the Chicago Crime Commission,[9] to coordinate Chicago civic groups, some of which had privately financed "a crusade against lawlessness and corruption."

Dawes rejected Loesch's offer, but local initiatives to dislodge Capone from Chicago were well in progress.[10] The day after Hoover's election, Dawes remarked, "in general it may be said, though to this some may demur, that the larger the vote cast, the more discriminating it is. This was true in Chicago, where the issue of good government and the alliance between crime and politics personified in minor candidacies determined the result in its local bearings."[11]

Federal investigators opened files on the Capone organization, but little substantive evidence sufficient to bring a tax fraud indictment had been collected. As dawn fell over the country on New Year's Day, 1929, New York City police reported that no arrests had been made in 115 of 337 total murders for 1928. Stock companies and banks were closed. In all probability, Al Capone was asleep at the family home on Prairie Avenue on Chicago's far south side. President-elect Herbert Hoover traveled on board the *USS Utah* enroute to Washington from a goodwill and trade tour to Central and South America. The 32,000 speakeasies in New York City had been open all night, visited by their small but powerful gangster clientele.[12] Most of the 573,000 federal workers took the day off.

In the final weeks of the Coolidge administration, the Bureau of Investigation, enlisted by Mabel Walker Willebrandt, assistant attorney general for Prohibition, prisons, and tax enforcement, pursued Capone's failure to appear before a federal grand jury in Chicago.[13] By March 1929, J. Edgar Hoover held evidence sufficient to indict Capone for contempt of court. The new president had other ideas for a comprehensive, multiple-agency investigation designed to seal off Capone's legal options. Almost immediately, President Hoover ordered Mitchell and Mellon to secure Capone's prosecution and imprisonment. Edgar Hoover's bureau was expected to assist, as were all other investigative branches with any government interest in Capone's enterprises.

Mabel Willebrandt's initiative in January to have Capone arrested was premised on successful prosecution under the Volstead Act. Despite an uncertain future in federal service, Willebrandt was determined to overcome Capone's obvious flouting of the Prohibition law.[14] A warrant charged Capone with smuggling liquor, and a subpoena was issued February 21 for his appearance in Chicago's federal district court on March 12. To get out of the trip north, he secured a letter from his Florida doctor, Kenneth Phillips, stating that he had "been suffering with broncho-pneumonia pleurisy with effusion of fluid into the chest cavity, and for six weeks was confined to his bed at his home on said Palm Island, and has been out of his bed only for ten days last past, but has not fully recovered from said disease; that in the professional opinion of affiant, the said Capone's physical condition is such at this time that it would be dangerous for him to leave the mild climate of southern Florida and go to the City of Chicago, State of Illinois, and that to do so would, in the professional opinion of affiant, imperil the safety of the said Capone, and that there would be a very grave risk of a collapse which might result in his death from recurrent pneumonia."[15] Phillips's diagnosis, certified by other Miami doctors, stated that Capone would be strong enough to travel to Chicago in thirty or forty days.

Chicago's U.S. attorney Johnson believed Dr. Phillips was lying: "If it can be proved to be [a] false [affidavit] it seems to me that both the doctor . . . and Al Capone . . . can be punished for contempt of court."[16] A week after Capone's scheduled grand jury appearance, Johnson filed information charging that Capone's petition had been based on a false affidavit. Oddly, Johnson turned to Arthur P. Madden, the Internal Revenue Bureau's intelligence unit chief, to verify the affidavit, a move suggesting that he and Edgar Hoover were not on cordial terms. Attorney General Mitchell was then notified that a follow-up was needed. Mabel Willebrandt wrote to Edgar Hoover on March 20: "As a personal matter of very great importance to me, I wish you would look into this Al Capone affidavit. It will be a tenstrike on a hugh [sic] case in Chicago if you are able to prove the falsity of this affidavit so that we can punish Capone and the Doctor for contempt. May I rely upon you to do so secretly and soon?"[17]

On March 21, Capone appeared before a Chicago grand jury to deny allegations that he was in the liquor business. On the same day,

Edgar Hoover notified Willebrandt that "the desired investigation to be made in a very discreet manner at the earliest possible moment."[18] This was code language to imply that bureau agents would take action on orders but that they had more important matters to investigate. On March 27, a warrant for Capone's arrest was issued for contempt of court. Field agents in Jacksonville and Chicago had produced information from several persons who had witnessed Capone's comings and goings from mid-January to mid-March 1929.[19]

Investigators gathered reports of Capone's travel by ship to Nassau in early February.[20] The manager of the Nassau office of the Munson Steamship Line wrote to the Miami office that "it is common knowledge with this Government that Alphonse Capone bears a bad reputation with the authorities in the United States. When he arrived here, they had not any advice of his proposed visit, and therefore was treated with the customary courtesy extended to visitors. I have now been officially advised that should Alphonse Capone pay another visit to Nassau he will be refused permission to land, under the Immigration Act, 1928."[21] Despite Capone's status as a pariah in the United States, his visit, reported by the *New York Times* as an expedition to buy a home in the Bahamas, attracted "several crowds in Nassau as a kind of curious transplant from the unknown world of gangsterdom."[22]

Bureau investigators discovered that Dr. Phillips had not been well advised to attest to Capone's faked illness. George Johnson decided upon possible criminal charges against Phillips for contempt of court. He wrote to Edgar Hoover that a contempt citation had been issued, although Capone had been released on bond. He thanked Hoover for the efficiency of bureau agents and said, "in dealing with persons like Capone my policy is to prosecute vigorously for every violation and this prosecution for contempt will be helpful in other ways." Edgar Hoover did not learn for a year what "other ways" were intended. For the moment, Johnson and Willebrandt seemed pleased with investigative progress, although Willebrandt and Edgar Hoover were frustrated by delayed resolution of the Prohibition and contempt of court charges.[23]

THE PRESIDENT ORDERS IRS INVESTIGATION

Capone, fresh from jail on March 17, 1930, relaxed at his Florida home awaiting mid-April trial on the contempt matter. On April 8, President Hoover wrote to Mitchell and Mellon: "The most important areas for the enforcement of the 18th Amendment should be directed toward those larger rings and conspiracies whose operations in illicit liquor are obvious, and whose manifestations apparently cover even more than single states." He directed them to prepare a report "as to the correctness of these assumptions and as to the advisability of organizing special corps of attorneys in the Department of Justice devoted to these large conspiracies, who would assemble material from the local district attorneys and prohibition agents and who would have as [their] own investigating staff special delegates from the Prohibition Bureau."[24] Capone-type organizations were, by then, known to be intricate, mobile cartels represented by competent legal counsel. Hoover was convinced that the government's methods, skills, and wit could compete with organized crime, using investigative innovations, diligent street work, and interagency cooperation. His law enforcement reorganization initiatives came none too soon, as Capone and other gangsters arranged a mid-May 1929 meeting in Atlantic City to restructure liquor distribution territories. Capone's gun-toting conviction in Philadelphia on May 17 gave the government an opportunity to build the tax case. In the same period, Johnson indicted Frank Nitti (or Nitto), Capone's enforcer, and Al's brother Ralph. Trial was set for April 1930.

On March 18, Walter Hope, assistant secretary of the treasury, called for a complete audit of Al Capone's tax-paying history.[25] The next day, commissioner of the internal revenue, Robert H. Lucas, reported Capone's tax history and outlined investigative progress. Lucas said that the earlier investigation had been opened by Treasury's Intelligence Division in October 1928. He said that "no record of filing of any return for any year was found in the Bureau and the investigation was for the purpose of determining to what extent he was delinquent in the payment of income tax." After a detailed recounting of the indictments in cases against Ralph Capone, Frank Nitti, and "Jack Gusick" (Jake Guzik), Lucas reported that Al Capone had purchased a home in Miami for $40,000 with a $30,000 mortgage. The deed to the property was in the name of his wife, Mae; and when the insurance companies discovered this fact, they retracted their policies "on the basis that the Capones' were not a good risk." He closed by saying that a search had been made for the real estate operator who had handled the house transaction.[26]

The major players were to be found at several levels in the executive branch. Herbert Hoover was handed regular summaries of the progress of the Justice and Treasury departments. Attorney General Mitchell and Assistant Attorney General G. A. Youngquist directed J. Edgar Hoover's contempt case and the prosecution efforts of George Johnson. Mellon gave primary operational responsibility to Elmer L. Irey, chief of Treasury's Enforcement Division. Success in convicting Al Capone's brother, Ralph Capone, of tax evasion on April 25, 1930, convinced Irey that the major investigation would also yield a conviction.[27] Field supervision of the tax case was given to Frank J. Wilson, including front-line investigations, planting of spies in the Capone organization, telephone wiretaps, surveillance of Capone's alleged properties and operations, and the documentation of investigative actions.[28]

On March 18, 1930, Youngquist drafted a curious office memo summarizing discussions of recent federal operations. Apparently, federal work against Capone had been dormant during the gangster's confinement. Youngquist telephoned the Prohibition Bureau's commissioner, James M. Doran, to inquire into any liquor law violations against Capone, only to be told that his bureau could never connect Capone to such illegalities. He telephoned George Johnson to learn that Johnson "had been much interested in Capone for a long time, but that the Federal authorities had not thus far been able to procure any tangible evidence of wrong-doing." Furthermore, Johnson commented that while he intended to investigate the contempt matter, "it is not a matter of seriousness or of importance." Youngquist concluded, "The difficulty seems to lie in the fact that Capone keeps himself two or three or four times removed from the actual operations. In that situation it is almost impossible to procure evidence unless his henchmen will talk—and they won't."[29]

On March 21, a special agent in charge of the Revenue Bureau's intelligence unit, Arthur P. Madden, drafted a lengthy "personal" memorandum concerning progress in Al Capone's tax case. Madden set a tone of urgency in his opening paragraph: "I know that the Commissioner is much interested in this matter. I am informed that the Attorney General is interested in it, and it has been intimated that the White House may be expressing a desire to see it brought to an early conclusion." For Madden the case appeared to have been easily developed, but "I have always had in mind the proposal to develop a criminal case that would stand up under a strong defense in court. Capone is represented by two or three of the best trial lawyers who regularly appear in the Federal Courts in Chicago. . . . Both of those individuals were employed for several years as Assistants to the United States Attorney here."[30] Efforts made in March 1929, said Madden, turned up several deposits by Al's brother Ralph at the Pinkert State Bank on the south side of Chicago.

While these deposits produced a guilty plea by Ralph, Madden warned that no hard evidence of transfer of funds to Al could be proved. Until the time of his memo, Madden said that the office had spent most of its time on investigations of Capone's accountant and enforcer, Jack Gusick/Guzik and Frank Nitto/Nitti, thereby indicating that the bureau originally had pursued a bottom-up strategy. Ralph Capone, it seems, had filed tax returns for several years, but at that time Madden's work could not prove a satisfactory case of under-reporting or a case showing links to brother Al. Nitto's case was more easily proven through a chain of checks cashed at several other banks, as revealed in grand jury testimony. Nitto, however, did not file any tax returns, thus leading to his indictment on the basis of check-cashing testimony. Madden believed that Nitto would be no help to the government since "he is the type of individual who would submit to a sentence of ten years in the penitentiary before he would inform on any of his associates." At the end of the report, Madden appears to contradict his first impressions of an easy case against Al Capone. He acknowledges Capone's shrewd actions to disguise the transfer of funds to Florida but adds that "apparently he prepared himself for almost every contingency." Evidence had been gathered from the manager of the Metropole Hotel, where the Capone organization had its headquarters, that "forty or fifty rooms . . . were occupied by Al Capone and various principals," concluding that "it is easy to see that a very great deal of money was required."[31] His memo closed with a note of realism, somewhat awkwardly stated, however: "I will keep you advised when anything of importance develops. The point that I am trying to make . . . is that no matter what has been done so far in this general investigation has led to the tracing of funds into the hands of members of the Capone organization and that is the end. So far the funds have not and could not be followed through."

In a memo on March 22, Madden commented in connection with the attorneys Capone had retained that Capone had considered filing delinquent tax returns if he could be assured that the government would not use them as evidence. A follow-up memo on March 25 informed Wilson that attorney Arthur Mattingly had notified the bureau that he was serving as Capone's counsel and that Capone (and others) "were very apprehensive" about the government's investigations, and "anxious to file delinquent returns and clear up any differences that there may be between him and the Government." Further, he reported that Capone had no records but wished to reach agreement on a figure the government considered appropriate. He made special mention that no arrangement had been agreed upon, either by the agent who spoke with Mattingly or by any other bureau employee. The bureau's intentions at this point were announced in Madden's closing remarks: "I do not see how [Mattingly] can accomplish much through any such plan as he has in mind. . . . [I]t appears to me that the only way in which he can dispose of his case is to file returns and take his chances. If he does decide to file returns, it would appear that in so doing he will furnish evidence to the Government which may be used in the prosecution of [Capone] for delinquency."[32]

Lawrence Richey, former Secret Service agent and President

Hoover's personal secretary,[33] passed confidentially to Youngquist the record of a phone conversation between columnist Mark Sullivan and James M. Cox, former governor of Ohio, Democratic candidate for president in 1920, and owner of the *Miami Daily News*. Cox had two suggestions: that since Capone was on bail in the contempt case, he could be forced by the federal court to remain within the Chicago federal district until his trial on other matters and that Capone should be investigated as to citizenship, and if not born in the United States, he should be deported. Other draconian methods were supported, such as forcible removal from the state of Florida upon his arrival there. Cox recommended to Sullivan, in a manner he knew would reach Hoover, that "the Department of Justice might profitably see whether they could do something which would be evidence to the public of determination to halt or rebuke the spectacle that Capone apparently is providing."[34]

On March 31, 1930, Youngquist phoned President Hoover to say that George Johnson had been appointed to lead the prosecution team. Youngquist told Hoover that "there is a possible prospect of getting a tax evasion indictment against [Capone], but they haven't got enough yet. He is very clever. He is two or three or four times removed from the actual operation. . . . There is just one small item. That is some money transmitted to him by telegraph in Florida in 1928, but even that was transmitted to someone else down there for him." Notes of a follow-up call to Hoover on or about the same day conveyed a sense of reassurance to Hoover that progress in small steps would eventually put Al Capone in prison: "They convicted Ralph Capone for tax evasions a week or two ago. We are working on the Al Capone tax matter and while [George Johnson] was here he got information which he thought might tie up Al Capone in it, and then prosecution could be started against him. I impressed upon him the one big job was to convict Al Capone for violation of the law if he could do it. I wanted you to know we are keeping after it."[35]

Special U.S. Attorney William J. Froelich wrote to Youngquist on April 3, 1930, that telephone conversations intercepted by investigators characterized Capone's negative financial situation. Capone, Froelich commented, "is desperate for money and wants to get away from what he terms 'heat' in Chicago." He expected to bring a witness in succeeding days who would be useful in an unidentified secret indictment then in progress.[36] Only two weeks later, the attorney general wrote to Senator Pat Harrison in response to Harrison's interest in pending criminal actions against Capone. On April 14, Mitchell told Harrison that he had been informed of Treasury Department inquiries into Capone's taxes, "but that matter has not reached a point where any definite conclusions have been reached and I cannot find that there is any proposal pending to compromise any criminal liability."[37]

A week later, Johnson notified Youngquist that he had been tied up with the Ralph Capone trial and would proceed immediately with the Al Capone prosecution. Johnson's tone expressed the tension in the Northern District stemming from case backlogs and the pressure to take the contempt case to prosecution:[38] "We have so many lengthy cases here that I am forced with the alternative of compromising many of them or never have an opportunity to try them, and the Al Capone case has been delayed with others on that account." He urged that Mitchell should give support to legislation to add judges to the Northern District of Illinois, otherwise "there is little prospect of gaining on the calendar year."[39] With the announcement of Ralph Capone's conviction on April 25, Walter E. Hope sent Hoover a newspaper account: "The enclosed represents a little progress even though the chief offender still goes unapprehended."[40]

Federal authorities gave defense attorneys high marks for their work in the Ralph Capone case. On April 28, 1930, Madden wrote to Wilson, proclaiming "I do not see how a better defense could have been made," while also praising methods used by federal prosecutors.[41] The effort, he said, had a "wholesome effect upon this [Chicago] community"; and succeeding prosecutions were likely to receive a similar reaction. Madden reported Al Capone's possible connections with the Roosevelt Finance Company, dominated, he said, by Louis Greenberg. He said that Capone might have been connected with "the purchase of a considerable number of cashiers checks at the Schiff State Bank" and one other bank. Capone had been asked why he had telephoned Greenberg on several occasions at the Roosevelt Finance Company, but investigators remarked that his responses were unconvincing. He concluded that Capone's wealth would be difficult to locate, but "I have no doubt that Al Capone and his associates received substantial income from the dog race track operated near Chicago. As a matter of fact, there is fairly convincing proof that substantial sums were paid to Frank Nitti, who is one of the principals in the Capone organization."[42] Although he was jubilant that two of the principals in the Capone group had been put under the jurisdication of the court, Madden concluded, "It would be hard to imagine any cases in which more difficulties were presented than arose out of the Ralph Capone and Frank Nitto investigations."[43] Larry Richey received the report in May 1930 with a covering note from Walter Hope suggesting that "The President might be interested in seeing this."

Capone had been declared persona non grata by Chicago's commissioner of police: "You'll be arrested as often as you show yourself to any of our detectives."[44] Nitti's indictment on March 23 encouraged Capone to return to his Palm Island estate in Miami. Even there, Capone was unwelcome. Within two months, the City of Miami passed a vagrancy ordinance phrased in a manner designed to exclude: "any person having visible means of support acquired by unlawful or illegal means or methods, or any person who is dangerous to the safety of the city of Miami, or any person or persons known or reputed to be crooks, gangsters or hijackers."[45] The governor of Florida, Doyle Carlton, tried to stop Capone's return to the state, but on April 25 Capone secured a federal injunction against anyone attempting to stop his travel to Palm Island.[46] On or about May 2, former Ohio governor James M. Cox called President Hoover to offer to aid in the 'get Capone' campaign. He reported that Capone had set up headquarters in Montreal and Havana to ship liquor into the United States and that Capone intended to use the port of Miami as a point of entry. Hoover recorded in his notes, "Cox's specific request is that the government at Washington send to Miami one of its best investigators from either the Department of Justice or the Prohibition Enforcement Department to cooperate with the local prosecuting attorney, *whose name, I think, is Hawthorne* [handwritten] and with Cox and his associates." Hoover then wrote that he thought it desirable to visit Cox and the *Daily News* before proceeding with such an investigation. He believed in Cox's initiative: "I imagine this would be a good thing for the government to do and I can see no objection to it." This kind of tactic, he wrote, was "a proper way of cooperating with local authorities for the suppression of racketeering gangs."[47]

Madden was pleased to report to Irey the progress made to uncover evidence of direct Capone control over the Roosevelt Finance Company.[48] His report of May 9 revealed that Louis Greenberg was the principal behind the company operations and that his two inside agents had effectively connected Greenberg with a loan to Al Capone. In an odd occurrence, however, while the two agents were assigned at the company, two men representing themselves as government agents entered the company in Greenberg's absence and seized all the records. Prior to the mysterious removal of records, agents uncovered a loan to Al Capone, part of which had already been paid.

Agents learned from Greenberg that the remainder of the loan was in certificates of indebtedness. The certificates were then traced through several banks and the Federal Reserve system back to the dog track owner E. (Edward) J. O'Hare. O'Hare, interviewed by agents several months earlier, reported "confidentially that it would have been out of the question for any one to attempt to operate such a business as his at or near Cicero without arranging for payments to the powers that be, which, of course, included the Capone organization." Madden was forthright in the conclusion that O'Hare was the source of government securities diverted from the assets of the dog track to Capone, but the evidence was largely circumstantial. This entire line of inquiry heartened the situation for Madden, causing him to ask Irey to have O'Hare's tax records sent for closer examination for possible implications in the Capone matter.

By May 21, the Capone organization was beginning to show the stress. Dwight H. Green, special assistant to George Johnson, notified Washington that men from the Capone crew had destroyed a tavern owned by an informant who had given information that money had been paid to Capone men "for Capone."[49] Ralph Capone's conviction on six counts of making false statements, concealment of assets, and failure to pay income taxes gave the IRB the confidence to continue the investigation of Frank "Netto" (Nitto), then to follow it with prosecution of Al Capone.[50]

Agent Frank Wilson traced the connections between E. J. O'Hare and the Hawthorne Dog Track.[51] Finding none of any legal value, he turned to John T. Rogers, a *St. Louis Post Dispatch* writer, to provide information on O'Hare. Rogers, well recognized for his communications channels to organized gangsters, was enlisted by revenue agents to get O'Hare to give "the low-down on the track."[52] O'Hare talked with agents "confidentially . . . as he is afraid of being knocked off." He told Wilson that when the track was incorporated in 1927, three persons (J. Patton, J. Cusick, and Frank Nitto) put up half the cash and O'Hare put up the other half. Stock certificates were then issued to the named persons and to Al Capone; but when word of this transaction was spread around Chicago, the negative publicity necessitated the production of new certificates without the names of Capone and Nitto. The new stock, Wilson reported, was put in the names of "Patton, Cusick, some members of their families and a small amount to P. Granada, a C.P.A. who audits the books of the corporation."[53] Wilson was encouraged by the leads he had developed, but he indicated that testimony from third-party associates was not likely as there was a distinct "chance of being knocked off for squealing."[54] Internal Revenue Commissioner Robert H. Lucas was more hopeful, however, when he forwarded Irey's report to Walter Hope, "In the Capone case, it looks as though the boys have at last found a clue which may lead to something."[55]

Statutory reorganization of the Justice and Treasury departments took effect July 1, 1930. Stepped up investigations were ordered, and additional agents and attorneys were sent to Chicago to assist in the Capone matter. William Froelich was dispatched to Chicago to coordinate efforts and to assist Johnson. The Capone case was becoming more complex. Hoover wrote to Mitchell on July 11, "I think it would hearten the situation a good deal if we could revive this idea and make such an organized staff under some special attorney. We are being criticized very severely around centers like Chicago for failure to do anything in the larger conspiracies."[56] Jake Lingle, a *Chicago Tribune* reporter with ties to Capone, had been murdered on June 30. A Northside gangster, Jack Zuta, was the prime suspect, and upon his murder in August 1, government agents required fast action to acquire any residual tidbits of information for the Capone work.[57]

In the summer of 1930, government investigators were given private funds and intelligence information by business organizations and newspapers. Depression economics strained federal investigative resources. The Wickersham Commission was denied additional funds, causing the president to declare that he would seek private funding. Hoover had always nurtured volunteer efforts, even in matters involving criminal justice. In keeping with his philosophy, the Chicago Association of Commerce, the parent organization that funded the "Secret Six" anticrime organization, offered to donate money to further the Capone investigation. On July 22, Robert I. Randolph, the association's executive director, wrote to Larry Richey expressing hope that a certain unnamed Department of Justice agent could continue his assignment with the association or in other forms of racketeering and Prohibition enforcement work.[58]

Mitchell also believed in the merits of closer association between private organizations, local government, and federal investigators. He instructed Youngquist to consult with a designated list of groups or individuals to make "inquiries into income tax returns, which may open leads into other fields and which may result in the discovery of other federal offenses or of state offenses."[59] Further, he suggested that these organizations form "a joint executive committee to cooperate wherever their services are desirable" and that the coordination of the links with the private sector be through Bureau of Internal Revenue agents. Progress in establishing private links was slow.

In mid-August, solicitor general and acting attorney general Thomas D. Thacher ordered Johnson to "cooperate to the fullest extent possible with local authorities in investigation with a view to prosecution of all offenses against Federal law which may be disclosed [by the state's attorney in Chicago]." Johnson, apparently finding this somewhat humorous at this late date, wrote back that the Cook County state's attorney and he were "personally on the friendliest terms; that we have been friends and neighbors for more than twenty years;

that we meet regularly once a week and confer on matters to be handled" and that he had been working with him and the Association of Commerce "on a plan for the investigation of police and gang activities in Chicago." Johnson could not resist the jab at Thacher for being entirely unaware of his activism in Chicago: "I am pleased to note that it is the policy of the Department that these things be done and I am happy to report that they were initiated before receiving the instructions of the department."[60]

On September 5, Thacher notified President Hoover confidentially that "the plans of the five leading Chicago newspapers and the ten or twelve civic organizations interested to gather a fund to be placed at the disposal of the Association of Commerce and expanded by the Association for investigative work have not yet been completed, and that it is likely to be several weeks before actual work of investigation is commenced by the Association." Thacher told Hoover that he had stepped up federal investigative actions by proposing a total force of fifteen agents to work on the Capone case.[61]

On September 12, Johnson notified Youngquist that he had made some private office space available in Chicago, "without expense to the government," for staff personnel sent from Washington to assist in the Capone investigation. He made it clear to Youngquist that he was secretly "procuring a lot of records through agencies organized for that purpose, the expense of which will be borne by civic bodies" and that he had "arranged for a secret investigation of municipal records through municipal officers, so that the fact will not be known."[62] On the same day, Johnson wrote an impassioned letter to the attorney general outlining the history of his work with the civic organizations, dating, he said, about two and one-half years from his recommendations to Mabel Willebrandt. He insisted that the key to cooperation here was absolute secrecy and that he wanted to select his own investigators and liaison personnel. Clearly, he was miffed by Youngquist's insistence that an assistant would be assigned to his staff from Washington.[63] On the seventeenth, Johnson confirmed his conversations with local newspaper publishers "for the joint endeavors of the Chicago publishers and the civic bodies, so that plans will proceed very much as we discussed them in Washington."[64] Johnson planned to use information acquired from five newspapers. A special writer for the Hearst newspapers was enlisted to supply any information to the Justice Department in the course of his confidential investigation of Capone's organization.[65]

The newly formed Association of Commerce Committees, by then fully in service of Johnson's office, had agreed to protect evidence and witnesses who had given information in several tax cases. Johnson told Youngquist that the association had offered a $1000 reward for the arrest of Frank Nitti and that it had paid the salaries of the guards used to protect key witnesses in the prosecutions of Jack Gusik, Nitti, and others.[66] By early November, Youngquist had authorized a leave of absence for Alexander Jamie, chief of special agents for the Bureau of Prohibition in Chicago, to head the investigative force of the Association of Commerce. Jamie took along his assistant who had resigned from the Prohibition Bureau.[67]

Internal revenue agent Arthur P. Madden pursued investigation of Jack Guzik for false reports of income for 1928 and 1929. Madden's boss, Frank Wilson, had uncovered evidence that Guzik had received $134,500 from gambling ventures not shown on his return. He indicated in a letter to Elmer Irey on September 4 that "if the Government will some time in the very near future take summary action against Guzik by obtaining a warrant for his arrest and by attempting to have a heavy bond fixed for him, that action in itself may influence [a] prospective witness . . . to tell the truth about the income which Al Capone is known to have received."[68] Madden stressed that the witness would probably not come forward without the achievement of the objectives he outlined. David Burnet, commissioner of the internal revenue wrote to George Johnson on the eighth, suggesting that Johnson should consider indicting Guzik on the information lying behind the Madden report. Further, he noted that the details of the Guzik case were not known in Washington, and if justice were to take action, the Guzik case "will probably have a far-reaching beneficial effect upon the Government's interests in this and related cases."[69] Youngquist immediately authorized Johnson to pursue the Guzik matter at his own discretion. Burnet was, in all probability, not entirely aware of the secret work being done to concentrate actions against the total Capone organization.

Mitchell and Froelich jealously guarded the direction of the Capone tax matter, clearly evident in correspondence concerning allegations that Capone controlled transshipments of grapes through the Chicago railyards. The footsteps of Mabel Willebrandt, by now in private law practice under retainer to protect the interests of California grape growers, could be heard in the background. The Federal Farm Bureau, headed by C. C. Teague, a former activist grape grower organizer, had developed information that he believed was useful in pursuing Capone on Sherman Antitrust law violations.[70] On September 24, John Lord O'Brian, assistant attorney general for antitrust, inquired of Mitchell how far the Justice Department was willing to extend resources to bring an antitrust prosecution. Mitchell informed O'Brian that it would be acceptable to proceed to develop an antitrust case as long as great caution was exercised not to interfere with other cases involving income tax, narcotics, prohibition, immigration, counterfeiting, or other federal crimes. O'Brian, a seasoned and highly respected lawyer,[71] pursued the matter with great care.[72]

J. Edgar Hoover, a loyal fan of Mabel Willebrandt, actively argued the merits of expediting an antitrust prosecution. By mid-October, eager to join Capone's pursuers, Edgar Hoover's Bureau had uncovered several witnesses who held information on alleged antitrust dimensions of Capone control over the grape juice situation. When they refused to testify before the federal grand jury, however, O'Brian and Mitchell could only give the antitrust matter passing regard amid the corpus of more fruitful cases.[73] Capone, of course, was highly incensed when he learned that the feds were trying to lay the grape juice conspiracy on his door step.[74] Government wiretaps were in good operating order. Youngquist wrote to Johnson on November 14. He had just been informed that Capone "telephoned to a Washington lawyer about the grape juice concentrate matter and appeared very much disturbed over the situation, apparently because one of his rackets might be affected."[75]

By November, Mitchell was overseeing directly all racketeering investigations in full swing in Chicago and New York. Included in the investigative agenda, and consistent with President Hoover's views, was Mitchell's plan to undercut labor racketeering. Writing to O'Brian on November 4, Mitchell promoted the use of the Sherman Act against corrupt unions: "labor racketeering is widespread. . . . It is an important phase of gangster rule and breakdown of law and order. The local authorities are often helpless or corrupt. In its campaign for law enforcement the federal government can perform a real public service by going after the racketeers, whenever they violate Federal law."[76] Chicago was the primary focus of attention. J. Edgar Hoover remained convinced that Capone could have been jailed and prosecuted successfully on the contempt charge. Mitchell and Youngquist were inclined to agree, and they believed that the contempt case, perhaps brought in a Florida state court, would yield a conviction.[77] Edgar Hoover was not eager, however, to assign more investigative resources to the Capone matter.[78] He was particularly sensitive to the use of his men to guard witnesses in various federal cases in Chicago.[79]

Capone was drawn out of his quarters at the Lexington Hotel for several meetings with IRS agent Frank Wilson. Negotiations were conducted with Capone, his attorneys, and government agents to secure payment for taxes on incomes for the years 1926 to 1929. Capone, apparently secure in the belief that even Frank Wilson could be manipulated, signed affidavits admitting to incomes ranging from $26,000 to $100,000 in these years. Attempts were made to bribe government officials.[80] Neither Capone nor his attorneys internalized the clear message they had been sent by government officials, perpetually diligent in their work to secure convictions. Brother Ralph had been convicted and incarcerated on June 16, 1930; Frank Nitti pleaded guilty and was sentenced on December 20, 1930; Jack Guzik was sentenced on December 30, 1930; Sam Guzik had been indicted on October 30, 1930. All were tax evasion cases; all were sentenced to the federal penitentiary at Leavenworth to sentences ranging from eighteen months to five years.

Criticism of Hoover's anticrime campaign heated up in November 1930. The charge was made that Hoover had usurped state law enforcement powers in the Capone case. He responded to the charges on November 25: "The Federal Government is assisting local authorities to overcome the hideous gangster and corrupt control of some local governments. But I get no satisfaction from the reflection that the only way this can be done is for the Federal Government to convict men for failing to pay income taxes on the financial product of crime against State laws. What we need is an awakening to the failure of local government to protect its citizens from murder, racketeering, corruption, and a host of other crimes, and a rallying to the support of those men in each locality who are making a courageous battle to clean up these localities."[81] By December 2, Hoover sought new authority in the deportation laws "so as to more fully rid ourselves of criminal aliens."[82] Hoover also wanted congressional support to widen federal authority to act against the *Unione Siciliano* and other Italian gangs in New York then engaged in deadly warfare.[83]

Mitchell granted George Johnson special approval to travel to Miami on December 15 to interview several witnesses who had given statements regarding the contempt case against Capone. Progress in this case had moved slowly, but Judge James H. Wilkerson had agreed to hear it late in January. Motions by Capone's attorneys to dismiss the case were rejected by the court and trial was set for February 25. Johnson told Youngquist that he had been advised that Capone would not seek appeal on the court's conviction because there were no questions of importance to be argued.

As Capone's fate was fully in the hands of federal authority, new levels of public disdain for racketeers surfaced. Judge John H. Lyle, the "fighting judge" and Republican candidate for mayor of Chicago, addressed the Chicago Safety Council in mid-December, claiming that he would send Capone to the electric chair. Further, he claimed that Capone had become "a very real and powerful political force"; allegedly, said Lyle, he had a member of Congress in his pocket and a "mouthpiece" in the Illinois legislature. "Capone has no right to live."[84] In more subtle terms, Elmer Irey published statements in the *Internal Revenue News* for February suggesting that in nearly all cases of tax evasion indictments are carried through the federal courts to conviction. He wrote, "knowledge that punishment follows attempted violations of the tax laws is a warning, certainly, to other possible tax evaders." Implying the Chicago successes, he said, "results obtained in one jurisdiction offer a definite idea of the situation throughout the country. In this jurisdiction, 13 indictments were returned against persons alleged to have evaded payment of income taxes over a period of years. Seven alleged violators, four of whom were indicted in the previous year, were brought to trial, and, upon conviction or a plea of guilty, were given prison sentences ranging from 18 months to 5 years. The remaining 10 of the 13 indicted during 1930 are awaiting trial."[85] This tone contrasted sharply with Youngquist's view that "the work in Chicago is progressing very well, but evidently we are not yet in sight of our goal."[86]

1931: HOOVER–CAPONE SHOWDOWN

Hoover suggested a shift in federal investigative talent away from Chicago and toward Prohibition and drug enforcement problems in New York City, by then the center of power for the Luciano crime group. Federal agents had broken up the largest narcotics ring in history during a raid on a New York dinner party in November 1930, netting several million dollars worth of opium smuggled from Turkey and Greece.[87] The emerging interest of crime groups in drug importation had received little press attention, but investigations into the November 1928 assassination of Arnold Rothstein suggested that drugs had become a new source of profit for organized crime. Although suggested in correspondence of George Johnson, Capone was never implicated in illicit drugs.

On March 5, adding to the legal talent to expedite both the tax and contempt cases against Capone, Dwight Green was appointed to open grand jury and civil or criminal proceedings to move the Capone matters along. Meanwhile, the Justice Department worried that Capone would file a petition for a writ of certiorari to the Supreme Court in a fashion that would leave the government short of time to oppose it. George Johnson was pressured to respond to or seek any prospective appeal in the Court of Appeals before the U.S. Supreme Court adjourned in June.[88]

Weighing in at 235 pounds, the dapper Al Capone walked up the steps to the federal courthouse on March 12, heavily guarded by local police. The government quickly made its case in the two-year-old contempt of court matter. Capone was found guilty and sentenced to six months in jail. Public reaction was mixed. Some viewed the judgment as a minor victory in a larger battle; others suggested that the action was an entirely insignificant and inappropriate decision for a gangster of Capone's reputation.[89] The prosecution's case involved professional testimony from Dr. James S. Williamson, dean of the medical department of the University of Illinois, and was according to George Johnson, a "case the Attorney General regarded as one of great importance."[90] Mabel Willebrandt, craving recognition in the Capone caper, wrote to Walter H. Newton, Hoover's legislative liaison, to brag about her role in starting the investigations in 1928. Newton, fully mindful of Hoover's reasons for firing Willebrandt yet also aware of her tricky personality, wrote back, "the Federal Government is about the only outfit trying to do something to this crowd. I am glad to know of your part in initiating it."[91]

With implied progress in Chicago and a need to shift resources to other crime centers, Hoover wrote to Mitchell on March 16: "The special organization set up for the prosecution of gangsters in Chicago has worked out most successfully and has been a contribution to the whole of that community. I am wondering if you would consider setting up such a special organization in New York with view to prosecution of evident grafters of federal courts. . . . I believe that such an activity might be salutary to the country and a contribution to the enforcement of other laws."[92] Mitchell, pressed by the workload of his office, responded on the twenty-fifth: "Considering the amount of crime at this point, the results may seem meagre, but in proportion to our responsibilities we have done much more than the State authorities in making a dent in gangster racketeering and corruption." He closed with a summation of Youngquist's efforts in "the New York City situation" which Hoover had inquired about, noting in particular that investigations had been significantly enlarged there.[93] Actually, Mitchell's confidence extended beyond reality of the New York initiatives. Youngquist's memo to Mitchell on March 24 mentioned only an "embryonic stage" in these new investigations and only tentative plans to organize them in a fashion similar to the Chicago team.[94]

On March 12, George Johnson addressed the gathered membership of the Better Business Bureau at the La Salle Hotel in downtown Chicago. Johnson opened his remarks with, "at some time in the future in a more advanced state of public morals, and with a keener interest on the part of our citizens in government, a history will be written of Chicago beginning with the year 1922 and ending with the year 1928, which will be designated as the period of the greatest corruption in local government. It will also mark the period of the development of organized crime, and when I use the term 'organized crime' I mean the type of violations which make a business of crime." Distinguishing organized crime from "crimes of passion and degeneracy and crimes committed for the purpose of vengeance," Johnson remarked that "organized crime derives its income from privilege. Privilege in this sense is immunity to violate the law granted by some law enforcement official with a consideration paid for protection." A recitation of cases he had prosecuted in recent months then brought him to his main proposal, legislation at the state level that would obligate a formal records management system for local governments doing business with contractors. Johnson suggested that numerous tax fraud cases initiated by the federal government had taught several valuable lessons. Prosecutors, Johnson argued, could bring indictments in speedy fashion if public bureaus of audits were granted unhindered access to contractor records and access by any citizen who wished to inquire into public expenditures.

Throughout the spring of 1931, Johnson and agents Madden, O'Rourke, and Wilson pieced together the evidentiary fragments of the complex Capone organization. On March 24, Youngquist drafted a summary report in which he outlined all the Chicago prosecutions to that point.[95] He emphasized that the New York investigations should proceed in the same manner as the Chicago work, including the assignment of special agents to the U.S. attorney.[96] Highlighting the competition between agencies, Youngquist was informed that "some of the Special Agents of the Bureau of Internal Revenue who have been doing very effective work in Chicago are resentful over the appearance of newspaper statements to the effect that the work has been done by Special Agents of the Department of Justice. I told Mr. Irey that I was sure no such statement had been given by you."[97]

Mitchell became defensive at the suggestion that he had been responsible for miscasting the credit for the work: "In press conferences on the Chicago situation I have repeatedly referred to the fact that the principal work there has been by agents of the Bureau of Internal Revenue and have never failed to mention their work and have explained that Bureau of Investigation, Prohibition Unit, Immigration Bureau, etc., have merely been supplementary. Please tell Mr. Irey so. I have just reported to the President that the principal work at Chicago has been by Bureau of Internal Revenue."[98] Concurrently, he wrote to Hoover, "Considering the amount of crime at that point [Chicago], the results may seem meagre, but in proportion to our responsibilities we have done much more than the State authorities in making a dent in gangster racketeering and corruption. The New York situation which you recently inquired about is also dealt with in Mr. Youngquist's statement. Efforts are being made to enlarge our activities there."[99] Irey was notified of Mitchell's sensitivity to the good work of the IRB the next day, and all was back on track.

Between March and the late summer of 1931, several grand juries met to consider the government's cases against Al Capone. Eliot Ness and other Prohibition agents continued to raid breweries and warehouses alleged to belong to the Capone organization, and some of these circumstances survived legal challenges to become successful prosecutions.[100] Howard T. Jones, acting director of the Prohibition Bureau, reported to Youngquist on May 5 that a conviction had been secured against Paul Morton, a "Bugs" Moran lieutenant, stating that the result was "probably the most important conviction in a Prohibition conspiracy case in Chicago since Prohibition."[101] Froelich, overseeing the Chicago cases, wrote to Mitchell that he was "happy with the way everything is going, and only hope we can deliver on the 'big boy' for you."[102] Capone's attorneys appealed the contempt of court conviction, arguing that the original grand jury subpoena was invalid. Their efforts picked up speed when they learned of the April seventeenth sentencing of Sam Guzik to one year in Leavenworth. On the government side, Youngquist sent a note and a *Chicago Tribune* clipping to Mitchell, "One more Chicago gangster=7." Mitchell responded, "Good work. I have sent the other clippings over to the White House." By early May, Froelich was calling for more investigators for Chicago and two more automobiles to work on the tax case and a liquor conspiracy charge.[103] Success in Capone's case meant that more demands would be placed on federal authorities to provide leadership and expertise.[104] On June 2, Youngquist received information from the United States attorney in Kansas City that interceptions of telephone conversations had revealed that the Capone people were supplying liquor to John Lazia, a Capone lieutenant in that city.[105]

On June 5, a federal panel indicted Capone for tax evasion for the years 1925 to 1928. The ink on the official indictment documents was barely dry when the attorney general wrote to the commissioner of the internal revenue to commend Irey and his investigators for the fine work done to acquire the evidence. Already there was jubilation, although Capone had not yet been put on trial to test the government's charges. The next day Capone plead guilty to multiple counts, assuming that if he faced time in prison it would be only a short duration. During the summer months, he shifted his pleas on different counts while the government prepared to present the case to a jury. Mitchell urged Johnson to consider negotiating with Capone's lawyers to get a signed agreement that Capone would not resume criminal activities in the United States after his expected sentences were served. This strategy, Mitchell suggested, would allow the federal court to impose new sentences should Capone fail to live up to the agreement, thus satisfying the public mind that justice had been served.[106]

THE GOVERNMENT'S NEAR-FATAL MISTAKE

The Literary Digest for June 27, 1931, reflected upon the government's successes in recent gangster cases. President Hoover's involvement in directing the Al Capone case was not easily recognized by the readership, and the White House made no special attempt to put Hoover at the center.[107] Frank J. Loesch, vice president of the National Crime Commission and member of Hoover's Law Observance Commission, wrote to Hoover on June 29, 1931, to mark the occasion of the government's preliminary victory and Hoover's role in it: "Locally, the indictment of Capone and his plea of guilty has taken first place, but there is a distinct undertone of dissatisfaction, which has been expressed to me a good many times, that there has some sort of an arrangement been made by reason of which he will be allowed to get off with a sentence of two and one-half years. I have had many expressions to the effect that 'Well, you got your man, you got him by law; that is better than his being murdered by the gangsters.' I hope that some day you will allow me to tell the public how much you had to do with it and how much impetus was personally given by you."[108] Hoover wrote back on July 1 acknowledging Loesch's kind letter, "Some time when the gentleman you mention is safely tucked away and engaged in very hard labor, you can tell all about it." Loesch, age 79 and "Chicago's most useful citizen," never published his inside story. It is, however, more than a reasonable certainty that neither Loesch nor Hoover was aware of how tenuous was the proposal of 'hard labor.'

Capone was granted bond in the amount of $50,000 on June 5. By mid-June, newspaper editorials across the nation expressed outrage over rumors that Capone had received a deal to get no more than three years in prison in exchange for his plea of guilty to liquor violations and tax evasion. If the rumor was true, wrote the editor of the *Boston Herald*, "the good efforts of the government's success in the prosecution will be half undone."[109] Letters to the attorney general were far less soft in tone, for example: "Do you wonder that the people of these United States have such a wide spread 'Contempt of the Law' when common gutter-bred crooks convicted beyond the shadow of a doubt can 'deal' with the United States."[110] The credibility of the Hoover administration's persistence was nearly lost, and explanations were demanded by a public tiring of Capone's skillful legal maneuvers.

Several of the principals were at the heart of the snafu: Mitchell, Youngquist, Johnson, Judge Wilkerson, and Al Capone's attorneys. Despite jubilation at Capone's indictment, justice and treasury officials questioned the strength of their evidence in the tax evasion and prohibition cases. According to Johnson's account, Capone announced that he could not get a fair trial, thus urging his attorneys to seek a plea agreement for a lighter sentence. Johnson, of course, would require approvals from Washington. He approached Mitchell and Youngquist in mid-May to present the Capone suggestions, but his bosses recommended delay for further details from Capone's attorneys. More meetings were held in late May, and the Capone lawyers sought an eighteen-month sentence in exchange for guilty pleas. Johnson could not agree with so short a sentence, fully reporting his discussions to Judge Wilkerson.

Wilkerson was apprised that the attorney general had been briefed and that serious consideration had been given to the Capone plea suggestion "by reason of the difficulties the government had encountered in the investigation and the hazardous nature of the government's case, particularly because two of the witnesses who were necessary to the government's case had been the bookkeepers of the gambling houses in which the defendant was interested." Johnson further apprised Wilkerson of matters of tax evasion law and procedure pending before the appellate court which could have a negative impact on the government's case against Capone. Wilkerson agreed to take the whole matter under advisement, noting that even if Johnson could acquire written approval of the plea agreement from the attorney general and the treasury secretary, "the ultimate responsibility would rest upon the court."

Johnson had further meetings with Capone's lawyers in which the latter refused to agree to a recommendation of more than two and one-half years confinement. He advised Youngquist of their intransigence, and he also shared the information with his assistants and intelligence unit officials Irey, Wilson, and Madden. Wilkerson was notified by Johnson that Mitchell and Youngquist agreed to the recommendation of two and one-half years, and he reminded him of "the hazards involved in a trial." At no time throughout the various negotiations up to the June 16 pleas of guilty and on to Wilkerson's withdrawal of the pleas on July 31 did Johnson have reason to believe that Wilkerson would change his mind. The newspapers got hold of the Capone plea agreement on June 16. Johnson believed that Capone had leaked the story to seal the deal, and the furor brought political pressure on Judge Wilkerson.

On July 13, after Johnson returned from a much-needed vacation, Wilkerson summoned him to his office. Johnson was surprised by Wilkerson's inquiry into the Prohibition conspiracy indictment, stating that he had not been apprised of the nature of the allegations. Johnson reminded the judge that the substance of the allegations had filled the newspapers for days, but the judge moved on to hesitation about allowing the Capone recommendations to proceed. Johnson bolted, saying that he was "honor bound to defendant's counsel to make a recommendation that I had agreed to make." Further, he told Wilkerson that Capone should be offered the opportunity to withdraw his pleas, but that to do so "because the case was hazardous for the government." Johnson then sought the written approval of Mitchell and the secretary of the treasury for a limited sentence of two and one-half years. Johnson had further reason to believe that Wilkerson would uphold the recommendations because one of his assistants, Mr. LaRue, was told by Wilkerson "that under no circumstances would he permit the defendant to withdraw his plea of guilty to the prohibition conspiracy indictment." Wilkerson went on vacation for several days, stating that "he would be guided by what would transpire at the hearing on July 30, 1931."

Johnson's negotiations with Capone's attorneys, therefore, had been guided by written approvals of the arrangement received from the attorney general and the assistant secretary of the treasury, Arthur A. Ballantine, on July 24, 1931: "You are authorized to advise the court that the Treasury Department concurs in the recommendation of the Attorney General that Alphonse Capone be sentenced to a term of two and one-half years in the aggregate under the indictments charging him with violations of the federal income-tax law in your district to which he has entered pleas of guilty, to run concurrently with the sentence the court may impose upon him on his pleas of guilty to the liquor conspiracy indictment there pending."[111] Fearing the possibility that Wilkerson would renege on accepting the pleas, Youngquist told Johnson to avoid a recommendation "unless the court would follow it." Johnson advised Wilkerson of this caution and Wilkerson replied "that the Attorney General should not impose such limitations on me under these circumstances." Johnson stood by his recommendation and noted for the record that he would not have made a recommendation if he believed Wilkerson would not uphold it.[112] Moreover, he was supported in the July 28 letter from the attorney general which stated, "I also approved of your proposal to recommend to the court that if Alphonse Capone dismisses his appeal in the contempt proceeding the six-months' sentence imposed upon him in that case should run concurrently with the sentences to be imposed in the income-tax and conspiracy cases."[113]

Youngquist's summation of the facts is similar to Johnson's, but there are both reinforcing and alternative perspectives on some key points. He said that the income tax indictment returned against Capone on March 12, 1931, was "not because there was enough evidence available but because the statute of limitations was about to run for the year in question, 1924." Regarding the negotiations with

Capone's attorneys, Youngquist was not offended by the process, since "the interests of the government would be excellently served by Capone's pleading guilty and being given a prison sentence, even for a relatively short term." To him, and reasonably apparent to the attorney general, "the length of sentence was of much less importance than the restoration of public confidence in law enforcement that would follow upon his actually being put behind the prison bars." He affirmed that Judge Wilkerson never agreed to give Capone a two and one-half year sentence, but he admitted that both he and Johnson had taken the matter for granted "in view of what had happened in the case of others of the Capone gang."

Youngquist emphasized that "the evidence against Capone was very weak [in the prohibition violation case], he having had no direct connection with the liquor activities so far as could be shown since 1924 or 1925." He was confident the tax evasion case would stand up in trial. Between mid-June and early July, Wilkerson's perspective on the possible arrangement changed drastically. Wilkerson, in further meetings with Johnson, seemed pressured by Elmer Irey's statements to the press that "the government had an 'iron bound' case on the income tax violation. He criticized the allegation of some five thousand overt acts in the liquor conspiracy indictment and the publicity given to that fact. He spoke of letters that he had received urging a lengthy sentence for Capone and . . . newspaper editorials to that effect." Referring probably to the Prohibition case, Youngquist agreed with Wilkerson that the court could not enter into an agreement with Capone, but he said that "it would be most unfortunate if that plea had to be withdrawn and the case go to trial (having in mind the slimness of our chance)."

Wilkerson, Youngquist reported, gave clear indication to Johnson that he would not follow the recommendations of Capone's attorneys as accepted by the government. Furthermore, he wanted Capone's attorneys notified of his position so that they would have an opportunity to withdraw their pleas. With a slightly different cast to Johnson's report of the facts, Youngquist said that Judge Wilkerson wanted to learn "whether Johnson could get letters from the Attorney General and the Secretary of the Treasury approving the recommendation (having in mind apparently the power of these two officers to compromise tax matters both civil and criminal)." On July 23, Johnson called Youngquist to say that he had received a call from Wilkerson. Youngquist took careful notes of his conversation with Johnson. In summary, the judge told Johnson that he wanted an unconditional plea of guilty from Capone, and if he did not get it from him in open court the trial on the tax matter could proceed. He wanted no prior formal arrangements with Capone, most reasonably related to reasons of judicial tradition and political pressure from a community insisting on harsh punishment. Johnson told Youngquist, "I can tell you and the Attorney General in confidence his exact words: 'A Judge would be a damned fool not to pay attention to that!'"

Capone's attorneys were notified of these transactions and that Capone would appear in a hearing on July 30 to give his unconditional plea of guilty. All bets were off on that day, however, when Capone's attorneys withdrew the pleas, which were, according to Youngquist, based on "a statement by Judge Wilkerson that he expected to put Capone on the stand and question him, plus the vicious way in which he said it."[114] Johnson's phone call to Youngquist on July 31 refers to Wilkerson's desire to have the grand jury "dispose of the idea that Capone committed 5,000 offenses against the liquor laws." He also noted that Capone's attorney, on learning from Wilkerson that Capone would be ordered to testify, "seemed to lose his head and made a number of extravagant statements."[115]

The entire intrigue reflected the skills of the principals in sensing, from Capone's point of view, the willingness of the government to engage in any form of negotiated solution, and from the government's view the tradeoffs of a potentially hazardous trial situation and a public seeking a harsh sentence, which might not have been possible. Judge Wilkerson, while highly supportive of the government's position against Capone, was keenly aware of remaining with judicial tradition not to bargain with criminals while equally aware of the risks attendant to a Capone victory, especially on the tax evasion charges.[116] Youngquist, in a blunt letter to an angry citizen, put the capstone on the matter: "Capone did not 'dicker' with the President, and his 'influence' did not reach anyone in this Department."[117]

HOOVER'S ENDS ACHIEVED

The sweet taste of victory permeated the halls of the Internal Revenue. The cover page of the August 1931 issue of the *Internal Revenue News* announced indictments of several gangsters. No additional information was included. The trial began on October 7. The trial proper was covered well in local and national newspapers. The government's case hung on its ability to present the jury with sufficient evidence that Capone was a wealthy person in contrast to the tax burden he claimed he could not owe from his business enterprises. On October 17, the jury found Capone guilty on three counts of tax evasion for the years 1925 through 1927, based on personal and business income of $650,000, and two counts of tax avoidance for the years 1928 and 1929.[118] Wearing a "screaming green suit" to hear the verdict, Capone darted from the courtroom to a waiting car. Unofficially, the Justice Department reported the cost of the investigation had been $100,000, a cost the government believed would sustain the integrity of the law's superiority over gangsters like Capone.[119] This was approximately half what the government said Capone owed in taxes for the years at issue. On October 24, Capone was sentenced to ten years in federal prison, one year in the Cook County Jail, and a $50,000 fine plus court costs.

By December 1931, almost a year had passed since Herbert Hoover requested a shift in manpower from the Chicago investigations to New York City. Irey was asked by the new commissioner of internal revenue, David Burnet, to prepare a report of the taxpayers, tax dollars owed, and penalties received as a result of the New York efforts. The long list of cases must have been good news to a White House nearly overrun with the rigors of deepening strains of the Depression.[120] Secretary of the treasury Mellon, in one of the few pieces of publicly available correspondence to Hoover on the Capone matter, recommended that Hoover write a personal and confidential letter of appreciation to Mr. John T. Rogers of the *St. Louis Post Dispatch* and to the owner of the newspaper, Mr. Joseph Pulitzer, for their contributions of valuable information on Capone throughout the investigation. Rogers, according to Irey's report, gave invaluable information during several visits to Chicago and Florida. He remained in close contact with Internal Revenue agents and put these agents in contact "with certain persons who were extremely helpful." The *Post Dispatch* bore all the costs of Rogers's work, and it received no special treatment in terms of late-breaking news. Irey emphasized that "Mr. Pulitzer would deeply appreciate recognition of their assistance in the form of a letter such as this, especially coming from the President with whom Mr. Pulitzer is personally acquainted. It will be readily understood that there will be no disposition on the part of the Post Dispatch to publish such a letter or to reveal its contents in any way. To do so would place their representative, Mr. Rogers, in a dangerous position before the gangster element of Chicago, I cannot but strongly urge that the President be requested to sign such a letter."[121]

From his Cook County jail cell, Capone challenged his convictions in early January 1932. In *Alphonse Capone* v. *United States of America*, attorneys argued that the government required Capone to plead on four separate counts of attempting to evade taxes, when in fact the U.S. attorney contended that there had been only one attempt at evasion. The argument addressed the question of whether an indictment for attempting evasion in the words of the law was adequate to support a sentence of imprisonment.[122] On February 27, the Seventh Circuit Court affirmed Capone's conviction. A week earlier, Johnson wrote to Mitchell reflecting upon confidential information that Capone was receiving undue privileges as a prisoner in the Cook County Jail. He reported that no record was maintained for Capone's visitors or other persons with whom he communicated. Urging Mitchell to authorize a full time guard in the jail, Johnson said that his informant revealed Capone's intentions to escape if the circuit court rejected his case.

Showing a touch of self-serving humanity, Capone offered to inter- vene in the recovery of the kidnapped son of Anne and Charles A. Lindbergh by paying a reward of $10,000 for the boy's recovery. The ploy posed an interesting irony: a hero of the underworld who could not afford to pay his taxes offered a hero of the legitimate world the money to recover his son. The proposition was given headline play in some newspapers, but no one in government took it seriously. By mid-March, Capone intended to appeal to the Supreme Court for a petition of certiorari. Movietone people appeared at the Cook County Jail to film Capone, and it was difficult for federal authorities to deny them access.[123] Frank Loesch wrote to Senator William E. Borah expressing his concern that Capone may have been capable of directing his criminal enterprises from a prison cell, and that the Capone dynasty reached into labor unions, small business, Illinois state government, the U.S. attorney's office, and even the federal bench.[124] All such concerns were set aside when Capone entered the federal penitentiary at Atlanta on the evening of May 3, 1932, and became convict number 40866 the next day.

Chapter 7

Federal Prison Reforms

*A rigorous, yet humane, scientific, yet commonsense, progressive,
yet protective, program of penal reform.*[1]

Hoover's administration was the first to give formal policy attention
to federal prisons and prisoners. Under his leadership, prison administration, historically ignored, was transformed from an antiquated
and rawly inadequate collection of penitentiaries into a model system.
Remarkably, reforms to facilities and practices introduced in 1929
were implemented by 1933. Moreover, federal correctional practices
were replicated, as intended, in several state prison systems. With
the formation of the Federal Bureau of Prisons in 1930, prison management was established as a formal policy function of the executive
branch.

LEGACIES OF PREVIOUS ADMINISTRATIONS

Before the mid-1920s, federal prison administration did not appeal
to scholars of criminology, the presidency, or social history. The
most physically obtrusive and costly branch of the Justice Department attracted only occasional journalistic interest. Low appeal to
students may be ascribed to the humdrum nature of prison routine
and the drab, harsh qualities of the Atlanta, Leavenworth, and McNeil
Island penitentiaries.[2] The few scholars, like Harry Elmer Barnes,
who engaged in prison studies aimed their research at state prisons.[3]
Prison management, including the Hoover reforms, is equally un-
appealing to scholars of the American presidency. Federal prisons

are comparatively benign agencies among the numerous cabinet-rank and noncabinet organizations in the executive branch, and they deliver inconsequential political value.

Presidents Harding and Coolidge emphasized criminal law enforcement and displayed little concern for prison expansion or facilities for drug-addicted or mentally ill federal offenders. Federal cops chased suspected anarchists and labor thugs, and their marching orders emphasized Prohibition enforcement, narcotics smuggling, and auto theft.[4] Successes appeared in rising workloads for U.S. attorneys, bulging federal court dockets, and increasingly crowded federal prisons. By 1928, Atlanta, Leavenworth, and McNeil Island remained the principal federal prisons. Federal probation was small and grossly underfunded; paroles were handled at each institution through an óften inequitable administrative system with no central authority in Washington that required the superintendent of prisons to travel to every parole meeting. Prison construction and alternatives to incarceration, topics of rare discussion in public forums,[5] lay dormant in academic and professional circles, contemplated only by young sociologists and the liberal press. Economic prosperity and Prohibition enforcement held greater appeal.

Hoover's reforms intended six major changes: selection of strong and innovative agency managers, elimination of abusive and unprofessional prison practices, reorganization of correctional functions, reduction of crowding through construction of new facilities, reduction of prisoner idleness through expansion prison industries, and expansion of diversity in federal corrections. Reform plans were aided by two major catalysts. First, ideas for correctional reform were plentiful, found mainly in the writings of academicians, prison administrators, and social critics. In publications and convention speeches, intellectuals and professionals recognized that the federal government bore responsibility for housing an increasing number of criminal offenders; and federal initiatives could serve as models for state reforms. Second, prison riots in the summer of 1929 brought overcrowded conditions to public attention, thereby improving Hoover's chances for his reform measures.

HOOVER APPOINTS SANFORD BATES

Sanford Bates was formally appointed superintendent of the Bureau of Prisons by President Hoover on April 23, 1929. The *New York Times* editorialized that the new superintendent was "by no means an amateur strategist nor only a scholarly theorist fussing with the baffling problems of the improvements of special institutions of the country and the making over [of] the minds and hearts of the criminal populations." The *Times* applauded Bates's appointment as one of "unusual significance." He was said to be "a pioneer" and a man capable of true reforms: "The whole 'context' [of planned prison reforms] indicates that his selection for this important post means that the Department of Justice wants the administration of the Federal prisons to be in the hands of a man who is both a scientific penologist and a practical man of affairs."[6]

Bates's first days in office were hectic. Upon the assurances of Assistant Attorney General Mabel W. Willebrandt that the "Congress would dispose to carry out the recommendations of its committee and provide for the establishment of a prison bureau on a larger and more effective scale," Bates believed his first task was to convince Hoover and Attorney General Mitchell "that the course we proposed to follow was sound." He envisioned a new penal policy "which looked beyond the date of a man's admission to a prison to the time of his discharge, and which justified the attempts which we proposed to make to improve, rehabilitate, and reestablish Federal prisoners as a move in the direction of ultimate public protection."

President Hoover was predisposed to this type of approach, Bates said. Over dinner at the White House, Hoover asked Bates, "which is the more important, to reform the [9]0,000 [referring to the combined federal and state prison and jail populations] or to teach the 122,000,000 that crime does not pay? To which effort should we give most attention?" Bates, writing from memory in 1936, responded: "Why not do both, Mr. President? Why not so contrive the punishment of the 90,000 that it will be both deterrent and constructive? A prison need not be dirty, or lax in its discipline; or managed by grafting officials, or overrun with idle men, to exercise a deterrent effect. Men can be punished, and at the same time their bodies can be rid of disease and their minds cleansed of delusions. They can be kept busy at productive tasks, and they can be given opportunities for education and betterment without weakening the sanctions of the law."[7]

His vision of a model prison system obligated political commitment to a mature approach to law enforcement, in particular to the social costs of criminal behavior: "So often we hear a specious cry, and I have no doubt many of you have echoed it in your own hearts: 'We have spent too much time on the criminal. Let's have some sympathy for his victim.' And my contention is that the more we change the criminal into a law-abiding citizen, and the more, through modern and scientific methods, we reduce the number of criminals, the more real sympathy we are showing for the unfortunate victim."[8] If history had taught the prison administrator and the society that crime could be deterred by punishment alone, Bates believed, then it would be "our duty to make prison as gloomy and painful as possible. It is because of our growing belief that such a policy has not been successful that we are turning to something different."⁹ Prisons, therefore, were tools supplied by a society committed as much to "realizing the newer ideals as there [would be] in carrying out the old [punitive methods]. We have ideals enough, but the accomplishments of the new program will require an extraordinary amount of perseverance, intelligence and faith in the ultimate worth of human nature."¹⁰

Bates was handed the executive management of all institutions and programs. Most of his time was spent on prison operations, but nights in the summer of 1929 were given to bureau plans for new facilities and programs. Other professional activities in his ordinarily full schedule of public speaking and writing were set aside. He was besieged with requests to join criminological research projects, to give speeches, to visit prisons, to review statistical studies, and to address graduation ceremonies.¹¹ The job put him in charge of an annual budget of $10 million, the reorganization of the bureau, and the drafting of legislation to construct new institutions. Congressional approval for some improvements to the prison system had already been granted, and these required immediated implementation.¹² His attitude remained enthusiastic and theoretically driven. Two weeks after taking over, he wrote to Frank Loveland, Jr.: "I may say that we have set up a very ambitious and extended organization here in the office, and that it has received the unofficial approval of the Attorney General. If we can get the money to carry it out, I think you will agree that it will be a long step in advance, and I have a special job waiting for you in connection with this new scheme."¹³

The mid-July 1929 prison reports carried surprising statistics of rapid population increase. He paused to consider the dilemma: "I suppose we could go on forever, putting men in jail, turning them out and taking them back again, without having very much permanent effect upon the stream of criminality. Either our social structure is hopelessly maladjusted, or else there must be causes which can be ascertained with sufficient accuracy to want to attempt to remove conditions which tend towards crime." With the reform plans completed by August 1, 1929, he seemed even more confident of progress. Meeting with the Wickersham Commission, he concluded, "they are taking a very promising attitude towards the subject [of prisons], and the contact that I had with them . . . indicated distinctly that they were taking a scientific and not a popular view." He was particularly impressed with the commission's secretary, Max Lowenthal.[14] Upbeat expressions were tempered but not destroyed by the events surrounding the Leavenworth riot on the last day of July.[15]

Between March and August, the pace of domestic activities restricted opportunity for Hoover to communicate with Bates. But through Attorney General Mitchell, Bates's legislative plans and personnel selections met with executive support. Objectives were clear: select competent personnel to manage daily operations of federal prisons and draft legislative proposals to strengthen all operational areas and programs, with special emphasis given to parole and probation.[16] The House Judiciary Committee report in January 1929 had urged new prison construction, but Hoover and Bates recognized limitations in the congressional plan. For Bates, expansion of the parole system was absolutely essential, in combination with new prisons and jails and diversified correctional programs.

The process of hiring key personnel and administrative staff was completed in one year. Two deputy superintendents were added to the executive staff: Austin H. MacCormick,[17] and James V. Bennett.[18] A new director of the Training School for Prison Officers, Jesse O. Stutsman, was also added.[19] One of Bates's special priorities was to improve employee education levels throughout the federal prison system.[20] Each superintendent and warden was required to have a college education, preferably in law or medicine. Also, he often announced, they should be outfitted with knowledge of the aims of psychiatry and penal sociology, with experience, with an infinite amount of tact, with patience and perseverance, with courage to withstand pressures from various corners, and with knowledge of current correctional methods, business acumen, and methods for dealing with various branches of government.[21] The latest in correctional thinking, he believed, could evolve from an institute located at a "high class university" where research could involve both university staff and consultants.[22]

Women were included in Bates's recommendations for employment in corrections. Writing to Guy Holcombe, vice president of the board of trustees for Pennsylvania's Eastern State Penitentiary, Bates advised that opportunities for women could be found in women's institutions, probation, parole, and juvenile courts. Holcombe's daughter, it turned out, was interested in a career in criminology and penology. Bates recommended that she receive training in social work, but if she was interested in institutional work she should train for a position in a medical department or for a psychology department as a social case worker. His strongest advice was for Holcombe's daughter to receive a college degree in psychology.[23]

ELIMINATING ABUSIVE AND UNPROFESSIONAL
PRISON MANAGEMENT

An important and pressing political matter for Hoover was to rid federal institutions of abusive operational methods. In particular, Hoover demanded elimination of the secretive system of spying on prisoners by agents of the Bureau of Investigation. Under direct authorization from the Justice Department in the mid-1920s, bureau agents were planted inside the three major federal prisons. They reported to their superiors, and ultimately to J. Edgar Hoover. The *New York Times* exposed this practice in a series of articles between March 13 and March 24, 1929, an exceptionally critical period in the new Hoover administration. Hoover believed that it was necessary to act quickly in order to contain infectious political reaction that would challenge the credibility of reform policies. Spy practices contradicted correctional goals and held no rehabilitative value. They had been applied liberally for years, however, by administrators who followed orders of the assistant attorney general, Mabel Willebrandt. Willebrandt's objectives were to ferret out information about bootleggers and drug smugglers and to assist in the control of prisoners to avoid staff additions. The practice originated at Atlanta in mid-1928 when prison superintendent Albert H. Conner informed Willebrandt of alleged internal corruption in the penitentiary. Willebrandt, Conner later reported, decided "to send an undercover man to the institution in the guise of a prisoner."[24]

The order was carried out. A Bureau of Investigation agent was escorted to Atlanta, clothed in prison garb and locked in a cell. Records were fabricated to show a court sentence of one year and one day. He remained undercover for several weeks while reporting secretly to bureau supervisors. When Atlanta prison warden John Snook discovered the plot, he was insulted that the secret operation had not been discussed with him. When the agent's identity was revealed to Snook, the warden denied his request for immediate release.[25] To fix the situation, a plan was born to effect the agent's discreet transfer from Atlanta to Leavenworth by sending in a United States marshal to transport him off the Atlanta reservation. On orders from Willebrandt, the agent was removed from prison and promptly disappeared.[26] A similar incident occurred at McNeil Island penitentiary, although on that occasion the would-be prisoner was locked in solitary confinement when he tried to identify himself to the warden. As it turned out, in all cases the agents, as later described by James Bennett, made no important criticisms and did not identify any major institutionally condoned corruption.[27] Regrettably for Willebrandt, the entire farce attracted unexpected political heat.

The political risks to the new Hoover administration could not be ignored. At very least, the undercover spy system implied cheap half-measures at a time when comprehensive changes had been announced. At best, the practice was unrelated to broader fundamental changes to improve the integrity of Prohibition enforcement and prison morale. The *New York Times* reported on March 13 that Warden Snook had threatened to resign in protest against Willebrandt's insistence that the spy system would be maintained. Snook, a wealthy former state assemblyman and Idaho prison warden, had close political connections with Senator William E. Borah. Borah's Judiciary Committee had received from Snook several documents pertaining to the system, thus enticing the committee to conduct a full investigation. Attorney General Mitchell was aware that the system had been only partially discussed in New York. Democratic congressman John J. Boylan's committee on prison conditions, saved from further exposure by the fact, said the *Times*, that committee members refused to report their findings.

Senator Borah had three objections to the spy system. First, spying on prisoners entailed planting agents by faking judicial commitment documents and contriving procedures to remove the bogus prisoners. Second, no prison warden ought to have been subjected to a spy setup supervised from the Justice Department without his approval. Borah argued that if trust and confidence had not been invested in Warden Snook, the facts of any allegations should have been laid before the Congress long before March 1929. And third, penologists were opposed to spy practices because they demoralized prisoners and contradicted the positive intentions of enlightened penal practice. Borah concluded that the practice was "based on a wrong theory," manifesting a debasement and prostitution of the federal courts, and "about three hundred years behind the times in prison management."[28]

Willebrandt was interviewed on March 16. She said that Snook had been asked to resign in early March "because of utter want of administrative ability." Moreover, she defended the spy system by arguing that it "seems the only way at present to find the facts necessary to keep conditions wholesome in the penitentiaries." She claimed that the practice had been instituted by Mitchell's predecessor, Attorney General John G. Sargent.[29] Snook was given until March 31 to be on a train back to Idaho. Ironically, Snook had succeeded Warden Albert E. Sartain in 1925, a man with whom several associates had been convicted of accepting bribes from wealthy prisoners in exchange for "soft" prison jobs.[30] Snook's firing implied to Hoover Democrats that the new president had reneged on private commitments to bring southerners into his administration. Southern newspapers castigated the Snook decision, but authors were generally careful to note that southerners, too, disapproved of prison spy systems.[31] Editors, eager to coin a new phrase, referred to Willebrandt's actions as evidence of government "snoopervision." Nine months after the incident, J. Edgar Hoover confirmed to a congressional committee that Willebrandt had ordered the undercover agents into the two institutions.[32]

Bates's philosophy of prison management differed greatly from Willebrandt's and Conner's. He supported the concept of developing wardens from the ground up and of nurturing depth in the personnel most likely to aspire to senior-level vacancies. Management leadership to induce staff development would, he believed, improve morale among institution employees.[33] In general, he opposed press inquiries, but occasionally he allowed reporters to enter institutions if they agreed to write "constructive articles" without talking to inmates or taking pictures.[34] According to James Bennett, the policy was selectively applied.[35]

Bates's policies insisted upon firm but humane administration of federal institutions. A glimpse into his humanitarian side was provided by his policy on using corporal punishment devices. In state institutions, solitary confinement, bread and water rations, and iron rings to force men to stand in their cells were not uncommon. Bates disapproved of such methods; and where he found them, he demanded their elimination in nearly all cases. Bates's letters in such matters demonstrated an obvious irritation with conditions he had hoped were removed from federal institutions. For example, he wrote to Warden T. B. White in June 1931 that he had discovered in the institution's punishment records for May the use of solitary confinement and bread and water as punishments for a wide variety of prisoner acts.

While Bates did not reject their use under all circumstances, he instructed that the staff should try to adjust "modes of punishment not only to individual prisoners but to varying types of offenders. For example, it would seem a reasonable punishment for violation of the mail privileges to deprive a man of such privileges, making exceptions perhaps in the case of letters to wives or mothers. Loss of good time would seem to be an appropriate punishment for some offenses, loss of recreation privileges for others, reduction in grade for others, and solitary or separate confinement for still others."[36] The following month, Bates visited McNeil Island where he found use of the iron ring. Reacting immediately, he wrote, "I don't know whether it was understood at the time I left your institution but this letter will confirm my understanding that the iron ring formerly used to secure men undergoing punishment in a standing position is to be removed. Please advise me when this is done."[37]

PRISON CROWDING AND IDLENESS

In Hoover's care in March 1929 were approximately 8,400 institutionalized prisoners. Contrary to general assumptions, only 18 percent of the prisoners in federal cells had been sentenced under Prohibition's Volstead Act. An additional 8,100 federal offenders were housed in state and local facilities, of whom approximately 63 percent were Prohibition violators. Between April 1 and June 30, 1929, the population in federal prisons increased to 10,000, including several hundred new Prohibition cases. The sharp increase severely crowded penitentiaries, and even more prisoners were expected in succeeding months.[38] Increasingly, the federal system housed a greater diversity of inmates: Prohibition offenders, major smugglers, bank robbers, drug pushers, car thieves, and gangsters. Federal prisons had become, therefore, repositories for a wider range of offenders, more of whom than ever before were youthful and prone to learn crime from hardened offenders.

Crowding stressed all conditions in federal institutions, making prisons vulnerable to riots or attacks on guards. For example, prisoners at McNeil Island penitentiary learned that the Public Health Service had investigated the quality of the institution's water supply; $200,000 was needed to expand and improve the water system. On learning of the situation, Bates asked Mitchell to make the Congress aware of the potential problems that could arise from inmate dissatisfaction. The institution was understaffed and demoralized by lack of attention to inmate and staff concerns.[39] Food quality and preparation facilities were alleged sources of the Leavenworth riot on July 31, 1929.

Institutional crowding also affected the female prison population. During the 1920s, an ever-increasing number of women, of whom a substantial proportion were black and poor, were sentenced to federal institutions for narcotics violations and prostitution. Mary B. Harris, superintendent of the Alderson Federal Industrial Institution for Women in West Virginia, wrote to Bates in July.[40] She called attention to difficulties she was having in accommodating so many new assignees, particularly black women, in a system that remained segregated by race: "It is especially . . . urgent that the commitments of colored be carefully selected. As I told you, we have a number of long-time colored women and the turn-over in that section is very slow. The color question, of course, we never raise, but our proportion of colored is already four times the proportion of colored to white in the country and I feel that we have already the quota."[41] Harris was sensitive to the political pressure put on the Hoover administration to audit the racial affiliations of sentenced prisoners, but space was in short supply.

Given no immediate solutions to the rapid population growth, the most pressing problem was the inability of institutional administrators to keep prisoners busy and out of their cells. Prison jobs were limited by the identifiable tasks to which an inmate could be assigned for a defined period of time when staff were available to provide supervision. Two types of work were available: institutional maintenance and prison-made goods. The former was entirely acceptable; the latter, "convict labor," historically had been contentious.

Convict employment to make products for the free market was a well-worn issue by 1929. Serious and sustained opposition to such manufacturing appeared in the late nineteenth century. By 1886, prison labor drew formal federal attention when the U.S. commissioner of labor devoted his entire annual report to the subject.[42] Labor groups led by Samuel Gompers supported state-use-only laws as long as finished products of convict labor would remain outside the free market. In 1905, President Theodore Roosevelt signed an executive order prohibiting both convict labor on levees and other convict assignments. In late 1916, Congress created the Commission on Manufactures in Penitentiaries in an attempt to estimate the total amount of work performed by convicts in federal institutions. The good intentions of Congress, labor, industry, and penologists notwithstanding, state prisons in the mid-1920s frequently overproduced goods destined for the marketplace. In reaction, Congress passed the Cooper-Hawes bill, signed into law by Coolidge on January 21, 1929, to remove prison products from interstate commerce. The entire history reflected a rare coalition of labor and manufacturers, each faction interested in eliminating prison-made products from free markets. Neither faction was concerned, however, with prisoner idleness, dissension, or other seeds of prison disorder. A way had to be found to expand prison industries without affecting local economies.[43]

SECURING NEW FEDERAL
CORRECTIONS LEGISLATION

The prison overcrowding situation was obvious to Hoover. By March 15, 1929, the attorney general had reviewed the House of Representatives survey on federal prisons. He then asked Bates to begin work on a comprehensive plan to improve the situation.[44] At the very least, the congressional report served to prepare the legislative branch for Hoover's expansion plans. Whole new federal institutions were needed. Alternative prison sites, such as military facilities or small urban institutions, required selection. Prison enterprises were needed to reduce idleness. New methods for holding and rehabilitating special classes of prisoners—such as juveniles, first offenders, recidivists, and drug addicts—would contribute to the long-term reduction of recidivism.[45] Bates carried these messages to congressional committee members throughout the summer of 1929.

Delayed congressional action meant that prison populations would expand uncontrollably. Reflecting upon the Leavenworth riot, Hoover spoke to the press on August 6: "Atlanta is 120 percent over capacity in inmates at the present time, and Leavenworth 87 percent, all of which is the cause of infinite demoralization and the direct cause of outbreaks and trouble." He said he would ask the Congress for $5 million not only to renovate old prisons and to add a new prison in the Northeastern area but also to add to the number of probation officers to help to alleviate prison space pressures.[46] Actually, proposals sent to Congress on August 13 called for more than the amount mentioned in the news conference.[47] The total construction cost would be over $6.5 million, distributed over a five-year period.[48] The budget for new institutions included plans for one new penitentiary at $3 million, one new reformatory at $2.8 million, and three new jails at $750,000 each. In the interim, Hoover announced on August 20 that he had arranged with the secretary of war and the attorney general to house more than 1,600 prisoners at Alcatraz, Blackwell's Island, and Fort Leavenworth army installations until new construction was completed.[49] The transfer of prisoners posed no special legal problems and was accomplished within a few days.[50]

From August 6, 1929, through April 1930, prison reform was persistently promoted by Hoover, Mitchell, and Bates. Early in November 1929, Mitchell spoke on radio, repeating that the total construction program for new facilities would cost $6.5 million, stressing the impact the riot had placed on housing and feeding facilities and pointing out that prisoner idleness was the norm rather than the exception. Public discussion was a strategy intended to overcome congressional lethargy in the face of potentially steep economic decline. Hoover added more pressure in his lengthy December 3 State of the Union message. He said, "our Federal penal institutions are overcrowded, and this condition is daily becoming worse. The parole and probation systems are inadequate. These conditions make it impossible to perform the work of personal reconstruction of prisoners so as to prepare them for return to the duties of citizenship." Reminding Congress of the temporary measures he had taken by opening military prisons, he pressed the need for approving the plans for new construction and creating within the Justice Department the Federal Bureau of Prisons, with added staffing.[51]

Adding even more public pressure, Bates followed the president's message with a radio statement in which he characterized federal prison conditions as "intolerable." On December 15, U.S. attorney Charles Tuttle addressed a church group in New York and called for more "scientific study" and enlightenment on crime control and prison reform. And on December 20, Mitchell appeared before the House subcommittee overseeing prisons to appeal for immediate attention to reform measures already in congressional hands.

Prison overcrowding also affected inadequate women's facilities. In October, Bates had instructed the U.S. marshals that "no woman . . . should be committed to Alderson [women's institution in Alderson, West Virginia] without first consulting the Department and as designation [is] secured."[52] It had not been uncommon for federal judges to ignore guidelines for sentencing women to Alderson, and their insensitivity to crowding problems irritated Bates. Within recent months, the institution had been overfilled, many women sleeping in the hospital facilities. Superintendent Mary Harris expressed her continued frustrations to Bates: "We have many who have served from five to ten sentences already, some of them so many that they have lost count. We have a number of women who have been keepers of disorderly houses, and many more who have been in commercialized prostitution fifteen or twenty years. One woman from the District [of Columbia] was 79 years old when committed. While none of these are disciplinary cases in the strict sense of the word, many of them are a pernicious moral influence in a quiet way difficult to detect."[53] She pleaded for attention to the overcrowding problem. By April 1930, the Alderson population had been sharply reduced. Harris then began absorbing women prisoners previously housed in state prisons.[54]

The women's institution at Alderson was segregated by race of the prisoner. Inspections of its operations, facilities, and practices had revealed that it was an efficient and professionally run institution. Difficulties evident in the all-male penitentiaries were not found at Alderson. Grace Abbott, chief of the Labor Department's Children's Bureau, reported to Bates in February 1933: "The colored women have separate cottages and other segregation is carried out as to the colored by separate classes and work assignments. They attend the general institution functions such as movies, church, etc., sitting apart on one side of the auditorium." Furthermore, Abbott reported, "only colored women are assigned to the institution laundry and, of course, receive training in this work. A class in laundry theory is sometimes given for white women if there is a demand for it."[55] The policy of segregation remained unresolved until well into the Roosevelt administration.

The year 1929 had been exceptionally busy for Bates. He could report to Mitchell that significant progress had been made toward the original goals, but he could not report acquisition of construction funds. Hopeful of more rapid progress in 1930, however, Bates outlined his objectives: a new penitentiary to hold twelve hundred inmates in the Northeast; a reformatory for young first offenders in the Southwest; a new prison hospital for severe psychiatric problems; a reorganized Bureau of Prisons; new programs for education, field service, and probation and parole; new institutional activities dedicated to prisoner needs, such as a system of schools, a social investigator, a morale officer, and vocational instructors; several new federal jails on existing federal properties to handle overcrowding and to absorb many of the ten thousand prisoners in eleven hundred county jails; probation system expansion; and a prison industries function to put every prisoner to work to raise morale, improve discipline, and turn out men who could succeed in the industrial workplace.

Regarding staff improvements, Bates also hoped the Congress would provide funds to establish a correctional officer training school in New York City, to stiffen entry requirements for officers, to establish a communications system between inmates and the Washington headquarters, to create a Washington-based morale officer to address institutional problems, to install a merit system for officers, to secure permanent transfer of the disciplinary barracks at Ft. Leavenworth to the Prison Bureau, and to study uses of unused government property for possible bureau applications.[56] The wish list was an impressive collection of innovations. Bates believed that each element was necessary to bring the correctional system up to the standards that his community of professional peers believed was minimally acceptable.[57]

The pace of accomplishment slowed in 1930, despite the fact that the construction program received congressional approval. Deepening economic depression, unemployment, and drained federal reserves placed the prison program lower on the priority list. Bates aimed his concerns at the commitment of the Congress to support the notion of a nationally recognized model in the Bureau of Prisons. His frustrations appeared in letters to colleagues. To Walter Scott he wrote, "one of the great trials in public life . . . is that due to public opinion, the limitations of appropriations, and traditions, it is hard to put these ideas into operation as promptly as we would like. I am afraid it will be some time before we accomplish even the limited program which we have already presented to Congress for approval." On the same day, he wrote to A. D. Baird, "one trouble with the whole prison problem is that it is quite possible to make some very penetrating and convincing statements about the whole thing and it is a much more difficult task to bring about any practical approach to the ideals upon which we are all pretty generally agreed. It is very difficult to get the Government to finance propaganda work and, as a matter of fact, it is much better to have this done by private associations if possible."[58] The latter remark was a reference to paying consultants to come to Washington to lobby for prison and other bureau resources.

Bates had been given wide latitude on facilities needs. His communications with Hoover and Mitchell stressed frugality and conservation of use of existing government buildings. Bates was particularly conscious of the need to pursue economy measures, noting in several of his letters to Mitchell the steps that he and his staff had taken to control costs. There is no evidence, however, that any effort was made to significantly reduce any of the original construction plans. As the new year proceeded, no congressional action was taken to deliver funds. On April 28, Hoover wrote to the Congress urging passage of all of his federal justice system reforms, including the prison work: "We have already 11,985 prisoners in federal establishments built for 6,946. The number of federal prisoners in federal and state institutions increased 6,277 in the nine months from June 30, 1929, to April 1, 1930. The Attorney General has stated that we cannot hope to enforce the laws unless we can have some point of reception for convicted persons. The overcrowding of the prisons themselves is inhumane and accentuates criminal tendencies."[59]

At last, between May 13 and 27, 1930, Hoover signed five measures to establish a hospital for defective delinquents, to create the United States Parole Board, to authorize the Public Health Service to treat federal prisoners, to create the Federal Bureau of Prisons and to establish federal jails, and to construct two new federal prisons. The construction program was designed with two objectives in mind: (1) to expand maximum security space in regions where a much larger influx of federal prisoners had occurred (the Northeast and the Northwest), thus relieving transportation costs and widening local opportunities for prison release programs; and (2) to distribute across the country a number of smaller facilities, such as jails, hospitals, and road camps, to deal with short-term offenders, offenders requiring special medical or physical care, and offenders whose legal transgressions were relatively minor and for whom learning industrial trades was deemed beneficial. Both these objectives were in keeping with professional views on prisoner classification, constructive rehabilitation, and efficiency.

NEW ORGANIZATION AND NEW DIVERSITY OF OPERATIONS

Reorganization, for all its obvious practicality, had not been easy to squeeze from the clutches of Congress. Executive-branch workload and congressional debate over the manner of change combined to delay action, even though the issue had been laid out for at least two years. With Bates in place to build the necessary congressional support, Hoover believed that eventually the reorganizational plan would be sent to him for signature. Early legislation proposed that a separate prisons bureau was needed, but it was to have only weak central control over institutions. The Judiciary Committee observed that the "penal institutions were, to all practical purposes, under the independent control of the wardens." The committee remarked further, "when the superintendent of prisons' office was originally established its primary duty was the inspection of jails and prisons." It was impossible, the committee concluded, for prison management to make any real progress until the superintendent of prisons (later director) was granted complete administrative and policy control.

Overhaul of the administrative design of the Justice Department's prison function achieved Hoover's objective of a more centralized and professional prison service. Prison management, separated from Prohibition enforcement, now carried equal departmental stature with the Bureau of Investigations. The persistent embarrassments of Prohibition enforcement could be isolated from the more pressing problems of institutional operations. Hoover found unacceptable the congressional recommendation to remove prison management from the Justice Department. Instead, he desired to delegate to the new Federal Bureau of Prisons the centralized authority needed to emphasize the unique and purposeful functions of prison organizations that could not be properly reformed if they remained on an organizational level that demeaned management, staff, clientele, and contributions to federal justice. On this point the Congress agreed: "in view of the extent and importance of its work [prisons should] be made a major bureau in [the Department of Justice] and that the superintendent of prisons be given an adequate organization to assist him."[60]

The administration's perseverence resulted in significant new diversity of facilities under the control of a new Bureau of Prisons system. The new penitentiary at Lewisburg, Pennsylvania "was designed with a view not only of the safekeeping of the prisoners but for their ultimate improvement and individual reconstruction." Proudly, Bates observed, "it was constructed at a cost substantially less than one-half the cost of other modern State prisons." It was constructed on one thousand acres, for which the government paid only $95,000. Mitchell informed the Congress that the decision to construct the prison in Pennsylvania was based on "its central location and proximity to large centers of population; the adaptability of the site for agricultural development and other purposes; the presence near by of cheap coal; the presence of superior facilities in the form of railroads, highways, gas and water supply; the climate and the length of the growing seasons."[61] Lewisburg was touted as the most advanced prison in the United States; and when it was opened, Bates and Mitchell were pleased that it represented expectations formed in 1929: "The prison of the future should be at once a disciplinary school for those who can be reformed, a place of segregation for the incorrigibles and a laboratory for the study of the causes of crime."[62]

System expansion included plans for an island prison and smaller facilities positioned around the country. An island prison for hardened criminals had been proposed in previous years, but a divergence of opinions held up legislative commitment. Bates remarked to Edith M. Rogers, "the idea of a convict island is not a new one, . . . and has undoubted advantages, also many practical disadvantages."[63] The Bureau of Efficiency was at that time surveying the possibility of constructing an institution on the Virgin Islands. Several camp-type and industrial reformatories, regional federal jails, special hospitals for defective delinquents and medical care cases, and farms for narcotics law violators were more appealing to Congress. Reformatories were needed to house minimum-security inmates, to reduce penitentiary populations, and to "provide stimulating and useful employment opportunities." Proposals to acquire land at military facilities such as Camp Benning in Georgia, Camp Bragg in North Carolina, and Camp Lee in Virginia were put forward late in 1929. Approval for their use came early in 1930, with plans to put approximately four hundred "younger type of prisoners" at Camp Lee to develop a saw mill, a farm, and a canning factory.[64] Useful opportunities sometimes attracted labor and business opposition, but Bates defended each of them by showing that they did not violate the government-use-only restrictions on prison labor and products. Congressional passage of the Prison Employment Act gave the Bureau of Prisons unrestricted authority to use prisoners at the camps in any manner deemed desirable.

While the road camp system generally received support from the Army, some Army officers came to expect a regular flow of prisoners transferred from the Atlanta penitentiary. But by the fall of 1930, the number of prisoners sent to camps decreased as a result of improvements in parole methods at Atlanta. The Army provided equipment, although sometimes slow in coming, and the prison camp supervisors supplied labor to clear and widen roads, wreck buildings to salvage lumber, construct golf links and tennis courts, cut wood, repair buildings and motor vehicles, and construct air fields.[65] Occasionally, the balance was upset, thereby producing a vitriolic exchange of correspondence between Bates and Army camp officials. In a relatively mild letter, Bates said, "our prison camps are proving very popular with various of your fellow officers and we are being besieged continuously by commanding officers of various Army posts, asking for assignments of men. Quite naturally being human our inclination is to favor those camps where every facility is afforded our men. You, nevertheless, can rest assured that we will do our utmost to retain a reasonable force at your camp since you were the first to give us a trial and we are not so fickle as to forget our friends."[66]

Road camps became sources of political snipping by mid-1931 when irate citizens, some of whom were upset because prisoners were alleged to be taking precious jobs in a depression economy, and local politicians perceived the camps as places of rest rather than work. Bates expected work days for each prisoner and staff member were eight hours long, and assignment to the camps was considered a privilege warranting proper conduct at all times.[67] Bates knew instinctively that if the perception of easy duty spread among politicians the camps were doomed to elimination in favor of return to the penitentiaries. He feared this as much for the guards and supervisors of the camps as he did for the prisoners who, he believed, would benefit from work in the fresh air. Accordingly, he cautioned camp supervisors, "A busy and conscientious guard usually means busy and conscientious inmates. It is hoped that inmates will realize the importance of success not only for themselves but as it effects the future of many other men now in the walls who are looking forward to their own possibility of going to a camp."[68] By March 1932, the camp at Fort Bragg housed two thousand prisoners, and Bates and his assistant directors, while often critical of camp operations, recognized the value of their place in the new bureau system.

The reformatory at Petersburg, Virginia, was constructed to house six hundred minimum-security prisoners at a cost of slightly more than $450 per man. Plans were made for a detention farm in Milan, Michigan, similar in size to the Petersburg facility. Located near Detroit, the Milan facility was designed to house prisoners awaiting trial and some who had received sentences. The camp at Ft. Eustis, Virginia, was the "least expensive but in some ways the most interesting of all the Federal penal institutions" because it was placed on government property once used by the War Department and salvaged for refurbishment. The industrial reformatory at Chillicothe, Illinois, was built at a cost of $2.6 million, and according to Bates it was "one of the most modern and complete reformatories for young men in the world." The reformatory at El Reno, Oklahoma, was similar to the Chillicothe facility, costing $1 million to construct and opening in the spring of 1933.

Bates believed that "our method of detaining people pending trial is cruel, medieval, unscientific and unncessary. If a group of determined and intelligent men should put their heads together for even a short time, I believe, it would be easy to establish a method for securing the attendance of suspected persons at the time set for trial with much less damage to themselves and expense to the public."[69] His thoughts evolved into a plan to construct a series of local jails to hold suspects under investigation and to allow a closer relationship with federal courts. Jails were constructed in New Orleans, Louisiana, and El Paso, Texas. El Paso was "designed to afford opportunities for labor of prisoners in the reclamation and irrigation of the dry land at that point."

Bates's plan to locate some federal jails in existing federal buildings met with opposition he willingly engaged. The architect for the Treasury Department issued a report on October 21, 1930, concluding that Bates's plan would interfere with the architectual beauty of federal buildings. Bates was incensed by this "prejudice." In a risky tactical maneuver, he fired off a letter in June 1931 to all U.S. district court judges to solicit opinions on the architect's views: "I do not need to tell you that the outstanding scandal in connection with American penal system is the condition of our local and county jails. We are making an earnest effort in the appointment of new inspectors, the raising of standards of cleanliness, discipline and segrgation, the condemnation of jails where unfit, and the solicitation of cooperation from local and State authorities to better this situation. In some places we are meeting with success, in others we come up against an impossible situation. Politics and the fee system have the county jails in their grip in many localities. Indifference to the situation is found among the best citizens of many communities." Entrenched views at the Treasury Department brought continued resistance. Assistant secretary of the treasury Ferry K. Heath wrote to Mitchell in August rejecting the results of Bates's surveys, then suggesting that jails be constructed inside federal buildings to save construction funds. In a brilliant stroke of imagination, Heath recommended new jail construction where land was inexpensive.

A hospital for defective delinquents was built in Springfield, Missouri, "devoted solely to the medical and hospital care of prisoners who are either mentally or physically incapacitated." Once again Bates called attention to cost effectiveness of such facilities. He pointed out that the Springfield facility had been constructed on 450 acres of land given to the government. He was particularly praiseworthy when he wrote that it was "without counterpart anywhere in the world and today it's the ultimate in advanced housing and treatment of this type of public charge."[70]

The federal probation system had been created in 1925, but by 1929 added caseloads had become absurdly contradictory to the original purposes. Only six probation officers served the entire federal court system, each supervising several thousand male first-time offenders spread over wide geographic distances. Expansion of the service was an absolute necessity because "a large number of persons convicted in [federal] courts for violation of federal statutes and [then confined] in various institutions might have been placed upon probation had [the system] the means and personnel to investigate their character and trustworthiness."[71] Proponents of federal probation-system expansion urged sharp increases in the number of officers, and they argued for personnel control over the officers by the civil service system rather than by the courts.[72] The latter suggestion challenged directly the discretionary authority of district judges. The final legislative solution displayed compromise in the interests of shared power between the judicial and executive branches. The civil service control provision was substantially modified. It stipulated that all probation officers were required to submit monthly written reports on their work activities to the attorney general. The bill also allowed judges to appoint officers, while the attorney general controlled salaries and expenses. Hoover's signature on the bill in mid-1930 added ten times the original number of probation officers, thus permitting approximately 12,300 cases to be placed on probation between July 1, 1930 and June 30, 1931; 15,700 cases were added in the same period from 1931 to 1932.[73]

Overcrowded conditions in federal prisons remained a serious problem awaiting solution by the completion of new facilities. Congressional approvals in mid-1930 did not mean that expansion institutions would be available immediately. Normal bureaucratic approvals to acquire land, secure contractors, and manage actual construction would have to be suffered before the pressures on prison populations could be alleviated. In the meantime, dangerous conditions existed in Atlanta and Leavenworth. On December 11, 1931, Leavenworth's warden, T. B. White, was kidnapped and shot by three prisoners who had acquired forged passes to get to his office. In running the gauntlet of several gates, four other prisoners joined in; and guns and a stick of dynamite were used to threaten guards. Hostages included Warden White, his secretary, and two typewriter repairmen. The escapees and the hostages were held at gunpoint to reach the front gate of the prison. Once outside, escapees commandeered a car belonging to several black soldiers on their way to go rabbit hunting. A harrowing high-speed chase ended with the nonfatal shooting of the warden, several minor injuries to guards, the capture of four of the seven escapees, the killing of two more, and a suicide by the last escapee, who had barricaded himself at a local farmhouse.

While Warden White recovered in the hospital, losing an arm in the process, the Bureau of Investigation conducted an inquiry into the immediate causes of the breakout. A report issued in January 1932, identified the conspiracy of several guards and recommended immediate prosecution. Two of three guards directly implicated in the escape plot committed suicide, a third was tried and convicted. Bates and J. Edgar Hoover defended most of Warden White's actions, but Mitchell seemed unwilling to accept their views. Bates focused on the laxity of measures that would permit the making of extra keys by inmates known to be locksmiths and the system of passes that remained inadequately supervised. Numerous weapons had been smuggled into the prison, and some evidence suggested that a recently released convict had given assistance. Evidence was also found of drug trafficking, but this seemed not to be a central concern.[74] Mitchell chastised White's handling of the matter: "the general tenor of the reports would suggest that he has been deficient in executive ability in the administration of the prison by lack of proper training of his subordinates and failure to establish discipline and proper methods to detect and avoid trouble of this kind." He urged a Justice Department review of all laws available for application in cases of this kind, including any statutes to punish guards who conspired and convicts who escaped by injuring or killing guards.[75] White's injuries forced his reassignment to the new penal farm at El Paso, but Bates stood by him in reports to Mitchell. To ensure control at Leavenworth, Bates recommended F. G. Zerbst as the new warden, prosecution of those involved, new training procedures, and legislation to increase penalties for illegal possession of firearms inside a prison.[76] Bates further demonstrated his loyalty to White by issuing a press release on February 7, 1932: "The Department has already expressed its belief that Warden White acted with great courage and presence of mind at the time of the break, and perhaps at the risk of his own life, saved the Institution from a major disaster. He is a man of unquestioned honesty and probity."

PRISON POPULATION REDUCTION: PAROLES AND PARDONS

New construction, prison management measures, and expanded system diversity all contributed to fundamental improvements in the quality of life at institutions. The essential factor in the success of institutional life, however, was the condition under which federal prisoners returned to society. The federal parole system had been created by the Federal Parole Act of 1910. Administrative controls upon the system had strangled administrative efficiency, and the participants in parole decisions affecting thousands of prisoners could no longer keep up.

By 1929, the federal parole system reached a state of near collapse. With all their other duties, the attorney general and the superintendent of prisons were also members of each federal institution's parole board. Other members of each parole board included the warden and the institution physician. Boards reviewed approximately 9,000 cases per year by 1928, compared with 674 in 1910. Bates, as superintendent of prisons, was required by law to visit each federal institution each year and to personally listen to individual requests for early release.[77] Congress had recognized in January 1929 that an independent parole board was essential to relieve prison overcrowding and that such a board required "full authority to act on parole applications without requiring the approval of the Attorney General."[78]

The bulk of the parole cases arose from the more mainstream areas of federal crimes, in particular violations of the Volstead Act (Prohibition). Prior to Hoover's approval of a new federal parole board in May 1930, thousands of case jackets were individually reviewed, and the superintendent was expected to consider cases whether or not their facts were particularly noteworthy.[79] Boards rated parole applicants on four criteria: (1) conduct, deportment, dependability, and trustworthiness; (2) attitude toward the institution, officers, other inmates, and society; (3) industry, diligence, attentiveness, energy, and application of duties; and (4) work output, speed of work performed, and work quality.[80] By December 1929, the inefficiencies inherent in a decentralized system were no longer acceptable. Bates's frustrations were expressed to Mitchell: "I am impatient for the time to come when we can begin some constructive improvement, not only in our parole consideration system in the institutions, but in the supervision [of parolees]. I wonder if you would consider the appointment of some high-class man at once to act as parole adviser to you and as a representative of the Bureau in the institutions sending the adoption of the legislation by Congress. There are 1486 applications at Atlanta next week and possibly even more than that at Leavenworth."[81] Mitchell, of course, was in full agreement with the Bates's views and frustrations.[82] The legislation to fix these problems languished in Congress.

Hoover and Mitchell insisted that once Congress approved the new centralized federal parole board the members should be persons with parole experience and contributions to parole policy advancement. He wished to draw to government service diversely capable people who could work together in teams. Recommendations were solicited from senators, congressmen, university scholars, and parole professionals. Bates was asked to screen applicants. Responses to Hoover's call reflected a rich collection of talent available for the difficult work of determining who should be released from overcrowded prisons at a time of heightened social concern for crime.

Professor Edwin H. Sutherland at the University of Chicago recommended Dr. Stuart A. Queen of the University of Kansas, Dr. Jesse F. Steiner of Tulane University, and Dr. Earle F. Young of the University of Southern California. Sutherland remarked, "No one of these can be regarded as an expert in the field of criminology, but all three of them have done considerable work in the field. From the point of view of temperament and personality, I believe that Steiner is the best of the three."[83] Bates wanted, however, a board composed of people representing three types of factors he considered essential to making good parole decisions: law enforcement and prosecution factors; sociological, medical, and psychiatric factors; and judicial factors. He found his law enforcement and prosecution member in Irwin B. Tucker, a former U.S. attorney. The judicial member was found in Arthur D. Wood, a lawyer and student of penology who had served as a member of the Michigan Commission of Pardons and Paroles and was well recognized by the National Prison Congress. Recalling Hoover's earlier remarks about Willebrandt's service, Bates was hesitant to recommend a woman for the third seat on the parole board. Checking with the White House, however, he learned that Hoover was pleasantly, even solicitously favorable to the idea of a woman on the new board.[84] Selection decisions and evaluations of capabilities and compatibility with other members remained with Bates and Mitchell.

A vigorous exchange of letters between Bates and Mitchell began in mid-May 1930. Hoover signed the law creating the board on May 13, giving strong private indication that he wanted a woman member. Mitchell instructed Bates on Hoover's desire that strong consideration be given to the appointment of a woman. On May 17, Bates responded that if one of the members was to be a woman, he had three recommendations: Edith M. Burleigh of Los Angeles; Katherine F. Lenroot, assistant chief of the Children's Bureau in Washington, D.C.; and Miriam Van Waters, a juvenile court referee in Los Angeles. Just ten days later, apparently somewhat uncertain about the appropriateness of a woman appointee, Bates recommended Dr. Gordon F. Willey, assistant director of mental health in Pennsylvania. In a May 27 memo, Bates also said that if a woman appointee was preferred by Hoover and Mitchell, he preferred one whose background was either in the sciences or in the law, including diverse professional training with no strong biases preferring either science or law. This was a tall order.

Mitchell and Hoover met to clear the air—a woman was to be selected. Selection remained with Bates. Hoover's final decision reached Bates while he inspected federal institutions in California. Assistant director Bennett telegramed Bates: "Attorney General wishes you to exhaust every possibility of obtaining suitable woman for parole board before proceeding further STOP Although I explained that proposal to appoint woman placed entirely different light on situation Attorney General seemed troubled about failure to organize board promptly STOP He wishes you canvas field as thoroughly as possible and recommend woman STOP."[85] Bates had been forthright in his search for a woman, but it was obvious that the White House wanted absolute assurances.

Additional complications followed. Travel and the heavy workload insured Bates's testy edge. In a less than cordial response to Mitchell, Bates wrote, "I have been working literally sixteen hours a day here to finish this investigation, clean up paroles, get some information with reference to next year's budget, and move on to McNeil Island . . . this evening." He reported that he had located another candidate, Ida Koverman, recommended by Mabel Willebrandt, but he warned that he knew "nothing of the political associations of any of [these two] women [assuming] that [neither] would be 'politically obnoxious.'" He added, however, that his attendance at several parole meetings had convinced him that "more than ever . . . it is no job for a woman, especially a lay woman or one who has not been professionally trained to take the kind of testimony we have to hear without a quiver."[86]

His lack of certainty about the appointment of a woman had not followed from any chauvinism. He had worked with women in the correctional context for several years and had often promoted their role in the field. Rather it seemed to follow from his concern that he could not easily locate a woman who would be substantively prepared and acceptable to parole professionals and who would avoid making decisions with emphasis on either too much science or too much law.[87] Bates could not ignore his observation, too, that the White House appeared to have contrived the search for a woman out of political fallout from the Willebrandt decision: "It is rather significant that we have not had one single woman applicant for the job but that we are put to it to dig out a woman who will accept it and yet be suitable. I do not believe it would be doing a kindness to the woman member and I believe she would find the job difficult, laborious and unsuitable. Neither do I think it would be any kindness to woman-kind in general to pick out one of their number for this kind of job. Would it be advisable for the president to make the announcement that he had been prepared to include a woman . . . if there seemed to be any general demand that he do so but inasmuch as the job was not suitable, that only four per cent of our total Federal prison population were women, and that no woman had volunteered for the position that he did not feel it advisable to force the issue."[88] The solution was ignored.

On June 6, 1930, Jessie F. Binford, a psychiatrist and director of

Chicago's Juvenile Protection Association, was solicited by telegram to apply for the position: "Federal appointment would offer unusual opportunity for independent constructive work and prestige STOP Urge acceptance if offered for sake of official national recognition of women and initiating right kind of program even if personal demands necessitate holding but one a year" (referring to the number of parole board meetings). Bennett telegramed Bates once again on June 10 that he had asked Walter N. Thayer, Jr., and Walter L. Treadway for their views on Binford, stressing that Binford had probably been ruled out: "Binford [is] willing [to] accept position provided her appointment would not be considered [a] reason for refusing [to] appoint [a] woman cabinet member STOP We think this reservation indicates type of personality undesisirable on parole board STOP Have submitted these facts [to the] Attorney General."[89] Binford's appointment was rejected.

On June 12, the lengthy and contentious search for the third member was resolved. Dr. Amy N. Stannard of Washington, D.C., a psychiatrist serving as a consultant to the St. Elizabeth's Federal Hospital for the Insane, was appointed to the board. Dr. Stannard held A.B. and M.D. degrees from the University of California. Not only did the appointment end the controversy, it reflected Bates's determination to find a woman with the precise credentials he required. Mitchell's edict, spurred by pressure from the White House, had been saluted by Bates and Bennett, and the result was pleasing to all concerned. On June 13, the deadline to find the third member had been barely met by the "appointment . . . of another woman to an important official post."[90] Bates wrote to Julia K. Jaffray, secretary of the National Committee on Prisons and Prison Labor and member of the Alderson federal women's prison: "You are absolutely correct in your supposition that the President himself insisted upon one member of the Board being a woman. He went further than this and stated . . . that he feels that as fast as women have had the experience in executive and administrative work that equips them to hold high public office, women who are not so qualified ought to be considered on an equal footing with men. I am sure that he was gratified that we found such a useful and scientifically trained woman as Dr. Stannard for this position."[91] Stannard's selection was no substantive depreciation of the professional standards held by Bates, Mitchell, or Hoover; but it was clearly an act to put a woman into a predominantly male bastion of government. At salaries of $7500 each, the newly formed federal parole board commenced work on June 13, 1930.

With the creation of the new federal parole board, individual institutional boards were abolished. Every parole case required review by the institution warden, then by the consolidated board in Washington. Federal prisoners housed in state institutions were entitled to federal parole board review. The board was ruled out of jurisdiction over parole cases at the National Training School for Boys in Washington, D.C., an institution governed by a separate board appointed by the president.[92] With legal authority in order, the board set about processing clearing cases at its first meeting on June 21. Mary Harris asked that the board come to Alderson first in order to address the caseload of numerous drug addicts.[93] In months to come, the board received high praise for its work, both in quantity of case accommodation and sensitivity to the public interest: "It might fairly be said that while the Board has freely utilized the parole machinery they have done so more in the interest of the public than in the interest of the prisoner and in many cases released him after the expiration of a considerable portion of his sentence in order that he might have the benefit of parole supervision and yet not receive any substantial diminution of his sentence."[94]

With the fundamental elements of prison reforms in operation by mid-1930, Hoover took aim at completing reforms to judicial procedures. At the end of 1930, he asked Congress for additional budgetary provisions for construction projects, including additional facilities.[95] By this time, the problems of economic management were consuming most of his administrative time. Judicial reforms, unlike correctional reforms, involved few new costs, but they held excellent potential for saving unnecessary judicial and prosecutorial resources. Hoover was pleased with his successes in prison, parole, and probation reform. He was convinced they had gone further than any administration "both of the physical necessities of delinquents [referring to inmates] and also putting into action very important moral forces that should be helpful."[96]

Chapter 8

Marginal Concerns: Lynching, Massie, Pardons, Lindbergh, and Bonus Army

The fears in the hearts of millions of mothers were lifted.[1]

Between their first days in office and their last, all presidents encounter marginal concerns, all of which take them away from priorities or detract from their positive historical legacies. Accordingly, presidents tend to avoid or delegate marginal concerns in the natural interest of time management or personal or political lack of interest. Of course, there are costs to avoiding marginal concerns, but they are not usually recognized in advance.

This chapter is devoted to five marginal events affecting Hoover's federal justice initiatives: lynchings of blacks, the Massie murder case, pardon requests in controversial cases, the Lindbergh kidnapping case, and the Bonus Army disturbance. The conceptual substance of these events was represented in Hoover's scheme of federal justice administration. But conditions of occurrence or challenges they posed to the philosophy of the policy agenda relegated each to marginal status.

LYNCHINGS

Hoover was in a better-than-average position of the presidents after Lincoln to have opposed lynchings, particularly lynchings of blacks. His attachment to progressive social reforms, his candor in support of black economic advancement, and his firm positions on law-based justice were ideal policy resources.[2] His problem, according to Lisio, was his dry, sterile utopianism; his detached, naive faith in a cooperative spirit between races.[3] He was unwilling in the 1928 campaign to assert a formal policy against racial violence, but this was also true of Al Smith. Each candidate avoided alienating southern Democrats. Lynching, despite its barbarity and illegality, was not an issue on which Hoover desired to contradict his philosophy of state law enforcement duty.

As president, Hoover found it nearly impossible to separate his interest in the future of blacks from black lynchings. Black leaders wrote to the White House regularly, and throughout the term they approached Hoover with their views. On the day before taking office, he received a request from the National Urban League for words of encouragement for a forthcoming conference. Hoover skirted the issue of lynching, instead remarking upon the fundamental need to build black economic independence: "The first step toward being a good citizen is to achieve economic independence. It is the soil in which self respect takes root, and from which may then grow all the moral and spiritual enrichments of life. The work of the National Urban League to train Negroes in the city to find new lines of occupation is fundamental to the progress of the race. I wish you successes in this undertaking."[4]

Hoover could not avoid pressures to remove long-standing policies of discrimination in federal employment or to consult with black leaders on other reform measures. To overcome some of these pressures, Hoover banned discrimination in Census Bureau hiring practices, an action that caused substantial southern political discord. Three months after taking office, Hoover and his wife invited Mrs. Jessie De Priest, the wife of a newly elected black congressman from Chicago, Oscar De Priest, to the White House for afternoon tea, stirring quite harsh racial bigotry.[5]

Difficulty in escaping the bigotry, indeed the volatility of any attempts to cross white-defined racial barriers, was demonstrated by the bitter reaction of Texas Governor Dan Moody. Moody signed a Texas legislative resolution indicting Hoover's invitation: "the people of the South, and particularly those of Texas, have never in the past and will never in the future, condone any act or conduct that would tend in the least to sanction social racial equality as between the white and negro races and particularly acts and conduct on the part of persons in high official position [that] will carry a semblance of national and governmental sanction."[6] Legislatures in Florida, Georgia, and Mississippi passed similar resolutions. Undaunted, De

Priest invited blacks and whites to a musical and reception at the Washington Auditorium on June 21. Polite declines from several white politicians were sent, Congressman J. C. Shaffer and his wife could not ignore an opportunity to snub De Priest for his boldness.[7]

A long-standing issue supported both by many black leaders and by Hoover, the extrication of U.S. troops from Haiti, offered a safer vehicle for advancing, albeit indirectly, on black issues. Since Wilson's deployment of troops in 1915, blacks frequently associated the Haitian occupation with lynching. Moving cautiously in December 1929, following internal disturbances in Haiti, Hoover inched toward removing the troops.[8] But before doing so, he wished to investigate conditions in Haiti out of "a necessity to build up an assurance of an effective and stable government so that life and property may be protected when we withdraw."[9] Appointments to study commissions were intended to link symbolically troop withdrawal with opposition to lynching. Furthermore, appointment of black leaders active in the antilynching campaign to positions on an investigatory commission would offer evidence of Hoover's interests in black issues in general and, by implication, an interest in lynchings.[10]

Oscar De Priest had been suggested to Hoover as a person to head a Haitian study commission. The suggestion met vigorous opposition, however, from Frank Loesch, a Wickersham Commission member. Loesch wrote confidentially to George Wickersham, and Wickersham forwarded Loesch's concerns to Hoover: "I [Frank Loesch] sincerely hope that the President will not appoint Oscar De Priest as the Commissioner from the United States in the Haitian situation. De Priest was the vice lord, and may be so today, for all I know, among the colored people for years past. His reputation smells to Heaven. I earnestly hope that the President will not make such an appointment even though Mr. Hamilton Fish [a New York Republican congressman], as reported by the papers, had suggested De Priest for that Commission."[11] Loesch provided no details on De Priest's alleged illegal affairs.

In February 1930, Dr. Robert R. Moton, president of the Tuskegee Institute, was appointed to head a study commission on Haitian education.[12] This, however, was not the main commission to investigate comprehensively the internal situation in Haiti. Distinguished from the Forbes Commission,[13] the Moton Commission performed its work in Haiti in June and early July 1930, only to confront added racial discrimination in their attempt to return home. The U.S. Navy refused to allow Moton and his commissioners to return aboard a Navy ship.[14] This insult could not have occurred at a more sensitive time for Hoover's intentions to advance, even hesitatingly, on black issues. In July 1930, just as the Moton Commission was trying to get back home, Hoover nominated circuit court judge John J. Parker for the Supreme Court, outraging black leaders. The July 19 issue of the *Cleveland Call and Post* editorialized, "Hoover has witnessed the lynchings of fifteen Negroes in America since December 1929, and has not only failed to interfere, but has said nothing against the un-American, savage trait."

Early in August 1930, Sam H. Reading, a national news service president, wrote to Hoover on the lynching matter. While he commended Hoover for his conference on the 1930 drought, he seemed more interested in urging him to put lynchings on the agenda of the forthcoming special governors' conference on drought relief. Calling attention to the fourteen lives lost in lynchings in 1930, Reading contrasted the president's drought position and his actions on black lynchings: "It may be only coincidental that many of the States most seriously affected by the drought have been among those States staging lynchings during the present year, but it would appear to the layman that the conference . . . would be a not inopportune time to discuss this perilous situation."[15]

Hoover believed otherwise: "In your call to the Governor's [sic] you state that one million families are affected by the drought. The lynching evil affects directly every one of the thirteen millions of Negro citizens, and indirectly reacts unfavorably on the entire 168 millions of our population in that it increases the already too great lack of respect for constituted authority." In closing, Hoover said, "every decent citizen must condemn the lynching evil as an undermining of the very essence of both justice and democracy." A week later Hoover asked his legislative secretary, Walter Newton, to respond to NAACP's president, Walter White, using the exact language that had been used in closing with Reading, insisting that discussion of the lynching issue at a special conference on an unrelated topic would be inappropriate.[16] Just a few days earlier, a seventy-year-old black man was flogged to death by a group of white masked men; he had been tortured and whiplashed. Thousands of crimes, including murders and assaults upon blacks, were listed in police records as merely "mysterious circumstances."

The pace of black outcry on the lynching issue increased in late 1930. In November 1930, black groups held their own antilynching conference in Washington, D.C. Four months later, on March 25, 1931, nine black hobos were arrested for the alleged rape of two prostitutes on a train traveling toward Scottsboro, Alabama. Three trials before all-white male jurors produced guilty verdicts, raising to the national level the specter of southern racism and rigged justice.[17] Leftist groups and the communist party thickened the atmosphere of opposition to the convictions, and the state guard was installed to curb potential violence.

Hoover, far from facts or a penchant to get involved, received letters and telegrams pleading for federal intervention.[18] He had no power to intervene, and the economic gloom of the moment seemed far more pressing. Once again, he took only an indirect course of action, referring to the Scottsboro case in a national radio hookup on April 14 on the fiftieth anniversary of the founding of Tuskegee Institute: "We have still many problems to solve in this matter [of overcoming racial inequities for Negroes] and no section of our country is without its responsibility or without room for progress and improvement. . . . There can be no solution either in the communities or government that is not based upon sympathetic understanding and absolute justice."[19]

By 1932, black disenchantment with Hoover's passive avoidance of the lynching issue reached its peak. Hoover continued to apply passive measures in spite of lost favor. He appointed black members to the White House Conference on Child Health and Protection, the National Advisory Committee on Education, the Committee on Unemployment and Housing, and several other bodies. On August 18, 1931, he wrote to Mitchell, "I have mentioned to you on one or two occasions the possibility of employing a colored attorney in the Department of Justice."[20] Blacks were, indeed, appointed to a few positions in the administration, including the justice and education departments. To show other types of action, although significantly late in his administration, Hoover appointed a special investigative commission in 1932 to probe charges that federal officials had condoned discrimination against black families dispossessed in the 1927 Mississippi flood.[21] But neither he nor the Congress supplied operating funds to the commission, thus deepening black alienation and frustration with inconsequential efforts. This stood in sharp contrast to his anonymous donation of $500 to the National Urban League, a practice followed by many white progressives.[22] The haze of appointments and other indirect methods deepened the marginalization of the lynching issue.

To show a modicum of action against the lynching of blacks, Hoover reviewed the 1931 report of the Southern Commission for the Study of Lynchings. Disturbed by what he read, he asked Mitchell to draft legislation to bring military forces into the equation of investigating and controlling lynching incidents. As Lisio has observed, the Congress would never have approved this extension of the president's powers. The proposal stirred Southern hatreds, but Hoover obviously intended to advance in small increments what some of his predecessors accepted as necessary but were unwilling to promote, even though the proposed legislation invited opposition. Noticing Hoover's interest in the Southern Commission's findings, Mrs. J. E. Andrews, president of the Women's National Association for Preservation of the White Race, fired off a telegram to Hoover: "No reason for this agitation as report of Commission state[s] that lynching[s] have decreased to exceeding[ly] low mark. We state frequent recurrence of criminal assault of white women is appalling. Nation shocked at crimes in every section. White supremacy and law enforcement issues in coming election. Women of white race organizing for self protection. Literature forwarded you which is going to heads of government and all organizations in every state in union with information concerning this conference. We ask your protection from combination of New York, Atlanta, Tammany, Liquor, Negro, Social Equality coalition. Women of white race have right to live in separateness in that peace and tranquility assured by the very preamble of the National Constitution."[23]

In December 1931, Hoover prepared for his annual message to Congress, and he intended to include a statement on lynching: "Under the question of 'Lynching' I have in mind adding a sentence at the end somewhat as follows: 'These actions are the negation of the Republican form of government guaranteed to our citizens by the Constitution. With the modern expedition, through aerial and motor forces of Federal troops located at all important centers throughout the country, it is possible to bring them almost instantly to the assistance of local authorities if a system were authorized by Congress that would make such action swift and possible.'"[24] He added that he was not satisfied that the section of the speech regarding Justice Department progress against lynchings was sufficiently strong, and he had hoped to "place the tremendous progress of the Department of Justice before the country." The message he ultimately delivered, however, contained no words pertaining to lynching. Hoover's last year in office was the most frustrating year of his entire private and public life. He had hoped to win back support from black leaders who had come to believe that he was not sincere, especially after his 1930 nomination of Judge John J. Parker.[25] The frustration reached into black veterans groups. On December 11, 1931, the *New York Times* carried an article, "Hoover Silence on Strengthening of Anti-lynching Laws in Message to Congress Denounced by Ex-Service Men's League and League of Struggle for Negro Rights." To recapture some of his losses, he asked Mitchell to reconstruct the Dyer antilynching law that had lost its way in the Senate in the Harding years. No action was taken by Hoover or Mitchell to put the issue before the national public in an election year that was surely to be difficult.

RAPE AND MURDER IN PARADISE: THE MASSIE CASE

Thalia Massie, the young wife of Navy Lieutenant Thomas H. Massie, claimed that she was raped by five men after she was abducted on a Honolulu, Hawaii, street in September 1931. Five men were arrested for the crime: Horace Ida and David Takai, Japanese-Americans; Benny Ahakuelo and Joseph Kahahawai, native Hawaiians; and Henry Chang; a Chinese-American.[26] All five men were well defended in the trial that began on November 21. On December 6, the court freed the defendants because of a hung jury. Anger and racial prejudice spread among Navy personnel who believed that an injustice had been done by a jury composed of no whites or women. Navy officials in Hawaii fanned the flames of discord by public charges of police and prosecutorial incompetence. Racial hatred ran high, and on December 12 Horace Ida was abducted and severely beaten by a group of sailors, including Albert Jones, a name that would reappear. The purpose of the beatings was to extract a confession.

President Hoover, Attorney General Mitchell, and Secretary of the Interior Ray Lyman Wilbur apparently did not consider the importance of the implications of the case before mid-December. The *New York Times* carried articles on rioting in Honolulu on December 14 and 15. However, even two full weeks after the trial outcome, Wilbur and Judd spoke calmly by new radio-telephone: "The opening of telephone communication with Hawaii, in addition to facilitating administration, enlarges the area to which people almost anywhere can talk with others far away."[27] Neither Hoover nor Wilbur mentioned the situation in their later autobiographies, despite Hoover's order in mid-December to call out U.S. Marines to restore order in Honolulu.[28]

Behind the case lay a history of racial unrest and discord between Navy people and the Hawaiian ethnic population. Despite its territorial status, Hawaii had received mild congressional attention about these tensions in 1930 when Governor Judd requested (and failed to receive) Senate approval for a crime commission to study problems on the islands. In response, Judd appointed his own commission to develop legislative proposals to improve the quality of justice administration.

Alarm bells sounded in Washington on January 10, 1932. Governor Judd telegramed Ray Wilbur to inform him of a new complication in the case:

Yesterday morning one of Ala Moana defendants, a Hawaiian, was kidnapped after reporting to court at Honolulu into a car rented by an enlisted Navy man after being pointed out by mother of complainant to the two men in car. About hour and half later same car apprehended in country with same woman driving and two men in rear, one being husband of complainant, other an enlisted Navy man with dead body of defendant in car. Search of home of complainants mother indicates conclusively defendant killed there. Shot heard there by neighbors and much evidence found. The three found with body charged yesterday with murder and at request Commandant turned over to Navy officials by territorial Circuit Court for custody. Indications another enlisted navy man implicated who is being held. Other four defendants Ala Moana case incarcerated at own request so no reason to anticipate further disorders. Reports from mainland this morning that militia called out absolutely false. No occasion for this or other such steps. Situation calm. Authorities are controlling situation and are able control all situations. Am informed by press that United States Senate has adopted resolution calling upon Attorney General to conduct investigation of conditions in Hawaii. If correct I urge Attorney General immediately send investigator as it is most important to all concerned that true facts be known.

The dead man, one of the defendants in the Massie rape allegation (collectively known as the "Ala Moana" case), was Joseph Kahahawai. The woman driving the car was Mrs. Grace R. Fortescue, Thalia Massie's mother, a niece of Alexander Graham Bell and stepdaughter of Robert B. Roosevelt of New York.[29] The accomplices were three Navy men, Thomas H. Massie, Edward J. Lord, and Albert O. Jones. Police investigation revealed that Kahahawai had been killed by a .32 caliber pistol at Mrs. Fortescue's home, apparently after the men extracted a confession from him. The weapon was never found, although cartridges for a .32 caliber were found on Jones when he was searched by the police. Both Mrs. Fortescue and Albert Jones had purchased .32 caliber pistols on December 15 and later acquired licenses to carry firearms on the basis of threats to their lives.[30]

The atmosphere surrounding the Massie-Fortescue family and permeating the local community was becoming increasingly tense. The resulting disorder included restricting Army and Navy personnel to their posts and the alerting of some units of military police to the possibility of rioting.[31] Hoover was offered a variety of opinions about the case and justifications for Massie's actions. He remained publicly silent on the matter, however, realizing that certain Democratic members of the Senate saw an opportunity to criticize the administration.

On January 11, Mark Sullivan, newspaper columnist, long-time friend, and member of Hoover's "medicine ball cabinet," wrote to Larry Richey and to Hoover with equally strident support for the vigilantism of Mrs. Fortescue and Lieutenant Massie. He said they "were completely justified in murdering the raper. This justification must be held to extend to the sailors who helped them." In tones of clear racism, he warned Hoover that the case would attract world-wide attention and might well threaten white dominance over the islands: "Hawaii is the place where the white and yellow portions of the race meet. At such a place, the protection by the whites of women of their race must be insisted upon. . . . [i]t must be assumed as a matter of course, and if necessary enforced, through sheer ruthless force. No white government can afford to take any other course. To do otherwise would not only destroy the white government within its own nation but would be a surrender of white standards which would have a bearing on the balance of power in the world as between white standards and non-white ones. . . . This may not be utopian justice but it is the only practicable way." Sullivan's letters to the White House had opened with, "I know nothing about that Hawaiian case except what I see in the newspapers. This is all the country knows, and it is on this that the country will base its emotion." On "this," Sullivan insisted that Hoover get rid of the territorial governor, judge, and prosecuting attorney and that he reconstruct the government in Hawaii after ordering martial law.[32]

On the same day, Victor S. K. Houston, the congressional delegate from Hawaii, wrote to Hoover his outline of conditions involved in the case. Houston summarized the facts of the trial and the resulting disorders, reported his investigation into the facts about rapes in Hawaii in the previous year, and noted that various racial groups had lived in relative harmony in years past. He concluded that "ineffective control of prohibition and vicious moving picture shows, have probably contributed in a degree to a development of the gangster situation." Balancing this statement was a more direct charge that publicized remarks by top naval officers, both in Washington and in Honolulu, had escalated the tension. His reference was to the chief of naval operations, Admiral William V. Pratt, who said, "American men will not stand for the violation of their women under any circumstances. For this crime they have taken the matter in their own hands repeatedly when they felt that the law has failed to do justice."[33]

By this time, Hoover had received several telegrams and letters, most but not all of which appealed for release of Fortescue, Massie, and the others, to be followed by diligent prosecution of the rapist. Neither the commandant of naval forces at Pearl Harbor, Yates Stirling, nor Admiral Pratt had made Hoover's job in sorting out his responsibility to act any easier. Stirling commented to the press early in December that "a certain portion of Honolulu's population refused to take cases of assault upon women seriously. . . . Honolulu may expect cases of assault upon women unless the better element gets to work to stamp out this condition."[34] Yates was a Virginian who stood by the code of the South, supporting without question the actions of Lieutenant Massie and the others. The only sane head in the Navy ranks appears to have been that of the secretary of the Navy, Charles Francis Adams, who ordered Fortescue, Massie, and the others held in custody aboard a Navy ship in the days following their arrest.

Hoover's complete avoidance of the Massie case in his *Memoirs* is unexplained. In the middle of the Senate hearings, he conducted meetings with Mitchell and Wilbur. Wilbur advised him that matters were under the good control of Governor Judd and the Hawaiian justice system and that newspaper reports of widespread civil unrest were exaggerated. There was no objection to Wilbur's point of view, but Hoover wanted his own investigation of the situation.[35] A cabinet meeting was also held on December 12. The attorney general argued against Secretary Adams's suggestion that the case be moved to the mainland, and Wilbur instructed that the Navy had not helped matters by boycotting island shops and allowing Admiral Pratt the opportunity to issue statements that incited the local populace.[36] Despite clamors from the press for Hoover to act in ways that were never clear, the president, in all probability, found no basis for doing more than leaving the situation to Mitchell, Wilbur, Judd, and local authorities. Beyond appointing Judd governor, a man in whom he had complete faith, Hoover had no legal authority to do more.

The Senate, on the other hand, added to the tension by passing Resolution 134. Southern senators in particular needed to get out front to proclaim righteous indignation for the plight of a sweet young southern girl. The resolution instructed Mitchell to report to the Senate "upon the administration and enforcement of criminal laws in the Territory of Hawaii by the police authorities, the prosecuting officers, and the courts of the Territory, and to suggest any changes in the organic law desirable in the interest of prompt and efficient administration of justice in the Territory." On January 14, 1932, the attorney general, sensing larger concerns for the political volatility of the case, sent an assistant attorney general, Seth W. Richardson, to Hawaii to study conditions affecting law enforcement under the Senate resolution. Senate concern waned after the sixteenth, but smoldered in the background without resolution. Then the House of Representatives followed suit, led by Georgia Congressman Carl Vinson, and opened hearings on the Ala Moana affair. The House report essentially applauded the actions of the Navy and took the opportunity to lay blame upon Governor Judd and the local authorities for, it alleged, allowing conditions of crime to get out of hand. Governor Judd cabled Wilbur on January 15 with detailed information in response to Navy charges of lax judicial administration in a 1929 case involving an alleged rape by and subsequent murder of a Navy seaman.[37] Ignoring all the information that justice was in the hands of local authorities, House Resolution 209 requested Hoover to pardon Massie.[38] Wilbur remarked to the press that he had faith in Judd and the local authorities.

In an apparent effort to get the correct facts to the White House about errors made by the press in reporting conditions on Hawaii, Wilbur wrote on the twentieth to Theodore Joslin, Hoover's second and not particularly pleasing press secretary, "You may be interested in glancing through this correspondence from the United Press, regarding the misquotation. It shows that once in a while we get the boys across the barrel." Joslin wrote back, "It was a pleasure to read the correspondence. . . . This is one that they had to eat their words. More power to your elbow."[39] The case received no further official attention from Hoover. The defendants were indicted on January 26 and arraigned on January 29. Mrs. Fortescue, Lieutenant Massie, and the others were imprisoned on the *U.S.S. Alton*, and there they awaited trial.

Seth Richardson investigated the case from February 4 to mid-April. He reported his findings on the Hawaiian investigation to Mitchell's office late in March. The report was made to the Senate in April 1932. It concluded that no crime wave had occurred in Hawaii in the previous year; work on improving the quality of the law enforcement agencies was, however, a major priority the islands could not afford to ignore without great social cost. The report also stressed the importance of senatorial action to mandate improvements in the Hawaiian justice system as an "extraordinary experiment" in making better justice in a place of such racially diverse population. When Judd read it, his only objection centered on Richardson's proposal that the Congress provide the president with the power to appoint the police chief and the local prosecutor. Hoover would be approached by Wilbur on these proposals, as Judd had urgently wired the interior secretary with a request that the president not promote such anti–home rule measures.[40]

In the meantime, the trial of Fortescue, Massie, and the others began on April 4. Mrs. Fortescue had hired the famed but retired seventy-five-year-old trial lawyer Clarence Darrow to defend her, Massie, and the others. There was little for the jury to consider. The witnesses were trotted out, admissions from Massie and his cohorts clearly revealed a revenge killing, and physical evidence was more than supportive of a conviction. Darrow's closing argument, broadcast to the mainland by radio, was fundamentally an appeal to the consciences of men who might put themselves in Massie's shoes if their wives had been raped. The jury was out for two days, returning with a verdict of guilty on April 29 to the charge of manslaughter with a request that Judge Charles S. Davis apply leniency. The defendants were sentenced to ten years in prison, but within one hour of their entering jail their sentences were commuted by Governor Judd.[41] Judd claimed that the pressure from members of Congress was so great that he had virtually no choice in the decision. He later wrote: "Had I possessed facts which I learned later, I doubt if I would have commuted the sentences."[42]

Governor Judd retained the Pinkerton Detective Agency early in June. He asked the company to look more closely at the details of Thalia Massie's allegations and to provide him with a report of findings. On August 25, 1932, Governor Judd sent a coded naval message to Ray Wilbur requesting authority to leave the territory in September to finish some work for acquiring funds for island construction from the Reconstruction Finance Corporation and to conclude with the Pinkerton representatives the investigation under way at that time.[43] Judd received the report in December 1932, and its contents questioned heavily the veracity of Thalia Massie's testimony. By January 1933, nothing more had come of the Pinkerton investigation, and Wilbur was inclined to let the matter drop. A nolle prosequi was accepted by Judge Davis on February 13, 1933. Both Mrs. Fortescue and the Massies had already departed from the island, thus leaving no accuser of the four remaining Ala Moana defendants from the original trial.

Writing a personal and confidential letter to Judd, Wilbur said, "the more time that elapses, the less apt there is to be any pursuit of the question. With Senator [Hiram] Bingham out of the road, and [Senator Kenneth] McKellar interested in other things, the next administration should be free from this difficulty. . . . I assume that some time before you resign, you will cover the question of those prosecutions and make some formal statement in the report of the Pinkertons."[44] The next month found Wilbur defending the Hawaiian criminal justice system against the exploitation of the press in the Massie case. He was convinced of local support for the rebuilding the police, prison, and jury systems through Governor Judd's progressive reforms; and he recognized that the Massie case was the catalyst for reforms that had been urged for years.[45]

PARDON REQUESTS IN CONTROVERSIAL CASES

By June 1932, President Hoover had considered pardons both in cases associated with World War I espionage and sedition and in cases attributed to the Teapot Dome scandal of the early 1920s.[46] On

July 6, John Lord O'Brian wrote to ACLU's executive director, Roger Baldwin, to advise that each case brought to the president's attention will have been initiated by the individual claimant.[47] No mass investigation would be initiated by the government because of shortages in investigative manpower at the FBI. Baldwin, unwilling to accept O'Brian's excuse, reminded the assistant attorney general that even presidents Harding and Coolidge had publicly referred to these offenders as "political prisoners" or "prisoners under the wartime emergency laws." By 1933, the investigative staffs of the FBI had been greatly reduced, thus slowing to a trickle the number of wartime pardon cases reviewed by Herbert Hoover.[48]

Distantly analogous to the emotions involved in the espionage and sedition cases was the controversial California case involving Tom Mooney and Warren Billings. Hoover's passing interest in the case became slightly more active in the summer of 1929. The ACLU and labor groups had by then organized new informational and political pressures to regain popular attention. Both men, they argued, had been unfairly convicted in the Preparedness Day bombing in San Francisco in July 1916 that killed ten people and wounded four dozen others. Prolabor factions in Congress, strengthened by the support of senators Garner Jackson and Burton Wheeler and religious groups favoring a Mooney-Billings pardon, attracted Hoover's attention.

In May 1929, three Wickersham Commission consultants, Zechariah Chafee, Jr., Walter Pollack, and Carl Stern, undertook an investigation of Mooney-Billings, supervised by Commissioner William S. Kenyon. Conducting their inquiries quietly but not entirely secretly, all were convinced from the beginning that Mooney and Billlings had been subjected to a travesty of justice. Hearing repeated mentions of the case from California friends, Hoover asked the Justice Department in September 1931 to look into the facts. Attorney General Mitchell reminded him that the case was a state matter. Labor factions insisted that the president had a responsibility to investigate the matter since he had tacitly approved the study and had paid for it with government funds. Mitchell and Wickersham stood their ground, however, refusing to publish the report; but in January 1932, a copy was leaked to the press. Consistent with the original philosophy of the researchers, the report concluded that there had been a frame-up of Mooney and Billings.[49] Hoover took no further action.

More potentially contradictory to Hoover's initiatives to clean out corruption from the federal justice system were the pardon cases of the Teapot Dome offenders. Hoover took office only seven years after the politically explosive Teapot Dome affair sent several corporate criminals to federal prisons. He knew personally the major defendants in the case, especially former Attorney General Harry M. Daugherty, former Secretary of the Interior Albert B. Fall, and California oil man Harry F. Sinclair. Justice Department cases against the principals in bribery and conspiracy trials of grand magnitude carried press and popular attention from 1924 to 1928, ending with the 1928 trial of Sinclair. Sinclair's wealthy friends stirred a resurgence of interest in the Teapot Dome offenders in 1929. This could not have pleased Hoover, since he had hoped to forget the scandal that destroyed his friend Harding.

The most contentious of the Teapot Dome offenders were Albert Fall, Harry Sinclair, and Harry Blackmer. Time had passed since the investigations had occurred, and some memories of the scandal had faded. These offenders, however, had the economic power to keep their appeals in the federal courts and to muster coalitions of supporters in the Congress who favored clemency. Fall was finally convicted of bribery in September 1929, but appeals stayed his prison sentence of one year and a fine of $100,000 until 1931. His attorney, former U.S. Senator Atlee Pomerene, was successful in claiming that Fall's health would be injured if he went to prison in the St. Elizabeth Hospital in Washington, D.C., or if he were to travel to Washington to testify against Sinclair. Fall received approval to serve his time in the New Mexico State Penitentiary near his home in El Paso. Allegations surfaced that Fall had received preferential treatment while in New Mexico, but investigation by the Marshal's Service found no evidence. It was characteristic of Fall's attitude with regard to his conviction that Pomerene sent a bill to the Justice Department for $140 in transportation costs for the trip from El Paso to his prison cell. Following Fall's release from prison in May 1932, Senator Pomerene sent President Hoover a bill for $50,000 for Fall's legal defense, since Fall had claimed indigency. Hoover had been apprised of Fall's legal manipulations, but he refused to grant Fall executive clemency in 1931 and a pardon thereafter.[50] Pomerene's request could not have angered Hoover, as the president appointed him in July 1932 to be a member of the board of the Reconstruction Finance Corporation.[51]

Sinclair began his sentence on May 9, 1929, waltzing into the District of Columbia Asylum and Jail from his chauffeur-driven limosine. In August 1929, one of Sinclair's supporters, Mr. Robert L. Owen, wrote to the attorney general with a claim that Sinclair was serving a six-month sentence for contempt of court for ordering the Burns Detective Agency to investigate the Teapot Dome jury. The court's sentence, said Owen, was factually baseless, and Mr. Sinclair had no "wrongful purpose and no conscious disrespect or contempt of court" in mind. Owen argued that Hoover had a "clear duty" to commute Sinclair's sentence, reasoning that the offense was "previously unknown to the law"; that the government had in previous years committed the same acts of surveillance; that Sinclair had already served three months and suffered "humiliation a man of his high character and fine associations deeply feels at being incarcerated in a common jail with ordinary felons"; and that the government was to blame for the original "unlawful" lease which caused Sinclair to lose $10 million over his "patriotism to promote the national defense."[52]

Mitchell wrote immediately to Hoover to outline the situation of the commutation and pardon requests of both Sinclair and another Teapot Dome defendant, Harry Mason Day. The barrage of letters to the White House favoring the pardons of Sinclair and Day, 135 and 57 respectively, caused Mitchell to take the matter seriously. Twelve newspapers across the country opposed Sinclair's appeal, as did several lawyers and judges. Day had been charged as Sinclair's employee to hire private detectives in 1927 to follow jury members during his boss's trial. No evidence was produced to demonstrate that the detectives intimidated any juror, but the District of Columbia trial court declared that obstruction of justice had occurred. The U.S. Supreme Court affirmed the lower court's decision. Sinclair's attorneys put forth the reasoning that Sinclair deserved clemency because there were no improper motives in the actions of the detectives and Sinclair had already suffered enough losses from his short time in prison away from an oil empire that needed him.

Mitchell took vigorous exception to such lame appeals and urged Hoover to steer clear of the matter: "For the President to now interfere with the judgment of the court without development of any new facts would be for the Executive to substitute his judgment for that of the courts as to what ought to have been the proper sentence." Regarding the impact any presidential pardon would have, Mitchell cut to the core of the issue: "the public interest requires that in criminal cases executive clemency [should] not [be] exercised so as to outrage public opinion. . . . I think the extension of executive clemency under these circumstances would have a very bad effect on the administration of justice and on the confidence of the people in the way justice is administered."[53] Mitchell flatly rejected the Sinclair-Day interpretation of their plight and advised Hoover to do the same. Hoover refused to pardon Sinclair on September 21.[54]

In November, reeling from the controversies in the Teapot Dome and other pardon cases, Hoover insisted upon a new Justice Department procedure for sending up pardon cases. Writing to Mitchell, Hoover said, "hereafter, in every case where pardon, commutation of sentence, or other executive clemency is granted, you are authorized, in response to inquiries by public officials, or the press, to make public the names of those who supported the application for clemency, and the reasons advanced by them for urging clemency."[55] The Teapot Dome crimes and the subsequent pardon requests had tested the limits of Hoover's patience. There was nothing to be done for men for whom Hoover had the greatest disrespect. To have given the cases any more attention would have heightened Hoover's vulnerability even more in the 1932 campaign.[56]

LINDBERGH KIDNAPPING AND LINDBERGH LAW

Charles Lindbergh was an American flying hero. He and his wife, the former Anne Morrow, counted among their friends in high places presidents Coolidge and Hoover. They had been honored by a White House visit after Charles's cross-Atlantic flight in 1927, and they were international celebrities of wide calling.[57] The Lindberghs led busy lives, traveling the world by air and being greeted and pawed over by throngs of people. Charles enjoyed the isolation and imagined security of their new home in Hopewell, New Jersey, away from merciless reporters who persisted in invading their privacy.[58] The house at Hopewell was occupied upon its completion in the winter of 1931, about the time Lindbergh was appointed by Hoover as a member of the National Advisory Committee for Aeronautics.

Within hours of the kidnapping of the Lindbergh baby on the evening of March 1, 1932, newspapers and radio commentators called for the president to make a radio appeal to the nation to assist in the recovery effort. Requests for Hoover's assistance ranged from expressions of sympathy and public prayers to use of federal resources to form organizations to clear up all crime in America. A lengthy telegram from a man in New York called for citizens, "regardless of their views on Prohibition to boycott hard liquor speakeasies and bootleggers until baby Lindbergh is returned safely to his parents. The loss to the underworld will in a few days be far greater than profit from kidnapping."[59] Another suggestion urged all school children to contribute a penny to the capture of the kidnapper. Others asked the president to declare a national baby day.

Hoover was shocked by the kidnapping upon learning of the incident in the early hours of March 2. His immediate instructions to other government officials can only be surmised; but by the morning on March 2, J. Edgar Hoover had already organized a squad of investigators to stand by to assist in the investigation.[60] The president wrote immediately to the Lindberghs: "My heart goes out to you in deepest sympathy in your distress, and I do pray that you may speedily have your son restored to you." He then ordered every federal investigative agency to lend assistance in the search for the

Lindbergh baby, among them the Bureau of Investigation, the Postal Service Inspectors, Secret Service, Prohibition Bureau, the Labor Department, the Washington Metropolitan Police Department, and the U.S. Coast Guard. Attorney General Mitchell maintained constant communications with the president, and announced to the press that "every officer of this Department of Justice has the deepest anxiety that the child will be quickly restored to its parents. Every agency of the department will cooperate to the utmost with the State authorities."[61]

Frank Loesch, Wickersham Commission member, visited with the president on the second to caution that federal agents had no statutory authority to investigate "professional kidnapping." Loesch, an arch advocate of private initiative, urged Hoover to promote sponsorship of an interstate organization of private persons, analogous to the Chicago "Secret Six," to hunt down the kidnappers. A month earlier Loesch had proposed the same plan in an interview with *New York Times* reporters. After his meeting with Hoover, Loesch further reinforced his suggestion: "You have to fight the kidnappers in a different way. Private individuals could band together to find out who is back of these rings. The organization should be perfected in each State and then affiliated into a national body. Men would have to lie around for months to get a line on the kidnappers through the underworld gossips. Perhaps 20 percent of the gossip would be useful, but there is where you would get your leads."[62] This was an entirely typical remark from Loesch who had allegedly faced down Al Capone to get a 'clean election' in Chicago in 1928.[63] Loesch's blusterings for presidential sponsorship of private action took its place in the massive public dialogue. Texas Congressman Hatton W. Summers remarked that the Lindbergh kidnapping "was no more important . . . than if the humblest child from the humblest home in America had been taken."[64] This was 1932, a year of deep economic depression during which the differences between the rich and famous and the poor and anonymous drew public attention.

On March 4, Hoover convened a cabinet meeting at which he reinforced the policy of assistance to the Lindbergh investigation. This confirmed his intense special interest in the case, his empathy for the Lindberghs, and his keen awareness that failure to act would anger an intensively concerned public. The governor of New Jersey, A. Harry Moore, requested Hoover's direct assistance in coordinating all federal efforts. Hoover sent Bureau of Investigation director J. Edgar Hoover to New Jersey to converse with Moore, but Edgar Hoover arrived to find a large room full of police officials and New Jersey State Police commissioner H. Norman Schwarzkopf clearly in charge. An offer was extended to intervene in a kidnapping of the twelve-year-old son of a wealthy Ohio contractor, despite the fact that some members of Congress challenged the possible intrusion upon state police authority.[65]

Throughout March and April, a bizarre series of events unfolded.[66] Democrats in New Jersey were reeling from the inability of the state police to solve the crime, and local Republicans, searching for a hook upon which to attack Governor Moore, charged incompetence.[67] The convicted and jailed Al Capone offered $10,000 for the return of the baby, a suggestion that did not have a ring of sincerity to IRS's intelligence unit director, Elmer L. Irey.[68] The Lindberghs decided to pay the $50,000 ransom demand on April 2, hoping that all their communications with characters ranging in presumed credibility from gangsters to private detectives would produce fruitful leads. Police jurisdiction for the investigation remained with Schwarzkopf's State Police, and Charles Lindbergh, insistent upon remaining in the middle of the action, added confusion to an already frustrating and politically heated situation. Bureaucratic politics festered in an atmosphere of unclear investigative jurisdiction. J. Edgar Hoover and others angled for pieces of the action, but Schwarzkopf refused to allow fingerprint evidence to be tested in the Bureau of Investigation laboratory.[69] Elmer Irey convinced Charles Lindbergh to leave him on the case. Irey claimed that Lindbergh was so insistent upon intelligence unit involvement that he phoned the secretary of the treasury, Ogden Mills, to ensure its implementation.[70] Interagency feuding over their roles in the investigation was resolved on May 13, 1932. The decomposed body of baby Charles was found within a few miles of the Lindbergh home on May 12. The finality refocused the problem on the kidnappers and away from a variety of hoaxsters and hangers-on, including an incompetent and corrupt agent of the Department of Labor.[71]

On May 13, the president wrote to Attorney General Mitchell to order a complete investigation into the case: "I am desirous that your investigation services should place themselves at the disposal of the New Jersey police for every possible assistance to them in interstate activity or any other fashion, and that you should keep this as a never to be forgotten live case until these criminals are implacably brought to justice. The three government departments having investigation services should at once coordinate themselves under the direction of the Department of Justice to this end and through this agency offer themselves to assist the police of New Jersey in every possible way."[72] Hoover's official statement on the same day reminded the public that "the Federal Government does not have police authority in such crimes, but its agencies will be unceasingly alert to assist the New Jersey police in every possible way until this end has been accomplished."[73]

It was clear that Hoover would assert the use of authority he did not have, except by way of indirect assistance. But no one in political or other circles was likely to object. In the manner of execution, he intended that federal investigators move to New Jersey and enter the center, not the periphery, of the inquiry. Following Hoover's orders, Mitchell immediately instructed J. Edgar Hoover to coordinate all federal involvement in the Lindbergh investigation. This meant that Elmer Irey at IRS would take his supervision from J. Edgar Hoover.[74] Echoing his boss, Edgar Hoover had not favored federal kidnapping authority "because of budget limitations and recent reductions in appropriations for the detective forces of the department."[75] But such hesitancy was inoperable upon the president's order.

Although Hoover's instruction to Mitchell and other federal investigative agencies was a clear extension of federal authority, it was not without executive branch precedent. Theodore Roosevelt had intervened directly in a kidnapping case in 1905, offering the use of federal investigators.[76] Senate bill S. 1525 and House Resolution 5657 lay on desks in the House and the Senate, with hearings in the House on February 26, 1932, just three days before the Lindbergh crime. S. 1525 had been on the Senate agenda since December 30, 1931. Members of Congress were not particularly favorable to the involvement of federal investigators in state matters such as kidnapping, fearing the effects of increasing the police powers of the federal government.

S. 1525, which had been passed by the Senate Judiciary Committee just days before the Lindbergh kidnapping, was mainly a response to the 1931 attempted kidnapping of General Charles G. Dawes, Hoover's president of the Reconstruction Finance Corporation and Coolidge's vice president. Kidnapping for ransom had grabbed the public attention in previous months. St. Louis police chief Joseph Gerk reported that 279 kidnappings had occurred in the United States in 1931.[77] An irresponsible report was published that two thousand ransom kidnapping events had occurred in the United States between 1930 and 1932, a figure that should have been closer to three hundred in the previous three years. Constance Morrow, Anne Morrow Lindbergh's sister, had even been targeted in 1929. Political rhetoric heated up in statehouses and legislatures, and some states installed death penalty statutes for abduction crimes.[78] New Jersey, like Illinois, had such a law at the time of the Lindbergh kidnapping. Chicago's state attorney, John A. Swanson, sought its application two months earlier against six men captured for the torture-kidnapping of a doctor and his wife.[79]

In the House, Resolution 5657, sponsored by Congressman John Cochran just four days before the Lindbergh crime, put forth the argument that state police forces were ill prepared to deal with the complexities and volume of ransom kidnap cases. Witnesses from police and private groups, including Robert I. Randolph of Chicago's Secret Six organization, told congressmen that states were impotent to carry on investigations across state lines and to force witnesses from other states to testify. They were pointed in their observations that although Postal Service and other investigators had no trouble crossing state lines, kidnapping was a state offense unrecognized by federal authorities. After the kidnapping, Cochran said in reaction to Hoover's order for federal investigative involvement, "every one will applaud the action of the President, but I can tell you he acted without any authority of law." Cochran insisted that Hoover apply the same logic to the protection of all children.[80]

Congressional hesitancy to expand federal policing authority was also the hesitancy of the attorney general and some legal scholars like Felix Frankfurter. Risking political repercussions, Mitchell announced on March 2 that he had ordered Edgar Hoover's involvement. But Mitchell included a caveat that assistance was rendered without any knowledge of a violation of federal law. Furthermore, he cautioned, "there are bills pending in Congress to make the transportation of kidnapped persons across state lines a federal offense. Because of budget limitations and recent reductions in appropriations for detective forces of the Department, I have not felt able to recommend such legislation but I have no objection to such a measure if Congress desires to pass it."[81] Sticking to this position, Mitchell addressed the nation by radio on March 5. Using the Tenth Amendment as his anchor, he said that ordinary crimes like murder, extortion, kidnapping, banditry, theft, blackmail, threats of violence, and frauds were, with few exceptions, related to exclusive federal sovereignty, not federal crimes, "and cannot be made such." Aside from the better situation of the states to enforce against these crimes, Mitchell pointed out that there were only 3,456 federal investigators to meet the expectations of federal law enforcement statutes. By reminding his listeners that the federal government should not be an entity of last resort in the solution of local crimes, Mitchell was obviously preaching White House opposition to the proposed federal kidnapping measures awaiting congressional review.[82]

Mitchell remained adamant in his opposition to the idea of federal jurisdiction in kidnapping cases. He offered his final public opinions on June 21: "If this law had been on the statute books at the time the Lindbergh case arose, there would have been an outcry demanding that the federal government take hold of the case; the local police authorities would have relaxed their activities and been glad to dump the responsibilities on the federal government; we would have spent thousands of dollars with no better results than the state authorities obtained, only to find out at the end that no federal crime had been committed as there had been no interstate transportation. . . . Indeed, in every kidnapping case that may arise, until the crime is solved no one knows whether there is any interstate transportation justifying interference by the federal government." Mitchell, however, advised the president and the public that the congressional insistence upon a federal jurisdiction should not be vetoed by Hoover, as this would have been an inappropriate use of the veto power.[83] Clearly, Mitchell agonized over federal takeover of crime jurisdictions that he believed would lead to even more federal court congestion and accusations by the states that encroachment on state prerogatives had occurred.

The federal kidnapping law was signed by President Hoover on June 22, 1932. Hoover's *Memoirs*, published twenty years after the Lindbergh incident, clearly imply an affirmative interest on his part in a federal kidnapping law: "The kidnapping and murder of the Lindbergh baby in March, 1932, brought public recognition of the necessity for Federal action. I was able to secure vigorous authority from Congress in the following June and July by two acts allowing the Federal government to pursue and prosecute when the kidnappers crossed state lines." In the same statement, Hoover acknowledged the "wave of kidnaping" that had occurred in previous years and added that organized gangs could easily cross state lines in automobiles to escape local police authority.[84]

THE BONUS MARCH DISASTER

Almost a full year after Hoover had suggested the need for veterans' assistance, tension between the White House and veterans' organizations had increased. Persistent lobby efforts to secure more veterans' benefits became increasingly irritating, as Hoover saw such strategies aimed at fulfilling narrow special interest. His agitation appeared in a speech in Boston on October 6, 1930, to the assembled membership of the American Legion. Of masterly construction, this speech linked Hoover's faith in law observance, voluntarism, self-sacrifice, citizen duty to serve in the military, and administration initiatives. He told his listeners, "you have recognized that the upholding of the Constitution and the enforcement of the laws must . . . not rest upon Government officials alone; it must rise from the stern demand and the loyal cooperation of good citizenship and individual responsibility." Hoover then reminded them of individual obligation for national defense service, that Americans had never favored "a large standing army," that the core of national defense had always been "citizen soldiers," and that "the economic burdens of war shall fall with equal weight upon every element of the citizenry." The American Legion, he said, had been out front in the effort to improve industrial mobilization while it had, by "mutual helpfulness," achieved "solicitude for your comrades, disabled both in war and peace." The nation had done its part also by improving veterans' benefits in several ways, as evidenced by the total annual budget outlay of $900 million.

The national treasury had limits, Hoover insisted, and those limits must result from a blending of citizen cooperation and government responsibility: "There is . . . a deep responsibility of citizenship in the administration of this trust of mutual helpfulness which peculiarly lies upon your members, and that is that the demands upon the Government should not exceed the measure that justice requires and self-help can provide. If we shall overload the burden of taxation, we shall stagnate our economic progress and we shall by the slackening of his progress place penalties upon every citizen." In polished terms, he told the legionnaires that they had already accepted the principles of good citizenship built on voluntary cooperation and military duty, thus they should expect to get from government only what they could not supply for themselves through 'mutual helpfulness.' Should they insist upon an alteration in this philosophy in the direction of new benefits, they would be responsible for injuring economic well-being. The lecture called on the legion to "renew and expand your mission of citizenship."[85]

Congressional and executive initiatives in 1930 and 1931 to provide new government facilities for sick and disabled veterans, as well as medical treatment of veterans without regard to source of illness, allayed veteran interest in pushing for the earlier guaranteed bonus money. But persistent revelations about gross inequities in benefits combined with news of discord within Hoover's administration about organization of veterans affairs. As the political pressure heated up in Congress, the number of supporters for the president's policy of delay on new benefits deteriorated rapidly. Hoover was portrayed as the leader of the opposition to new treasury allocations for veterans, even though many veterans and members of Congress were aware of their direct and indirect complicity in prior years in producing benefit inequities.[86] Mixed reactions in the circle of beneficiaries and in the Congress conveyed an impression to Hoover that the bonus issue held no seeds of significant political discord. Hoover apparently had been willing to concede benefits to veterans of the most deserving class, but in April 1932 he announced his rejection of the House bill with particular emphasis upon provisions containing implied cases of graft and inequities.[87]

For Hoover, the matter was simple logic drawn heavily from his commitment to guard the treasury as times got tougher. He insisted that a government faced with numerous other demands should not be obligated to pay veterans' benefits on demand. The original agreement to pay the veterans their bonus in 1945 should have been accepted as a matter of law requiring no further explanation. Furthermore, he believed the Congress was caving in to lobbyist demands to increase benefits to veterans whom he did not believe were entitled to further government support.[88] Accordingly, the president vetoed legislation in mid-1930 and early 1931 that he firmly believed would contradict the concept of veterans' benefits, as well as worsen the Depression. In both cases, Congress overrode his vetoes, and the battle lines were drawn. Democrats persisted, as Hoover described, for "political purposes," offering legislation to increase veterans' benefits. The matter was also taken up at the September meeting of the American Legion.

Hoover did not help himself by delivering another speech to the American Legion in October 1931. Legionnaires were told, "in these circumstances it is those who work in the fields, at the bench and desk who would be forced to carry an added burden for every added cent to our expenditures; [and] today a great service to our country is the determined opposition by you to additional demands upon the Nation until we have won this war against world depression. I am not speaking alone of veterans' legislation . . . but I am speaking equally of demands for every other project proposed in the country which would require increased Federal expenditure."[89] Veterans were marginalized by these words, even though legion conventioners voted down by a difference of 902 to 507 the proposals written into legislation.[90] Again, a mixed message gave Hoover continued justification to ignore the harder elements of the probonus benefit groups.

The congressional and press dialogues continued in the early months of 1932. As thousands of veterans arrived in Washington, among them a small contingent of Communist party organizers, Hoover ordered the Army to supply equipment and facilities to defuse tension. Marches took place almost daily at the White House, and encampments on public property were gradually filled to capacity. As weeks went by, Hoover's quiet support for provisioning the marchers reaped new criticism from members of the Congress and the military, who feared that others would demand equal treatment.[91] As inconsequential threats were whispered about assassinating Hoover, the gates of the White House were ordered padlocked and the guard force was strengthened.[92] Conspiracy theories, including allegations of complete Communist influence over the motivations and actions of the marchers, were discussed on the street and in the offices of the executive branch. Demonstrations by jobless people in several other cities convinced intelligence personnel in the War Department that insurrection was the intended outcome.

The summer heat intensified feelings in the camps in several locations in Washington, including a large camp at Anacostia and lesser gatherings in scattered federal buildings. Superintendent of police for the District of Columbia, Pelham D. Glassford, made valiant and repeated efforts to treat the marchers with respect and to provide them with provisions that he, too, hoped would quell their hostility.[93] In contrast, Army chief of staff Douglas MacArthur grew impatient with the lack of direct action to rout the encampments. Hoover had appointed MacArthur on Secretary of War Patrick Hurley's recommendation two years earlier, announcing that his choice had given him "a great deal of pleasure to promote so brilliant a soldier."[94] Glassford's efforts had the secret support of Hoover; but as June passed into July, the medical and emotional health of the marchers was labeled self-destructive. Added to the physical conditions so frequently described in newspaper articles and photographs was the fear of a Communist conspiracy. Talk of revolution piqued the concern of General MacArthur and J. Edgar Hoover. MacArthur wanted to enter the fray;[95] Edgar Hoover wanted to steer clear of it.[96]

By July 28, 1932, tensions ran high at the White House. Hoover had reached the end of his patience, refusing to meet with marchers or to acknowledge any features of their allegations of government intolerance to their plight. Consistently rainy weather in July made the camps susceptible to the spread of contagious diseases, and it had become clear that the longer the delay on definitive action the greater the chances of injury to men, women, and children. Police chief Glassford, despite support for the ideals of the marchers in earlier weeks, came to accept the city commissioner's view that law and order had deteriorated to the point of requiring federal troop intervention. General MacArthur later described the situation, clearly in terms designed to justify his intervention wishes: "A mob of 5,000 strong began to move up Pennsylvania Avenue toward the Treasury Building and the White House. The police were outnumbered five to one. Glassford was mauled and stripped of his police superintendent's gold badge, gunfire broke out, two men were killed and a score or more badly injured. It was evident that the situation had gotten beyond the control of the local authorities."[97]

By this time, Hoover's special bill to get return transportation expenses for the veterans had been implemented. Marchers who had lost patience with the process and others who wanted to escape the increasingly divided and violent inner core departed on government funds. Beyond train fare home, Hoover was unwilling to support any further legislative initiatives. Spending programs would not be accepted, he argued, especially in a campaign year.[98] He was also unwilling to let the city government suffer property losses and potential loss of life, recognizing that he would bear ultimate responsibility for failure to act. Having met with the city commissioners, Secretary of War Patrick J. Hurley, and General MacArthur, Hoover's order to dispatch troops had been indeed predicated on contemplation of the consequences of inaction. A plea for assistance from the city commissioners, he announced, caused him to call out the Army to assist the district authorities. Appearing also to have been swayed by intelligence reports on the composition of the marchers at that time, he announced that "a considerable part of those remaining are not veterans; many are communists and persons with criminal records. . . . The veterans amongst these numbers are no doubt unaware of the character of their companions and are being led into violence which no government can tolerate."[99]

Bayonets, tanks, and tear gas were unfortunate solutions to the marchers' protests. To Hurley and MacArthur, this meant the mustering of troops in full battle gear to push the marchers out of their camps. This was accomplished that afternoon. Few injuries were reported, and MacArthur reported to the press that evening that the "insurrectionists fired their billets" at Anacostia, not the Army.[100] As Lisio has pointed out, once Hoover gave the order to clear the marchers, he lost control over the events.[101] Stopping short of issuing a decree of insurrection, which would have enabled MacArthur to apply sweeping military maneuvers, Hoover gave every indication that military action had been permitted to proceed. Those close to Hoover later said that the president's orders had been disobeyed, while MacArthur understood no other instruction than a direct order to clear the camps.[102] Hoover could not have avoided responsibility for the violent outcome, and he never blamed MacArthur for overreacting. In later years, MacArthur flatly asserted the president's responsibility for the military action in the situation.[103] Some have argued that MacArthur's arrogance of mind brought him to shun any orders contrary to the most vigorous actions to sweep the camps.[104] Affirmative action of some sort was clearly demanded, but an exaggerated flavor of insurrection and conspiracy had infected the decision-making processes of all concerned. Postevent justifications, reports, and memoirs issued by several of the key players, however, made no concessions to the likelihood that smaller, less strident actions could have taken place in earlier months, such as establishment and supervision of a special site on public property where demonstrators could convene and earlier investigations of the criminal elements perceived to be at the core of the most violence-prone membership.[105] Hoover took responsibility for an outcome that contradicted his reasoned, humane, and systematic approaches to all earlier law enforcement issues.

Chapter 9

March 4, 1933: Report Card on Crime and Justice Reforms

Impartial justice has offered mankind its most certain escape from arbitrary power. Justice is also the safest cornerstone upon which peoples may erect their entire social organization.[1]

The ride from the White House to the Capitol steps was a somber affair for Hoover and Roosevelt.[2] An overcast and windy day, at least there was no rain to dampen an already strained circumstance. As Hoover and the throngs listened to the words of the inaugural address, they heard nothing of crime or of the federal justice system. Only mild reference was made to "a conduct in banking and business" in terms of "the likeness of callous and selfish wrongdoing." The words of Roosevelt's inaugural spoke of hope and containment of "fear itself."

Two weeks before leaving office, Hoover gave his final public speech to onlookers at the laying of the cornerstone for the new U.S. Department of Justice building in Washington. Law, democracy, and justice formed the cornerstones of civilized society, he implied: "Justice . . . knows neither station, position, wealth, nor poverty; and justice can act only with the most efficient, honest organization of the enforcement machinery. For this, public officers and equipment are indispensable, but equally indispensable to their success are the self-discipline and cooperation of the people." Modifying the inscription on the stone, which read, "Let justice prevail, though the heavens fall," Hoover substituted, "Justice shall prevail, because that is the people's will."[3]

Hoover's bid for reelection was launched under circumstances no incumbent could have imagined before October 1929. Those were years of economic boom, success in war and international relations, and popular support for organizational responses to social problems. The perceived harshness of military deployment against the Bonus marchers capped an already dramatic shift in the public's patience with organizational responses and with speeches about competent and enlightened administration of justice.

Unlike the upbeat proposals in his first months in office, Hoover's campaign speeches offered no new proposals for crime control or federal justice administration. Indeed, aside from stubborn insistence to continue Prohibition enforcement, law observance and system improvements disappeared as policy objectives. Hoover's acceptance speech on August 11 repeated his original theme, that the federal government should not relieve individuals, states, or private institutions of responsibilities to enforce the constituted law. His message, by then considerably worn and out of step by virtue of general disenchantment with his economic policies, ministered to law and to the control of crime without mention of the many practical achievements of his administration. New directions in federal justice lay unclaimed; instead came a preaching reminder of a policy that had little to do with real, community-divisive threats to law observance.

Hoover stood flatfooted in favor of the continuation of the Eighteenth Amendment, an albatross policy. His opening words to the Republican conventioneers rang as they had rung for four years: "I desire to speak so simply and so plainly that every man and woman in the United States who may hear my words cannot misunderstand." The long acceptance speech, so characteristic of Hoover's dry thoroughness, reminded the crowd of the "economic calamity" of the previous years, born in "reckless boom" and worsened by "weeds of waste, exploitation, and abuse of financial power." He then acknowledged the work of a bipartisan Congress in the construction of economic measures that had evolved from the "intrepid soul of our people." To all but the economically secure listener, these were hollow words to a nation filled with unemployment and despair. Relations between government and citizens, he preached, must emphasize responsibilities of each person to preserve the balance between "great national power" and the individual "freedom through local self-government." This philosophy had played out most ideally in the private initiatives of Chicago's citizen groups in bringing down Al Capone. But it amounted to nothing in the uniform enforcement of the Prohibition; and it was entirely incomplete in the charade of the Lindbergh kidnapping investigation. In these matters, federal agents were invested either with too little power to control the conditions under which violations of law occurred or with insufficient authority to resolve what states and localities might have agreed to do for themselves.

On Prohibition, Hoover recognized the abuses that resulted from "practical nullification of the Constitution," and a regime of "subsidized crime and violence" to which he could not subscribe. He said that he could not accept a "return to the old saloon with its political and social corruption, or on the other [destiny] to endure the bootlegger and the speakeasy with their abuses and crime." Clearly absent from the speech was any mention of the panoply of initiatives to improve federal law enforcement, judiciary, and prisons. The context of his words pertaining, once again, to the president's duty to enforce the law, was limited to the "elimination of the evils of this [liquor] traffic from this civilization by practical measures."[4] He wanted only to find ways of encouraging the states to renew their pledge to enforce the Constitution and to find ways to "awaken a sense of national consciousness of the purposes of life itself."[5] Many other topics were laboriously examined, of course, but none other so symbolized Hoover's rigid reasonableness before an uninterested audience.

On October 12, Hoover spoke more directly, although no more comprehensively about his criminal justice successes, in a speech to the American Bar Association. Paying homage to the "incalculable practical value" of the Supreme Court in mitigating injury to people and to controlling "excessive disturbance to political equilibrium," he returned to the theme of local initiatives against crime. "Fundamentally," he argued, "our capacity to extinguish criminality and lawlessness lies in the moral training and moral stature of our people." Equating regulation of crime with regulation of economic change, Hoover said, "Crime is a more personal, a more individual thing, than economics. I have often said that you cannot overtake an economic law with a policeman. But the only thing that can overtake a criminal is a policeman. The facts of most crimes are localized; they must be investigated at the scene. The pursuit of the criminal must be directed from the community whose peace has been broken, and the evidence for his trial can most effectively and most justly be presented to his neighbors and judges in the community. Thus, in spite of the fact that crime also has frequently become interstate, the suppression of crime is still most effectively accomplished locally . . . and should not be shifted to the Federal Government."

Aiming directly at proposals for modification of federal rules of criminal procedure, which had languished in the Senate Judiciary Committee for three years, Hoover captioned the impact of unwieldy and untimely court delays. "One of the most disheartening difficulties of zealous officers of government is the law's delays, during which evidence loses its value, witnesses die, and criminals are encouraged to believe that through its maze of technicalities justice can be neither swift nor sure." Naturally, he hoped that the lawyers association would line up behind proposals to simplify federal criminal procedures "to make the administration of law a terror to evildoers by its promptness and certainty."[6]

With nearly equal the speed of its appearance in March 1929, the crime issue faded from Hoover's official words during the last days of the 1932 campaign. The missing element, of course, was the credit he could have taken for policies already implemented. The opportunities for doing so were frequent, his material so voluminous. Instead, like the limited remarks he made to the Republican convention in August and the ABA meeting in October, few words addressed such profound changes in federal justice. Perhaps in symbolic recognition of his victory over gangster Al Capone, on November 5 Hoover returned to the theme of local control: "I think you are all conscious of the humiliation that comes to our countrymen when the Federal Government must deliberately use the violation of income tax laws to collect gains on crime in order to curb these criminals who are uncontrolled, unprosecuted, and unconvicted by the States and municipalities." Jabbing at Governor Roosevelt, he opposed more activism on the part of the federal government to take over the "burden" of state and local responsibility. He warned that the "gangster life" had become "one of the most dangerous elements to the whole of our civilization. It would seem that [with] the opportunities that were given the Governor of New York . . . he might have made a larger contribution in these last 3 years to the solution of the gang life in that State, under the great powers conferred and the obligations bestowed by the constitution and laws of his own State."[7]

After voting in his home state of California and after a long night of disappointing election returns, Hoover conceded the election to Franklin Roosevelt at 9:30 P.M. on November 8.[8] Again, neither of his December annual messages to Congress mentioned crime or other recommendations for further criminal justice reforms. An important bill to reform federal criminal procedures remained in congressional committees, signed finally in February 1933. A final success, for which there was little fanfare, transferred to the Supreme Court the power to formulate rules for practice to be followed by lower federal courts in criminal cases. The measure had taken four years to pass: "It realizes, in part, a quarter of a century of demands for reform in Federal criminal procedure. It should prevent well-endowed criminals, who have been convicted by juries, from delaying punishment by years of resort to sharp technicalities of judicial procedure. It will increase respect for the law."[9]

Hoover's unwillingness to glory in the advancements of federal justice administration is to be comprehended only through closer consideration of his personal and political views. First, he had always been clear about the need for fairness and justice in transactions between individuals or business partners. These values were taken for granted in relations between individuals and between individuals and government. His duty was limited to leading the installation of government systems to enhance law-based social relations; and beyond completion of this task, there was no need to credit personal or political accounts. Second, Hoover held firmly to a philosophy that federal leadership was less important than solutions by individuals or states, a viewpoint that perhaps should have been recognized as obsolete amidst the difficulties encountered in convicting Capone and in maintaining effective leadership in the Lindbergh case. Third, as Theodore Joslin observed, over the life of Hoover's public service, "the number of times he reversed himself or modified an important position could be counted on the fingers of one hand."[10] And finally, Hoover was a man of executive action toward positive ends in the administration of justice, leaving operational decisions and credit for jobs well done to competent administrators. He considered such matters as the pardon cases, including those brought by elitists like Fall and Sinclair, as details warranting no more than efficient management and minor administrative attention. He believed that the Massie assault, rape, and murder case, despite all the political heat from southern Democrats, was a marginal crime warranting local administration of justice in a territory over which he had little control. The assumption that others would automatically comprehend the correctness of his minimalist, self-effacing approach to the presidency was, perhaps, his principal failure, especially as it relates to the weight of his policy interest in justice administration.

A key question comes to mind, however, in Hoover's defense. What other practical course of action could have been expected from Hoover with respect to federal law enforcement and justice system improvements? Expanded federal authority was unacceptable to a Congress that had only begun to consider overcrowded conditions in the federal prisons and the unworkability of the Volstead Act. There was no groundswell of popular interest in expanding federal law enforcement. The electorate was wholly uninformed on both the degree of disarray in the federal system and the informed proposals for improvement that lay unused in the intellectual and practitioner communities. Indeed, Hoover came to office with a mandate to enforce federal law; but to accomplish this, he determined the necessity of soliciting the views of knowledgeable thinkers and doers and of reorganizing federal police, court, and prison functions. By January

1932, this work was well in the hands of competent administrators. The announced agenda had been implemented.

Two lessons had been learned over the life of the Hoover administration with respect to justice reform initiatives. First, Hoover's initiatives to redirect a limited federal response to crime could have been clarified and formulated only in the early months of his administration. Federal criminal justice reforms, despite intellectual and popular support on March 4, 1929, were vulnerable to displacement by unanticipated events. Second, Hoover's determination to change the face and substance of federal justice administration guaranteed recognition by insiders to law and legal process but relative obscurity to the public and to the history of the modern presidency.

No fair evaluation would give all credit for federal justice initiatives to Hoover's one-term administration. Prior to 1929, federal legislation created the federal court system and the Justice Department, added criminal laws to the meagre list of crimes offered by the Framers, and extended policing authority to carry out a presidential duty to enforce laws and protect domestic tranquility. Several law enforcement organizations were established and experienced before 1929. New federal drug, alcohol, and other statutes instituted after the Civil War pressured involvement by the federal courts in criminal matters, and federal prisons took in an increasing federal prisoner population. Federal justice administration lacked organizational codification and direction; it lacked focus; and it lacked a reform agenda for succeeding years. The first weakness sapped energy, the second weakness injured identity and morale, and the third weakness limited adaptation to new crimes and new burdens on agencies.

What Hoover contributed was a timely recognition of these weaknesses and an intention to craft the miscellaneous parts of federal justice administration into a comprehensive whole. To do so implied the choice of a competent and hard-working attorney general; White House secretaries; commissioners; Justice Department deputies; and countless line personnel in law enforcement, U.S. attorneys' offices, courts, and prisons. There was need to publicly declare the value of efficient justice administration as the critical factor in law observance; to promote the responsibility of government to serve as ultimate insurer of honesty and fairness in business transactions, including enforcement against monopolies; to chase down abuses of authority by government agents and to fire incompetent personnel; to incorporate scientific investigation of the federal system of justice at a time when science and social policy had merged interests; to introduce reorganized and strengthened federal investigative branches to better assist local police authorities; to encourage by procedural reforms the federal courts to take a managerial approach to the processing of ever-increasing civil and criminal caseloads; and to instill greater faith in combined actions of individuals, states, and the federal government in containing the causes of crime.

The action ingredients of Hoover's recognition of weaknesses included involvement of academics and practitioners in the assessment of theories and research on crime causation and the establishment of priorities for federal justice policy implementation. Intellectual and practitioner resources were there for the picking. Their critical mass in law schools, university departments, federal agencies, police departments, and other justice system functions at all levels, as well as those among the press and independent consultants could, with executive leadership, reach beyond the manufacture of good ideas to implementation of social reforms. Hoover tapped these resources, thereby legitimating their role in fulfilling the ideals of law observance and justice administration. Naturally, it is impossible to evaluate with precision the individual or collective contributions of these resources to the overall changes implemented by the end of the Hoover administration. But comparisons between federal justice conditions before his administration and at its end can be reasonably traced to the ideas, plans, and operational work of the thinkers and doers employed to make improvements. By 1933, federal agencies showed significant improvements in law enforcement professionalism; the federal courts showed new competencies in prosecution, linkages with policing functions, and expeditiousness in sentencing offenders; and the federal corrections system had become greatly diversified and expanded in ways that permitted classification and securing of prisoners, probationers, and parolees.

Legal system reforms, including alterations to practices believed to induce some criminality (e.g., "third degrees tactics of police," inconsistent sentencing, or harsh prison conditions), were pursued for their relevance to crime causation. The operating assumption was that the seedbed of crime causation was also the place to find more efficient social control mechanisms. If nothing else could be said for the simplicity of such associations, at the very least the political and social interests had begun to sense the social construction of crime. Prohibition enforcement brought grudging acceptance of the unfriendly links between morality and law. Popular expectations about the role of law in society, especially American society, cracked under repeated discoveries that much criminality was going unchecked by legal means. Somehow, adjustments to the legal system would strengthen comprehension of crime's causative roots, thereby giving the social control system the advantage in making legal expectations fit reality.

His associative state envisioned collaboration between local organizations, such as civic, business, and labor groups, and government organizations chartered to encourage them to find their own solutions to problems. Intensely idealistic at heart, Hoover believed strongly in the voluntaristic spirit of a well informed American public.[11] Such a theory would be clearly demonstrated in his approach to the Wickersham Crime Commission as mainly an informational device, and to the initiation of the Al Capone investigation. As an ideal, the theory was fundamentally correct with respect to Prohibition enforcement and the necessity of broad social acceptance of the law. But Hoover failed to understand that alcohol and its marketplace popularity were forces that voluntary associations and law would never be able to repress.

The Wickersham Commission's investigative efforts were purposely promoted to enlighten informed approaches to crime and justice. They were pioneering efforts to attract leading scholars across the spectrum of emerging social and behavioral sciences. Scholars were asked to prioritize issues and to screen the evidence of successful ways to improve upon knowledge of the causes of crime and upon administrative practices for responding to it. Given the narrowness of Prohibition politics and resistance to an undertaking that had no predecessor, intellectual credibility was essential to shoring up Hoover's ultimate interest in reshaping federal justice administration. Furthermore, the commission's work directly informed Hoover's policy of expanding the field of research questions, of calling for greater precision in federal statistical management, and of publicizing conditions of justice agency performance. Scholarship had not been systematically applied to questions of federal concern, nor had it been given political recognition as a tool of policy design and implementation. The commission had achieved the objectives of teaching the president, but more important, of teaching the public that complex policy issues must be carefully considered. As C. H. Willard observed in June 1929, "In dealing with the social disease called crime the country is now at the stage at which England found itself a hundred and fifty years ago when public sanitation in towns was born, first as a groping idea, and later maturing into a science." The commission, Willard believed, could accomplish three objectives in the course of its limited life: it could assemble and judge existing facts; it could educate the public with respect to the facts; and, it could "help make possible the future program for getting facts and applying the treatment which can be deduced from such new facts."[12]

Hoover's avoidance of a black appointment to the commission seems odd by modern standards, but pragmatism governed the outer limits of his progressivism. He could not have sustained popular support for a commission targeted at discovery of the scientifically based middle depths on Prohibition while casting a liberal profile on an issue with no national policy platform. It was not an unrecognized tradeoff,[13] but furor created by Hoover's White House dinner party for Oscar DePriest symbolized the volatility of the racial issue that ran far deeper in the public psyche than Prohibition or the comprehension of the causes of crime. Black avoidance of the Wickersham results was understandable, based perhaps on perceived insensitivities to certain special issues that were arguably important to complete fulfillment of Hoover's precepts about law observance and federal justice. It was a call he made to save the commission process from the racism that underlay the politics of the times.

The ends of Hoover's policy to secure the arrest, conviction, and imprisonment of Alphonse Capone were achieved, first, by labeling Capone's crimes as national integrity and security threats, second, by retaining law enforcement and prosecutorial talent determined to overcome Capone's intimidation of legitimate government, and finally, by permitting his staff the discretion to use all legal authority to carry out the policy in an uncompromising manner. Hoover transformed policy against organized crime by combining a relatively thin veneer of federal authority with skilled and eager investigators and a political will to penetrate a crime group with an equally thin veneer of power. Capone's conviction weakened criminal conspiracies and encouraged new opportunities for state and local crime control measures to flourish.

Law's necessary enforcibility, of course, was uppermost in Hoover's sense of social control. At minimum and within his executive reach, the federal government was obligated to organize and supervise in ways that would accomplish police agency tasks and avoid loss of public confidence. Organization was Hoover's best suit; supervision, including discipline and training of federal agents, was delegated to competent administrators he chose to head agencies like the Prohibition Bureau, and the newly formed Border Patrol and the Bureau of Narcotics. Realignment of these agencies, he was convinced, would put them in the best position to carry out policing duties, not simply revenue enhancement duties as earlier conceived.[14] Closer association with U.S. attorneys and direct oversight by the attorney general would ensure law-based enforcement.

Hoover's first objective in reforming the federal criminal courts was to raise the level of judicial integrity. Rooting out corrupt or inefficient prosecutors and judges was the method of choice, as Hoover believed that no time could be wasted on those uncommitted to a new order of federal court business. His second objective was to deliver to U.S. attorneys and the courts, mainly by congressional authorization, additional personnel and modified procedures for expediting criminal and civil case loads. The objectives were set forth in his inaugural address and doggedly pursued during his term. Integrity was achieved by firing incompetent or corrupt prosecutors and by instructing the Justice Department to undertake discreet investigations of federal judges where allegations of misconduct arose. Hoover's faith in the integrity and diligence both of Attorney General Mitchell, and of those selected to head the investigative branches enhanced his capability to proceed with the occasional distasteful task of firing executive department personnel. At the time, however, significant advancement in the development of federal justice administration could not have occurred without an effort to clean out the deadwood.

Reforms to court administration proposed during Hoover's term were made mainly on the strong but reserved advice of the attorney general. Mitchell remained one of Hoover's most diligent and trusted insiders—not bad for a Minnesota "Hoover Democrat." Hoover never presumed to know the intricacies of the criminal law or pretended that he could single-handedly advise the judiciary on matters of complex procedure. Mitchell could, however, and this allowed Hoover to take his crime control policies across lines of constitutionally and traditionally regulated arenas of power. His perspective was relatively simple: find ways to improve the ability of the federal courts to more efficiently administer justice by removing unnecessary procedural blockages to enforcement objectives. On the surface, Hoover's philosophy appeared to favor the dominance of policing over judicial scrutiny of police and prosecutors. Hoover's reforms, however, were considered constructively modest and were supported by legal scholars like Roscoe Pound, the attorney general, the Wickersham Commission, and bar associations.

Not all of Hoover's actions involved negative house cleaning. He appointed district, circuit, and Supreme Court judges, many of whom served in public service capacities with high distinction. For example, upon resignation of Supreme Court Justice William Howard Taft, Hoover nominated Charles Evans Hughes. Judicial experience, integrity, and legal scholarship were Hoover's priorities for appointments; and in nearly all cases his appointments have been viewed with high regard. Upon the death of Supreme Court Justice Edward T. Sanford, Hoover appointed North Carolina Circuit Court Judge John J. Parker. Parker's nomination encountered immediate opposition from labor organizations, which had been opposed to him as antilabor, and by the NAACP, which insisted he had spoken racist words.[15] Failing confirmation of Judge Parker, Owen J. Roberts, who had been the Justice Department's special prosecutor in the Teapot Dome case, was nominated and approved. Upon resignation of the elderly Oliver Wendell Holmes in January 1932, Hoover nominated Benjamin I. Cardozo, who received immediate Senate approval. Hughes and Cardozo have been rated as "great" justices, while Roberts is rated "average."[16]

President Hoover, as well, took no special interest in prison management through the period of his commerce secretaryship. But by the campaign of 1928, his practical attitudes about law enforcement took on clear support for prison reforms as integral features of an effective crime control policy. He believed it was impossible to ignore the rapid growth of prison populations attributable to Prohibition and drug law enforcement, which he supported as proper objectives of federal authority. He was aware that public sentiment favored longer criminal sentences and that press accounts lauded police and judicial efficiency in destroying liquor operations, in rounding up labor dissidents, and in containing prostitution rings. As a mining engineer of world travel, however, he was fully familiar with the implications of overloading one element of a process to the detriment of another. He understood points of stress on properties arranged in systems, and he had long experience addressing predictable outcomes of growing system pressures. Acclaim piled on Hoover for his Belgian food relief work during World War I was sufficient evidence of his comprehension of, and subscription to, dynamics of organizational incoherence—and the repairs for it. As commerce secretary, he remained knowledgeable of state and federal prison conditions, gradually forming an opinion that law, enforcement, punishment, and rehabilitation would become important public management concerns in later years.

Hoover also considered that he and the Congress recognized that federal prison administration, given its pronounced growth in the previous ten years, required coequal administrative standing with the enforcement and prosecutorial components of federal justice. Further neglect of the institutions to which criminals were sentenced and housed implied their inutility as places of punishment or reform. Federal prisons, Hoover believed, were constructed to punish, deter, and correct through modest but humanitarian means. If these objectives were demeaned, the purposes of law enforcement and prosecution were less clear.

And finally, Hoover had personal and scientific allegiances to the philosophical underpinnings of corrections. Personal commitment arose from his Quaker religion; scientific commitment developed from his experiences as a mining engineer and his adherence to the principles of scientific management. For Hoover, prison management was only an essential administrative arena in a relatively small federal bureaucracy in which favorable policy implementation was presumed to follow a matching of competent administrators with adequate financial and physical plant resources.[17]

From the intentions of the Wickersham Commission to modifications of all aspects of the administration of justice, policies were rooted in a principle of coordination of enforcement with judicial and sanctioning functions of the criminal law. Hoover understood the limits of the president's domestic policy agenda, particularly with respect to reforms in administrative areas where there was no coalition of interests over purely administrative matters. Construction of new prison facilities and programs, for example, may have made good management and economic sense, but it did not translate into broad political recognition or support. Hoover's support for new developments in federal administration, prisoner classification systems, improvements in probation and parole, and formal prison industries could not have attracted high political acclaim. But they demonstrated commitment to the exercise of his constitutional responsibilities and to his philosophical allegiance to the potency of all aspects of the justice system as means for promoting the rule of law.

Notes

Manuscripts and records used in the course of this research book are located in scattered federal agencies or private collections. To save space in the notes, I have abbreviated references to records as follows: (DOT-ATF) Al Capone records, Department of the Treasury, Alcohol, Tobacco, and Firearms Unit; (DOJ-Tax) Al Capone records, Department of Justice, Tax Division; (FBI) Al Capone records, Department of Justice, Federal Bureau of Investigation; (FS-HHPL) French Strother papers, Herbert Hoover Presidential Library; (HHPL) Herbert Hoover Presidential Library; (MWW-FBI) Mabel Walker Willebrandt records, Federal Bureau of Investigation; (BOP) Sanford Bates records, Department of Justice, Bureau of Prisons; (SHSU) Sanford Bates records, Sam Houston State University; and (WDM-MHS) William D. Mitchell records, Minnesota Historical Society. Litigation was brought against the Internal Revenue Service in 1986 to open the IRS tax investigation records of Alphonse Capone. The United States Court of Appeals (5th Circuit) ruled, however, to permit the government continued secrecy over records more than sixty years old for a deceased and convicted federal felon. See J. D. Calder, "Al Capone and the Internal Revenue Service: State-sanctioned Criminology of Organized Crime," *Crime, Law and Social Change* 17 (April 1992): 33–46.

CHAPTER 1

1. "Message to Congress Transmitting Report of the National Commission on Law Observance and Enforcement," 1/20/31, *Public Papers of the Presidents of the United States, Herbert C. Hoover (1929–1933)* [hereafter *Public Papers*] (Washington, D.C.: Government Printing Office, 1976).

2. For excellent background on Hoover and historical perceptions, see E. W. Hawley et al., *Herbert Hoover and the Historians* (West Branch, Iowa: Herbert Hoover Library Association, 1989).

3. W. K. Klingaman, *1929: The Year of the Great Crash* (New York: Harper & Row, 1989), pp. 139–142.

4. Inaugural Address, 3/4/29, *Public Papers*.

5. Ibid.

6. Hoover's early life and career are thoroughly examined in G. H. Nash, *The Life of Herbert Hoover: The Engineer, 1874–1914* (New York: W. W. Norton, 1983).

7. Ibid., pp. 228–232.

8. Ibid., pp. 245–276.

9. Ibid., p. 479. Richard Norton Smith points to the influence of Thorstein Veblen, a Stanford professor in the early twentieth century, on Hoover's desire for a socially conscious class of engineer. Hoover, Smith argues, "embellished Veblen's notion of the engineer as society's management consultant, disinterested enough to know what was best, forceful enough to realize the age-old ambition of a standard combining generosity with practicality. No mere disciple of mechanical utopias would do." R. N. Smith, *An Uncommon Man: The Triumph of Herbert Hoover* (New York: Simon and Schuster, 1984).

10. G. H. Nash, *The Life of Herbert Hoover: The Humanitarian, 1914–1917* (New York: W. W. Norton, 1988), pp. 25–33.

11. Ibid., pp. 165–168.

12. D. Burner, *Herbert Hoover, A Public Life* (New York: Alfred A. Knopf, 1978), p. 160.

13. J. Brandes, "Product Diplomacy: Herbert Hoover's Anti-Monopoly Campaign at Home and Abroad," in *Herbert Hoover As Secretary of Commerce: Studies in New Era Thought and Practice*, ed. E. W. Hawley, pp. 185–216 (Iowa City: University of Iowa, 1981).

14. J. H. Wilson, "Herbert Hoover's Agricultural Policies, 1921–28," in Hawley, op. cit., pp. 118–120. See also D. Burner, op. cit., p. 172.

15. C. Gentry, *J. Edgar Hoover: The Man and the Secrets* (New York: W. W. Norton, 1991), p. 125.

16. H. C. Hoover, *The Memoirs of Herbert Hoover: The Cabinet and the Presidency, 1920–1933* [hereafter *Memoirs*] (New York: Macmillan, 1952), p. 171.

17. F. Russell, *The Shadow of Blooming Grove: Warren G. Harding in His Times* (New York: McGraw-Hill, 1968), pp. 507–513.

18. Accounts of the circumstances surrounding installations of the first police radio systems vary considerably. For example, Detroit's police chief, William Rutledge, reported in his June 4, 1929 address to the International Association of Chiefs of Police that "in the early part of 1921 . . . we placed our first car, equipped with a receiving set, on the streets of Detroit. In 1922 I arranged for a statewide broadcast of the license numbers of stolen cars." Rutledge titled his presentation "Radio in Police Work." V. A. Leonard, acclaimed police science professor, took credit for convincing Berkeley, California's chief of police, August Vollmer, to design and install the first police owned and controlled radio system in the United States in 1926. The Mel-

bourne, Australia, police department, said Leonard, had been the absolute first location for police radios in 1923. V. A. Leonard, *The New Police Technology* (Springfield, Illinois: Charles C. Thomas, 1980), pp. 166–169. G. T. Payton differs: "On April 7, 1928, the world's first workable police radio system went on the air. The Detroit Police Department went on the air as station W8FS. . . . This was the climax of seven years of work and development under the direction of Police Commissioner William P. Rutledge." Payton adds that bureaucratic resistance with the Federal Radio Commission (now the Federal Communications Commission) caused delays in securing licensing. G. T. Payton, *Patrol Procedure* (Los Angeles: Legal Books, 1971), p. 123.

19. Burner, op. cit., p. 163.
20. A. Vollmer to G. W. Wickersham, 8/19/30, Archives.
21. A. G. Theoharis and J. S. Cox, *The Boss: J. Edgar Hoover and the Great American Inquisition* (Philadelphia: Temple University Press, 1988), pp. 82–98.
22. R. G. Powers, *Secrecy and Power, The Life of J. Edgar Hoover* (New York: Free Press, 1987), pp. 142–143.
23. H. J. Abraham, *Justices and Presidents: A Political History of Appointments to the Supreme Court* (New York: Oxford University Press, 1974), p. 182.
24. Hoover, op. cit., pp. 41, 54.
25. F. J. Cook, *The FBI Nobody Knows* (New York: Macmillan, 1964), pp. 138–139.
26. G. E. White, *The American Judicial Tradition: Profiles of Leading American Judges* (New York: Oxford University Press, 1976), p. 217.
27. R. K. Murray, *Red Scare: A Study in National Hysteria, 1919–1920* (New York: McGraw-Hill, 1955), pp. 190–195.
28. R. E. Morgan, *Domestic Intelligence: Monitoring Dissent in America* (Austin: University of Texas Press, 1980), pp. 27–30. A summary of circumstances of how J. Edgar escaped the corruption in the Justice Department between 1921 and May 1924 is found in Russell, op. cit., pp. 518–520.
29. See also the account by S. J. Ungar, *FBI: An Uncensored Look behind the Walls* (Boston: Atlantic Monthly Press, 1975), pp. 47–55.
30. Powers, op. cit., pp. 161–163. Herbert Hoover's FBI file contains a collection of miscellaneous documents dating to 1921. Herbert Hoover and J. Edgar Hoover maintained a close and long association.
31. J. M. Dorwart, *Conflict of Duty: The U.S. Navy's Intelligence Dilemma, 1919–1945* (Annapolis: Naval Institute, 1983), p. 3. See speculations about this matter in Gentry, op. cit., p. 153.
32. Gentry, op. cit., p. 125.
33. M. Medved, *The Shadow Presidents: The Secret History of the Chief Executives and Their Top Aides* (New York: Times Books, 1979), p. 185.
34. T. Sugrue and E. E. Starling, *Starling of the White House* (Chicago: Peoples, 1946), p. 297.
35. A. C. Brown, *The Last Hero: Wild Bill Donovan* (New York: Times Books, 1982), pp. 112–113. Donovan rejected the governorship and returned to private law practice.
36. Hoover, *Memoirs*, p. 192.

37. Ibid., pp. 322, 326.

38. Ibid., p. 185.

39. He was author of *Policeman and Public* (New Haven: Yale University Press, 1919); and *Crime Prevention* (Princeton: Princeton University Press, 1918).

40. R. K. Murray, "Herbert Hoover and the Harding Cabinet." In Hawley, op. cit., p. 26.

41. Burner, op. cit., pp. 166, 265–266.

42. W. F. Swindler, *Court and Constitution in the 20th Century: The Old Legality 1889–1932* (Indianapolis: Bobbs-Merrill, 1969), p. 232.

43. Hoover, *Memoirs*, p. 219.

44. Hoover's handwritten notes cite his reasons for rejecting Donovan: "a. He was wet; opposed 18th Amendment, was in favor of repeal or change. Any Atty Genl publicly opposed to the laws he was called to enforce could neither command public confidence nor the support of his own staff in vigorous action. In other words, in endeavor to *force* a member. b. Has never had an administrative experience. c. Is a soldier before soldiers, not a restraining civilian. d. Refused to agree that he would accept such re-organization plans as administration called for. e. Developed vast capacity for intrigue which resulted in starting of opposition press campaigns. f. His enforcement of the Sherman Act as Asst. Atty Genl has been very bad. g. He could not be confirmed in the Senate for above reasons." Regarding consideration for secretary of war, Hoover wrote that Donovan had attempted to force his own appointment by press manipulation and that he was too dictatorial in demeanor: "Showed immaturity of mind[,] needs to be 10 years older." H. C. Hoover to file, undated 1929, HHPL.

45. Russell, op. cit., pp. 433–434.

46. Robert Murray observed that Mellon's great wealth may have intimidated Hoover when they both served in Coolidge's cabinet, and it is equally likely they disagreed on tax policies. R. K. Murray, "Herbert Hoover and the Harding Cabinet." In Hawley, op. cit., p. 32. Hoover and Mellon appear to have corresponded only infrequently on the Capone investigation from 1929 to 1932. John Kobler's assertion that Hoover ordered Mellon to go after Capone at a morning gathering of the "medicine ball cabinet" on the White House lawn in January 1929 is implausible. See J. Kobler, *Capone: The Life and World of Al Capone* (New York: G. P. Putnam's Sons, 1971), pp. 270, 277. Mellon's personal demeanor of superiority among men of equal rank would more reasonably have been expressed as ambivalence toward Capone, and any order from Hoover would more reasonably have been a cordial request in a private setting. Mellon was not part of the medicine ball group: R. L. Wilbur, *The Memoirs of Ray Lyman Wilbur, 1875–1949* (Stanford: Stanford University Press, 1960), p. 543. Hoover's *Memoirs* do not identify Mellon as an attendee of the morning medicine ball exercise sessions.

47. Hoover, *Memoirs*, p. 274.

48. See letter Willebrandt sent to Mitchell outlining her contributions to federal prison management in response to a Hearst paper conclusion that her work was only in the area of prohibition enforcement. D. M. Brown, *Mabel Walker Willebrandt: A Study of Power, Loyalty, and Law* (Knoxville: University of Tennessee Press, 1984), pp. 98–99.

49. She characterized Wittpen as "well and favorably known for her interest in penology. ('Hoover Democrat')." M. W. Willebrandt to H. C. Hoover, 4/2/29, HHPL.

50. H. C. Hoover to W. H. Taft, 4/7/29, HHPL.

51. Swindler, op. cit., pp. 136–139.

52. W. B. Gatewood, Jr., *Theodore Roosevelt and the Art of Controversy: Episodes of the White House Years* (Baton Rouge: University of Louisiana Press, 1970), p. 283.

53. H. C. Hoover, *The New Day: Campaign Speeches of Herbert Hoover, 1928* (Stanford: Stanford University Press, 1928), p. 98.

54. Ibid., p. 70.

55. "Change in the Constitution can and must be brought about only by the straightforward methods provided in the Constitution itself. There are those who do not believe in the purposes of several provisions of the Constitution. No one denies their right to seek to amend it. They are not subject to criticism for asserting that right. But the Republican Party does deny the right of anyone to seek to destroy the purposes of the Constitution by indirection.

Whoever is elected President takes an oath not only to faithfully execute the office of the President, but that oath provides still further that he will, to the best of his ability, preserve, protect, and defend the Constitution of the United States. I should be untrue to these great traditions, untrue to my oath of office, were I to declare otherwise." Ibid., p. 30.

56. Hoover, op. cit., p. 200.

57. The inaugural address set the tone for this broad issue orientation: "I propose to appoint a national commission for a searching investigation of the whole structure of our Federal system of jurisprudence, to include the method of enforcement of the eighteenth amendment and the causes of abuse under it."

58. H. C. Hoover to G. W. Wickersham, 5/27/29, HHPL.

59. G. W. Wickersham to the assembled Commission, 5/28/29, HHPL.

60. H. C. Hoover to R. P. Lamont, 6/1/29, HHPL.

61. H. C. Hoover to G. W. Wickersham, 6/1/29, HHPL.

62. W. D. Mitchell, press release, 3/29, HHPL.

63. H. T. Jones to W. H. Newton, 10/31/31, HHPL.

64. Of the federal prisoners housed in federal institutions on June 30, 1929, 19 percent had been sentenced under the Volstead Act and 27 percent for Harrison (drug) Act violations.

65. W. S. Myers and W. H. Newton, *The Hoover Administration: A Documented Narrative* (New York: Charles Scribner's Sons, 1936), p. 535.

66. H. C. Hoover (ed. William S. Myers), *The State Papers and Other Writings of Herbert Hoover* [hereafter *State Papers*] (New York: Doubleday, Doran, 1934), p. 14. The *State Papers* single out the termination of William A. De Groot, chief prosecutor, Office of the U. S. Attorney, Eastern District of New York.

67. *New York Times*, 3/29/29.

68. M. W. Willebrandt to L. Richey, 3/27/29, HHPL. Willebrandt wrote: "Here is a memorandum of United States Attorneys who should be removed and of United States Attorneys who should be called in and made to function

better, which was requested of me. It may be handy for The Chief to have it unsigned. It consequently is in form suitable to be lost or handed to anyone else."

69. G. W. Wickersham to H. C. Hoover, 5/29/29, HHPL.

70. "Annual Message to the Congress on the State of the Union," 12/2/30, *Public Papers.*

71. Quoted in Smith, op. cit., p. 159.

72. H. F. Pringle, "Profiles—The President—III," *New Yorker,* 1/10/31, p. 22.

73. See K. F. Gerould, "Jessica and Al Capone," *Harper's Monthly Magazine,* 6/31, pp. 93–97. Capone was described as a "straight shooter" by Louis Adamic, *Dynamite: The Story of Class Violence in America* (New York: Viking, 1931).

74. F. D. Pasley, *Al Capone: The Biography of a Self-Made Man* (New York: Ives Washburn, 1930), p. 84.

75. Hoover, *Memoirs,* pp. 276–277.

76. There is something of an irony in this meeting. It was convened by Hoover to chase a gangster believed to have violated the tax laws and other federal laws. Huston later resigned under fire as Republican chairman because he could not recall from whom he had borrowed campaign funds to gamble, both privately and in the stock market. He had been Hoover's assistant secretary of commerce in the Coolidge administration. See Burner, op. cit., p. 308.

77. George E. Q. Johnson wrote to Attorney General Mitchell in July 1929 outlining, among several details, the steps he would take to attack the gangs, enforce the prohibition law and maintain the integrity of his office staff. He said he had worked out a plan "to reach gangs by cutting off their revenue, since money is the only thing that holds lawless gangs and organizations together." He said that gang money was derived mainly from gambling and prohibition, but the only way to get results was to instill cooperation with the state's attorney's office to rebuild the "continuity of interest" lost by the Prohibition department and the local police. He concluded that "what they really need is intelligent leadership and direction and this is lacking." He considered intimidation of witnesses as the "greatest, single difficulty in the administration of the law" in his district, thus calling for a new system of "protection of witnesses when they testify from threats made against them and who are placed in real danger." Further, he suggested that the attorney general was wholly dependent on information supplied by government agencies. He wanted Mitchell to supply him with two or three investigators "who would investigate conditions under his direction when he has reason to think that he is being mislead or that something is covered up." G. E. Q. Johnson to W. D. Mitchell, 7/26/29, Archives.

78. Unauthored file memo, 9/20/29, DOJ-Tax. The list of those under investigation included Al Capone, Ralph Capone, Terrence Druggen, Frank A. Lake, Gene Garfield Oliver, Jake Gusick, Johnny Patton, Louis Lipschultz, Louis Cowan, Joseph Fusco, George Howlett, Homer T. Ellis, Oliver J. Ellis, Hawthorne Kennel Club, Illinois Kennel Club, and E. J. O'Hare.

79. G. E. Q. Johnson to W. D. Mitchell, 9/21/29, DOJ-Tax. Johnson wrote,

"The frauds are against the United States as well as against the citizens of these municipalities. In my judgment, prosecution should be expedited and should be vigorously forceful. Any laxity on the part of the United States Attorney in Chicago in the prosecution of these frauds would subject me to much criticism."

80. S. Bates to W. D. Mitchell, "Accomplishments of the Bureau of Prisons Since March 4, 1929," 2/15/33, HHPL.

81. *Outlook Magazine*, 11/25/11. Gatewood has argued that Roosevelt's position on vigilantism viewed the danger to white people as a greater concern for law and order than for justice for blacks. Gatewood, op. cit., p. 38.

82. Zangrando, op. cit., pp. 41–45.

83. Warren Harding had, in earlier years, favored lynchings under certain circumstances and later justified others. See R. C. Downes, *The Rise of Warren Gamaliel Harding, 1865–1920* (Columbus: Ohio State University Press, 1970), pp. 51–52, 536–537, 548–550, 561.

84. C. E. Swartz to H. C. Hoover, 6/24/29, HHPL.

85. Records at HHPL do not establish any correspondence with Hoover and the White House until December 1931.

86. *Literary Digest*, 1/23/32.

87. *New York Times*, 3/2/32.

88. Lindbergh had traveled in 1927 to all forty-eight states to promote commercial aviation, construction of local airports, and airport safety measures with funding from the Daniel Guggenheim Fund for the Promotion of Aeronautics. T. D. Crouch, *Charles A. Lindbergh: An American Life* (Washington, D.C.: Smithsonian Institution Press, 1977), pp. 40–41.

89. For an analysis of the news reporting of the event, see H. M. Hughes, "The Lindbergh Case: A Study of Human Interest and Politics," *American Journal of Sociology* 42 (July 1936): 32–54.

90. A. M. Lindbergh, *Hour of Gold, Hour of Lead: Diaries and Letters of Anne Morrow Lindbergh, 1929–1932* (New York: Harcourt, Brace Jovanovich, 1973), pp. 211–212.

91. *New York Times*, 3/3/32.

92. Idem, 2/27/32.

93. The definitive account of conditions before, during, and after the march is found in D. J. Lisio, *The President and Protest: Hoover, Conspiracy, and the Bonus Riot* (Columbia: University of Missouri Press, 1974).

CHAPTER 2

1. Hoover, *Memoirs*, p. 198.

2. D. B. Burner, "Before the Crash: Hoover's First Eight Months in the Presidency," in *The Hoover Presidency: A Reappraisal*, ed. M. L. Fausold and G. T. Mazuzan, (Albany: State University of New York Press, 1974), pp. 50–68.

3. G. T. Allison, *Essence of Decision: Explaining the Cuban Missile Crisis* (Boston: Little, Brown, 1971), pp. 28–35.

4. G. H. Nash, *The Life of Herbert Hoover: The Engineer, 1874–1914* (New York: W. W. Norton, 1983), p. 481.

5. Ibid., pp. 570–576.

6. G. H. Nash, *The Life of Herbert Hoover: The Humanitarian, 1914–1917* (New York: W. W. Norton, 1988), pp. 362–378.

7. J. A. Schwarz, *The Interregnum of Despair: Hoover, Congress, and the Depression* (Urbana: University of Illinois Press, 1970), pp. 230–238.

8. R. N. Smith, *An Uncommon Man: The Triumph of Herbert Hoover* (New York: Simon and Schuster, 1984), p. 99. As Smith observes, Hoover "presided over an endless round of public conferences and private think tanks, all designed to educate decision makers, inspire legislation or promote grass-roots cooperation" (p. 100).

9. Best, op. cit., p. 103.

10. E. E. Robinson and V. D. Bornet, *Herbert Hoover: President of the United States* (Stanford: Stanford University Press, 1975), pp. 25–38.

11. Smith, op. cit., p. 94. As one recent author characterized the thinking of Taylor and Gantt, "the system must be first"; T. P. Hughes, *American Genesis: A Century of Invention and Techno-Logical Enthusiasm* (New York: Penguin, 1989).

12. See "The Progressive as Domestic Dynamo," in J. H. Wilson, *Herbert Hoover: Forgotten Progressive* (Boston: Little, Brown, 1975), pp. 79–121.

13. Nash, 1988, op. cit., p. 377.

14. G. D. Best, *The Politics of American Individualism: Herbert Hoover in Transition, 1918–1921* (Westport: Greenwood, 1975), p. 178.

15. Wilson, op. cit., pp. 68–69.

16. J. Brandes, "Product Diplomacy: Herbert Hoover's Anti-Monopoly Campaign at Home and Abroad," in *Herbert Hoover As Secretary of Commerce: Studies in New Era Thought and Practice*, ed. E. W. Hawley et al. (Iowa City: University of Iowa Press, 1981), pp. 186–192.

17. D. R. McCoy, "To the White House: Herbert Hoover, August 1927–March 1929," in Fausold and Mazuzan, op. cit., pp. 32–33.

18. D. Burner, *Herbert Hoover: A Public Life* (New York: Alfred A. Knopf, 1979), pp. 192–199.

19. McCoy, op. cit., p. 36.

20. See his acceptance speech, A. E. Smith, *Campaign Speeches of Governor Alfred E. Smith* (Washington, D.C.: Democratic National Committee, 1929), pp. 1–26.

21. Ibid., p. 1.

22. Robinson and Bornet, op. cit., pp. 20–24.

23. R. V. Peel and T. C. Donnelly, *The 1932 Campaign: An Analysis* (New York: Farrar & Rinehart, 1935), p. 4.

24. R. C. Silva, *Rum, Religion and Votes: 1928 Re-Examined* (University Park: University of Pennsylvania Press, 1962).

25. H. C. Hoover, *The New Day: Campaign Speeches of Herbert Hoover, 1928* (Stanford: Stanford University Press, 1928), p. 5.

26. Ibid.

27. Ibid, p. 30.

28. In this context, I can agree with some scholars who have referred to Prohibition as the "phony referendum" of the 1928 election. See A. J. Lichtman, *Prejudice and the Old Politics: The Presidential Election of 1928* (Chapel Hill: University of North Carolina Press, 1979), p. 92.

29. Ibid., p. 32.

30. Ibid., p. 36.

31. Ibid.

32. It is reasonable to speculate that Hoover had found some facetious humor in the irony of former attorney general Harry M. Daugherty's speech to the 1924 American Bar Association meeting, titled "Respect for the Law."

33. Hoover, *The New Day*, p. 70.

34. Ibid., p. 98.

35. Ibid., p. 104.

36. Ibid., p. 106.

37. Ibid., p. 107.

38. Ibid.

39. Ibid., p. 110.

40. Ibid., p. 111.

41. Ibid., p. 166.

42. Ibid., p. 208.

43. Ibid., p. 212.

44. While relaxing in Florida in January 1929, Hoover expressed fear that the nation had excessive expectations about his ability to solve domestic problems. See quotation in Burner, op. cit., p. 211.

45. A. DeConde, *Herbert Hoover's Latin-American Policy* (New York: Octagon, 1970), pp. 13–24.

46. Speech upon arrival in Peru, 12/5/28, *Public Papers*.

47. Inaugural Address, 3/4/29, *Public Papers*.

48. "Address to the Associated Press: Law Enforcement and Respect for the Law," 4/22/29, *Public Papers*.

49. Ibid.

50. "Annual Message to the Congress on the State of the Union," 12/3/29, *Public Papers*.

51. News conference, 12/27/29, *Public Papers*. The use of the word 'fire' is interesting in the context of events. On December 24, 1929, a major fire in the executive office wing of the White House forced Hoover to move to other office quarters for several weeks.

52. P. Way, *The Encyclopedia of Espionage: Codes and Ciphers* (London: Danbury, 1977), pp. 126–131.

53. Ibid., p. 128.

54. R. L. Jones, *The Eighteenth Amendment and Our Foreign Relations* (New York: Thomas Y. Crowell, 1933), pp. 78–85.

55. *Literary Digest*, 4/6/29, 5/11/29.

56. K. C. Frazer, "The 'I'm Alone' Case and the Doctrine of 'Hot Pursuit,'" *North Carolina Law Review* 7 (1929): 413–422.

57. L. Englemann, *Intemperance: The Lost War Against Liquor* (New York: Free Press, 1979), p. 119.

58. C. E. Stewart to W. D. Mitchell, 3/20/28, Archives.

59. J. B. Reynolds to J. Marshall, 3/21/28, Archives.

60. This is an excellent case to demonstrate the attorney general's lack of power to terminate the employment of a U.S. attorney. See J. Eisenstein, *Counsel for the United States: U.S. Attorneys in the Political and Legal Systems* (Baltimore: Johns Hopkins University Press, 1978), pp. 9–13.

61. H. V. Kaltenborn, 5/2/29, Archives. A year later, De Groot sued the *Brooklyn Daily Eagle* for defamatory comments.

62. H. C. Hoover to W. D. Mitchell, 1/18/30, HHPL.

63. Public safety director Lemuel B. Schofield interviewed Capone immediately after the arrest. The interview contained several obvious contradictions, including Capone's alleged statement that he was more secure than he had been in years. Articles containing the most detailed reporting of the incident appeared in the *Philadelphia Inquirer*, 5/17/29 and thereafter.

64. It was reported that Capone admitted he had just come from an Atlantic City "peace conference." A news magazine reported that "an agreement was reached, he revealed, that gang slayings in Chicago should cease." *Literary Digest*, 6/15/29.

65. *New York Times*, 8/18/29. On September 8, Capone had his tonsils removed, and on September 22 the *New York Times* reported he had filed his third appeal of his conviction. The public safety director's dialogue with Capone appears contrived for publication.

66. Philadelphia police records of the Capone gun-toting case have been destroyed. No evidence has ever been offered to establish possible collusion between federal agents and local police to secure Capone's arrest outside Chicago, away from Miami and close to Washington, D.C.

67. F. D. Pasley, *Al Capone: The Biography of a Self-Made Man* (New York: Ives Washburn, 1930), pp. 334–335.

68. George Nash observed this characteristic in Hoover's earlier days as a mining executive: "The capacity to select able lieutenants and to inspire their devotion was one of his notable talents. It was, he knew, the foundation of his own success." Nash, 1983, op. cit., p. 571.

69. *New York Times*, 6/3/29.

70. D. Burner, op. cit, p. 205.

71. M. W. Willebrandt to L. Richey, 5/6/29, HHPL.

72. *New York World*, 5/6/29. M. W. Willebrandt to L. Richey, 5/14/29, HHPL. Mark Requa was a Hoover loyalist and insider from the Food Relief era.

73. See M. W. Willebrandt, "Federal and State Control of Air Carriers by Certificates of Convenience and Necessity," *Journal of Commerce and Air Law* 3 (April 1932): 159–166.

74. M. W. Willebrandt to H. C. Hoover, 5/26/29, HHPL.

75. H. C. Hoover to M. W. Willebrandt, 5/28/29, HHPL.

76. H. C. Hoover to J. Richardson, 5/31/29, HHPL.

77. H. C. Hoover to L. Richey, 6/3/29, HHPL.

78. See feature article by H. H. Hart in *New York Times*, 4/30/30. Dr. Hart was a consultant to the Wickersham Commission.

79. S. Bates to F. Loveland, Jr., 6/17/29, Archives.

80. W. D. Mitchell to A. M Hyde, 6/24/29, Archives.

81. R. N. Smith, op. cit., p. 112. An excellent and detailed source of information on Hoover's first months in office is found in D. B. Burner's "Before the Crash: Hoover's First Eight Months in Office." In Fausold and Mazuzan, op. cit., pp. 50–68.

82. S. Bates to S. Glueck, 8/1/29; S. Glueck to S. Bates, 8/6/29, Archives.

83. He also wrote: "All of the colored cell houses and dormatories [sic] maintained good order during the riot and there was none of this class of population that took any big part in the demonstration and all were taken to the dining room today and fed. We almost filled the dining room with the colored population and outside gangs, as well as the work gangs on the inside industries." Fifteen ring leaders were identified, and their biographies were supplied to Bates for possible movement to other institutions. T. B. White to S. Bates, 8/2/29, Archives. Of the three wounded inmates, two recovered quickly and the third had a leg amputated.

84. S. Bates to A. H. MacCormick, 8/3/29, Archives. MacCormick reported three days later, "that the prison is so far beyond its physical capacity and is undermanned is the real reason for the food, the curtailment of mail, and the curtailment of outdoor recreation. It is also causing men to be dealt with in such masses that there are unquestionably just causes for complaint that their personal troubles, here and at home, are not given enough attention. There is little time to devote to the individual." A. MacCormick to S. Bates, 8/5/29, Archives.

85. S. Bates to A. H. MacCormick, 8/9/29; A. H. MacCormick to S. Bates, 8/25/29, Archives. Regarding Alcatraz, MacCormick observed, "it would be much more difficult to take over than the D. B. at Leavenworth because it could not well be operated as a branch of any other institution." MacCormick wrote to Bates two weeks earlier with observations of the disciplinary barracks and their great potential for housing at least 900 inmates: "I cannot believe that if President Hoover would walk through this institution and then walk through that one [Leavenworth main institution] he would lose fifteen minutes in deciding to tell the Army to close up shop and give the whole institution to us until the contemplated program of expansion can be put through. It certainly made the Warden and me weep to see that hugh [sic] plant, . . . which there is no finer in the Country, being used at half capacity and supplied with all the facilities which we so greatly need here and at Atlanta." He concluded, "I think you will have a tough fight with the War Department, but it is worth it."

86. In a food allocation report for July 1, 1928 to June 30, 1929, it was clear that food rations had been reduced at Leavenworth. Archives.

Food Rations, Leavenworth, 1928 v. 1929

1928		1929	
July	$24,342.04	January	$23,037.74
August	22,752.72	February	20,701.54
September	24,685.18	March	22,092.46
October	25,938.41	April	21,329.99
November	27,726.72	May	22,652.02
December	26,697.23	June	20,440.93

The total decrease of $21,887.62 was an economy move.

CHAPTER 3

1. E. H. Sutherland, *Criminology* (Philadelphia: J. B. Lippincott, 1924), p. 11.

2. D. F. Henderson, *Congress, Courts, and Criminals: The Development of Federal Criminal Law, 1801–1829* (Westport: Greenwood, 1985), pp. 3–16.

3. Ibid. See also A. J. Dodge, *Origin and Development of the Office of the Attorney General* (Washington, D.C.: U.S. Government Printing Office, 1929), p. 73.

4. M. K. B. Tachau, *Federal Courts in the Early Republic: Kentucky 1789–1816* (Princeton: Princeton University Press, 1978), p. 11.

5. J. C. Furnas, *The Americans: A Social History of the United States, 1587–1914* (New York: G. P. Putnam's Sons, 1969), pp. 208–209, 378–380.

6. W. S. Bowen and H. D. Neal, *The United States Secret Service* (Philadelphia: Chilton, 1960), pp. 12–17; D. R. Johnson, *American Law Enforcement: A History* (St. Louis: Forum, 1981), pp. 73–86.

7. W. S. McFeeley, *Grant, A Biography* (New York: W. W. Norton, 1981), pp. 368–369.

8. E. Foner, *Reconstruction: America's Unfinished Revolution, 1863–1877* (New York: Harper & Row, 1988), pp. 454–459; see also H. M. Hyman, *A More Perfect Union: The Impact of the Civil War and Reconstruction on the Constitution* (Boston: Houghton Mifflin, 1975), pp. 478–515.

9. A. W. Trelease, *White Terror: The Ku Klux Klan Conspiracy and Southern Reconstruction* (New York: Harper & Row, 1971), pp. 415–416.

10. F. M. Kaiser, "Origins of Secret Service Protection of the President: Personal, Interagency, and Institutional Conflict," *Presidential Studies Quarterly* 18 (Winter 1988): 101–128; M. Leech, *In the Days of McKinley* (New York: Harper & Row, 1959), pp. 231–232.

11. F. S. Calhoun, *The Lawmen, United States Marshals and Their Deputies, 1789–1989* (Washington, D.C.: Smithsonian Institution Press, 1989), p. 150.

12. Ibid., pp. 201–227.

13. L. D. Ball, *The United States Marshals of New Mexico and Arizona Territories, 1846–1912* (Albuquerque: University of New Mexico Press, 1978), pp. 239–244.

14. Ibid., p. 235.

15. Conclusions about linkages between law enforcement and military intelligence functions, and about the origins of new law enforcement agencies have been drawn from W. B. Gatewood, Jr., *Theodore Roosevelt and the Art of Controversy: Episodes of the White House Years* (Baton Rouge: Louisiana State University Press, 1970); J. M. Dorwart, *Conflict of Duty: The U.S. Navy's Intelligence Dilemma, 1919–1945* (Annapolis: Naval Institute Press, 1983); J. M. Dorwart, *The Office of Naval Intelligence: The Birth of America's First Intelligence Agency, 1865–1918* (Annapolis: Naval Institute Press, 1979); M. B. Powe, *The Emergence of the War Department Intelligence Agency: 1885–1918* (Manhattan: American Military Institute, 1975); R. G. Powers, *Secrecy and Power: The Life of J. Edgar Hoover* (New York: Free Press, 1987).

16. J. M. Myers, *The Border Wardens* (Englewood Cliffs: Prentice-Hall, 1971), pp. 13–40.

17. There were hundreds of shooting incidents. As violence got closer to Washington, D.C., skepticism about enforcement competence became more vocal. Senator Frank L. Greene was shot in the head on a Washington street in February 1924 by Prohibition Bureau agent O. E. Fischer. After undergoing two surgeries and nearly dying, Senator Greene partially recovered. See *New York Times*, 2/16/24–3/15/27.

18. J. S. Berman, *Police Administration and Progressive Reform: Theodore Roosevelt As Police Commissioner of New York* (Westport: Greenwood, 1987). An early work that suggests the direction of New York's reforms is W. McAdoo's *Guarding a Great City* (New York: Harper & Brothers, 1906). McAdoo was police commissioner from 1904 to 1906. Even Chicago had called in a group of academic and legal scholars to look into police problems and committed to a thorough study of their implications. See L. D. White and the Citizens' Police Committee, *Chicago Police Problems* (Chicago: University of Chicago Press, 1931).

19. A. V. Lashly, *Professional Criminal and Organized Crime* (New York: American Bar Association, 1928).

20. The literature on this topic is thin, but some scholarly sources include W. A. Tidwell, J. O. Hall, and D. W. Gaddy, *Come Retribution: The Confederate Secret Service and the Assassination of Lincoln* (Jackson: University of Mississippi Press, 1988), pp. 155–170, 212–222; D. Kahn, *The Codebreakers: The Story of Secret Writing* (New York: Macmillan, 1967), pp. 214–350; Dorwart, 1979 op. cit.; W. R. Corson, *Armies of Ignorance: The Rise of the American Intelligence Empire* (New York: Dial, 1977), pp. 41–76.

21. See an excellent overview of the emergence of private detectives, such as Allan Pinkerton, in C. A. Siringo, *A Cowboy Detective: A True Story of Twenty-two Years with a World-Famous Detective Agency* (Lincoln: University of Nebraska Press, 1988). Reprint of 1912 edition.

22. J. D. Calder, "Industrial Guards in the Nineteenth and Early Twentieth Centuries: The Mean Years," *Journal of Security Administration* 8 (December 1985): 11–22.

23. The development of internal intelligence functions prior to the twentieth century is reviewed in R. E. Morgan, *Domestic Intelligence: Monitoring Dissent in America* (Austin: University of Texas Press, 1980), pp. 15–36.

24. T. H. Price and R. Spillane, "The Commissioner of Internal Revenue As a Policeman," *Outlook* (11/27/18): 498–505.

25. G. T. Marx, *Undercover: Police Surveillance in America* (Berkeley: University of California Press, 1988), p. 31. The *Olmstead* case in 1928 was the first to test wiretapping. See E. J. Lapidus, *Eavesdropping on Trial* (Rochelle Park: Hayden, 1974), pp. 16–18.

26. K. A. Kerr, *Organized for Prohibition: A New History of the Anti-Saloon League* (New Haven: Yale University Press, 1985), pp. 222–235.

27. See generally, P. Sayre, *The Life of Roscoe Pound* (Iowa City: University of Iowa Press, 1948).

28. R. Pound, "The Causes of Popular Dissatisfaction with the Administration of Justice," *American Bar Association Report* 29 (1906): 395–417.

29. S. Walker, *Popular Justice: A History of American Criminal Justice* (New York: Oxford University Press, 1980), pp. 170–172.

30. The preface to the 1929 edition was dated November 7, after his appointment to Hoover's Commission on Law Observance and Enforcement. He noted the passage of time and implied that some conditions may have changed. Referring to his service on the Hoover Commission, he wrote: "This caution seems expedient lest [the lectures] should appear to pass a present judgment on what I am now required to look into more deeply."

31. Walker, op. cit., p. 171.

32. R. Pound, *Criminal Justice in America* (New York: Henry Holt, 1930), pp. 213–215.

33. E. H. Sutherland, *On Analyzing Crime*, ed. K. Schuessler (Chicago: University of Chicago Press, 1973), p. xi.

34. M. S. Gaylord and J. F. Galliher, *The Criminology of Edwin Sutherland* (New Brunswick: Transaction, 1988), pp. 96–98. Sutherland delivered an address at the 1928 American Prison Association meeting titled "Crime and the Conflict Process." See *American Prison Congress Proceedings, 1928*.

35. See, for example, L. Wirth, *The Ghetto* (Chicago: University of Chicago Press, 1928); J. F. Fishman, *Crucibles of Crime* (New York: Cosmopolis, 1923); L. Lewis and H. J. Smith, *Chicago: The History of Its Reputation* (New York: Harcourt, Brace, 1929).

36. Among them *Sociology Before Comte* (1917); *History of the Penal Reformatory and Correctional Institutions of New Jersey* (1918); *Social History of the Western World* (1921); *Progress of American Penology* (1922); *Sociology of Political Theory* (1923); *The New History and the Social Studies* (1924); *History and Social Intelligence* (1926); *The Repression of Crime* (1926); *The Evolution of Penology in Pennsylvania* (1927); co-authored *An Economic and Social History of Europe* (1927), *In Quest of Truth and Justice* (1928), and *L'Angleterre et la Guerre Mondiale* (1928).

37. His iconoclasm, however, carried him into efforts to rewrite the history of World War I, and his "penchant for writing counterpropaganda disguised as history" was probably the characteristic that separated him from Sutherland and others. See R. Turnbaugh, "The FBI and Harry Elmer Barnes," *Historian* 42 (May 1980): 385–398.

38. Other early books confirmed his diversity of thought, as well as his formal training in economics and political science: *The Labor Movement* (1921); *Darker Faces of the South* (1924), and *The Mexican Revolution* (1928).

39. Herbert Hoover was a trustee of the institute, along with Raymond B. Fosdick, Frank O. Lowden, and Charles E. Merriam.

40. In 1915, Gault was asked to study crime in Chicago for the Chicago Council for Investigation of Crime.

41. B. D. Karl, *Charles E. Merriam and the Study of Politics* (Chicago: University of Chicago Press, 1974), p. 144; see also R. Seidelman and E. J. Harpham, *Disenchanted Realists: Political Science and the American Crisis, 1884–1984* (Albany: State University of New York Press, 1985), pp. 109–126.

42. L. Kalman, *Legal Realism at Yale, 1927–1960* (Chapel Hill: University of North Carolina Press, 1986), pp. 45–46.

43. H. N. Hirsch, *The Enigma of Felix Frankfurter* (New York: Basic Books, 1981), p. 72.

44. D. Smith, *Zechariah Chafee, Jr.: Defender of Liberty and Law* (Cambridge: Harvard University Press, 1986), p. 5.

45. R. Moley, *Our Criminal Courts* (New York: Minton, Balch, 1930), p. xv; see also W. L. Morse and R. C. Moley, "Crime Commissions as Aids in the Legal-Social Field," *Annals of the American Academy of Political and Social Science* 145 (September 1929): 68–73.

46. S. B. Warner, "Crimes Known to the Police—An Index of Crime?" *Harvard Law Review* 45 (1931): 307–317.

47. S. Bates, "Criminal Records and Statistics," *Journal of Criminal Law and Criminology* 19 (December 1928–1929): 8–14.

48. G. E. and E. H. Carte, *Police Reform in the United States: The Era of August Vollmer* (Berkeley: University of California Press, 1975).

49. This history is summarized by J. P. Kenney, *The California Police* (Springfield: Charles C. Thomas, 1964).

50. "School for Police as Planned at Berkeley" [with A. Schneider] (1917); "The Convicted Man—His Treatment While Before the Court" (1918); "The Policeman as a Social Worker" (1919); "Revision of the Acherley *Modus Operandi* System" (1919); "Bureau of Criminal Records" (1920); "Practical Method for Selecting Policemen" (1921); "Aims and Ideals of the Police" (1922); and "Narcotic Control Association of California" (1922).

51. Carte and Carte, op. cit., pp. 19–21, 129–130.

52. J. Liss and S. Schlossman, "The Contours of Crime Prevention in August Vollmer's Berkeley," *Research in Law, Deviance and Social Control* 6 (1984): 79–107.

53. Cited in Carte and Carte, op. cit., p. 57.

54. Ibid., pp. 56–57.

55. D. R. Johnson, *American Law Enforcement: A History* (St. Louis: Forum, 1981), p. 70.

56. *New York Times*, 5/5/29.

57. S. Bates, "Address" *American Prison Association Proceedings* (1926): 22–24.

58. S. Bates to W. F. Ogburn, 4/19/32, Archives.

59. After addressing the National Fire Prevention Association in May, 1932, Bates remarked, "They seemed quite struck with the analogy which I made between fire fighting and crime fighting to the effect that prevention is much more effective than attempting to remedy the situation after it is too late."

60. S. Bates to W. M. Tippy, unknown date/1931, Archives. Tippy was executive secretary of the Federated Council of the Church of Christ.

61. S. Bates, "Scientific Penology," *Prison Journal* 10 (January 1930): 1–2; "A Program of Protective Penology," *Prison Journal* 10 (October 1930): 16–18; "Address," *American Prison Association Proceedings, 1927*, pp. 220–225.

62. Bates believed that such associations could encourage politicians to address risky political issues, such as prisoner idleness, prisoner employment, and reforms necessary to aid prisoner readmission to society.

63. See a comprehensive critique of criminal statistics and the politics of their use by the notorious trial attorney, Clarence Darrow, "Crime and the Alarmists," *Harper's Monthly Magazine* 153 (October 1926).

64. The British had moved in the same direction toward an institutionally based applied criminology. See D. Garland, "British Criminology Before 1935," *British Journal of Criminology* 28 (Spring 1988): 1–18. An American

236

article fitting this tradition was written by F. H. Warren, "Crime—A Complex or a Crisis," *Notre Dame Lawyer* 9 (December 1928): 146–177.

65. Moley, op. cit., p. 747.

66. L. N. Robinson, *History of Criminal Statistics* (Boston: Little, Brown, 1911).

67. IACP urged measurements of change in crime over time, centralization of records, ongoing statistical research, and establishment of uniform definitions for personal and property crimes.

68. N. Timasheff, *Sociological Theory: Its Nature and Growth* (New York: Random House, 1964), p. 104.

69. R. Gault, *Criminology* (Boston: D. C. Heath, 1932), p. 27.

70. E. H. Sutherland, *Criminology* (Philadelphia: J. B. Lippincott, 1924), p. 11.

71. H. E. Barnes, *The Repression of Crime* (New York: George E. Doran, 1926), p. 344.

72. Ibid., p. 345.

73. Gaylord and Galliher, op. cit., p. 66.

74. Sutherland, op. cit, p. 590.

75. Ibid.

76. Ibid., p. 599.

77. Ibid., p. 618.

78. J. H. Laub, *Criminology in the Making: An Oral History* (Boston: Northeastern University Press, 1983), p. 168.

79. T. Sellin, "Is Murder Increasing in Europe?" *Annals of the American Academy of Political and Social Sciences* 219 (May 1926): 241.

80. F. E. Haynes, *Criminology* (New York: McGraw-Hill, 1930), p. 4.

81. Ibid., p. 6.

82. Ibid., p. 396.

83. J. L. Gillen, *Criminology and Penology* (New York: Century, 1926, rev. 1945), p. 599.

84. Ibid.

85. Ibid., pp. 530–545.

86. Ibid., p. 499.

87. New York: Thomas Y. Crowell, 1922.

88. Ibid., p. 284.

89. W. C. Reckless, *Vice in Chicago* (Chicago: University of Chicago Press, 1931), p. viii.

90. Ibid., p. ix.

91. Ibid., p. 270.

92. Ibid.

93. Ibid., p. 277.

94. F. M. Thrasher, *The Gang: A Study of 1,313 Gangs in Chicago* (Chicago: University of Chicago Press, 1927), pp. 487–532.

95. Goddard's *The Criminal Imbecile* (1915), Weidensall's *The Mentality of the Criminal Woman* (1916), Jacoby's *The Unsound Mind and the Criminal Law* (1918), Healy and Healy, *Pathological Lying, Accusation, and Swindling* (1922), Hoag's *Crime, Abnormal Minds, and the Law* (1923), Smith's *The Psychology of the Criminal* (1923), Singer and Krohn's *Insanity and Law*

(1924), Glueck's *Mental Disorder and the Criminal Law* (1925), Sullivan's *Crime and Insanity* (1925), Healy and Bronner's *Delinquents and Criminals: Their Making and Unmaking* (1926), Murchison's *Criminal Intelligence* (1926).

96. Gault, op. cit., pp. 21, 33, 34.

97. R. Moley, "The Collection of Criminal Statistics in the United States" *Michigan Law Review* 26 (May 1928): 748.

98. Ibid., p. 751.

99. Ibid., p. 752. Suggested categories were nationality, occupation, age, marital status, and previous criminal record.

100. Ibid., p. 753.

101. Ibid., p. 760.

102. Ibid., p. 759.

103. Ibid., p. 762.

104. In 1917, he published an extensive prison history titled *History of the Penal Reformatory and Correctional Institutions of the State of New Jersey*, a book that proclaimed the capacity of the individual to reform and the institutional practices best suited to aid reform. In 1927, he published another state-level study, *Evolution of Penology in Pennsylvania*, that stressed the role of good political and economic salesmanship in introducing New York's Auburn prison experiment into Pennsylvania and the appeal of the Pennsylvania system instituted by Quaker reformers who viewed the inmate first as human and second as economic contributor.

105. Barnes, op. cit., 1926, p. 377.

106. Consider *Greed* (1924); *Condemned* (1929); *Spies* (1928); *Sherlock Holmes* (1922); *The Mysterious Dr. Fu Manchu* (1929); *A City Gone Wild* (1928), *Underworld* (1929); *The Racket* (1929).

107. Sayre, op. cit., p. 253.

CHAPTER 4

1. F. Frankfurter to N. D. Baker, 7/20/29, Archives.

2. T. E. Cronin, "On the Separation of Brain and State: Implications for the Presidency," in M. Landy, *Modern Presidents and the Presidency* (Lexington: Lexington Books, 1985), p. 52.

3. Ibid., p. 51. This refers to the transformation of the president from informed candidate to sophisticated policy maker.

4. The 257 boxes of commission records are stored at the National Archives and Records Administration facility in Suitland, Maryland.

5. The meeting was held in the Department of Justice building because the commission's new offices in the Tower Building at 14th and K Streets were not yet complete.

6. H. C. Hoover to the commission, 5/30/29, Archives.

7. Ibid.

8. News conference, 3/19/29, *Public Papers*.

9. "Special Message to the Congress Proposing a Study of the Reorganization of Prohibition Enforcement Responsibilities," 6/6/29, *Public Papers*.

10. News conference, 10/1/29, *Public Papers*.

11. "White House Statement about a Proposed Joint Select Committee to Study Prohibition Enforcement," 1/10/30, *Public Papers*.

12. Minutes of the commission's meeting, 5/28/29, Archives.

13. W. S. Kenyon to G. W. Wickersham, 3/23/31, Archives.

14. D. J. Lisio, *Hoover, Blacks, & Lily-Whites: A Study of Southern Strategies* (Chapel Hill: University of North Carolina Press, 1985), pp. 73–75.

15. Minutes, 5/28/29, Archives.

16. S. W. Livermore, *Woodrow Wilson and the War Congress, 1916–18* (Seattle: University of Washington Press, 1968), especially the chapter on Wilson's defense of Baker's management of the War Department, "The Badgering of Baker," pp. 91–104. Like Hoover as Wilson's food administrator, Baker faced a persistently critical Congress during World War I. Baker's abilities to survive such conditions and to have recognized Hoover's contributions to the policy of feeding the Belgians made him one of the most likely and qualified persons to head a potentially controversial crime commission. On the matter of Baker's sentiments about Hoover during the war, see G. H. Nash, *The Life of Herbert Hoover: The Humanitarian, 1914–1917* (New York: W. W. Norton, 1988), p. 372.

17. Pound's career can be traced through his writings, some of which include "The Causes of Popular Dissatisfaction with the Administration of Justice," *American Bar Association Reporter* 29 (1906): 395–411; "Law in Books and Law in Action," *American Law Review* 44 (1910): 12–36; "The Scope and Purpose of Sociological Jurisprudence," *Harvard Law Review* 25 (1912): 510–526; "Courts and Legislation," *American Political Science Review* 7 (1913): 365–374; "The Call for a Realist Jurisprudence," *Harvard Law Review* 44 (1931): 697–711. A biography appears in D. Wigdor, *Roscoe Pound* (Westport: Greenwood, 1974).

18. H. F. Pringle, *The Life and Times of William Howard Taft: A Biography*, vol. 2 (Hamden: Archon, 1964), p. 662.

19. W. F. Swindler, *Court and Constitution in the 20th Century: The Old Legality 1889–1932* (Indianapolis: Bobbs-Merrill, 1969), p. 137.

20. Hoover's long absences from the United States, some suggested, had disqualified him for office. Wickersham argued successfully for Hoover's efforts to keep his home in the United States. See E. S. Corwin, *The President: Office and Powers 1787–1957*, 4th ed. (New York: New York University Press, 1957), p. 330.

21. Wickersham sent Pound a "confidential report," which had also been sent to Hoover, regarding the progress of the commission over the first five months of operation: "I think it will refresh your memory as to things you know of, and will give you some of the things done by committees of which you are not a member and which have not been brought to your attention." G. W. Wickersham to R. Pound, 10/29/29, Archives.

22. R. Pound to M. Lowenthal, 8/3/29, Archives. A few days later, Pound had learned more about Hutcheson: "I confess Judge Hutcheson did not look good to me on paper in Who's Who. I am much relieved to hear that he is the right sort of man." R. Pound to M. Lowenthal, 8/9/29, Archives. Lowenthal told Pound that all the commissioners favored Hutcheson's selection and that Pound would find him "different from the judges you recently encoun-

tered in Virginia." M. Lowenthal to R. Pound, 8/5/29, Archives. Lowenthal was apparently not aware at this time of Commissioner Kenyon's objection to Hutcheson: "It seems [Hutcheson] made some expression from the Bench reflecting on the prohibition agents that cut very deeply into their feelings, and they regard him as very hostile. I think this is the most unfortunate appointment that the Commission has made." W. S. Kenyon to M. Lowenthal, 10/21/29, Archives. In contrast, Supreme Court justices Brandeis and Holmes spoke highly of Judge Hutcheson.

23. Judge Hutcheson was a sitting federal district judge for the Southern District of Texas, appointed by President Wilson.

24. R. Pound to G. W. Wickersham, 8/22/29, Archives. Pound's comment was a reflection upon reading Glueck's article on the causes of crime in the September 1929 issue of *Harper's Monthly.* Glueck had completed his study of 1000 criminals, about which a book was later published.

25. R. Pound to M. Lowenthal, 8/14/29, Archives. Felix Frankfurter also supported her appointment and urged that the work be done at the University of Chicago. F. Frankfurter to G. W. Wickersham, 7/1/29, Archives.

26. G. W. Wickersham to J. Michael, 8/22/29, Archives.

27. The list is lengthy, but their collective stature may be properly represented in such names as Robert M. Hutchins, president of the University of Chicago; Mary van Kleeck, director of industrial research for the Russell Sage Foundation; Dean Edith Abbott of the Graduate School of Social Science Administration at the University of Chicago; Sanford Bates, former commissioner of corrections for the State of Massachusetts and U.S. superintendent of prisons; Dr. Rufus von Kleinsmid, president of the University of Southern California. William Ellis, New Jersey commissioner of institutions and agencies; Lewis Lawes, warden of Sing Sing prison; Carl Stern, a New York trial lawyer; and justice of the New York Court of Appeals, Joseph M. Proskauer.

28. In an internal memo by Roscoe Pound, Vollmer was mentioned as the most logical person to do law enforcement research: "Vollmer is recognized everywhere as a remarkable man in respect to experience, wide information and sound sense." 6/17/29, Archives.

29. G. W. Wickersham to A. Vollmer, 6/12/29, Archives.

30. A. Vollmer to G. W. Wickersham, 6/15/29, Archives. Vollmer's doctor, Hubert N. Rowell, told Vollmer that his heart condition required his constant monitoring. Additional work and a long trip east would therefore be out of the question. H. N. Rowell to A. Vollmer, 6/25/29, Archives. Vollmer suggested that Wickersham find a replacement among other police officials he recommended. "Another very logical choice is Colonel Arthur Woods, formerly police commissioner of New York City." A. Vollmer to G. W. Wickersham, 6/26/29, Archives.

31. Just before leaving Berkeley, Vollmer provided Wickersham with an outline of the report of the police consultants, too voluminous for publication here. It demonstrates Vollmer's attention to detail. A. Vollmer to G. W. Wickersham, 9/28/29, Archives.

32. M. Lowenthal to R. Pound, 6/27/29, Archives.

33. G. W. Wickersham to P. J. McCormick, 8/13/30, Archives. He was replaced by his able assistant W. F. Barry in October 1930. Apparently,

Lowenthal quit over the congressional funding issue in the spring of 1930. Zachariah Chafee wrote to Lowenthal just before the latter departed: "May I say that I particularly appreciate all that you have put into this enterprise and realize what a disappointment to you personally the outcome must be." Z. Chafee to M. Lowenthal, 6/27/30, Archives.

34. In a letter to Wickersham, van Kleeck wrote in reference to a new book by Dr. Charles S. Johnson, "The facts here brought together seem to me to indicate that, in view of the disproportionate amount of crime among Negroes, the undependability of the records and the false conclusions often drawn upon them, we cannot entirely ignore the problem as though there were nothing special to say about Negroes in relation to law observance and enforcement. As a matter of fact, the only dependable conclusion which can at this moment be drawn is that crimes and crime statistics regarding Negroes are a very special problem not covered in a general discussion of the whole population." M. van Kleeck to G. W. Wickersham, 2/19/30, Archives. A month later, Walter White, acting secretary of the NAACP emphasized to van Kleeck that a study was necessary of police propensity to arrest Negroes, thus giving the false impression of high levels of Negro crime. W. White to M. van Kleeck, 3/19/30, Archives.

35. Z. Chafee to M. Lowenthal, 6/7/30, Archives. Wickersham wrote on June 12 to say that the budget did not permit an inquiry into the subject of Negroes and criminal justice administration. A few days later, Chafee wrote back: "I hope very much that the solution in the autumn will permit a reconsideration of the relation of the Negro to criminal justice. . . . The situation of the Negroes is comparable in importance to that of the foreign born." Z. Chafee to G. W. Wickersham, 6/18/30, Archives.

36. C. Murphy to H. C. Hoover, 4/20/29, Archives.

37. For a more complete discussion of lynching as political and social concern, see R. L. Zangrando, *The NAACP Crusade against Lynching, 1909–1950* (Philadelphia: Temple University Press, 1980). Communications with Wickersham are mentioned on p. 90.

38. M. Lowenthal to N. D. Baker, 10/21/29, Archives.

39. Lisio, op. cit., p. 194.

40. Bettman had graduated from Harvard Law School in 1898, moving on to become assistant prosecuting attorney in Hamilton County, Ohio, then special assistant to the United States attorney general on matters of enforcing the espionage law and the alien enemy law. Thereafter, Roscoe Pound employed him to work on the prosecution portion of the Cleveland Crime Survey and a similar survey in Boston. Felix Frankfurter, a principal researcher on the Cleveland study urged Wickersham to conduct a thorough review of the Cleveland recommendations to see "what recommendations were adopted and what remained mere print and why, and what effect it has had on Cleveland, now that eight years have elapsed since the Survey." F. Frankfurter to G. W. Wickersham, no date/1929, Archives.

41. Hoover wrote: "I congratulate the Chicago Daily News on its splendid new building and the fifty-four years of distinguished public service which has made it possible. I congratulate Chicago on the fact that one of its great institutions has made such an important contribution to the beauty of the

city and by establishing the principle of air rights construction opened the way to a greater development of its business and commercial resources." He closed with a hope that the *News* "will continue to be a leader of public enterprises and a moulder of sound opinion valuable alike to its community and the nation." The letter to Strong was read during the dedication of the new *News* building. "Message to the Chicago Daily News on the Dedication of Its New Building," 7/8/29, *Public Papers.*

42. Loesch suggested that Colonel Arthur Woods, former New York police commissioner and Hoover insider, was "one of the best equipped to deal with this subject."

43. News conference, 7/19/29, *Public Papers.*

44. "In a business so vast and complex as that of the Federal Government a large part of the research work necessarily is carried out by special commissions and committees, delegated to investigate a given subject and to report to the President or to the Congress. . . . A great majority of these commissions are created, not by the President but, by the Congress upon its own motion."

	By Congress	President	Total
President Roosevelt			107
President Taft			63
President Wilson	75	75	150
President Harding			44
President Coolidge	74	44	118
President Hoover	22	20	42

"White House Statement on Committees and Commissions," *Public Papers,* 4/24/32.

Hoover's executive committees were temporary, and none specifically addressed the question of crime. The research committee on social trends included crime as one of several broad social problems, and a paper contained in its final report published in 1933 was written by sociologist Thorsten Sellin. The social trends committee was led by Wesley C. Mitchell, member of the board of directors of the Social Science Research Council and professor of economics at Columbia University; Charles E. Merriam, chairman of the political science department at the University of Chicago; William F. Ogburn, president of the American Sociological Society and professor of sociology at the University of Chicago; Howard W. Odum, professor of sociology at the University of North Carolina and editor of *Social Forces;* and Shelby M. Harrison, director of the U.S. Department of Surveys and Exhibits and vice-general director of the Russell Sage Foundation. "White House Statement on the Appointment of a Research Committee on Social Trends," 12/19/29, *Public Papers.*

45. M. Lowenthal to D. Stevens, 8/unknown/29, Archives.

46. Cleveland, 1 to 575; Chicago, 1 to 450; New York, 1 to 446; St. Louis, 1 to 417; Detroit, 1 to 380; Philadelphia, 1 to 368; London, 1 to 365; Paris, 1 to

276; Vienna, 1 to 275; Berlin, 1 to 225; Brussels, 1 to 205; Rome, 1 to 129. Survey results for June and July 1929, Archives.

47. Minutes of the commission's meeting, 5/28/29, Archives.

48. Ibid.

49. H. C. Hoover to W. D. Mitchell, 6/5/29, HHPL. Mitchell wrote back on the tenth to advise that short of declaring martial law, Congress had not approved military force to prevent smuggling.

50. H. C. Hoover to W. D. Mitchell, 2/1/32, HHPL.

51. Undated handwritten note, probably early 1932, HHPL.

52. G. W. Wickersham to E. G. Grace, 1/20/30. E. G. Grace to G. W. Wickersham, 1/27/30, Archives.

53. N. D. Baker to M. Lowenthal, unknown date/1930, Archives.

54. C. N. Bliss to G. W. Wickersham, 3/7/30, Archives.

55. F. Frankfurter to N. D. Baker, 7/20/29, Archives.

56. F. Frankfurter to G. W. Wickersham, 9/6/29, Archives.

57. G. W. Wickersham to F. Frankfurter, 9/10/29, Archives.

58. S. B. Warner to B. Smith, 7/5/29, Archives.

59. Herbert Hoover was secretary of commerce in 1927 and was in receipt of the 70-page Census Bureau report entitled "Instructions for Compiling Criminal Statistics." Nine chapters were included: Classification of Offenses, Prisons and Reformatories, Parole Agencies, Jails and Workhouses, Police Departments, Courts, Prosecutors, Probation Departments. The preamble set forth several guiding principles of the Census Bureau, among them was "Statistics form a unified whole." There was no intention to create a "complete system, in the sense of containing all the criminal statistics that it is desirable to publish." Rather, the intention was to construct a "unified system" to "present a picture of the administration of criminal justice that is free from overlapping and from important omissions." Archives.

60. M. Lowenthal to R. Pound, 7/28/29, Archives. Bettman had previously been assistant to assistant attorney general John Lord O'Brian in the Justice Department's war legislation division.

61. Other members included Alfred F. Foote, commissioner of the Massachusetts State Police; Jacob Graul; Cleveland chief of police; Thomas Healy, superintendent of police for New Orleans; George G. Henry, Baltimore chief of police; James W. Higgins, Buffalo police commissioner; L. V. Jenkins, Portland chief of police; and John H. Alcock, Chicago deputy commissioner of police. An advisory committee included Lent D. Upson, Robert H. Gault, Charles E. Gehlke, Leonard V. Harrison, William Healy, J. Edgar Hoover, R. R. C. Kieb, George W. Kirchwey, C. M. Osborn, and W. M. Steuart.

62. Reflecting upon the ill feelings that had developed between himself and Bruce Smith, Warner wrote to Lowenthal: "In dealing with me you need not fear that you will hurt my feelings or injure my pride of authorship if you disagree with me and turn down any report I make you. A person cannot deal long with Mr. Frankfurter without losing any ideas he may ever have had about the perfection of his or anybody else's ideas or writings." S. B. Warner to M. Lowenthal, 7/16/29, Archives.

63. The Census Bureau's Manual of Instruction for Compiling Criminal Statistics had been issued in 1926, approved by signature of commerce

secretary Herbert Hoover. Leonard Harrison was a perpetual critic of the census data-collection efforts, arguing that the organization had never been adequately staffed and that it had done little to encourage reporting or coordinating. L. V. Harrison to G. W. Wickersham, 7/11/29, Archives.

64. G. W. Wickersham to N. D. Baker, 10/30/29, Archives.

65. William P. Rutledge, chief of police in Detroit, Michigan, and executive vice president of the International Association of Chiefs of Police, chaired IACP's committee on uniform crime records. Linked to the foundation was the Bureau of Social Hygiene, Inc. of New York City, on whose board of directors sat Leonard V. Harrison, John D. Rockefeller, Jr., Arthur Woods, Raymond B. Fosdick, Winthrop W. Aldrich, and John D. Rockefeller, III.

66. Notes for the meeting, 3/12/30, Archives.

67. Only on rare occasions did cities keep information on race, nationality, or country of birth of offenders, data that Sam Warner wanted to collect. It was suggested that nativity data in connection with Prohibition violations might be the way to encourage the retention of nativity data for all offenses. C. H. Willard to S. B. Warner, 11/26/29, Archives.

68. G. W. Wickersham, address to the Boston Chamber of Commerce, 3/12/31, Archives.

69. B. Smith to L. V. Harrison, 7/9/29, Archives.

70. Ibid.

71. B. Smith to S. B. Warner, 7/24/29, Archives.

72. R. B. Fosdick to G. W. Wickersham, 7/10/29, Archives.

73. M. Lowenthal to R. Pound, 8/5/29, Archives.

74. B. Smith to A. Vollmer, 9/7/29, Archives.

75. S. B. Warner to A. Vollmer, 9/19/29, Archives.

76. A. Vollmer to M. Lowenthal, 10/9/29, Archives.

77. A. Vollmer to B. Smith, 9/27/29, Archives.

78. A. Vollmer to S. B. Warner, 9/27/29, Archives. Later in November, Lowenthal conversed with Vollmer: "Mr. Vollmer stated that so much feeling had developed in the subject of police statistics and crime statistics in general that he thought it might be hurtful to his work if he went into the matter of statistics with the police chiefs when he called them into a conference here some time ago." M. Lowenthal to F. J. Loesch, 11/14/29, Archives.

79. G. E. Carte and E. H. Carte, *Police Reform in the United States: The Era of August Vollmer* (Berkeley: University of California Press, 1975), pp. 55–56. See also, D. E. J. MacNamara, "August Vollmer, the Vision of Police Professionalism," in P. J. Stead, *Pioneers in Policing* (Montclair: Patterson Smith, 1977), pp. 178–190. J. Edgar Hoover wrote to Vollmer congratulating him on the appointment as adviser to the commission: "I well realize that you have before you quite a large task and I want you to feel that if there is any assistance that either this Bureau or I can be to you, you have but to command me." J. E. Hoover to A. Vollmer, 9/10/29, Archives.

80. This group was created with federal administration assistance in 1925 and modeled after the Chicago Crime Commission. By 1929, however, it had conducted no original research. In July, Louis Howe, New York governor Franklin Roosevelt's key assistant, visited with Max Lowenthal to determine whether he could get some money for research from Hoover's law

observance commission and to have all local and state commissions share crime information. He recorded for the file, "On neither point did I make any statement committing the Commission in any way." M. Lowenthal to file, 7/31/29, Archives.

81. R. Moley to N. D. Baker, 10/25/29, Archives.

82. R. Moley, "The Collection of Criminal Statistics in the United States," *Michigan Law Review* 26 (1928): 747–762.

83. R. Moley to N. D. Baker, 10/14/29, Archives.

84. Unknown authorship and newspaper clipping sent by N. D. Baker to M. Lowenthal, 9/26/29, Archives.

85. N. D. Baker to R. Moley, 10/28/29, Archives.

86. R. Pound to G. W. Wickersham, 8/21/29, Archives.

87. Lowenthal observed in November that Wickersham was doing everything he could to insure that the commission "will be in a position to consider matters on the merits, and that the merits may not be disregarded because of any other factor." M. Lowenthal to F. J. Loesch, 11/14/29, Archives.

88. R. Moley to N. D. Baker, 10/14/29, Archives.

89. N. D. Baker to R. Moley, 10/28/29, Archives.

90. M. Lowenthal to S. B. Warner, 9/23/29, Archives.

91. B. Smith to R. Pound, 10/13/29, Archives.

92. See T. A. Reppetto, "Bruce Smith, Police Reform in the United States," in P. J. Stead, *Pioneers in Policing* (Montclair: Patterson Smith, 1977), pp. 191–206.

93. S. B. Warner, "Crimes Known to the Police—An Index of Crime?" *Harvard Law Review* 45 (December 1931): 307–317.

94. M. Lowenthal to R. Pound, 6/27/29, Archives.

95. G. W. Wickersham to Commission, 6/3/30, Archives.

96. C. Kelsey, "Immigration and Crime," *Annals of the American Academy of Political and Social Science* 214 (May 1926): 165–174.

97. Report of her conclusions, Archives.

98. M. Lemann to M. Lowenthal, 6/26/29, Archives.

99. Ibid. This view is also reflected in her later work, *The Tenements of Chicago, 1908–1935* (Chicago: University of Chicago Press, 1936).

100. At the end of the 'foreign born' commission report, organized crime was briefly mentioned as a topic in need of careful, reasoned examination. A young assistant professor at the University of Illinois, John Landesco, had conducted formal investigations into organized crime's role and influence in American society. On May 20, 1929, just three days after Al Capone was arrested, tried, and convicted in Philadelphia on a charge of carrying a concealed weapon, Landesco delivered a paper in Chicago titled "The Making of the Gang and of the American Mafia." He was, as Mark Haller has described, "an immigrant boy on Chicago's West Side and his subsequent wide contacts with immigrant communities in a number of American cities gave him a background that made it possible for him to gain the confidence of the men he wished to study. He could speak their language as well as the language of academia." M. H. Haller, Introduction to J. Landesco, *Organized Crime in Chicago: Part III of the Illinois Crime Survey 1929* (Chicago: University of Chicago Press, 1968), p. xv. Reprint of 1929 volume. Landesco's findings were not formally recognized by the commission.

101. G. W. Wickersham to K. Mackintosh, 7/18/30, Archives. Chafee often complained that he was perpetually forced to lay out money from his own pocket to fund his research for the commission, then to endure the tedious process of recovering costs from the budget allocations. He disliked being "banker for the United States." Lowenthal told him he would be glad to have Chafee's expenses paid directly from the headquarters fund and added, "Fortunately for the people and myself, I am not the entire government, and am not in a position to have things done wholly to my own preference." Z. Chafee to M. Lowenthal, 2/21/30, Archives. M. Lowenthal to Z. Chafee, 2/25/30, Archives. The two were good friends.

102. Preliminary report, "Non-Observance of Law by Government Officials Engaged in Enforcing Laws," 7/30/29, Archives.

103. G. W. Wickersham to L. Friedman, 4/3/30, Archives.

104. G. W. Wickersham to N. D. Baker, 6/17/31, Archives.

105. Wickersham was particularly disturbed. He believed that the study did not reflect an "accurate analyses of the facts, quite independent of the broader question of how we could deal with such a complicated state of facts in the short time at our disposal." G. W. Wickersham to W. S. Kenyon, 6/17/31, Archives. Roscoe Pound had favored Chafee's studies and provided him with an assistant to carry on Chafee's classes at Harvard so that the research could continue. W. S. Kenyon to G. W. Wickersham, 3/10/31, Archives.

106. Dennison insisted that no publicity be given to his project. Lawrence Richey wrote back: "We will give out no statement and endeavor to protect you against any publicity, although, of course, little birds have ways of singing sometimes when unexpected; but so far as we can control it, nothing shall be said until after you get here" (to Washington). L. Richey to H. S. Dennison, 11/21/29, Archives.

107. "Specifically, we should like to know how much of a factor the use of liquor is among workmen at the present day and how it compares with conditions before prohibition." G. W. Wickersham to L. R. Crandall, president of the George A. Fuller Company.

108. Minutes of the commission meeting, 5/30/29, Archives.

109. M. Lowenthal to M. Lemann, 6/28/29, Archives.

110. C. H. Wilcox to B. L. Melvin, 5/12/31, Archives.

111. Lowenthal told Kenyon not to make her work public: "This matter is not ripe for public announcement as a request has been made to the county authorities of Los Angeles County to grant Miss Van Waters a year's leave of absence and formal decision by the county authorities has not yet been reported to the Commission." M. Lowenthal to W. S. Kenyon, 11/21/29, Archives.

112. G. W. Wickersham to P. J. McCormick, 12/26/29, Archives.

113. Monte Lemann wrote to Wickersham: "My first reaction upon reading of the action of the House this morning was one of personal relief since the elimination of the appropriation would mean no further responsibility, anxiety or expenditure of time by us." M. Lemann to G. W. Wickersham, 6/21/30. Wickersham responded: "I have just had a talk with the President about it and he is by no means discouraged. He thinks he will get the money to carry on our work somehow." G. W. Wickersham to M. Lemann, 6/24/30, Archives.

114. G. W. Wickersham to N. D. Baker, 6/27/30, Archives.

115. N. D. Baker to G. W. Wickersham, 5/29/30, Archives.

116. "Statement on the National Commission on Law Observance and Enforcement," 6/27/30, *Public Papers.*

117. H. W. Anderson to G. W. Wickersham, 6/30/30, Archives. Anderson had met privately with Hoover at the White House on June 12, obviously not persuading the president to change his position.

118. W. S. Kenyon to M. Lowenthal, 10/29/29, Archives. Wickersham told Kenyon that he thought public hearings were valueless: "that kind of hearing which . . . rambles over the whole face of the earth, and is an example of the futility of unregulated, unprepared inquiries. The only effective public hearings . . . are those which are preceded by careful inquiry, preparation and arrangement." G. W. Wickersham to W. S. Kenyon, 9/17/29, Archives.

119. A. L. Comstock to G. W. Wickersham, 11/2/29, Archives.

120. Preliminary report of the commission, 10/25/29, Archives.

121. G. W. Wickersham to A. L. Comstock, 11/19/29, Archives.

122. A bill was introduced on December 19, 1929, to get the demand and immediate progress report from the commission.

123. "Special Message to the Congress Proposing Administrative Reforms in Federal Law Enforcement and Judicial Machinery," 1/13/30, *Public Papers.*

CHAPTER 5

1. "Inaugural Address," 3/4/29, *Public Papers.*

2. W. J. Ritz, *Rewriting the History of the Judiciary Act of 1789: Exposing Myths, Challenging Premises, and Using New Evidence* (Norman: University of Oklahoma Press, 1990), pp. 98–116.

3. I do not suggest that citizen enlightenment emerged solely at this point. For a perspective on the gradual emergence of controls on local police, see W. B. Miller, "Police Authority in London and New York City 1830–1870," *Journal of Social History* (Winter 1975): 81–101; M. H. Haller, "Historical Roots of Police Behavior: Chicago, 1890–1925," *Law & Society Review* 10 (Winter 1976): 304–323; R. Lane, *Policing the City—Boston, 1822–1885* (Cambridge: Harvard University Press, 1967); J. R. Richardson, *The New York Police, from Colonial Times to 1901* (New York: Oxford University Press, 1970).

4. E. D. Graper, *American Police Administration: A Handbook of Police Organization and Methods of Administration* (New York: Macmillan, 1921).

5. R. B. Fosdick, *American Police Systems* (New York: Century, 1920), pp. 80–109.

6. T. Roosevelt, *American Ideals and Other Essays Social and Political* (New York: G. P. Putnam's Sons, 1910); T. Roosevelt, *An Autobiography* (New York: Macmillan, 1913); G. W. Walling, *Recollections of a New York City Chief of Police* (New York: Caxton, 1887); W. McAdoo, *Guarding a Great City* (New York: Harper & Brothers, 1906); L. Fuld, *Police Administration: A Critical Study of Police Organizations in the United States and Abroad* (New York: G. P. Putnam's Sons, 1909); A. Woods, *Policeman and Public* (New Haven: Yale University Press, 1919); C. F. Cahalane, *The Policeman* (New York: E. P. Dutton, 1923).

7. N. Douthit, "Police Professionalism and the War against Crime in the United States, 1920s–30s," in *Police Forces in History*, ed. G. L. Mosse (Beverly Hills: Sage, 1975).

8. H. B. Chamberlin, "The Chicago Crime Commission—How the Businessmen of Chicago Are Fighting Crime," *Journal of Criminal Law and Criminology* 11 (November 1920): 386–397; E. Connor, "Crime Commissions and Criminal Procedure in the United States since 1920: A Bibliography, January, 1920–June, 1927," *Journal of Criminal Law and Criminology* 21 (May 1930): 129–145; J. Pfiffner, "The Activities and Results of Crime Surveys," *American Political Science Review* 23 (November 1929): 930–956.

9. The horrors of the Prohibition enforcement experience are nicely summarized in A. Sinclair, *Prohibition: The Era of Excess* (Boston: Little, Brown, 1962), pp. 182–190.

10. Treasury Department's branches of Border Patrol, Coast Guard, Customs, Narcotics, Prohibition, the Intelligence Unit of the Internal Revenue Bureau, and the Secret Service; in the Labor Department's Immigration Patrol; in the Justice Department's Bureau of Investigation; in the Postal Department's Division of Postal Inspectors; in the War Department's Military Intelligence Department; in the Navy Department's Intelligence Division; and in the Interior Department's General Land Office.

11. Exceptions include L. F. Schmeckebier, *The Bureau of Prohibition: Its History and Organization* (Washington, D.C.: Brookings Institution, 1929). Comprehensive study of federal agencies did not appear until the 1930s. A detailed listing of regulatory and investigative activities appeared in C. H. Woody, *The Growth of Federal Government, 1915–1932* (New York: McGraw-Hill, 1934). The most thorough work was published three years later, A. C. Millspaugh, *Crime Control By the National Government* (Washington, D.C.: Brookings Institution, 1937).

12. D. M. Brown, *Mabel Walker Willebrandt: A Study of Power, Loyalty, and Law* (Knoxville: University of Tennessee Press, 1984), pp. 53–56.

13. An example of J. Edgar Hoover's revamping of the bureau is found in a 1926 memo to assistant attorney general John Marshall. The 8-page memo outlined selection criteria, the economy measures of the bureau, establishment of the identification division, cooperative relationships with local police chiefs, successes with fingerprint technology, and various cases in which his agents conducted outstanding investigations. J. E. Hoover to J. Marshall, 10/8/26, Archives.

14. Sinclair, op. cit., p. 182.

15. Schmeckebier, op. cit., pp. 43–57.

16. "Message to the 33rd Convention of the National Congress of Parents and Teachers," 5/5/29, *Public Papers*.

17. "Message to the Congress Transmitting Report of the National Commission on Law Observance and Enforcement," *Public Papers*, 1/20/31.

18. "If law can be upheld only by enforcement officers, then our scheme of government is at an end." Address to the Associated Press, "Law Enforcement and Respect for the Law," 4/22/29, *Public Papers*.

19. H. C. Hoover to E. Boole, 9/17/29, HHPL.

20. H. C. Hoover to I. Smith, 8/12/30, HHPL.

21. H. C. Hoover to R. L. Durham, 9/21/32, HHPL. Mr. Durham had praised Hoover for not mentioning in a speech the revenues that might result to the federal treasury from legalized liquor sales. Hoover wrote: "The moral issue in that question outweighs all other considerations. The problem is how most practically to preserve the moral gains already made."

22. J. Edgar Hoover, for example, was appointed to his position on commerce secretary Herbert Hoover's recommendation in 1924. Hoover was ordered by his boss, Attorney General Stone, to limit investigations to violations of federal law and to improve the professional stature of bureau agents. Edgar Hoover was philosophically committed to these objectives, as were leaders in several other enforcement branches. See R. G. Powers, *Secrecy and Power: The Life of J. Edgar Hoover* (New York: Macmillan, 1987), pp. 144–178. Similar improvements had taken place in the Secret Service: W. S. Bowen and H. E. Neal, *The United States Secret Service* (Philadelphia: Chilton, 1960); and in the U.S. Marshal's Service: F. S. Calhoun, *The Lawmen: United States Marshals and Their Duties, 1789–1989* (Washington, D.C.: Smithsonian Institution Press, 1989), pp. 245–251.

23. J. Kobler, *Ardent Spirits: The Rise and Fall of Prohibition* (New York: G. P. Putnam's Sons, 1973), pp. 271–300.

24. C. Merz, *The Dry Decade* (New York: Doubleday, Doran, 1930), pp. 130–157.

25. R. L. Solomon, "Regulating the Regulators: Prohibition Enforcement in the Seventh Circuit," in D. E. Kyvig *Law, Alcohol, and Order: Perspective on National Prohibition* (Westport: Greenwood, 1985), pp. 88–89. Questions of the lawfulness of federal and state agents, often working together, constituted a major category of cases clogging appellate courts.

26. Woodcock distributed a "letter of instruction" to all levels of supervision in the Bureau outlining improvements he desired in the methods of operation against Prohibition violators. A. W. W. Woodcock to All Prohibition Administrators, 3/3/31, Archives.

27. A. E. Sawyer to G. W. Wickersham, 12/8/30, Archives. There were never more than 3,000 field agents in the Prohibition Bureau to cover the entire nation.

28. W. M. Provine to W. D. Mitchell, 7/2/29, Archives. Provine was U.S. attorney for the Southern District of Illinois.

29. H. S. Nelli, "American Syndicate Crime: A Legacy of Prohibition," and M. H. Haller, "Bootleggers as Businessmen: From City Slums to City Builders." In D. E. Kyvig, op. cit., pp. 123–157.

30. See an interesting accounting of the Miami situation at the time, including the use of deadly force by the Coast Guard, in P. Buchanan, "Miami's Bootleg Boom," *Tequesta* (June 1978): 13–31.

31. A. S. Everest, *Rum Across the Border: The Prohibition Era in Northern New York* (Syracuse: Syracuse University Press, 1978).

32. Report of Division of Western European Affairs, "Cooperation in the Prevention of Liquor Smuggling," U.S. State Department, 2/6/33, HHPL.

33. Mrs. Lillian De King was shot to death in her own home in early April 1929, her husband clubbed violently, and her son forced to fire a pistol to

wound an invading sheriff. The incident resulted from false information given to police by an informant. The incident was reported nationally and raised even more questions about deaths occurring from liquor enforcement: "What Mr. Hoover called a noble experiment was never in greater danger of frustration than it is just now, when the very eagerness of the Administration to forward it is leading to abuses and woes that may yet excite a counter-movement infinitely more potent because it would embody the demands of all outraged people." *Literary Digest*, 4/13/29.

34. News conference, 4/5/29, *Public Papers.*

35. *Literary Digest*, 4/20/29.

36. In July, Hoover also ordered the removal of machine guns, rifles, and shotguns from Coast Guard boats. Boats were armed with small cannons, and individual guardsmen were armed with pistols. *Nation*, 9/4/29.

37. For all the popular hype about Ness's activities, there is little primary-source information about him. For a brief biography of his life and sources for additional investigation, see J. D. Calder, "Eliot Ness, 1903–1957," in *Book of Days 1988*, ed. H. N. Kronick (Ann Arbor: Pierian, 1988), pp. 224–225. Poorly documented popularization of the Ness story is found in E. Ness and O. Fraley, *The Untouchables* (New York: Julian Messner, 1957). A new biography of Ness, more thoroughly researched than the last one, is expected.

38. H. C. Hoover to A. Mellon, 4/8/29, HHPL.

39. D. E. Koskoff, *The Mellons: The Chronicle of America's Richest Family* (New York: Thomas Y. Crowell, 1978), pp. 240–243.

40. Cited in E. E. Robinson and V. D. Bornet, *Herbert Hoover, President of the United States* (Stanford: Hoover Institution, 1975), p. 88.

41. "I think it would hearten the situation a good deal," he wrote to Mitchell, "if we could revive this idea and make such an organized staff under some special attorney. We are being criticized very severely around centers like Chicago for failure to do anything in the larger conspiracies." H. C. Hoover to W. D. Mitchell, 7/11/30, HHPL.

42. Some articles carried the spelling as Wirkkula.

43. *Nation*, 7/24/29.

44. Ibid.

45. *Literary Digest*, 6/29/29.

46. "Letter to the International Falls City Council on Its Protest against Prohibition Enforcement Incidents," 6/21/29, *Public Papers.*

47. *New York Times*, 6/12/29.

48. Officers G. Jennings and F. Beck mistook Hanson for a rum runner on a road in Niagara Falls, New York. Hanson did not stop on the order of the guardsmen, whom he believed to be robbers. New York's Senator R. S. Copeland demanded a congressional investigation into the Prohibition enforcement practices of the Coast Guard, but such action was stalled to await the outcome of state criminal trials of the two officers. The officers were tried on two occasions by state authorities, and the jury acquitted them on May 24, 1929. Hanson remained alive from May to August, blinded by shotgun pellets to the head.

49. S. Lowman, testimony, 6/21/29, Archives.

50. *U.S. Daily*, 6/18/29.

51. *New York World*, 6/13/29. This piece was appropriately titled, "Rum Killings Begin to Pull on Hoover and Some of Drys."

52. *New York Herald Tribune*, 6/23/29.

53. *New York Times*, 7/5/29.

54. *New York World*, 7/6/29.

55. R. White to W. D. Mitchell, 8/6/29, Archives.

56. O. R. Luhring to W. D. Mitchell, 8/10/29, Archives.

57. See an excellent early social science study of opium consumption in urban areas. B. Dai, *Opium Addiction in Chicago* (Chicago: University of Chicago Press, 1937). The act outlawed the manufacture, sale, purchase, or gift of narcotic drugs and imposed licensing requirements on druggists. The act was a good-faith response to resolutions drawn up at the 1912 Hague Convention, mainly aimed at controlling opium exporting.

58. S. Graham-Mulhall, *Opium, the Demon Flower* (New York: Montrose, 1926). At the time this book was published, Sara Graham-Mulhall was the former first deputy commissioner of the New York State Department of Narcotic Drug Control.

59. "Statement on Plans for Federal Prison Reform," 8/6/29, *Public Papers*.

60. Testimony of S. Lowman, 6/21/29, Archives.

61. Evidence of an increasingly severe drug problem was presented in several books, including E. Bishop's *Narcotic Drug Problem*, 1920; W. Black's *Dope: The Story of the Living Dead*, 1928; J. Gavit's *Opium*, 1925; R. A. Haynes' *Present Status of Narcotic Enforcement in the United States*, 1923; A. Hosie's two volume study *On the Trail of the Opium Poppy*, 1921; E. N. La Motte's *The Opium Monopoly* and *Ethics of Opium*, 1924; C. E. Terry and M. Pellens' *Opium Problem*, 1928; W. W. Willoughby's *Opium as an International Problem: The Geneva Conferences*, 1925; W. T. Dunn's, *The Opium Traffic in Its International Aspects*, 1920; S. Graham-Mudhall's, *Opium, the Demon Flower*, 1926; and E. MacCallum's, *Twenty Years of Persian Opium*, 1928. Congressional hearings were conducted on at least nine occasions from 1920 to 1929 on narcotics issues, and the Bureau of Narcotics published five pamphlets in 1930 titled "Traffic in Opium and Other Dangerous Drugs, 1926–1929." In consideration of a continuous flow of publications, especially those that focused on opium, the testimony of Seymour Lowman before the Wickersham Commission in June 1929 seems truly uninformed: "Our records show that the smuggling of raw opium has been very nearly suppressed."

62. As secretary of commerce, he sat on the Federal Narcotics Control Board (a drug importation commission) with the secretaries of state and treasury. International control of smuggling was a regular subject of discussion.

63. A. H. Taylor, *American Diplomacy and the Narcotics Traffic, 1900–1939* (Durham: Duke University Press, 1969), pp. 123–145.

64. Statement to the commission by D. W. MacCormack, 6/6/29, Archives.

65. News conference, 1/14/30, *Public Papers*.

66. News conference, 11/25/30, *Public Papers*.

67. Andrew J. Volstead wrote to Mabel Willebrandt two days after the inaugural address: "A reorganization such as is proposed would practically

paralyze our efforts for many months. The one thing that has happened to the Prohibition Unit that has done more harm than anything else is the frequent reorganising [sic] that has taken place. It has been organized and reorganised almost to death." A. J. Volstead to M. W. Willebrandt, 3/6/31, Archives. Without question, Volstead held pride of ownership in his Volstead Act, which in 1920 had produced the nightmare of Treasury Department enforcement.

68. News conference, 4/12/29, *Public Papers.*

69. *Public Papers,* 4/22/29.

70. W. D. Mitchell to M. W. Willebrandt, no date but presumed to be immediately after 5/3/29, Archives.

71. Patrol of coastal, northern, and southern borders had been performed by three separate federal departments: Treasury's Coast Guard (since 1790), Treasury's Customs Service (since 1886 on the Mexican border; since 1925 on the northern border), and Labor's Immigration Border Patrol (since 1925). A. C. Millspaugh, *Crime Control by the Federal Government* (Washington, D.C.: Brookings Institution, 1937), pp. 60–86.

72. Minutes of the meeting, 5/7/29, Archives.

73. W. D. Mitchell to file, 5/17/29, Archives.

74. H. R. 11204 was introduced in May, 1929 by Michigan congressman Hudson. H. R. 8574 was introduced nearly simultaneously to put the patrol in the Justice Department.

75. J. E. Hoover to M. W. Willebrandt, 4/16/29, Archives.

76. News conference, 5/28/29, *Public Papers.*

77. *Washington Herald Tribune,* 5/28/29. *New York Times,* 6/3/29.

78. Merz, op. cit., p. 251.

79. Anslinger began government service in the State Department's Foreign Service immediately after World War I, moving over to the Treasury Department to work for Secretary Mellon. He became assistant commissioner of Prohibition in 1929.

80. Koskoff, op. cit., p. 241. Anslinger married a relative of Mellon's, Martha Denniston. His early years are described in J. C. McWilliams, *The Protectors: Harry J. Anslinger and the Federal Bureau of Narcotics, 1930–1962* (Newark: University of Delaware Press, 1990), pp. 25–37.

81. D. C. Kinder, "Bureaucratic Cold Warrior: Harry J. Anslinger and Illicit Narcotics Traffic," *Pacific Historical Review* 50 (May 1981): 169–191.

82. D. F. Musto, *The American Disease: Origins of Narcotic Control* (New Haven: Yale University Press, 1973), pp. 210–212.

83. Hoover's budget increase proposal appears in *Public Papers,* 6/18/30. The *New York Times* covered Anslinger's appointment on 9/24/30 and the approval of his position by the Senate Finance Committee on 12/10/30. He was not mentioned in the *Times* index by name for 1931 and 1932, but under "drugs" for 1931 he was mentioned in connection with grand jury testimony, 3/21/31. The Bureau of Narcotics, the immediate predecessor to Anslinger's Division of Narcotics put out five pamphlets in 1930 on different topics of public education, all titled "Traffic in Opium and Other Dangerous Drugs, 1926–1929."

84. H. C. Hoover to the organizations, 2/21/30, HHPL.

85. *Public Papers*, 2/20/31, 1/18/32.

86. Hoover had recommended, unsuccessfully, in 1921 the appointment of Elizabeth W. Wright to serve at the Hague Convention as an authority on narcotics. She was appointed in 1924 to the Second Opium Conference, became the first woman to receive diplomat status, and worked for the Bureau of Narcotics for a short while in 1930. See A. H. Taylor, *American Diplomacy and the Narcotics Traffic, 1900–1939* (Durham: Duke University Press, 1969), pp. 303–304.

87. E. J. Epstein, *Agency of Fear: Opiates and Political Power in America* (New York: G. P. Putnam's Sons, 1977), pp. 23–29.

88. E. Rickard to H. C. Hoover, 1/10/30, HHPL.

89. W. R. Castle to H. C. Hoover, 8/14/30, HHPL.

90. P. G. Fish, *The Politics of the Federal Court System* (Princeton: Princeton University Press, 1973), pp. 95–98.

91. *New York Times* coverage of the De Groot matter is found between January 1 and July 12, 1929.

92. Fish, op. cit., pp. 107–108.

93. W. D. Mitchell to M. W. Willebrandt, 6/29/29, Archives.

94. J. E. Hoover to C. P. Sisson, 5/6/30, Archives.

95. W. D. Mitchell to K. McKellar, 6/11/30, Archives.

96. W. D. Mitchell to C. P. Sisson, 6/14/30, Archives.

97. After leaving office in 1933, Mitchell evaluated each of Hoover's appointments to the federal trial and appellate benches, comparing them with those of Harding and Coolidge. He had five labels for the categories: "very good," "good," "fair," "poor," and "bad."

98. H. C. Hoover to C. Howard, 8/18/30, HHPL.

99. Writing to Mitchell on 9/18/29, he said: "I see by the papers this morning that another large investment trust has been created, apparently of interstate character. I am wondering if it would be desirable to investigate this one to see whether or not it is within the law." John Lord O'Brian, assistant attorney general, was asked by Mitchell to investigate the trust, Marine Midland Corporation. Mitchell asked O'Brian on October 10, "Am I safe in telling the President that there is nothing about the banking and investment security business which can be considered interstate commerce?" An investigation was conducted and the company was found to be not within the scope of the antitrust laws because it did not manufacture or distribute in interstate commerce. Archives.

100. Lucas was replaced without prejudice by David Burnet in August 1930. In March 1931, Senator George Norris wrote to Mitchell alleging that Lucas may have violated the Corrupt Practices Act regarding the reporting of campaign funds. The matter pertained to an alleged account that Lucas was to have established using campaign funds for personal benefit. Mitchell was ordered to investigate; and when he wrote to Nugent Dodds on 10/10/31, he was emphatic: "I want to be sure [the charges] are sifted to the bottom and if there has been any violation of law, that it not be overlooked." Dodds conducted a thorough investigation and determined that there were absolutely no grounds on which to bring any federal prosecution. Archives.

101. H. C. Hoover to G. W. Wickersham, 11/11/29, HHPL.

102. H. C. Hoover to W. D. Mitchell, 9/18/29, HHPL.

103. W. D. Mitchell to H. C. Hoover, 10/22/29, HHPL. Hoover may not have taken Mitchell's advice, although he respected it. There is reason to believe that the delinquent judges were informally asked to step down.

104. W. D. Mitchell to T. D. Schall, 1/28/31, HHPL. Schall was a senator from Minnesota who, according to Hoover, held up Hoover's appointments and thereby delayed resolution of the court congestion problem in that state. See *Memoirs*, op. cit., p. 269.

105. H. C. Hoover to T. D. Schall, 2/3/31, HHPL.

106. "Letter to Senator Thomas D. Schall about the Appointment of a District Judge for Minnesota," 2/6/31, *Public Papers*.

107. "Letters to Senator Thomas D. Schall about the Appointment of a District Judge for Minnesota," 2/20/31, *Public Papers*.

108. Circular 2043 from W. D. Mitchell to all United States Attorneys, 6/8/29, Archives.

109. W. M. Provine to W. D. Mitchell, 7/2/29, Archives.

110. G. E. Q. Johnson to W. D. Mitchell, 7/26/29, Archives.

111. C. Sisson to G. E. Q. Johnson, 11/15/29; G. E. Q. Johnson to W. D. Mitchell, 12/14/29; G. E. Q. Johnson to C. Sisson, 12/18/29, Archives.

112. J. W. Gardner to C. P. Sisson, 6/2/30, Archives.

113. News conference, W. D. Mitchell, 1/24/31, HHPL.

114. "Special Message to the Congress on Reform of Judicial Procedure," 2/29/32, *Public Papers*.

115. H. C. Hoover to L. Richey, 12/9/30; A. R. Crozier to C. P. Sisson, 12/11/30; A. R. Crozier to C. P. Sisson, 12/12/30; W. D. Mitchell to H. C. Hoover, 12/11/30, Archives.

116. G. W. Wickersham, address to the Cincinnati Regional Crime Committee, 4/16/31, Archives.

117. G. W. Wickersham to W. S. Kenyon, 5/23/30, Archives.

118. W. D. Mitchell to N. Dodds, 12/30/31, Archives.

119. In September 1929, Senator Howell, District of Columbia Commissioner Doherty, Police Superintendent Pratt, U.S. Attorney Rover, and Prohibition Agent Blandford were not enforcing the Prohibition law in Washington. Hoover issued a press release on 9/22/29: "The President will have the matters vigorously investigated, for it is the intention not only to secure the fullest enforcement in the District possible under the organization of enforcement agencies as provided by law, but to make it a model in the country."

120. "Address to the White House Conference on Child Health and Protection," 11/19/30, *Public Papers*.

121. Regarding appeals, Hoover said, "Respect for the law and the effect of convictions as a deterrent to crime are diminished if convicted persons are observed by their fellow citizens to be at large for long periods pending appeal." "Special Message to the Congress on Reform of Judicial Procedure," 2/29/32, *Public Papers*.

122. Press statement and attorney general's letter to the president, dated respectively 2/5/33 and 2/24/33, are found in *State Papers of Herbert Hoover*, pp. 600–602.

CHAPTER 6

1. *Literary Digest*, 10/31/31, "Gangdom's King Guilty as a Tax Dodger."

2. E.g., J. Kobler, *Capone: The Life and World of Al Capone* (New York: G. P. Putnam's Sons, 1971); F. D. Pasley, *Al Capone: A Biography of a Self-Made Man* (New York: Ives Washburn, 1930); F. Spiering, *The Man Who Got Capone* (Indianapolis: Bobbs-Merrill, 1976).

3. In the same month, Elmer L. Irey published an article in the *Internal Revenue News* (vol.4, no. 8), titled "Patience Has Its Reward," in which he discussed the good work of the intelligence unit of the Internal Revenue Bureau. The article focused on efforts to track down taxes owed by an amusement company. In the course of the investigation, an agent commented publicly, "The taxpayer who camoflages [*sic*] his books and records for the purpose of deceiving the investigating officer is riding for a fall." Irey regarded the agent's statement as a constructive message with great symbolic enforcement value.

The Prohibition Bureau of the Treasury Department was also looking into the possible relocation of Capone gang members to the Washington, D.C. area. One report, in October 1928, from an informer named George Cole told agents that one of Capone's enforcers was moving away from Cleveland, Ohio, and New York City because he had a disagreement with the New York gang: "Due to recent activities, as concerns the operation of 'racketeers' in New York City, I believe it possible that some of the gangsters involved might try locating in Washington. It is quite evident that any of Capone's gang who might be in this vicinity are here for no good reasons." D. D. Mayne to E. C. Wilcox, 10/22/28, ATF.

4. Investigation by Internal Revenue revealed that Vidor had filed false and fraudulent income tax returns for 1925 to 1927 with the intent to evade taxes. A. H. Diebert to S. M. McNabb, 2/23/29, Archives. The Justice Department wanted to press the charge of conspiracy to evade taxes against Tom Mix in January 1930, because Mix was alleged to have lied to investigators. In March 1930, Mix pleaded guilty to three misdemeanor counts for failure to pay tax. When Vidor also plead guilty to failure to pay taxes for 1925, he was fined $400. Referring to the Justice Department case against actor Raymond Griffith for false returns, the following observation was made inside the Internal Revenue Bureau: "Informally, some of the agents here have told me that there would be a great many more of these cases reported to us from their department in Washington within a short time and I would therefore like to have you take the matter up with the Commissioner and find out about how long a time will elapse before we receive the balance of reports." The collection of cases was known in the IRB as the "Moving Picture Actors' Tax Cases." Most such case were completed for trial by June 15, 1929. S. M. McNabb to W. R. Mitchell, 5/27/29, Archives.

5. On October 31, 1928, he wrote to James F. Burke, general counsel of the Republican National Committee: "I have personally inspected the returns of Mr. Hoover for the years 1914 to 1925, inclusive, and I am informed by the Commissioner of the Internal Revenue that the records of the Bureau show

that the returns for the years 1926 and 1927 are now in the hands of the Internal Revenue Agent in Charge for the usual checking up, and that the taxes have been paid to date." A. W. Mellon to J. F. Burke, 10/31/28, Archives.

6. He started the year fresh from forcible ejection from Los Angeles in 1927, and the Miami mayor and council members attempt to toss him out of the city. Capone sought and received a restraining order to stay in Miami, but in September he shot himself in the leg in a rather undignified discharge of the pistol he carried in his pants pocket. *New York Times*, 9/21/28.

7. 274 U.S. 259. Manly S. Sullivan had refused to file a tax return on net income for 1921. The Fourth Circuit Court of Appeals held that Sullivan's income from the sale of illegal booze in violation of the Volstead Act must be reported but that completion of a tax return would mean that Sullivan would give up his Fifth Amendment right not to incriminate himself. Overruling the Fourth Circuit and writing for the Supreme Court, Justice Oliver Wendall Holmes suggested that the circuit court's interpretation, while correct on the obligation to report all income, carried the Fifth Amendment's application too far: "It would be an extreme if not an extravagant application of the Fifth Amendment to say that it authorized a man to refuse to state the amount of his income because it had been made in crime. But if the defendant desired to test that or any other point he should have tested it in the return so that it could be passed upon. He could not draw a conjurer's circle around the whole matter by his own declaration that to write any word upon the government blank would bring him into danger of the law. . . . In this case the defendant did not even make a declaration, he simply abstained from making a return. . . . It is urged that if a return were made the defendant would be entitled to deduct illegal expenses such as bribery. This by no means follows but it will be time enough to consider the question when a taxpayer has the temerity to raise it." Sullivan's conviction was upheld, and he was sentenced to six months in jail. See E. L. Irey brief of the case in *Internal Revenue News* (1).

8. 48 Sup. Ct. 564 (1928). The Fourth Amendment's protections against unreasonable searches and seizures did not extend to conversations conveyed by telephone.

9. Commission members included Frank J. Loesch, president; Robert H. Hunter, Gustave F. Fischer and Gerhardt F. Meyne, vice presidents; Charles R. Napier, secretary; Charles W. Berquist, assistant secretary; Joseph R. Noel, treasurer; George W. Rossetter, assistant treasurer; Henry B. Chamberlin, operating director; R. W. Dvorak, assistant operating director.

10. Dawes wrote on August 1, 1928 that "it is impossible for me to undertake the work while occupying my present office, but I have a sincere feeling of regret that I cannot help in the fight upon the lawless element there." C. G. Dawes, *Notes As Vice President 1928–1929* (Boston: Little, Brown, 1935), p. 77.

11. Ibid., p. 150.

12. W. K. Klingaman, *1929 The Year of the Great Crash* (New York: Harper & Row, 1989).

13. The bureau's work in this matter, long treated as a sideshow, was used by U.S. attorney George E. Q. Johnson as leverage in the planned tax

evasion case. J. Edgar Hoover's bureau was not legally empowered to attack the heart of Capone's criminal enterprises, thereby leaving it out of a controlling investigative position.

14. A summary of her work in the Justice Department is found in D. M. Brown, *Mabel Walker Willebrandt: A Study of Power, Loyalty, and the Law* (Knoxville: University of Tennessee Press, 1984), pp. 49–116.

15. A substantial amount of information in the contempt case was located in FBI file 69-180-4.

16. Johnson to Mitchell, 3/18/29, FBI file 69-180.

17. FBI file 69-18.

18. Ibid.

19. A police officer said he saw Capone in the company of New York's former governor Al Smith, claiming that Capone's profile in the local newspapers made him recognizable. A theatre usher said he saw Capone at the Miami Jockey Club at least thirty times during the period, while a stenographer said she witnessed an interrogation of Capone by County Solicitor Robert Taylor. Taylor told agents he "questioned Alphonse Capone for about two hours and . . . from all appearances [he] was in good health, and did not complain of being ill." FBI file 69-18, various dates, 1929.

20. Affidavits declare that fifty-one people were on board the New Northland on February 8, 1929, among them Al Capone, Philip D. Andrea, Wen Phillips, Fred Girton, and William McCabe.

21. The last paragraph of the act, clause 2 provided the title of "Undesirables," that such person shall not be allowed in the Colony "whose presence . . . would not be conducive to the public good." The governor council had the power to refuse admittance to anyone labeled an undesirable. FBI file 69-180-15.

22. *New York Times*, March 27, 1929.

23. On July 24, 1929, Johnson wrote to the attorney general to request that perjury charges against Dr. Phillips be delayed for two reasons: "first, I expect to use Dr. Phillips as a witness in the Capone matter here when it is tried; second, an investigation has been under way here for the past six months going into the income tax account of Alphonse Capone and his brother Ralph Capone which I expect to present to the grand jury some time early in the fall." Archives.

24. H. C. Hoover to W. D. Mitchell and A. Mellon, 4/8/29, HHPL.

25. "I would like to secure as soon as possible a report on the income tax record of Al Capone, — what income tax returns, if any, he has filed, what they disclose, what tax has been paid, etc." W. E. Hope to R. H. Lucas, 3/18/30, Archives.

26. R. H. Lucas to W. J. Hope, 3/19/30, HHPL.

27. E. L. Irey and R. J. Slocum, *The Tax Dodgers* (New York: Greenberg, 1948), p. 35.

28. See F. J. Wilson and B. Day, *Special Agent: A Quarter Century with the Treasury Department and the Secret Service* (New York: Holt, Rinehart & Winston, 1965). Spiering, op. cit.

29. G. A. Youngquist to file, 3/18/30, DOJ-Tax. The *Washington Post*

reported on March 17 that Johnson said he had two possible cases against Capone, "one involving the alleged nonpayment of income taxes and the other based on a contempt-of-court charge."

30. Benjamin Epstein and William Waugh.

31. A. P. Madden to F. J. Wilson, 3/21/30, Archives.

32. A. P. Madden to F. J. Wilson, 3/25/30, Archives. Madden's report was given special attention by his superiors. Irey passed it to Lucas: "The attached letter refers to the retention of a man named 'Mattingly,' of the firm of Mattingly and Nutt of New York City, as attorney for Al Capone in Chicago. It may interest you to know that Mr. Mattingly is a son-in-law of Colonel Nutt, and that the 'Nutt' in his firm is a son of Colonel Nutt. This firm was recently the subject of investigation by the Grand Jury in New York City, which expressed criticism of Colonel Nutt as Head of the Narcotic Division, which criticism resulted in the demotion of Colonel Nutt." E. L. Irey to R. H. Lucas, 3/28/30. Lucas passed this information to Hope: "The attached will throw some more light on the Capone case. Mr. Mattingly, referred to herein, has talked with Mr. Boyd of our Penalty Section. I have advised Mr. Boyd that no negotiations are to be entered into with Capone with the idea that his case may be settled for money alone!" R. H. Lucas to W. E. Hope, 3/29/30, Archives.

33. For a brief description of Lawrence Richey, see C. Gentry, *J. Edgar Hoover: The Man and the Secrets* (New York: W. W. Norton, 1991).

34. L. Richey to G. A. Youngquist, 3/24/30, accompanied by the undated draft memo by Mark Sullivan to H. C. Hoover, DOJ-Tax. Richey's memo read: "The President has asked me to forward to you confidentially the enclosed memorandum which has just been received by him."

35. G. A. Youngquist to H. C. Hoover, 5/31/30, HHPL.

36. W. J. Froelich to G. A. Youngquist, 4/3/30, DOJ-Tax.

37. W. D. Mitchell to P. Harrison, 4/14/30, DOJ-Tax.

38. "I write to inquire whether any further action has been taken in the proceeding against Al Capone for contempt of court. My recollection is that you expected to present the matter to the court about the middle of April." G. A. Youngquist to G. E. Q. Johnson, 4/21/30, DOJ-Tax.

39. G. E. Q. Johnson to G. A. Youngquist, 4/23/30.

40. W. E. Hope to H. C. Hoover, 4/26/30. Hope had acquired the article from R. H. Lucas. On the same day, Hope wrote to Lucas, "Many thanks for the clipping regarding Ralph Capone. More power to your elbow! If we could get the chief offender it would be a tremendous achievement." Lucas's note to Hope read, "I thought you might be interested in knowing what happened to Ralph Capone, Al's brother. The outcome of this case will no doubt give Al something else to worry about." R. H. Lucas to W. E. Hope, 4/26/30, Archives.

41. Ralph Capone claimed to have been a "poor race-horse man" with no income. Federal agents turned up evidence of bank accounts of more than $2 million for use in convicting him of tax evasion.

42. A. P. Madden to E. Irey, 4/28/30, HHPL. Madden commented that a revenue agent had been assigned to work in the office at Roosevelt Finance Company, but no evidence emerged from the efforts. Apparently telephone

records indicated that Al Capone had called Greenberg on several occasions in 1929. "Mr. Greenberg," Madden said, "is very much disturbed about something, and the indications are that there is important evidence in connection with his transactions, if the evidence can be obtained." The same memo indicates that substantial evidence had been gathered against Frank Nitto, and the "head of the dog track, a man named O'Hare."

43. Ibid. Madden also commented that Al Capone's attorney had called his office several times. "Evidently," Madden wrote, "he wants to reach a settlement, but the indications are that the desires to accomplish it in a way that would prevent the prosecution of his client."

44. *New York Times*, 3/22/30.

45. *New York Times*, 5/24/30.

46. Pasley, op. cit., pp. 352–353.

47. J. M. Cox to H. C. Hoover, on or about 5/5/30, HHPL.

48. It appears that the commissioner of the Internal Revenue, Robert H. Lucas, consistently sat on the end of his chair awaiting good news. He read Madden's report of May 9 and sent it along to his superiors: "The attached [Madden's report] has reference to the Al Capone matter. I believe our men are making progress. Following a conference yesterday with Mr. Irey and Mr. Boyd, arrangements have been made to assign two of our most competent investigating Revenue Agents from New York, and an experienced Intelligence Agent from Baltimore, to Chicago to take up the Al Capone investigation. I have hopes we shall be able to uncover something worth while." R. H. Lucas to W. E. Hope, 5/14/30, Archives.

49. D. H. Green to file, 5/21/30, DOJ-Tax.

50. G. A. Youngquist to W. R. Mitchell, 5/19/30, DOJ-Tax.

51. He found that O'Hare was a lawyer who had come to Cicero early in 1927 from St. Louis to manage the track. O'Hare managed tracks in other cities, as well; and he had been "a defendant in the Jack Daniels case, was convicted and served fifty-eight days at Leavenworth." His conviction had been overturned. Substantial efforts had been invested, without success, by the U.S. attorney's office in Chicago to learn whether O'Hare had any interest in the Hawthorne track.

52. When physician Isaac D. Kelley, Jr. was abducted and held for ransom in May 1931, John T. Rogers was the person to whom the St. Louis gang released their victim at 2 A.M. out of sight of police. *Literary Digest*, 5/23/31, p. 11.

53. "Patton" was John Patton, one of the managers of the Cicero dog track. "Granada" was actually Peter C. Granata, a Capone insider and later a Republican congressman.

54. F. J. Wilson to E. L. Irey, 6/22/30, Archives.

55. R. H. Lucas to W. E. Hope, 7/2/30, Archives.

56. H. C. Hoover to W. D. Mitchell, 7/11/30, Archives.

57. Youngquist notified Johnson "of the advisability, if it is possible, of our having a man in constant attendance upon the investigations in the Zuta matter, or at least to arrange to have made available to us all of the material that is unearthed by that investigation." G. A. Youngquist to G. E. Q. Johnson, 8/24/30, Archives.

58. R. Randolph to L. Richey, 7/22/30, HHPL.

59. Mitchell identified the following organizations or individuals: the Civic Safety League; the Crime Commission; the Secret Six; the Citizens Association; the Civic Federation; the Employers Association; the Better Government Association; Illinois Vigilance; Committee of Fifteen; and Drs. Arthur Burage and Herman Bundeson.

60. G. E. Q. Johnson to T. G. Thacker, 8/19/30, Archives.

61. T. G. Thacher to H. C. Hoover, 9/5/30, Archives.

62. G. E. Q. Johnson to G. A. Youngquist, 9/12/30, DOJ-Tax.

63. He said he brought the plans to Willebrandt in concert with his work on the Titus Haffa tax violation case. Haffa was a Chicago alderman. Early in 1928, with unrevealed cooperation in place, the civic organizations withdrew assistance hoping that the new state's attorney would take up the torch. The state's attorney, while successful in closing down several dog-racing tracks owned by gangsters, could not go it alone, thus new assistance was required. Johnson did not want a Washington assignee for three reasons: first, he did not want the press to ask the assigned why he was in Chicago; second, the assignee would be unacquainted with the manner of the investigations; and third, it was of no special prestige to Johnson to have an assistant to supervise his work. G. E. Q. Johnson to W. D. Mitchell, 9/12/30, Archives.

64. G. E. Q. Johnson to G. A. Youngquist, 9/17/30, DOJ-Tax.

65. Youngquist was introduced to this writer, whose name was blacked out on DOJ–Tax Division records supplied to this author, on September 24. The writer's activities in Chicago were, he said, not widely known, and he could be reached through the publishers of the Chicago *Examiner* or the Chicago *American.* He reported information that Youngquist said he already knew, with the exception that "one of the assistants in the office of the United States Attorney is corrupt and in very close contact with the Capone forces. He said he would obtain evidence to support the charge, but would in the mean time withhold the name of the assistant. Johnson's honesty and integrity is not questioned." The memo goes on to describe the system of graft involving three members of the board of assessors who were also coal dealers. The writer found that these dealers charged more for coal in exchange for reduced property tax assessments by coal purchasers. G. A. Youngquist to file, 9/26/30, DOJ-Tax.

66. G. E. Q. Johnson to G. A. Youngquist, 10/1/30, Archives.

67. G. A. Youngquist to W. D. Mitchell, 11/5/30, DOJ-Tax. Alexander Jamie married Eliot Ness's sister Clara, and the relationship is believed to have aided Ness's advancement in the Bureau of Prohibition. See S. Nickel, *Torso: Eliot Ness and the Hunt for the Mad Butcher of Kingsbury Run* (New York: Avon, 1989), p. 33.

68. A. P. Madden to E. L. Irey, 9/4/30, Archives.

69. D. Burnet to G. E. Q. Johnson, 9/8/30, Archives.

70. "Our information is that the Northwestern [unloading track] is under complete control of rackets controlled by the Bugs Moran and Capone gangs; that before grapes can be unloaded a tribute is exacted by representatives of these gangs; that the control is still further being perfected by extending it to the other unloading tracks. It is clear to us that this is interference with

interstate commerce and should be immediately and thoroughly investigated. The effect is that the potential purchasing of fresh grapes by home owners is being discouraged, resulting in leaving as the principal purchasers the organized bootleggers, who buy the product, process it in their wineries, and sell it to the foreign population through illicit channels." C. C. Teague to N. Dodds, 10/9/30, Archives. See Brown, op. cit., pp. 179–189, for an overview of the entire matter of Willebrandt's involvement in this caper.

71. See description of O'Brian's career in A. C. Brown, *Wild Bill Donovan: The Last Hero* (New York: Times Books, 1982); R. G Power, *Secrecy and Power: The Life of J. Edgar Hoover* (New York: Free Press, 1987).

72. "I have directed that the present inquiry into grape racketeering be conducted with unusual caution and secrecy; because if the fact becomes known that this Department is taking over the investigation of rackets at Chicago it may result in the local authorities attempting to unload their responsibility on the Department in other 'rackets' as well." J. L. O'Brian to W. D. Mitchell, 9/24/30, Archives.

73. Numerous pieces of correspondence found in the Archives address the coloquy on the grape-juice matter. All date from September to November 1930.

74. J. L. O'Brian to file, 11/4/30, Archives.

75. G. A. Youngquist to G. E. Q. Johnson, 11/14/30, DOJ-Tax.

76. H. Cummings and C. Mc Farland, *Federal Justice: Chapters in the History of Justice and the Federal Executive* (New York: Macmillan, 1937), p. 460.

77. Mitchell's handwritten note to Youngquist: "This memo of Hoover's suggests (unless there is some reason for delay we don't know about) that we have slipped a chance to get Capone in prison. His way is defying the government. Every body knows he is violating federal laws, & whereever a chance appears to convict him, not a minute should be lost. The US Atty of Chicago may have felt he wanted to wait for a bigger case, but doubt prosecution of any case would tend to break down the barriers in the way of getting proof on bigger cases. Besides, this may have been a felony charge in Florida, where the doctor's affidavit was one for use in a judicial proceeding. A false one would be perjury, & Capone procuring it, would be guilty of subornation. A Florida jury would make short work of him if given a fair chance." W. D. Mitchell to G. A. Youngquist, 11/7/30, DOJ-Tax. Youngquist noted at the base of Mitchell's memo that he had talked with E. Q. Johnson the day before to suggest "the advisability of bringing the Capone contempt case in for trial." On November 5, Youngquist had written to Johnson, "I wish you would consider also the advisability of bringing Al Capone before the court on the contempt charge pending in your district. Action upon it has been deferred by reason of the pendency of investigation in other matters; but I am approaching the conclusion that action should be taken in the contempt proceedings without reference to further investigation." G. A. Youngquist to G. E. Q. Johnson, 11/5/30, DOJ-Tax.

78. Writing to G. A. Youngquist on 10/23/3?, J. E. Hoover said that the bureau "could best aid law enforcement in general by properly performing

its investigative work in the extremely large number of instances of considerable importance which have been brought to the attention of the Bureau with the past few months." Archives.

79. Youngquist wrote to Hoover on September 25, caustically reminding him both that he was warranted in asking for Hoover's assistance in such guarding activities on a temporary basis and that it might be necessary in the future to ask for further assistance. G. A. Youngquist to J. E. Hoover, 9/25/30, DOJ-Tax.

80. A personal and confidential memo dated 12/18/30 from D. Burnet to W. E. Hope recorded the bribery attempts: "With reference to the Capone investigation in Chicago, I have to advise that perhaps six weeks ago Mr. Harry Curtis called upon me personally and suggested that it was now time to stop all prosecutions in the Chicago gang group. His suggestion was that he would be glad to spread the word in Chicago that there would be no further prosecutions and he stated that he would guarantee that at least $3,500,000 would be paid to the Collector of Internal Revenue at Chicago voluntarily by various racketeers, gangsters, etc., if they could be assured there would be no attempt at prosecution.

An attorney of the Capone case, named Lawrence P. Mattingly, called upon me and made the same general suggestion in the very indirect manner.

There have been other slight intimations, but all of such a nature that they could not be regarded as more than a very delicate hint. . . .

I have been informed that approaches have been made from time to time to various Federal officials in Chicago in the interest of these gangsters with a view to having their cases settled in other than a regular manner." HHPL.

81. News conference, 11/25/30, *Public Papers.*

82. "Annual Message to the Congress on the State of the Union," 12/2/30, *Public Papers.*

83. Capone's involvement in the Castellammarese war is outlined in interviews with Meyer Lansky in D. Eisenberg, U. Dan, and E. Landau, *Meyer Lansky: Mogul of the Mob* (New York: Paddington, 1979), pp. 123, 132. A new account of the Lansky group is found in R. Lacey, *Little Man: Meyer Lansky and the Gangster Life* (Boston: Little, Brown, 1991).

84. *New York Times,* 12/19/30.

85. *Internal Revenue News,* 2/31, vol 4., no. 8. Archives.

86. G. A. Youngquist to W. J. Froelich, 12/26/30, DOJ-Tax.

87. *Literary Digest,* 11/29/30. Seventeen men and women were arrested in the raid, believed by federal authorities to represent a $2-million-per-year enterprise.

88. "Please do all you properly can to enlist the cooperation of the courts toward an early disposition, for if certiorari be not applied for in time for action at this term, and if a stay order be made, the sentence can not in any event be executed until next fall." G. A. Youngquist to G. E. Q. Johnson, 3/3/31, DOJ-Tax.

89. *Literary Digest,* 3/14/31.

90. Johnson's request for funds to pay Dr. Williamson for his services was submitted after Capone's conviction with an explanation that a rebuttal of Dr. Phillips's statements on behalf of Capone could not remain unchallenged in court. G. E. Q. Johnson to W. D. Mitchell, 3/18/31, Archives.

91. W. H. Newton to M. W. Willebrandt, 3/9/31, HHPL. It is worth noting that Willebrandt formed her own law firm of Willebrandt, Horowitz & McCloskey. Willebrandt was retained by the Fruit Industries, Ltd., a marketing agency for the benefit of growers of grapes and other fruits. The mission was to stabilize the California grape crop and the distribution of grapes by avoiding as much waste as possible. Naturally, she had a vested interest in moving grapes to the market, and obstructions to such movement, including strikes or gangster-imposed tariffs, would come to her attention for legal action.

92. H. C. Hoover to W. D. Mitchell, 3/16/31, HHPL. Several criminal tax cases had been opened in New Jersey. E. C. Grouter to G. A. Youngquist, 3/19/31, DOJ-Tax.

93. W. D. Mitchell to H. C. Hoover, 3/25/31, Archives.

94. G. A. Youngquist to W. D. Mitchell, 3/24/31, DOJ-Tax.

95. The listed successes were Ralph Capone, sentenced to three years; Jack Guzik, sentenced to five years; Frank Nitti, sentenced to eighteen months; Terry Druggan, pleaded guilty but not yet sentenced; Frank Lake, pleaded guilty but not yet sentenced; Al Capone, sentenced to six months for contempt of court. He described the composition of the Capone organization; various criminal cases involving the board of assessments, building commissioners, and public contractors; and an investigation of a former member of the Illinois legislature. Youngquist pointed out that the Treasury Department had some history of settling some cases with alleged tax evaders: "Some time ago the Treasury Department compromised a case with Frank Hague, mayor of Jersey City, New Jersey, upon his paying a considerable sum of money. It developed that the money was advanced by Theodore M. Brandle. . . . Brandle and Hurley are ostensibly in the bonding and insurance business, but the investigation indicates that they are labor racketeers." He urged, therefore, the early assignment of special agents to New York to proceed in the manner used in Chicago.

96. When Dutch Schultz, the Bronx beer baron, was arrested by New York City police on June 18, 1931, they found $18,645 in cash in his pockets. Immediately, the detectives who made the arrest notified the U.S. Attorney's office which suggested that federal charges against Schultz might follow if local charges did not hold. A *New York Times* article on June 19 reported that "There were some in the Federal Building, however, who held that the money found on Schultz was probably income for 1931, which is not yet taxable" (p. 1). The comment was made thatWilliam Froelich's management of the new teams of agents and U.S. attorneys was not yet available to New York "because the drive against gangsters in the mid-Western city is far from ended, and more indictments are expected there." Days later, the U.S. attorney served a lien on the money seized from Schultz, having developed evidence that Schultz had banked $856,000 in the last six months of 1930.

Schultz was compared to Capone by a local judge who remarked, "Chicago has its Scarface Al Capone and New York has its Dutch Schultz. We don't want fellows like Schultz to come in here and run our courts" (*New York Times*, 6/25/31, p. 13).

97. G. A. Youngquist to W. D. Mitchell, 3/24/31, HHPL.

98. W. D. Mitchell to G. A. Youngquist, 3/25/31, DOJ-Tax.

99. W. D. Mitchell to H. C. Hoover, 3/25/31, Archives.

100. Kobler, op. cit., p. 322.

101. H. T. Jones to G. A. Youngquist, 5/5/31, DOJ-Tax.

102. W. J. Froelich to W. D. Mitchell, 4/15/31, DOJ-Tax.

103. W. J. Froelich to G. A. Youngquist, 5/7/31, DOJ-Tax.

104. Attorney General Mitchell received vigorous criticism from the wet press concerning statements he made in a radio speech on organized crime. Mitchell said that organized crime received only 20 percent of its income from prohibition violations and that gangsters committed ten times as many violations of state statutes as they did federal laws. The thrust of his speech urged states to take a more active role in prosecution of gangsters. *Literary Digest*, 5/30/31.

105. W. L. Vandeventer to G. A. Youngquist, 6/2/31, DOJ-Tax. Vandeventer reported that the information was acquired "by the interception of telephonic communications between Chicago and Kansas City."

106. W. D. Mitchell to G. E. Q. Johnson, 6/26/31, DOJ-Tax.

107. "And several news articles hint that President Hoover himself is behind the patient, thorough campaign which now nears its completion." *Literary Digest*, 6/27/31.

108. F. J. Loesch to H. C. Hoover, 6/29/31, HHPL.

109. 6/30/31, DOJ-Tax.

110. Respectively: Unknown writer to Attorney General, 8/3/31; Unknown writer to Attorney General, 8/1/31, DOJ-Tax. Names are blanked out pursuant to the Freedom of Information Act exemption on privacy, even after sixty years.

111. A. A. Ballantine to G. E. Q. Johnson, 7/24/31, Archives.

112. G. E. Q. Johnson to G. A. Youngquist, 12/31/31, DOJ-Tax. Youngquist had called for this report on November 13: "I should like to have from you a report as to what information the court had of the proposed arrangement for plea of guilty and sentence and what reason you had to think that the court would adopt the recommendation."

113. W. D. Mitchell to G. E. Q. Johnson, 7/28/31, DOJ-Tax.

114. Memorandum of G. A. Youngquist, 4/5/32, DOJ-Tax. The DOJ–Tax Division blacked out two full paragraphs and one additional sentence in this memo, now sixty years old.

115. G. A. Youngquist to W. D. Mitchell, 7/31/31, DOJ-Tax.

116. Testifying on March 8, 1932, before the Senate Judiciary Committee upon Judge Wilkerson's nomination for the Seventh Circuit Court of Appeals, Frank Loesch offered the following insights: "As a result of focusing public attention, the law officers got busy, and we got some of them, and then came the indictment in the United States Court, of Capone. Some of his fellows

had been convicted there, his brother and others, and I learned that virtually [a] bargain had been made with Capone that he should be sentenced for two and one-half years. . . . I supposed that trial would go through, that Capone would plead guilty and get two and one-half years in jail. I cannot put upon paper, nor can I put into testimony, gentlemen, the thrill that went over the City of Chicago when Judge Wilkerson said he would not be bound by any such bargain as that, but he would put the man on trial. He allowed Capone to withdraw his plea of guilty to the Prohibition violation, and then tried him on failure to make his income tax return."

When Senator Walsh of Montana asked him who made the bargain with Capone, Loesch answered George E. Johnson. He continued, "He must have had his support and the reason that was given to me was they were doubtful about their proof." When pressed on this answer, Loesch said, "I say the reports that afterwards reached me where the government case was not as strong as they thought it ought to be, and they thought it was best to give him a light sentence, rather than put him on trial." Senator Blaine pressed for more insight, and Loesch said, "I do not know what the facts are, except the government officers thought the case was weak, and therefor they had better take what they could get on the bargain of two and one-half years, rather than to try a case and fail for lack of proof, and allow him to escape."

117. G. A. Youngquist to Unknown citizen, 5/11/32, DOJ-Tax.

118. Of the complete set of twenty-two counts, Capone was convicted on three felony counts (one, five, and nine), attempt to evade tax; and two misdemeanor counts (thirteen and eighteen), failure to make return. He was not convicted on two counts of attempt to evade tax for 1928 and 1929; not convicted on five counts to attempt to evade tax in that he concealed income, failed to make return, and failed to pay tax for 1925 to 1929; not convicted on five counts of attempt to evade payment of tax for 1925 to 1929; and not convicted on five counts of attempt to evade payment of tax in that he concealed income and assets, failed to make return, and failed to pay tax for 1925 to 1929.

The law permitted Judge Wilkerson to sentence Capone to five years and a $10,000 fine for each of the three felony counts and one year and a $10,000 fine for each of the two misdemeanor counts. He chose, however, to sentence him to ten years for counts one and nine, allowing count five to be concurrent with the others, and to add one year for the misdemeanors and one fine of $10,000. This maneuvering allowed the judge and the Justice Department to claim to the press that Capone had been given the maximum sentence on each count. G. A. Youngquist to W. D. Mitchell, 4/13/32, DOJ-Tax. This memo also contains two blacked out paragraphs.

119. *New York Times*, 10/18/31. On 3/1/32 the *Times* concluded that had the Internal Revenue Service failed to seek Capone's conviction "a class of tax-exempt citizens would be created, and the government was not concerned with whether the income had been unlawfully obtained. The tax laws applied to profits no matter what their source."

120. The report is titled "Special Drive Against Racketeers, Intelligence Unit, Case Reported November 1931." Archives.

Case No.	Taxpayer	Tax Years	(Dollars) Taxes	(Dollars) Penalties
SI-9949-F*	H. Rosoff	3	152.14	114.11
SI-9926-F	Battipaglia & Bros.	12	6070.73	4553.08
SI-9826-F	M. Matranga	10	1256.06	942.06
SI-9825-F	M. Sabatelli	5	1327.50	995.62
SI-9630-F	Luigi Pagano	4	361.81	200.25
SI-9739-F	John Semler	2	19701.39	12868.44
SI-9763-F	F. Zagarino	4	22831.88	11415.95
SI-9625-F	Frank Casello	4	28209.88	14104.94
SI-9626-F	Frank Magistro	3	733.08	366.53
SI-9807-F	Frank DePalermo	4	24207.81	12103.91
SI-9632-F	Charles Rao	3	113.40	56.70
SI-9634-F	G. Sindona	4	270.21	135.11
SI-9622-F	Ignazio Milone	4	63299.20	47478.14
SI-9631-F	Guiseppe Carbo	3	1061.21	750.28
SI-9627-F	G. Alberti	4	14786.35	7393.17
SI-9893-F	W. D. Allen	6	39.54	29.63
Totals		75	184422.19	113507.93

*Special intelligence file

121. E. L. Irey to D. Burnet, 11/24/31. The suggested letter written by Irey read: "The Secretary of the Treasury has called my attention to the valuable assistance rendered to the Intelligence Unit of the Bureau of Internal Revenue by Mr. John T. Rogers of the St. Louis Post-Dispatch staff in the investigation at Chicago resulting in the conviction of Alphonse Capone and his lieutenants for income tax evasions. I am informed that the aid of Mr. Rogers was a large factor in the successful consummation of these cases. I appreciate and commend the great public service so performed by the Post-Dispatch and Mr. Rogers." Mellon's endorsement recommended that a letter from Hoover to Pulitzer would be helpful, "As I know this general subject is of much interest to you." A. A. Mellon to H. C. Hoover, 12/4/31, Archives.

122. S. Key and J. H. McEvers to G. A. Youngquist, 1/12/32.

123. G. E. Q. Johnson to W. D. Mitchell, 3/17/32, DOJ-Tax.

124. Loesch made his remarks to Borah in connection with Hoover's appointment of Judge Wilkerson to the federal appeals court. He said that the Chicago labor unions were virtually in the hands of the Capone organization. Capone, Loesch said, had two "adherents" in the Illinois state senate: Senator James B. Leonardi [Leonardo], who had been convicted of conspiracy to murder and to kidnap and other crimes and Senator Daniel A. Serratella, who had been indicted for vote fraud while he was employed in the voting office in Chicago. Loesch highlighted the fact that Serratella's attorney was a member of the Illinois House of Representatives while Peter C. Granata, a member of the U.S. Congress, had been "elected on the face of the returns by frauds so gross that the County Judge sent a number of the judges and clerks

of election committing the frauds to jail." He described William Parrillo, an assistant U.S. attorney, as a Capone supporter because it was feared that Parrillo would be nominated to Republican ward committeeman, thus giving him political control over liquor and vice activities in Chicago. He claimed that Capone had about 185 men under his control who were paid between $100 and $300 per week. In conclusion, Loesch said that Capone would consider it a great victory if Judge Wilkerson were not appointed to the court of appeals. F. J. Loesch to W. E. Borah, 3/23/32, HHPL.

CHAPTER 7

1. *New York Times*, 12/13/29.

2. The three institutions were created by Congress in the "Three Prisons Act," signed into law by President Benjamin Harrison in March 1891. Atlanta became operational in 1902. Leavenworth became operational in 1906. McNeil Island became operational in 1907.

3. More recently, the Federal Bureau of Prisons and its reform administrators have garnered new academic and historical recognition. In 1991, a conference was held in Washington, D.C., commemorating fifty years of Bureau of Prisons operations. A dedicatory collection of papers was designated for publication in 1993.

4. F. J. Donner, *The Age of Surveillance: The Aims and Methods of America's Political Intelligence System* (New York: Alfred A. Knopf, 1980), pp. 32–51; C. Gentry, *J. Edgar Hoover: The Man and the Secrets* (New York: W. W. Norton, 1991), pp. 70–144; R. G. Powers, *Secrecy and Power: The Life of J. Edgar Hoover* (New York: Free Press, 1987), pp. 36–143; C. S. Darrow, "The Ordeal of Prohibition," *American Mercury* 2 (August 1924): 419–427; W. Seagle, "Criminal Syndicalism," *American Mercury* 3 (June 1925): 36–42; R. S. Moley, "Politics and Crime," *Annals of the American Academy of Political and Social Science* 75 (May 1926): 78–84.

5. Clarence Darrow attempted to stir popular interest in capital punishment and harsh prison conditions. Darrow was not regarded as a mainstream authority on prisons, however, and the public mind seemed to be divided on matters of appropriate punishment.

6. *New York Times*, 5/5/29.

7. S. Bates, *Prisons and Beyond* (New York: Macmillan, 1936), pp. 14–17.

8. Quoted from radio remarks in June 1930 as published in the Osborne Society *News Bulletin*, June 1930.

9. S. Bates, "Architectural Environment in Relation to Prisoners," *Journal of Criminal Law and Criminology* 22 (November 1931): 544.

10. S. Bates, "Have Our Prisons Failed?" *Journal of Criminal Law and Criminology* 23 (November-December 1932): 574.

11. In several brief notes to requestors, Bates said that he had been forced by the weight of his responsibilities to avoid engagements for at least one year. Felix Frankfurter at Harvard Law School urged New York's Governor Franklin Roosevelt to ask Bates to serve on a commission to study the New

York prison system, saying, "I know that he would bring a good deal of authority to the results of such an investigation." Again, the rigors of the job in Washington obligated a letter of declination to Frankfurter. F. Frankfurter to F. D. Roosevelt, 7/25/29, SHSU.

12. *New York Times*, 4/23/29.

13. S. Bates to F. Loveland, 6/17/29, Archives.

14. S. Bates to S. Glueck, 8/1/29, Archives.

15. Representative of Bates's philosophy of prison administration was an article titled "What May Be Done to Forward the Judicious Application of the Principle of Individuation of Punishment by the Judge Who Assigns the Penalty to be Inflicted on the Offender," published in the *Journal of Criminal Law and Criminology* in 1926. Bates offered a system for classifying prisoners based upon their offenses. He argued that the classification system must attempt to match the prisoner with a treatment program, an idea that had been gaining favor with prison progressives since 1915. B. McKelvey, *American Prisons: A History of Good Intentions* (Montclair: Patterson Smith, 1977), p. 267. The plan called for building formal links between judges and prisons so that a sentence could be tailored to the individual's circumstances and the offender could grasp individual responsibility for actions. Bates concluded that "the judge should order such treatment of each individual criminal as will be most likely to effect his economic independence, intellectual integrity, and moral regeneration," Bates, "What May Be Done," p. 486. The notion of linking institutional assignments to judicial sentencing was characteristic of Bates's reform orientation and well within the general reform progressive correctional theories of the 1920s. Bates published the following articles or papers from 1920 and 1929: "The Possibilities and Methods of Increasing Parental Responsibility for Juvenile Delinquency," *American Prison Association Proceedings* (1920), pp. 267–282; "Do You Approve of Any So-Called Honor System for Inmates of Prisons and Reformatories?" *American Prison Association Proceedings* (1921), pp. 299–306; "Report of the Committee on Criminal Law and Statistics," *American Prison Association Proceedings* (1922), pp. 239–245; "Present Status of the Jail Movement," *American Prison Association Proceedings* (1923), pp. 293–296; "Care of Defective Delinquents at Bridgewater, Mass.," *Mental Hygiene* 8 (1924): 530–534; "What Should Be the Relation of the State to the County Prison System?" *American Prison Association Proceedings* (1924), pp. 269–286; with S. B. Warner, "Information Concerning Adult Male Criminals Which Should Be Published by Reformatories, Penitentiaries, and State Prisons," *Journal of Criminal Law and Criminology* 15 (1924–25): 177–238; "Report of the Committee on Criminal Law and Statistics," *American Prison Association Proceedings* (1925), pp. 117–143; "Parole and the Crime Wave," Address before the Joint Committee on Judiciary of the Massachusetts Legislature, March 3, 1926; "Parole of Prisoners," *Massachusetts Law Quarterly* 11 (1926): 1–17.

16. *New York Times*, 4/23/29.

17. MacCormick had been the executive officer at the U.S. naval prison in Portsmouth, New Hampshire, from 1917 to 1918. His superior was Thomas Mott Osborne. Under Osborne's tutelage, MacCormick moved on to study all

naval confinement facilities for the secretary of the navy. Linking educational and prison environments, MacCormick held positions as both an evaluator of prison systems and a college teacher. From 1921 to 1928, he taught courses in government at Bowdoin College in Brunswick, Maine, and served as the first alumni secretary of the college. Keeping contact with Osborne, he was asked in 1925 to survey the Vermont State Prison and with Osborne to investigate the brutality and mismanagement of the Colorado State Prison. In 1926, in honor of Osborne, MacCormick formed the Osborne Society and published, with Paul W. Garrett, the society's *Handbook of American Prisons*. Taking leave from Bowdoin in 1928, he then served as a fundraiser for a year as assistant to the president of Bennington College in Vermont. As a New Englander in the prison evaluation field, MacCormick was destined to associate with Bates, and in 1929 Bates asked him if he would come to Washington to become the assistant superintendent of the Bureau of Prisons. Impressed with MacCormick's achievements in the field of institutional education, Bates asked him in July 1929 to take charge of all responsibilities associated with welfare, education, medical services, libraries, social work, religion, food, and discipline. In 1931, MacCormick published a highly acclaimed and pioneering book, *The Education of Adult Prisoners: A Survey and a Program* (New York: National Society of Penal Information).

18. Bennett replaced Bates as the second director of the Bureau of Prisons, later publishing an autobiography, *I Chose Prison* (New York: Alfred A. Knopf, 1970).

19. Stutsman was superintendent of the federal detention facility in New York City and author of *Curing the Criminal: A Treatise on the Philosophy and Practices of Modern Correctional Methods* (New York: Macmillan, 1926). See T. Schade, "Prison Officer Training in the United States: The Legacy of Jessie O. Stutsman," *Federal Probation* 50 (December 1986): 40–46.

20. Whenever and wherever he found an open ear to this objective, he encouraged college graduates to seek employment in prisons and reformatories and, in particular, with the Bureau of Prisons. For example, in October 1929, he wrote to professor Edith Abbott at the University of Chicago, "if you have opportunities to suggest to some of your male workers that there is a real career ahead of them in the Federal prison service this will be a great assistance to us." S. Bates to E. Abbott, 11/12/29, Archives. The June 1931 issue of the Osborne Society *News Bulletin* observed: "The Visitors Book [at institutions] and questionnaires received indicate that much study is being given to the subject of criminology by university students."

21. S. Bates to M. E. Goodrich, 4/15/30, Archives. Goodrich was commissioner of penal institutions for New York.

22. S. Bates to J. Michael, 7/26/30, Archives.

23. S. Bates to G. T. Holcombe, unknown date/1930, Archives.

24. In a draft of *I Chose Prison* by Bennett dated 3/9/59, SHSU.

25. James V. Bennett's account of what followed is best quoted for its humorous cast on the warden's flat refusal to release the agent: "'How can I release you' thundered that highly indignant official. 'You came here under

a legal commitment and you haven't served your time out by any means! Do you think I can just open up the door and let any prisoner out when he decides he's tired of our bill of fare?' The special agent pleaded, explained, and tried to persuade. The warden was adamant. He knew the law! Finally he was persuaded to get in touch with the Department in Washington. But no argument, or even orders could move him to set the man free. Either he saw no way in which this could be done without violating the letter of the law or he was in a panic concerning what might be recorded in the agent's report."

26. Ibid.

27. Ibid.

28. *New York Times,* 3/17/29.

29. Ibid.

30. Sartain actually served time in the penitentiary he once managed.

31. *New York Times,* 3/24/29.

32. *New York Times,* 1/23/30. Further testimony by Hoover added, "The three agents who went into the Federal penitentiaries at Atlanta, Leavenworth and McNeil Island were college men." After pointing out Willebrandt's order to remove the agents on the inside, Hoover testified, "I will say that that practice is not indulged in at the present time. In fact, I received orders from the present Attorney General that that was not to be done." Hoover closed with a remark he couldn't have meant seriously, "We have a very definite rule in the bureau that any employe engaging in wire-tapping will be dismissed from the service of the bureau."

33. S. Bates to F. A. Butten, 5/8/30, Archives.

34. S. Bates to W. J. Harris, 5/15/30, Archives.

35. For example, Atlanta's Warden Aderhold granted a *Chicago Tribune* reporter an interview with prisoner H. L. Goldhurst of New York. FBI file 36-51-65 contains extensive reports on the Goldhurst case. Apparently Goldhurst alleged he had been promised immunity from prosecution and a parole agreement. There was pressure on the Bureau of Prisons to clear up media accounts suggesting that the Justice Department had given him special favors.

36. S. Bates to T. B. White, 6/9/31, Archives. Two months later, Bates inquired of Justice Department attorneys, "There is apparently nothing in the United States Statutes governing the right of the warden to inflict solitary confinement. Is there any memorandum, or are there decided cases, in any way restricting the right of the warden to inflict solitary confinement for punishment, or to provide separate confinement for prisoners who have shown themselves unable to get along in association with others." S. Bates to H. T. Jones, 8/8/29, Archives. The correspondence back and forth raised legal questions about the right of the warden to administer such punishments, but a rule promulgate at Atlanta in 1910, never challenged in court, granted authority to the wardens for "confinement in solitary cells with or without hard labor." Therefore, the department attorneys resolved, authority existed. B. R. Gary to H. T. Jones, 8/15/29, Archives.

37. S. Bates to F. R. Archer, 7/30/31, Archives.

38. The statistics are as follows:

Number of Persons per Million Population Sent to Federal Prisons and Reformatories and Number of Federal Prisoners

Year	No. per Million	Federal Prisoners
1910	11.4	2,043
1920	26.2	3,889*
1926	40.6	7,080
1929	58.9	10,068
1930	80.6	12,332

Source: Address by Attorney General Mitchell, to the University of Minnesota Law School Association, 4/15/31, HHPL.
*Number located in other DOJ source

39. S. Bates to W. D. Mitchell, 11/25/29, Archives.

40. The institution was opened in 1927 with Harris as the first warden.

41. M. B. Harris to S. Bates, 7/30/29, Archives. By February 1933, Alderson's official commitment authorization described the facility as a place of confinement for all female prisoners over the age of eighteen convicted of an offense against the United States and sentenced to more than one year with the following exceptions: (1) persons who had previously served a sentence in the institution either by direct commitment or by transfer, and (2) persons who appear to be psychopathic or mentally unbalanced.

42. S. Walker's section on "convict labor" provides an excellent summary of this important issue. *Popular Justice: A History of American Criminal Justice* (New York: Oxford University Press, 1980), pp. 71–73.

43. Congress had acted in 1923 to create the Joint Committee to Determine What Employment May Be Furnished Federal Prisoners. Late in 1924 Herbert Hoover, then secretary of commerce, convened the first federal conference to address "Competition between Prison-made Products and Free Industry and Labor." Both bodies addressed the use of convicts in piece-rate contract work as a source of repeated objection by labor groups and private manufacturers. State prison administrators and politicians avoided where possible any public discussions about defraying public costs through prisoner labor. Nonetheless, labor groups often instigated such debates and posed counterarguments on humanitarian and labor displacement grounds. Not unexpectedly, and befitting their traditional commitment to profiteering, manufacturers proclaimed interest in production at the lowest possible labor costs. With subtle but persistent expansion of labor power by the mid-1920s and a creeping spirit of prison reform regarding prison-goods-for-hire, several states outlawed contract prison labor. By 1929, prison contract labor had almost disappeared. McKelvey, op. cit., p. 292.

44. W. D. Mitchell to J. Taber, 3/15/29, Archives.

45. The survey revealed the following demographic information pertaining to the federal penitentiary population: In terms of race/ethnicity: White, 6303; Colored, 1386; Mexican, 319; Indian, 76; Chinese, 109; Japanese, 24; Eskimo, 3; other Orientals, 7. In terms of age: under 20, 388; 20–30, 3148; 30–40, 2804; 40–50, 1282; 50–60, 484; over 60, 121. In terms of first offender versus repeat offender: first time, 5,535 (67.3%); repeat, 2,692 (32.7%). Of 8,277 total federal penitentiary inmates at Atlanta, Chillicothe, Leavenworth, and McNeil Island, 4,699 (57%) were serving sentences of five years or less.
46. News conference, 8/6/29, *Public Papers.*
47. S. Bates to Bureau of Budget, 8/13/29, Archives.
48. Ibid.
49. The formal statement on the same day modified the locations to include Alcatraz, Leavenworth, and Governors Island. "Statement on the Use of Army Prisons to Relieve Overcrowding in Federal Prisons," *Public Papers,* 8/20/29.
50. News conference, 8/23/29, *Public Papers.*
51. "Annual Message to the Congress on the State of the Union," 12/3/29, *Public Papers.*
52. On October 24, 1929, Bates wrote this instruction to U.S. attorneys, U.S. marshals, and district judges.
53. M. B. Harris to S. Bates, 12/12/29, Archives.
54. S. Bates to M. B. Harris, 4/14/30, Archives.
55. G. Abbott to S. Bates, 2/2/33, Archives.
56. S. Bates to E. G. Lowry, 12/6/29, Archives.
57. This did not include elimination of segregation among federal prisoners or the policy of building separate prison facilities for blacks and whites: "A camp for colored prisoners has been set up in Chatham, Georgia, and as soon as authority has been obtained it is planned to set up many other such camps." S. Bates to W. D. Mitchell, 12/1/29, Archives.
58. S. Bates to W. B. Scot, 1/25/30. S. Bates to A. D. Baird, 1/25/30, Archives.
59. "Special Message to the Congress Urging Enactment of Recommendations for Criminal Law Enforcement," 4/28/30, *Public Papers.*
60. U.S. Congress, House of Representatives, "Report on Federal Penal and Reformatory Institutions," Report 2303, p. 5.
61. *New York Times,* 8/1/30.
62. *New York Times,* 11/4/29.
63. S. Bates to E. M. Rogers, unknown date/fall 1929, Archives.
64. S. Bates to A. C. Aderhold, 3/1/30, Archives.
65. J. J. Ryan to S. Bates, 11/19/30, Archives.
66. S. Bates to K. S. Perkins, 10/4/30, Archives.
67. S. Bates to J. J. Ryan, 9/15/30, Archives.
68. S. Bates to J. J. Ryan, 6/16/31, Archives.
69. S. Bates to J. Michael, 7/26/30, Archives.
70. S. Bates to W. D. Mitchell, 2/15/33, HHPL.
71. U.S. Congress, House of Representatives, House Report No. 2303.
72. U.S. Congress, House of Representatives, "Amend Probation Law," Report No. 2666, 1929.

73. Bates, *Prisons and Beyond*, p. 285.

74. F. G. Zerbst to S. Bates, 12/20/31; S. Bates to W. D. Mitchell, 12/23/31; S. Bates to F. G. Zerbst, 12/29/31; J. E. Hoover to S. Bates, 12/30/31, Archives. Austin MacCormick disagreed with Bates and argued that White was responsible for allowing conditions that produced the riot to exist. A. H. MacCormick to S. Bates, 12/29/31, Archives.

75. W. D. Mitchell to S. Bates, 12/24/31, Archives.

76. S. Bates to W. R. Mitchell, 12/29/31, Archives.

77. U.S. Congress, Senate, "Parole of United States Prisoners," Senate Report No. 537, 1930.

78. U.S. Congress, House of Representatives, House Report No. 2303.

79. For example, Bates was asked regularly to deal with the question of announcing parole decisions to the press. Since the attorney general was not part of the process of parole review, he was frequently unprepared to respond to press inquiries resulting from publication of the list of board decisions sent over to the attorney general's office. Later legislation creating the new parole board eliminated this problem by making all decisions final upon the attorney general's approval. S. Bates to W. D. Mitchell, 10/5/29, Archives.

80. J. V. Bennett to S. Bates, 11/6/29, Archives.

81. S. Bates to W. D. Mitchell, 12/30/29, Archives.

82. W. D. Mitchell to C. B. Slemp, 12/30/29, Archives. This memo reads, in part, that Mitchell and Bates were unhappy with "the present method of handling this difficult branch of correctional work."

83. E. H. Sutherland to S. Bates, 4/17/30, Archives.

84. Just a few days after Hoover had appointed Bates, he appointed Mrs. Caroline Bayard Wittpen as commissioner to the International Prison Commission.

85. J. V. Bennett to S. Bates, 5/28/30, Archives.

86. S. Bates to W. D. Mitchell, 6/2/30, Archives.

87. S. Bates to W. D. Mitchell, 5/27/30, Archives.

88. S. Bates to W. D. Mitchell, 6/2/30, Archives.

89. J. V. Bennett to S. Bates, 6/10/30, Archives.

90. J. V. Bennett to S. Bates, 6/10/30, Archives.

91. S. Bates to J. K. Jaffray, 7/12/29, Archives.

92. G. A. Youngquist to J. J. Byrnes, 7/2/30, Archives. Some controversy developed around the provision pertaining to the National Training School. On October 7, 1930, Youngquist reversed himself when notified by Mitchell that the board could rule on the school's cases. Mitchell agreed. The author had the pleasure of an undergraduate internship at the National Training School for Boys in 1965.

93. M. B. Harris to J. V. Bennett, 7/1/30, Archives.

94. S. Bates to W. D. Mitchell, 1/14/32, Archives.

95. He asked for $100,000 for the Atlanta Penitentiary; $214,000 for the McNeil Island Penitentiary; $1,000,000 for the industrial reformatory at Chillicothe, Illinois; $500,000 for a new reformatory west of the Mississippi; $500,000 for new federal jails; and $200,000 for the D.C. youth crime facility known as the National Training School for Boys. See "Annual Budget Message to the Congress, Fiscal Year 1932," *Public Papers*, 12/3/30.

96. News conference, 5/27/30, *Public Papers*.

CHAPTER 8

1. H. C. Hoover, *Memoirs*, p. 274.

2. J. H. Wilson, *Herbert Hoover: Forgotten Progressive* (Boston: Little, Brown, 1975), p. 136.

3. D. J. Lisio, *Hoover, Blacks, & Lily-Whites: A Study of Southern Strategies* (Chapel Hill: University of North Carolina Press, 1985), pp. 274–282. By briefing this concept, I hope I have not overly simplified Lisio's scholarship.

4. National Urban League to H. C. Hoover, 3/3/29. H. C. Hoover to National Urban League, 4/1/29, HHPL.

5. Several congressional wives had been invited to the White House, a tradition in previous administrations. For Mrs. Hoover to have discriminated by not inviting Mrs. De Priest would have contradicted the Hoovers' personal attachment to black progress and invited northern political criticism. The tea party occurred without a hitch, and it was soon a forgotten event, but not without the ordinary response of the South. Southern racists and the southern press castigated the Hoovers' party invitation, even though many knew of previous visits by blacks, including Booker T. Washington, to the White House. In contrast, the Chicago *Tribune* editorialized, "if Mrs. Hoover's tea party has driven the southern fanatics away from union and association with northern fanatics, it has been the best use of tea since the night it was thrown into Boston harbor." Chicago *Tribune*, 6/19/29.

6. Texas House Journal, 41st Leg., 2d sess, Texas State Legislature, June 18, 1929.

7. "Permit me to say that I am a Republican Member of Congress and that I have observed your course in the House, and it has been retiring and exemplary. The continuance of the course would have won you the admiration and respect of your colleagues and of the country. Every courtesy has been accorded to you to which you are entitled by virtue of your high office.

You are now embarking on a perilous course which will, if you continue, disturb relations which have long been amicably settled in the South. The people of the country are in sympathy with the development and advancement of your race, and I strongly favor this course.

Any movement or attempt by you in the direction of social equality is not a true interpretation of the attitude of both peoples. It will not be tolerated by the white people of the country, nor is it desired by the negro race.

The white people have their position, and are respected in it. The colored race has its place and is respected in it. No one desires to disturb these relations. To do so might lead to disaster." J. C. Shaffer to O. De Priest, 6/18/29, HHPL.

8. "Message to the Congress Requesting Authorization for a Commission to Investigate Conditions in Haiti," 12/7/29, *Public Papers*.

9. News conference, 2/4/30, *Public Papers*.

10. The independent commission was known as the United States Commission on Education in Haiti. The all-white independent commission to

study overal conditions in Haiti for purposes of informing Hoover's foreign policy was known as the President's Commission on Haiti, or Forbes Commission after its chairman W. Camerson Forbes. See A. DeConde, *Herbert Hoover's Latin-American Policy* (New York: Octagon, 1970), pp. 84–89; H. Schmidt, *The United States Occupation of Haiti, 1915–34* (New Brunswick: Rutgers University Press, 1971), p. 208.

11. G. W. Wickersham to H. C. Hoover, 12/21/29, HHPL.

12. Other members were Mordecai W. Johnson, Leo M. Favrot, W. T. B. Williams, and Benjamin F. Hubert.

13. Chairman W. Cameron Forbes and members Henry P. Fletcher, Elie Vezina, James Kerney, and William Allen White. The Forbes Commission was intended to advise Hoover on conditions in Haiti and the methods of extrication.

14. Eventually, the commissioners were granted passage on a mine sweeper. See Schmidt, op. cit., p. 185.

15. S. H. Reading to H. C. Hoover, 8/9/30, HHPL.

16. H. C. Hoover to S. H. Reading, 8/13/30; W. Newton to W. White, 8/20/30, HHPL. See Hoover's response to Reading, 9/23/30, *Public Papers.*

17. See D. T. Carter, *Scottsboro: A Tragedy of the American South* (Baton Rouge: Louisiana State University Press, 1979), pp. 11–50.

18. E. R. Matthews to H. C. Hoover, telegram, 6/22/31, HHPL.

19. "Radio Address on the 50th Anniversary of the Founding of Tuskegee Institute," 4/14/31, *Public Papers.*

20. H. C. Hoover to W. D. Mitchell, 8/18/31, HHPL.

21. See R. L. Zangrando, *The NAACP Crusade against Lynching* (Philadelphia: Temple University Press, 1980), p. 106. The story of Hoover's involvement in the 1927 flood matter is found in P. Daniel, *Deep'n As It Come: The 1927 Mississippi River Flood* (New York: Oxford University Press, 1977).

22. National Urban League to L. Richey, 7/25/32, HHPL.

23. J. E. Andrews to H. C. Hoover, unknown date/1931, HHPL.

24. H. C. Hoover to W. D. Mitchell, 12/31/31, HHPL.

25. J. A. Schwarz, *The Interregnum of Despair: Hoover, Congress, and the Great Depression* (Urbana: University of Illinois Press, 1970), p. 9.

26. Ethnic affiliations were central to the events that followed Massie's charges.

27. Press release, 12/21/31, HHPL.

28. R. L. Wilbur, *The Memoirs of Ray Lyman Wilbur, 1875–1949,* ed. E. E. Robinson and P. C. Edwards (Stanford: Stanford University Press, 1960), pp. 496–500; Hoover, *Memoirs.*

29. Mrs. Fortescue had been a Washington, D.C., socialite with family relations that extended north to New York and south to Virginia and Kentucky. She was married to former Major Granville Roland Fortescue, war correspondent and adopted cousin to, and White House aide of, Theodore Roosevelt. Thalia's father had ridden with Roosevelt up San Juan Hill in the Spanish American war, and Mrs. Frotescue maintained a home in Franklin Roosevelt's state.

30. P. V. Slingerland, *Something Terrible Has Happened* (New York: Harper & Row, 1966), p. 131; *New York Times,* 1/12/32.

31. Newspapers screamed that a great injustice had been done by the governor's willingness to cave in to congressional pressures so horrendously racist in tone and volume. Some editorials blamed Republican administration of the Hawaiian Islands for introducing the setting for the events, and naturally this charge caught Hoover's eye. On January 11, 1932, the *New York Evening Post* editorialized the volatility of the case in its off-handed insistance that Hoover assert more direct involvement in the situation: "Were Theodore Roosevelt still President of the United States, the impulse of every red-blooded man is to believe that he would order a United States battleship to bring to the American mainland [those] accused of the murder of the Hawaiian, Kahahawai. Because the fact is that with a Kanaka, or mixed-blood jury, these four people cannot have a fair trial in Honolulu. It is also a fact that in every State of the Union they would be acquitted for taking into their own hands the justice that was denied them by the Hawaiian courts." Civil unrest, charges of racism, and vigilantism caused Hoover to employ military police patrols and to order the attorney general to carry out an investigation.

32. M. Sullivan, *Our Times* (New York: Charles Scribner's Sons, 1938), p. 92.

33. Report is found at HHPL.

34. *New York Times*, 12/4/31.

35. P. V. Slingerland, op. cit., p. 177.

36. Ibid., p. 178.

37. L. M. Judd to R. L. Wilbur, 1/15/32, HHPL.

38. A memo from W. D. Mitchell to assistant attorneys general St. Lewis and Finch, 5/6/32, is informative with respect to Mitchell's thoughts on the proposed pardon for Massie.

> This is an interesting constitutional question and the memorandum should be preserved in the files. The question is whether the constitutional power of the President to pardon "offenses against the United States" is limited to violations of acts of Congress, or refers more broadly to offenses against the sovereignty of the United States and thus applies to offenses in areas in which the sovereignty of the United States is exclusive, consisting of violations of criminal statutes enacted under authority of Congress by local legislative bodies created by Congress.
>
> My offhand impression is that the broader interpretation of the constitutional power is to be preferred. So far as the precedents are concerned, it is about a stand off. The question is to be considered an entirely open one. If the President has power to pardon violations of territorial laws, Congress may not take it away. If he has not the power under the constitution, Congress may confer it on him by statute. As a matter of policy, especially because of the doubt as to power, the President ought not to attempt to deal with territorial offenses, (where acts of Congress do not confer on him power to do so) unless in the most extraordinary case of emergency such as a death sentence.

39. R. L. Wilbur to T. Joslin, 1/20/32. T. Joslin to R. L. Wilbur, 1/20/32, HHPL.

40. P. V. Slingerland, op. cit., p. 221.

41. C. Darrow, *Attorney for the Damned: Clarence Darrow in His Own Words*, ed. A. Weinberg (New York: Simon and Schuster, 1957), pp. 104–118.

42. L. M. Judd and H. W. Lytle, *Lawrence M. Judd & Hawaii, An Auto-biography* (Rutland: Charles E. Tuttle, 1971), p. 168.

43. L. R. Judd to R. L. Wilbur, 8/25/32, HHPL.

44. R. L. Wilbur to L. R. Judd, 1/28/33, HHPL.

45. *U.S. Daily,* 2/21/33.

46. Hoover was elected president only a decade after a wartime and conspiracy-driven Justice Department, headed by A. Mitchell Palmer, had taken espionage and sedition cases to federal courts. Approximately 1500 people had been convicted under the espionage and sedition laws of 1917 and 1918. A Senate resolution passed in February 1929 called for a general amnesty for these people, despite the fact that there were no longer any prisoners in federal institutions for these crimes. Hoover seemed amenable to granting full pardons, but according to Justice Department reports of 1929, no one had applied for relief. Hoover's general policy was to urge individual investigations of each case, a horrendous task for the Bureau of Investigation. This was accomplished, although it is not unreasonable to assume that the agency (and its director, J. Edgar Hoover) responsible for building indictable cases against possible pardon claimants had no incentive to turn up evidence of pardon worthiness.

47. It was John O'Brian and Alfred Bettman, as assistant attorneys general under A. Mitchell Palmer, who slowed prosecutions applying the Espionage Act against dissidents. See P. Lamson, *Roger Baldwin: Founder of the American Civil Liberties Union* (Boston: Houghton Mifflin, 1976), p. 78. Hoover, according to Baldwin, was not an exceptionally good friend of the ACLU, but not opposed to the organization either.

48. J. L. O'Brian to R. Baldwin, 7/6/32. R. Baldwin to J. L. O'Brian, 7/12/32, Archives.

49. C. Gentry, *Frame-up: The Incredible Case of Tom Mooney and Warren Billings* (New York: W. W. Norton, 1967), pp. 358–361.

50. The Archives file 226016 contains a wealth of information and case examples worthy of further investigation for their insights into white collar crimes. Pomerene had asked Hoover in June 1931 if the president would approve Fall's transfer to a jail near El Paso. Hoover sought Mitchell's advice on the matter: "The President wonders if he might have your advice on the enclosed communication from Mr. Pomerene." Fall claimed illness as the reason for the transfer. L. Richey to W. D. Mitchell, 6/19/31, Archives. Pomerane's bill for Fall's defense arrived at the White House in June 1932.

51. "Statement Announcing the Appointment of Atlee Pomerene as Chairman of the Reconstruction Finance Corporation," 7/26/32, *Public Papers.*

52. R. L. Owen to W. D. Mitchell, 8/5/29, HHPL.

53. W. D. Mitchell to H. C. Hoover, 8/27/29, HHPL.

54. "White House Statement Announcing the President's Refusal to Pardon Harry F. Sinclair," 9/21/29, *Public Papers.* The statement was terse: "Mr. Sinclair will not be pardoned by the President."

55. H. C. Hoover to W. D. Mitchell, 11/9/31, HHPL.

56. One of the best pieces of scholarship on the details of the Teapot Dome case is provided by B. Noggle, *Teapot Dome: Oil and Politics in the*

1920's (Baton Rouge: Louisiana State University Press, 1962). Noggle suggests that Hoover cut off potential political vulnerability to the legacy of Teapot Dome by significantly cutting oil leases in the months immediately after March 1929.

57. I. H. Hoover, *Forty-Two Years in the White House* (Boston: Houghton Mifflin, 1934), pp. 157–166.

58. Charles disliked crowds, having had several bad experiences upon arriving at places where he looked out to thousands of well-wishers. C. A. Lindbergh, *We* (New York: G. P. Putnam's Sons, 1927). See the chapter titled "An Epochal Flight" in which he describes the crowd reactions to his arrival in Paris in 1927. The constant nagging attention of reporters, no doubt, formed his opinion that press people were predatory and shallow, a view he would modify, although not relinquish, as later events unfolded in which the press became useful. K. S. Davis, *The Hero: Charles A. Lindbergh and the American Dream* (Garden City: Doubleday, 1959), p. 309.

59. Telegram to H. C. Hoover, 3/2/32, HHPL.

60. C. Gentry, *J. Edgar Hoover: The Man and the Secrets* (New York: W. W. Norton, 1991), pp. 150–151. The "Lindbergh squad" was headquartered in New York City and included special agents L. G. Turrou, T. H. Sisk, W. Merrick, W. Seery, J. E. Seykora, A. Sandberg, and H. Leslie. L. G. Turrou, *Crusade against Crime* (New York: Bernard Geis, 1962), p. 147.

61. *New York Times*, 3/3/32.

62. *New York Times*, 3/2/32.

63. The *New York Times* reported on January 30, 1932, "Secret Six Working to Stop Kidnappings," and no doubt Loesch's connections with the organization influenced his faith in similar private actions sponsored by federal authorities. For the Loesch–Capone meeting, see J. Kobler, *Capone: The Life and World of Al Capone* (New York: G. P. Putnam's Sons, 1971), pp. 13–14.

64. *New York Times*, 3/2/32.

65. *New York Times*, 3/5/32.

66. A very readable account of the case is found in G. Waller, *Kidnap: The Story of the Lindbergh Case* (New York: Dial, 1961). More serious attention to the details of the investigation is found in L. Kennedy, *The Airman and the Carpenter: The Lindbergh Kidnapping and the Framing of Richard Hauptmann* (New York: Penguin, 1986). Close attention to the trial of Hauptmann is paid in S. B. Whipple, *The Trial of Bruno Richard Hauptmann* (Garden City: Doubleday, Doran, 1937).

67. Davis, op. cit., p. 326.

68. E. L. Irey and W. J. Slocum, *The Tax Dodgers* (New York: Greenberg, 1948), p. 68.

69. Kennedy, op. cit., p. 87.

70. Irey and Slocum, op. cit., p. 67.

71. Ibid., p. 72.

72. H. C. Hoover to W. D. Mitchell, 5/13/32, HHPL.

73. "Statement on the Lindbergh Kidnapping," 5/13/32, *Public Papers*.

74. J. Fisher, *The Lindbergh Case* (New Brunswick: Rutgers University Press, 1987), p. 123.

75. *New York Times*, 3/3/32.

76. E. K. Alix, *Ransom Kidnapping in America 1874–1974* (Carbondale: Southern Illinois University Press, 1978), pp. 24–26.

77. *New York Times*, 1/27/32.

78. The *New York Times* reported statistics for kidnapping cases as follows: California, 25 cases; Indiana, 20 cases; Illinois, 49 cases; Kansas, 8 cases; Michigan, 26 cases; Oklahoma, 9 cases; Wisconsin, 8 cases; Nebraska, 6 cases; Massachusetts, 15 cases; New Jersey, 10 cases.

79. *New York Times*, 1/3/32.

80. *New York Times*, 3/3/32.

81. W. D. Mitchell, press statement, 3/2/32, HHPL.

82. W. D. Mitchell, radio address on the National Broadcasting System, sponsored by the American Bar Association, 3/6/32, HHPL.

83. H. Cummings and C. McFarland, *Federal Justice: Chapters in the History of Justice and the Federal Executive* (New York: Macmillan, 1937), p. 479.

84. Hoover, *Memoirs*, p. 274.

85. "Address to the American Legion," 10/6/30, *Public Papers*.

86. D. J. Lisio, *The President and Protest: Hoover, Conspiracy, and the Bonus Riot* (Columbia: University of Missouri Press, 1974), pp. 7–17.

87. "Veto of a Bill to Veterans' Pensions," 4/27/32, *Public Papers*.

88. Hoover, *Memoirs*, pp. 285–286.

89. Ibid., p. 288.

90. *Literary Digest*, 10/3/31.

91. D. MacArthur, *Reminiscences* (New York: McGraw-Hill, 1964), p. 93.

92. D. C. James, *The Years of MacArthur, 1880–1941* (Boston: Houghton Mifflin, 1970), p. 386.

93. Lisio, op. cit., pp. 70–71.

94. News conference, 8/5/30, *Public Papers*.

95. W. Manchester, *American Caesar: Douglas MacArthur, 1880–1964* (Boston: Little, Brown, 1978), pp. 149–152.

96. R. G. Powers, *Secrecy and Power: The Life of J. Edgar Hoover* (New York: Free Press, 1987), pp. 167–168.

97. MacArthur, op. cit., p. 94.

98. Furthermore, Hoover's time in July alone had been taken up with vetoing wage rates for contractors in public buildings (July 1), delivering a message to Congress on unemployment relief (July 5), delivering a major message on emergency relief and construction legislation (July 6), recommending alterations in the board of directors of the Reconstruction Finance Corporation (July 11), addressing the conference of smaller industries (July 11), reaching closure on a treaty with Canada for the St. Lawrence Seaway project (July 13 and 18), dedicating the International Peace Garden in Manitoba, Canada (July 14), cutting salaries of his cabinet and himself (July 15), holding a news conference on the Federal Home Loan Bank Act, (July 22), meeting with the New England Conference on Reemployment (July 23), addressing a message to the Boy Scouts of America (July 26), and—on the morning of the bonus disturbance—presenting the distinguished flying cross to two aviators.

99. "Statement about the Bonus Marchers," 7/28/32, *Public Papers*.

100. News conference with Secretary Hurley and General MacArthur, 7/28/32, *Public Papers.*

101. Lisio, op. cit., p. 192.

102. Secretary Hurley's order stated in part, "Surround the affected area and clear it without delay. Turn over all prisoners to the civil authorities. In your orders insist that any women and children who may be in the affected area be accorded every consideration and kindness. Use all humanity consistent with the due execution of this order." "Statement about the Bonus Marchers," 7/28/32, *Public Papers.*

103. "If President Hoover had not acted when he did he would have been faced with a serious situation. Another week might have meant that the government was in peril. He had reached the end of an extraordinary patience and had gone to the very limit to avoid friction before using force. Had the President not acted when he did he would have been derelict in his duty." MacArthur, op. cit., p. 95.

104. M. L. Fausold, *The Presidency of Herbert C. Hoover* (Lawrence: University of Kansas Press, 1985), pp. 200–202. Manchester, op. cit., pp. 149–152. An excellent account of street-level action is also found in M. Blumenson, *The Patton Papers, 1885–1940,* vol. 2 (Boston: Houghton Mifflin, 1972), pp. 975–980.

105. Attorney General Mitchell's report dated September 9, 1932 indicated that one-fourth of the Bonus marchers could not be identified as war veterans and that many had police records. No one questioned the adequacy or honesty of the search of War Department, Veterans Bureau, or Justice Department files to ascertain veteran status. No one questioned the relative importance of having a "criminal record," and no one raised doubt that criminal records bore any relationship to the outcome. Furthermore, the appropriateness of participation in the demonstrations by nonveterans, labeled by the attorney general as "imposters," was regarded only as a factor conducive to insurrection. See "Statement on the Justice Department Investigation of the Bonus Army," 9/10/32, *Public Papers.*

CHAPTER 9

1. "Message to the American Conference of Institutions for the Establishment of International Justice," 5/2/32, *Public Papers.*

2. F. Freidel, *Franklin D. Roosevelt: Launching the New Deal* (Boston: Little, Brown, 1973), pp. 196–212.

3. "Remarks upon Laying the Cornerstone of the Department of Justice Building," 2/23/33, *Public Papers.*

4. "Address Accepting the Republican Presidential Nomination," *Public Papers,* 8/11/32.

5. "Letter to Reverend Daniel A. Poling," 8/23/32, *Public Papers.*

6. "Address to the American Bar Association," 10/12/32, *Public Papers.*

7. Speech in Madison, Wisconsin, 11/5/32, *Public Papers.*

8. "Message Congratulating Franklin D. Roosevelt on His Victory in the Presidential Election," 11/8/32, *Public Papers.*

9. "Statement about Signing an Act on Reform of Criminal Procedures in Federal Courts," 2/25/33, *Public Papers.*

10. C. N. Degler, "The Ordeal of Herbert Hoover," *Yale Review* 52 (Summer 1963): 33.

11. A. U. Romasco, *The Poverty of Abundance: Hoover, the Nation, the Depression* (New York: Oxford University Press, 1965), pp. 10–23.

12. C. H. Willard to file, 6/10/29, Archives. Willard was Lowenthal's assistant.

13. Columnist Victor Yarros, writing in the July 17, 1929, issue of *The Nation,* offered the commission several suggestions for research investigation. Pointing to the many laws regularly violated, he emphasized that "millions of white persons in the Sunny South trample upon the Fourteenth and Fifteenth amendments of the Federal Constitution and ruthlessly disenfranchise millions of black citizens of the United States" (p. 60).

14. This earlier assumption was that the Treasury Department should house these functions, including the Coast Guard, as revenue enforcers was obsolete. Prohibition had evolved beyond revenue regulation to a police action, except for the industrial alcohol component. The quantity and methods of transportation of illegal narcotics into the country were no longer a simple matter of checkpoints and inspections of legitimate druggists.

15. Senate opposition avoided considerations of judicial credentials. Parker was highly regarded as an experienced and capable jurist of the first order. H. J. Abraham, *Justices and Presidents: A Political History of Appointments to the Supreme Court* (New York: Penguin, 1975), p. 189.

16. Ibid., pp. 289–290.

17. George Nash's chapter, "The Master of Efficiency," provides an excellent summary of Hoover's characteristics as a leader and analyst of both engineering and social problems. G. H. Nash, *The Life of Herbert Hoover: The Humanitarian, 1914–1917* (New York: W. W. Norton, 1988), pp. 362–378.

Bibliography

BIBLIOGRAPHIES

Brown, R. M. "Recent Contributions in the Field of Crime and Criminal Justice." *Social Forces* 6 (June 1928): 645–648.

Conner, E. "Crime Commissions and Criminal Procedure in the United States: A Bibliography, January 1920–June 1927." *Journal of Criminal Law and Criminology* 21 (May 1930): 129–144.

Conover, H. F. "Select List of Recent References on Crime and Criminal Justice, 1932–1934." Washington, D.C.: Library of Congress (1935) (mimeo).

Culver, D. C. (1934; 1939). *Bibliography of Crime and Criminal Justice, 1927–1931; and 1932–1937* (2 vols.). New York: H. W. Wilson.

Eaton, A., and S. M. Harrison (1930). *A Bibliogrpahy of Social Surveys: Reports of Fact-finding Studies Made As a Basis for Action.* New York: Russell Sage.

Iddings, E. S. (1930). *Current Research in the Law for the Academic Year 1929–1930.* Baltimore: Johns Hopkins University Press.

Kuhlman, A. F. (1929). *A Guide to Material on Crime and Criminal Justice.* New York: H. W. Wilson.

McCarthy, K. O. "Racketeering: A Contribution to a Bibliography." *Journal of Criminal Law and Criminology* 22 (November 1931): 578–586.

Nicholson, D. C., and R. Graves (1931). *Selective Bibliography on the Operation of the Eighteenth Amendment.* Berkeley: University of California, Bureau of Public Administration.

Sellin, T. "Brief Guide to Penological Literature." *Annals of the American Academy of Political and Social Science* 157 (September 1931): 224–232.

"Students' Dissertations of Criminological Interest." *Journal of Criminal Law and Criminology* 10 (May 1928): 95–97.

Vollmer, A. "Bibliography on Police Organization and Administration, Criminal Identification and Investigation." *American Journal of Police Science* 2 (January 1931): 76–79.

GOVERNMENT DOCUMENTS

National Commission on Law Observance and Enforcement. *Reports.* Washington, D.C.: 1931. (14 volumes).

U.S. Congress. House. *Origin and Development of the Office of the Attorney General.* 70th Cong. 2d sess. House Doc. 510, January 16, 1929 (Arthur J. Dodge).

U.S. Congress. House. Committee on the Judiciary. *To Reorganize Administration of Federal Prisons, to Authorize Attorney General to Contract of Care of United States Prisoners, to Establish Federal Jails, Report to Accompany H. R. 7832.* 71st Cong. 2d sess. H. Rep. 106, January 6, 1930.

BOOKS

Abels, J. (1969). *In the Time of Silent Cal.* New York: G. P. Putnam.

Abraham, H. J. (1974). *Justices and Presidents: A Political History of Appointments to the Supreme Court.* New York: Oxford University Press.

Adamic, L. (1931). *Dynamite: The Story of Class Violence in America.* New York: Viking.

Alix, E. K. (1978). *Random Kidnapping in America 1874–1974.* Carbondale: Southern Illinois University Press.

Allen, F. L. (1931). *Only Yesterday: An Informal History of the Nineteen-Twenties.* New York: Harper & Brothers.

———. (1940). *Since Yesterday: The Nineteen-Thirties in America.* New York: Harper & Brothers.

Allen, T. (1932). *Underworld: The Biography of Charles Brooks, Criminal.* New York: McBride.

Allison, G. T. (1971). *Essence of Decision: Explaining the Cuban Missile Crisis.* Boston: Little, Brown.

Allsop, K. (1961). *The Bootleggers and Their Era.* Garden City: Doubleday.

Anslinger, H. J., and W. F. Tompkins (1953). *The Traffic in Narcotics.* New York: Funk & Wagnalls.

Arnold, T. W. (1935). *Symbols of Government.* New York: Yale.

Asbury, H. (1928). *The Gangs of New York: An Informal History of the Underworld.* New York: Alfred A. Knopf.

———. (1933). *The Barbary Coast: An Informal History of the San Francisco Underworld.* New York: Alfred A. Knopf.

———. (1936). *The French Quarter: An Informal History of the New Orleans Underworld.* Garden City: Garden City.

———. (1940). *Gem of the Prairie: An Informal History of the Chicago Underworld.* New York: Alfred A. Knopf.

Baker, L. (1984). *Brandeis and Frankfurter: A Dual Biography.* New York: Harper & Row.

Ball, L. D. (1978). *The United States Marshals of New Mexico and Arizona Territories, 1846–1912.* Albuquerque: University of New Mexico Press.

Barnes, H. E. (1926). *The Repression of Crime.* New York: George E. Doran.

———. (1928). *Living in the Twentieth Century.* New York: Bobbs-Merrill.

Bates, S. (1936). *Prisons and Beyond.* New York: Macmillan.

Beito, D. T. (1989). *Taxpayers in Revolt: Tax Resistance During the Great Depression.* Chapel Hill: University of North Carolina Press.

Bennett, J. O. (1929). *Chicago Gangland: The True Story of Chicago Crime.* Chicago: Chicago Tribune.

Bennett, J. V. (1970). *I Chose Prison.* New York: Alfred A. Knopf.

Berger, R. (1975). *Executive Privilege: A Constitutional Myth.* New York: Bantam.

Berman, J. S. (1987). *Police Administration and Progressive Reform: Theodore Roosevelt As Police Commissioner of New York.* New York: Greenwood.

Bernstein, I. (1960). *The Lean Years: A History of the American Worker, 1920–1933.* Boston: Houghton Mifflin.

Best, G. D. (1975). *The Politics of American Individualism: Herbert Hoover in Transition, 1918–1921.* Westport: Greenwood.

Bilbo, J. (pseud.) (1932). *Carrying a Gun for Al Capone: The Intimate Experiences of a Gangster in the Bodyguard of Al Capone.* New York: Putnam.

Black, J. (1926). *You Can't Win.* New York: Macmillan.

Block, A. A. (1975). *Lepke, Kidtwist and the Combination: Organized Crime in New York City, 1930–1944.* Ann Arbor: University Microfilms.

———. (1985). *East Side–West Side: Organizing Crime in New York, 1930–1950.* New Brunswick: Transaction.

Blumenson, M. (1972). *The Patton Papers, 1885–1940* (volume 2). Boston: Houghton Mifflin.

Bowen, W. S., and H. D. Neal (1960). *The United States Secret Service.* Philadelphia: Chilton.

Brauer, C. M. (1986). *Presidential Transitions: Eisenhower to Reagan.* New York: Oxford University Press.

Brodie, F. M. (1974). *Thomas Jefferson, An Intimate History.* New York: W. W. Norton.

Brown, A. C. (1982). *Wild Bill Donovan: The Last Hero.* New York: Times Books.

Brown, D. M. (1984). *Mabel Walker Willebrandt: A Study of Power, Loyalty, and Law.* Knoxville: University of Tennessee Press.

Bruce, A. A. (1929). *The Administration of Justice in Illinois: A Summary of the Crime Survey of the Illinois Association of Criminal Justice.* Evanton: Northwestern University Press.

Burner, D. (1979). *Herbert Hoover: A Public Life.* New York: Alfred A. Knopf.

Burns, W. N. (1931). *The One-Way Ride: The Red Trail of Chicago Gangland from Prohibition to Jake Lingle.* New York: Doubleday, Doran.

Cahalane, C. F. (1923). *The Policeman.* New York: E. P. Dutton.

Calhoun, F. S. (1989). *The Lawmen: United States Marshals and Their Deputies, 1789–1989.* Washington, D.C.: Smithsonian Institution Press.

Callahan, J. (1928). *Man's Grim Justice: My Life Outside the Law.* New York: J. H. Sears.

Cantor, N. F. (1932). *Crime, Criminals and Criminal Justice.* New York: Henry Holt.

Carte, G. E., and E. H. Carte (1975). *Police Reform in the United States: The Era of August Vollmer, 1905–1932.* Berkeley: University of California Press.

Carter, D. T. (1979). *Scottsboro: A Tragedy of the American South.* Baton Rouge: Louisiana State University Press.

Cashman, D. (1981). *Prohibition: The Lie of the Land.* New York: Free Press.

Catton, B. (1948). *The Warlords of Chicago.* New York: Harcourt, Brace.

Cecchini, L. (1972). *Al Capone.* Milano: Giovanni De Vecchi.

Chafee, Z. Jr., W. H. Pollak, and C. Stern (1969). *The Third Degree.* New York: Arno.

Cherrington, E. H. (1920). *The Evolution of Prohibition in the United States.* Westerville: American Issue Press.

Clarke, D. H. (1929). *In Reign of Rothstein.* New York: Vanguard.

Cohen, A. K., A. Lindesmith, and K. Schuessler (eds.) (1956). *The Sutherland Papers.* Bloomington: Indiana University Press.

Cook, F. J. (1964). *The FBI Nobody Knows.* New York: Macmillan.

Corson, W. R. (1977). *Armies of Ignorance: The Rise of the American Intelligence Empire.* New York: Dial.

Corwin, E. S. (1957). *The President, Office and Powers, 1787–1957: History and Analysis of Practice and Opinion* (4th ed.). New York: New York University Press.

Cressey, P. C. (1932). *The Taxi-Dance Hall.* Chicago: University of Chicago Press.

Crouch, T. D. (1977). *Charles A. Lindbergh: An American Life.* Washington, D.C.: Smithsonian Institution Press.

Cummings, H., and C. McFarland (1937). *Federal Justice: Chapters in the History of Justice and the Federal Executive.* New York: Macmillan.

Dai, B. (1937). *Opium Addiction in Chicago.* Shanghai: Commercial.

Daniel, P. (1977). *Deep'n As It Come: The 1927 Mississippi River Flood.* New York: Oxford University Press.

Daniels, R. (1971). *The Bonus March: An Episode of the Great Depression.* Westport: Greenwood.

Darrow, C. S. (1902). *Resist Not Evil.* Chicago: C. H. Kerr.

——. (1922). *Crime: Its Causes and Treatment.* New York: Thomas Y. Crowell.

——. (A. Weinberg, ed.) (1957). *Attorney for the Damned: Clarence Darrow in His Own Words.* New York: Simon and Schuster.

Davidson, K. E. (1972). *The Presidency of Rutherford B. Hayes.* Westport: Greenwood.

Davis, K. S. (1959). *The Hero: Charles A. Lindbergh and the American Dream.* Garden City: Doubleday.

Davis, R. L. (ed.) (1972). *The Social and Cultural Life of the 1920's.* New York: Holt, Rinehart and Winston.

Dawes, C. G. (1935). *Notes as Vice President, 1928–1929.* Boston: Little, Brown.

DeConde, A. (1970). *Herbert Hoover's Latin American Policy.* New York: Octagon.

Dexter, W. F. (1932). *Herbert Hoover and American Individualism: A Modern*

Interpretation of a National Ideal. New York: Macmillan.

Dobyns, F. (1932). *The Underworld of American Politics*. New York: Fletcher Dobyns.

Dodge, A. J. (1929). *Origin and Development of the Office of the Attorney General*. Washington, D.C.: U.S. Government Printing Office.

Donner, F. J. (1980). *The Age of Surveillance: The Aims and Methods of America's Political Intelligence System*. New York: Alfred A. Knopf.

Dorris, J. T. (1953). *Pardon and Amnesty Under Lincoln and Johnson*. Chapel Hill: University of North Carolina Press.

Dorwart, J. M. (1979). *The Office of Naval Intelligence: The Birth of America's First Intelligence Agency, 1865–1918*. Annapolis: Naval Institute Press.

———. (1983). *Conflict of Duty: The U.S. Navy's Intelligence Dilemma, 1919–1945*. Annapolis: Naval Institute Press.

Downes, R. C. (1970). *The Rise of Warren Gamaliel Harding, 1865–1920*. Columbus: Ohio State University Press.

Duke, H. (1977). *Neutral Territory*. Philadelphia: Dorrance.

Eisenberg, D., U. Dan, and E. Landau (1979). *Meyer Lansky: Mogul of the Mob*. New York: Paddington.

Eisenstein, J. (1978). *Counsel for the United States: U.S. Attorneys in the Political and Legal Systems*. Baltimore: Johns Hopkins University Press.

Emerson, E. (1932). *Hoover and His Times*. Garden City: Garden City.

Englemann, L. (1979). *Intemperance: The Lost War Against Liquor*. New York: Free Press.

Epstein, E. J. (1977). *Agency of Fear: Opiates and Political Power in America*. New York: G. P. Putnam's Sons.

Everest, A. S. (1978). *Rum Across the Border: The Prohibition Era in Northern New York*. Syracuse: Syracuse University Press.

Faris, R. E. (1967). *Chicago Sociology 1920–1932*. San Francisco: Chandler.

Fausold, M. L. (1985). *The Presidency of Herbert C. Hoover*. Lawrence: University of Kansas Press.

Fausold, M. L., and G. T. Mazuzan (eds.) (1974). *The Hoover Presidency: A Reappraisal*. Albany: State University of New York Press.

Fish, P. G. (1973). *The Politics of the Federal Court System*. Princeton: Princeton University Press.

Fishman, J. F. (1923). *Crucibles of Crime*. New York: Cosmopolis.

Flexner, J. T. (1969). *George Washington and the New Nation: (1783–1793)*. Boston: Little, Brown.

Flynn, J. T. (1931). *Graft in Business*. New York: Vanguard.

Foner, E. (1988). *Reconstruction: America's Unfinished Revolution, 1863–1877*. New York: Harper & Row.

Fosdick, Raymond B. (1920). *American Police Systems*. New York: Century.

Furnas, J. C. (1969). *The Americans: A Social History of the United States, 1587–1914*. New York: G. P. Putnam's Sons.

Gatewood, W. B., Jr. (1970). *Theodore Roosevelt and the Art of Controversy: Episodes of the White House Years*. Baton Rouge: Louisiana State University Press.

Gault, R. H. (1932). *Criminology*. Boston: D. C. Heath.

Gelfand, L. E., and D. T. Critchlow (1979). *Herbert Hoover: The Great War and Its Aftermath*. Iowa City: University of Iowa Press.

Gentry, C. (1967). *Frame-up: The Incredible Case of Tom Mooney and Warren Billings*. New York: W. W. Norton.

———. (1991). *J. Edgar Hooover: The Man and the Secrets*. New York: W. W. Norton.

Gillen, J. L. (1926). *Criminology and Penology*. New York: Century.

Glueck, S. (1925). *Mental Disorder and the Criminal Law*. Boston: Little, Brown.

Glueck, S., and E. T. Glueck (1930). *500 Criminal Careers*. New York: Alfred A. Knopf.

Goodwin, J. C. (1923). *Insanity and the Criminal*. London: Hutchinson.

Graham, O. (1971). *The Great Campaigns: Reform and War in America, 1900–1928*. Englewood Cliffs: Prentice-Hall.

Graham-Mulhall, S. (1926). *Opium the Demon Flower*. New York: Montrose.

Graper, E. D. (1921). *American Police Administration*. New York: Macmillan.

Gusfield, J. R. (1963). *Symbolic Crusade: Status Politics and the American Temperance Movement*. Urbana: University of Illinois Press.

Hall, K. L. (1989). *The Magic Mirror: Law in American History*. New York: Oxford University Press.

Handlin, O. O. (1958). *Al Smith and His America*. Boston: Little, Brown.

Harpham, E. J. (1985). *Disenchanted Realist: Political Science and the American Crisis, 1884–1984*. Albany: State University of New York Press.

Haynes, F. E. (1930). *Criminology*. New York: McGraw-Hill.

Hawley, E. W., and T. Badger (eds.) (1981). *Herbert Hoover as Secretary of Commerce: Studies in New Era Thought and Practice*. Iowa City: University of Iowa Press.

Hawley, E. W., P. G. O'Brien, P. T. Rosen, and A. DeConde (1989). *Herbert Hoover and the Historians*. West Branch: Herbert Hoover Presidential Library Association.

Healy, W., and A. F. Bronner (1926). *Delinquents and Criminals*. New York: Macmillan.

Henderson, D. F. (1985). *Congress, Courts, and Criminals: The Development of Federal Criminal Law, 1801–1829*. Westport: Greenwood.

Hinshaw, D. (1950). *Herbert Hoover: American Quaker*. New York: Farrar, Straus.

Hirsch, H. N. (1981). *The Enigma of Felix Frankfurter*. New York: Basic Books.

Hoover, H. C. (1922). *American Individualism*. New York: Doubleday, Page.

———. (1928). *The New Day: Campaign Speeches of 1928*. Stanford: Stanford University Press.

———. (1933). *Hoover After Dinner: Addresses Delivered by Herbert Hoover before the Gridiron Club of Washington, D.C.* New York: Charles Scribner's Sons.

———. (1934). *The State Papers and Other Writings of Herbert Hoover* (ed. William S. Myers). New York: Doubleday, Doran.

———. (1952). *The Memoirs of Herbert Hoover, I, The Cabinet and the Presidency*. Washington, D.C.: U.S. Government Printing Office.

———. (1974–1977). *Public Papers of the Presidents of the United States,*

Herbert C. Hoover (1929–1933). Washington, D.C.: U.S. Government Printing Office.

Hoover, I. H. (1934). *Forty-Two Years in the White House.* Boston: Houghton Mifflin.

Hoover, J. E. (1938). *Persons in Hiding.* Boston: Little, Brown.

Hopkins, E. J. (1931). *Our Lawless Police.* Chicago: Les Quin.

Hostetter, G. L., and T. Q. Beesley (1929). *It's A Racket!* Chicago: Les Quin.

Hughes, T. P. (1989). *American Genesis: A Century of Invention and Techno-Logical Enthusiasm.* New York: Penguin.

Hyman, H. M. (1975). *A More Perfect Union: The Impact of the Civil War and Reconstruction on the Constitution.* Boston: Houghton Mifflin.

Hynd, A. (1945). *The Giant Killers.* New York: Robert M. McBride.

Inciardi. J. A., A. A. Block, and L. A. Hallowell (1977). *Historical Approaches to Crime: Research Strategies and Issues.* Beverly Hills: Sage.

Irey, E. L., and R. J. Slocum (1948). *The Tax Dodgers.* New York: Greenberg.

James, D. C. (1970). *The Years of MacArthur.* Boston: Houghton Mifflin.

Janney, O. E. (1911). *The White Slave Traffic in America.* New York: National Vigilance Committee.

Jennings, D. (1967). *We Only Kill Each Other: The Life and Bad Times of Bugsy Siegal.* Englewood Cliffs: Prentice-Hall.

Johnson, D. R. (1981). *American Law Enforcement: A History.* St. Louis: Forum.

Jones, D. A. (1986). *History of Criminology: A Philosophical Perspective.* New York: Greenwood.

Jones, R. L. (1933). *The Eighteenth Amendment and Our Foreign Relations.* New York: Thomas Y. Crowell.

Joslin, T. (1934). *Hoover Off the Record.* New York: Doubleday, Doran.

Judd, L. R., and H. W. Lytle (1971). *Lawrence M. Judd & Hawaii, An Autobiography.* Rutland: Charles E. Tuttle.

Kahn, D. (1967). *The Codebreakers: The Story of Secret Writing.* New York: Macmillan.

Kalman, L. (1986). *Legal Realism at Yale, 1927–1960.* Chapel Hill: University of North Carolina Press.

Karl, B. D. (1974). *Charles E. Merriam and the Study of Politics.* Chicago: University of Chicago Press.

Kavanagh, M. A. (1928). *The Criminal and His Allies.* Indianapolis: Bobbs-Merrill.

Kenney, J. P. (1964). *The California Police.* Springfield: Charles C. Thomas.

Kerr, K. A. (ed.) (1973). *The Politics of Moral Behavior: Prohibition and Drug Abuse.* Reading: Addison-Wesley.

———. (1985). *Organized for Prohibition: A New History of the Anti-Saloon League.* New Haven: Yale University Press.

Keve, P. W. (1984). *McNeil Century: Life and Times of an Island Prison.* Chicago: Nelson-Hall.

Klingaman, W. K. (1989). *1929: The Year of the Great Crash.* New York: Harper & Row.

Kobler, J. (1971). *Capone: The Life and World of Al Capone.* New York: G. P. Putnam's Sons.

———. (1973). *Ardent Spirits: The Rise and Fall of Prohibition.* New York:

G. P. Putnam's Sons.

Koskoff, D. E. (1978). *The Mellons: The Chronicle of America's Richest Family.* Thomas Y. Crowell.

Krog, C. E., and W. R. Tanner (eds.) (1984). *Herbert Hoover and the Republican Era: A Reconsideration.* New York: University Press of America.

Krout, J. A. (1925). *The Origins of Prohibition.* New York: Alfred A. Knopf.

La Motte, E. N. (1924). *The Ethics of Opium.* New York: Century.

Lamson, P. (1976). *Roger Baldwin: Founder of the American Civil Liberties Union.* Boston: Houghton Mifflin.

Landesco, J. (1929). *Organized Crime in Chicago* (Pt. III, Illinois Crime Survey). Chicago: University of Chicago Press.

Lapidus, E. J. (1974). *Eavesdropping on Trial.* Rochelle Park: Hayden.

Lashly, A. V. (1928). *Professional Criminal and Organized Crime.* New York: American Bar Association.

Laub, J. H. (1983). *Criminology in the Making: An Oral History.* Boston: Northeastern University Press.

Lavine, E. H. (1930). *The Third Degree: A Detailed and Appalling Expose of Police Brutality.* New York: Vanguard.

Lawes, Lewis E. (1928). *Life and Death in Sing Sing.* New York: Doubleday, Doran.

———. (1932). *Twenty Thousand Years in Sing Sing.* New York: R. Long and P. R. Smith.

Leech, M. (1959). *In the Days of McKinley.* New York: Harper & Row.

Leonard, V. A. (1980). *The New Police Technology.* Springfield: Charles C. Thomas.

Leuchtenburg, W. E. (1958). *The Perils of Prosperity, 1914–32.* Chicago: University of Chicago Press.

Lewis, L., and H. J. Smith (1929). *Chicago: The History of Its Reputation.* New York: Harcourt, Brace.

Lichtman, A. J. (1978). *Prejudice and the Old Politics: The Presidential Election of 1928.* Chapel Hill: University of North Carolina Press.

Lindbergh, A. M. (1973). *Hour of Gold, Hour of Lead: Diaries and Letters of Anne Morrow Lindbergh, 1929–1932.* New York: Harcourt, Brace Jovanovich.

Lippmann, W. (1932). *Interpretations 1931–1932.* New York: Macmillan.

Lisio, D. J. (1974). *The President and Protest: Hoover, Conspiracy, and the Bonus Riot.* Columbia: University of Missouri Press.

———. (1985). *Hoover, Blacks, & Lily-Whites: A Study of Southern Strategies.* Chapel Hill: University of North Carolina Press.

Livermore, S. W. (1968). *Woodrow Wilson and the War Congress, 1916–1918.* Seattle: University of Washington Press.

Lloyd, C. (1972). *Aggressive Introvert: A Study of Herbert Hoover and Public Relations Management, 1931–1932.* Columbus: Ohio State University Press.

Lowenthal, M. (1950). *The Federal Bureau of Investigation.* William Sloane Associates.

Lowitt, R. (1971). *George W. Norris: The Persistence of a Progressive, 1913–1933.* Urbana: University of Illinois Press.

Lyle, J. H. (1960). *The Dry and Lawless Years.* Englewood Cliffs: Prentice-Hall.

Lynch, D. T. (1932). *Criminals and Politicians.* New York: Macmillan.

MacArthur, D. (1964). *Reminiscenes.* New York: McGraw-Hill.

MacCormick, A. H. (1931). *The Education of Adult Prisoners: A Survey and a Program.* New York: National Society of Penal Information.

Malinowski, B. (1926). *Crime and Custom in Savage Society.* New York: Harcourt Brace.

Malone, D. (1974). *Jefferson the President: Second Term, 1805–1809.* Boston: Little, Brown.

Manchester, W. (1978). *American Caesar: Douglas MacArthur, 1880–1964.* Boston: Little, Brown.

Mannheim, H. (1972). *Pioneers in Criminology.* Montclair: Patterson Smith.

Mansfield, J. (1932). *True Tales of Kidnapings in America—in China—in Mexico.* New York: Business Bourse.

Marx, G. T. (1988). *Undercover: Police Surveillance in America.* Berkeley: University of California Press.

McAdoo, W. G. (1931). *Challenge: Liquor and Lawlessness versus Constitutional Government.* New York: Century.

McBain, H. L. (1928). *Prohibition: Legal and Illegal.* New York: Macmillan.

McConaughy, J. (1931). *From Cain to Capone—Racketeering Down the Ages.* New York: Brentano's.

McFeely, W. S. (1981). *Grant, A Biography.* New York: W. W. Norton.

McKelvey, B. (1977). *American Prisons: A History of Good Intentions.* Montclair: Patterson Smith.

McKenna, M. (1961). *Borah.* Ann Arbor: University of Michigan Press.

McPhaul, J. (1970). *Johnny Torrio: First of the Gang Lords.* New Rochelle: Arlington House.

McWilliams, J. C. (1990). *The Protectors: Harry J. Anslinger and the Federal Bureau of Narcotics, 1930–1962.* Newark: University of Delaware Press.

Medved, M. (1979). *The Shadow Presidents: The Secret History of the Chief Executives and Their Top Aides.* New York: Times Books.

Merriam, C. E. (1929). *Chicago: A More Intimate View of Urban Politics.* New York: Macmillan.

Merz, C. (1930). *The Dry Decade.* New York: Doubleday, Doran.

Messick, H. (1969). *Secret File.* New York: G. P. Putnam's Sons.

———. (1971). *Lansky.* New York: G. P. Putnam's Sons.

Millspaugh, A. C. (1937). *Crime Control by the National Government.* Washington, D.C.: Brookings Institution.

Moley, R. (1929). *Politics and Criminal Prosecution.* New York: Minton, Balch.

———. (1930). *Our Criminal Courts.* New York: Minton, Balch.

Moore, E. A. (1930). *A Catholic Runs for President: The Campaign of 1928.* New York: Ronald.

Morgan, R. E. (1980). *Domestic Intelligence: Monitoring Dissent in America.* Austin: University of Texas Press.

Mosley, L. (1976). *Lindbergh: A Biography.* Garden City: Doubleday.

Mosse, G. L. (1975). *Police Forces in History.* Beverly Hills: Sage.

Mueller, G. (1969). *Crime, Law and the Scholars.* Seattle: University of Washington Press.

Murphy, P. L. (1972). *The Constitution in Crisis Times, 1918–1969.* New York: Harper & Row.

Murphy, W. F. (1965). *Wiretapping on Trial: A Case Study in the Judicial Process.* New York: Random House.

Murray, G. (1975). *The Legacy of Al Capone: Portraits and Annals of Chicago's Public Enemies.* New York: G. P. Putnam's Sons.

Murray, R. K. (1955). *Red Scare: A Study in National Hysteria: 1919–1920.* Minneapolis: University of Minnesota Press.

———. (1973). *The Politics of Normalcy: Governmental Theory and Practice in the Harding-Coolidge Era.* New York: W. W. Norton.

Musto, D. F. (1973). *The American Disease: Origins of Narcotic Control.* New Haven: Yale University Press.

Myers, J. M. (1971). *The Border Wardens.* Englewood Cliffs: Prentice-Hall.

Myers, W. S. (1936). *The Hoover Administration: A Documented Narrative.* New York: Charles Scribner's Sons.

Nash, G. H. (1983). *The Life of Herbert Hoover, The Engineer 1874–1914.* New York: W. W. Norton.

———. (1988). *The Life of Herbert Hoover, The Humanitarian 1914–1917.* New York: W. W. Norton.

Nash, R. (1970). *The Nervous Generation: American Thought, 1917–1930.* Chicago: Rand McNally.

Nelli, H. S. (1970). *Italians in Chicago, 1880–1930.* New York: Oxford University Press.

———. (1976). *The Business of Crime: Italians and Syndicate Crime in the United States.* New York: Oxford University Press.

Ness, E., with O. Fraley (1957). *The Untouchables.* New York: Julian Messner.

Nickel, S. (1989). *Torso: Eliot Ness and the Hunt for the Mad Butcher of Kingsbury Run.* New York: Avon.

Noggle, B. (1962). *Teapot Dome: Oil and Politics in the 1920's.* Baton Rouge: Louisiana State University Press.

O'Connor, J. J. (1928). *Broadway Racketeers.* New York: Liveright.

Odegard, P. H. (1928). *Pressure Politics.* New York: Columbia University Press.

Olson, J. S. (1977). *Herbert Hoover and the Reconstruction Finance Corporation, 1931–1933.* Ames: Iowa State University Press.

Ostrander, G. M. (1957). *Prohibition Movement in California, 1848–1933.* Berkeley: University of California Press.

Owings, C. (1925). *Women Police: A Study of the Development and Status of the Women Police Movement.* New York: Frederick H. Hitchcock.

Parks, L. R. (1961). *My Thirty Years Backstairs at the White House.* New York: Fleet.

Parks, R., E. Burgess, and R. McKenzie (1928). *The City: The Ecological Approach to the Study of the Human Community.* Chicago: University of Chicago Press.

Pasley, F. D. (1930). *Al Capone: A Biography of a Self-Made Man.* New York: Ives Washburn.

———. (1931). *Muscling In.* New York: Ives Washburn.

Payton, G. T. (1971). *Patrol Procedure.* Los Angeles: Legal Books.

Peel, R. V., and T. C. Donnelly (1935). *The 1932 Campaign: An Analysis.* New York: Farrar & Rinehart.

Peterson, V. W. (1952). *Barbarians in Our Midst.* Boston: Little, Brown.

Pound, R. (1922). *Criminal Justice in Cleveland.* Cleveland: Cleveland Foundation.

———. (1930). *Criminal Justice in America.* New York: Henry Holt.

Powe, M. B. (1975). *The Emergence of the War Department Intelligence Agency: 1885–1918.* Manhattan: American Military Institute Press.

Powers, R. G. (1983). *G-Men: Hoover's FBI in American Popular Culture.* Carbondale: Southern Illinois University Press.

———. (1987). *Secrecy and Power: The Life of J. Edgar Hoover.* New York: Free Press.

President's Research Committee on Social Trends (1933). *Recent Social Trends in the United States: Report of the President's Research Committee on Social Trends* (2 vols.). New York: McGraw-Hill.

Pringle, H. F. (1964). *The Life and Times of William Howard Taft: A Biography* (2 vols.). Hamden: Archon.

Proskauer, J. J. (1934). *Suckers All.* New York: Macaulay.

Pryor, H. B. (1969). *Lou Henry Hoover: Gallant First Lady.* New York: Dodd, Mead.

Pusey, M. J. (1963). *Charles Evans Hughes.* New York: Columbia University Press.

Raper, A. F. (1933). *The Tragedy of Lynching.* Chapel Hill: University of North Carolina Press.

Reckless, W. C. (1931). *Vice in Chicago.* Chicago: University of Chicago Press.

Relyea, H. C. (ed.) (1981). *The President and Information Policy.* New York: Center for the Study of the Presidency.

Rich, B. M. (1941). *The Presidents and Civil Disorder.* Washington, D.C.: Brookings Institution.

Ritz, W. J. (1990). *Rewriting the History of the Judiciary Act of 1789: Exposing Myths, Challenging Premises, and Using New Evidence.* Norman: University of Oklahoma Press.

Robinson, E. E., and V. D. Bornet (eds.) (1975). *Herbert Hoover, President of the United States.* Stanford: Stanford University Press.

Romasco, A. U. (1965). *The Poverty of Abundance: Hoover, the Nation, the Depression.* New York: Oxford University Press.

Robinson, L. N. (1911). *History of Criminal Statistics.* Boston: Little, Brown.

Roosevelt, T. R. (1910). *American Ideals and Other Essays Social and Political.* New York: G. P. Putnam's Sons.

Rowles, B. J. (1962). *The Lady at Box 99: The Story of Miriam Van Waters.* Greenwich: Seabury.

Rumbarger, J. J. (1989). *Profits, Power, and Prohibition: Alcohol Reform and the Industrializing of America, 1800–1930.* Albany: State University of New York Press.

Russell, F. (1968). *The Shadow of Blooming Hill: Warren G. Harding in His Times.* New York: McGraw-Hill.

Sann, P. (1971). *Kill the Dutchman: The Story of Dutch Schultz.* New Rochelle: Arlington House.

Sayre, P. (1948). *The Life of Roscoe Pound.* Iowa City: University of Iowa Press.

Schlapp, M. G., and E. H. Smith (1928). *The New Criminology.* New York: Boni & Liveright.

Schlesinger, A. M., Jr. (1957). *The Crisis of the Old Order, 1919–33*. Boston: Houghton Mifflin.

Schmeckebier, L. F. (1929). *Bureau of Prohibition: Its History Activities and Organization*. Washington, D.C.: Brookings Institution.

Schmidt, H. (1971). *The United States Occupation of Haiti, 1915–1934*. New Brunswick: Rutgers University Press.

Schmidt, J. R. (1992). *"The Mayor Who Cleaned Up Chicago": A Political Biography of William E. Dever*. Dekalb: Northern Illinois University Press.

Schwarz, J. A. (1970). *The Interregnum of Despair: Hoover, Congress and the Depression*. Urbana: University of Illinois Press.

Sears, L. M. (1927). *Jefferson and the Embargo*. Durham: Duke University Press.

Seldes, G. (1965). *The Years of the Locust, America, 1929–33*. Boston: Little, Brown.

Seidelman R. (1985). *Disenchanted Realists: Political Science and the American Crisis, 1884–1984*. Albany: State University of New York Press.

Sellin, J. T. (1937). *Crime in Depression*. New York: Social Science Research Council.

Sharpe, M. C. (1928). *Chicago May: Her Story*. New York: Macmillan.

Shaw, C. R. (1930). *The Jack-Roller, a Delinquent Boy's Own Story*. Chicago: University of Chicago Press.

Sherman, R. B. (1973). *The Republican Party and Black America: From McKinley to Hoover, 1896–1933*. Charlottesville: University of Virginia Press.

Silva, R. C. (1962). *Rum, Religion and Votes: 1928 Re-Examined*. University Park: Pennsylvania State University Press.

Silver, T. B. (1982). *Coolidge and the Historians*. Durham: Carolina Academic Press.

Simpson, H. D. (1930). *Tax Racket and Tax Reform in Chicago*. Evanston: Northwestern University Press.

Sinclair, A. (1962). *Prohibition: The Era of Excess*. Boston: Little, Brown.

Siringo, C. A. (1912) [1988 ed.]. *A Cowboy Detective: A True Story of Twenty-two Years with a World Famous Detective Agency*. Lincoln: University of Nebraska Press.

Slaughter, T. P. (1986). *The Whiskey Rebellion: Frontier Epilogue to the American Revolution*. New York: Oxford University Press.

Slawson, J. (1926). *The Delinquent Boys: A Socio-Psychological Study*. Boston: R. G. Badger.

Slingerland, P. V. (1966). *Something Terrible Has Happened*. New York: Harper & Row.

Smith, A. (1929). *Campaign Addresses of Governor Alfred E. Smith*. Washington, D.C.: Democratic National Committee.

Smith, B. (1925). *The State Police: Organization and Administration*. New York: Macmillan.

———. (1934). *Chicago Crime Problems: An Approach to Their Solution*. New York: Institute of Public Administration.

Smith, D. (1986). *Zechariah Chafee, Jr.: Defender of Law and Liberty*. Cambridge: Harvard University Press.

Smith, G. (1970). *The Shattered Dream: Herbert Hoover and the Great Depression.* New York: William Morrow.

Smith, R. N. (1984). *An Uncommon Man: The Triumph of Herbert Hoover.* New York: Simon and Schuster.

Spiering, F. (1976). *The Man Who Got Capone.* Indianapolis: Bobbs-Merrill.

Steffens, L. (1931). *The Autobiography of Lincoln Steffens.* New York: Harcourt, Brace.

Stourzh, G. (1970). *Alexander Hamilton & the Idea of Republican Government.* Stanford: Standford University Press.

Stutsman, J. O. (1926). *Curing the Criminal: A Treatise on the Philosophy and Practices of Modern Correctional Methods.* New York: Macmillan.

Sugrue, T., and E. E. Starling (1946). *Starling of the White House.* Chicago: Peoples.

Sullivan, E. D. (1929). *Rattling the Cup on Chicago Crime.* New York: Vanguard.

————. (1930). *Chicago Surrenders.* New York: Vanguard.

Sullivan, M. (1938). *The Education of an American.* New York: Doubleday, Doran.

Sumner, W. T. (ed.) (1911). *The Social Evil in Chicago: A Study of Existing Conditions by the Vice Commission of Chicago.* Chicago: The Commission.

Sutherland, E. H. (1924). *Criminology.* Philadelphia: J. B. Lippincott.

Sutherland, E. H. (K. Schuessler, ed.) (1973). *On Analyzing Crime.* Chicago: University of Chicago Press.

Swindler, W. F. (1969). *Court and Constitution in the Twentieth Century: The Old Legality 1889–1932.* Indianapolis: Bobbs-Merrill.

Tachau, M. K. B. (1978). *Federal Courts in the Early Republic: Kentucky 1789–1816.* Princeton: Princeton University Press.

Tannenbaum, F. (1922). *Wall Shadows: A Study of American Prisons.* New York: G. P. Putnam's Sons.

————. (1933). *Osborne of Sing Sing.* Chapel Hill: University of North Carolina Press.

————. (1938). *Crime and the Community.* Boston: Ginn.

Taylor, A. H. (1969). *American Diplomacy and the Narcotics Traffic, 1900–1939.* Durham: Duke University Press.

Taylor, T. (1955). *Grand Inquest: The Story of Congressional Investigations.* New York: Simon and Schuster.

Terrett, C. (1930). *Only Saps Work—A Ball for Racketeering.* New York: Vanguard.

Theoharis, A. G., and J. S. Cox (1988). *The Boss: J. Edgar and the Great American Inquisition.* Philadelphia: Temple University Press.

Thrasher, F. M. (1927). *The Gang: A Study of 1,313 Gangs in Chicago.* Chicago: University of Chicago Press.

Tidwell, W. A., J. O. Hall, and D. W. Gaddy (1988). *Come Retribution: The Confederate Secret Service and the Assassination of Lincoln.* Jackson: University of Mississippi Press.

Timasheff, N. (1964). *Sociological Theory: Its Nature and Growth.* New York: Random House.

Train, A. (1912). *Courts, Criminals and the Camorra.* New York: Charles Scribner's Sons.

———. (1925). *On the Trail of the Bad Men.* New York: Charles Scribner's Sons.

Trelease, A. W. (1971). *White Terror: The Ku Klux Klan Conspiracy and Southern Reconstruction.* New York: Harper & Row.

Ungar, S. J. (1975). *FBI: An Uncensored Look Behind the Walls.* Boston: Atlantic Monthly Press.

Van Waters, M. (1925). *Youth in Conflict.* New York: New Republic.

———. (1927). *Parents on Probations.* New York: New Republic.

Walker, S. (1980). *Popular Justice: A History of American Criminal Justice.* New York: Oxford University Press.

Wallace, E. (1930). *On the Spot.* Garden City: Doubleday, Doran.

Waller, I. (1965). *Chicago Uncensored: Firsthand Stories about the Al Capone Era.* New York: Exposition.

Ware, L. (1938). *Jacob A. Riis: Police Reporter, Reformer, Useful Citizen.* New York: D. Appleton-Century.

Warren, H. G. (1959). *Herbert Hoover and the Great Depression.* New York: Oxford University Press.

Washburn, C. (1934). *Come into My Parlor: A Biography of the Aristocratic Everleigh Sisters of Chicago.* New York: National Library Press.

Waterman, W. C. (1932). *Prostitution and Its Repression in New York City, 1900–1931.* New York: Columbia University Press.

Waters, W. W. (1933). *B.E.F.: The Whole Story of the Bonus Army.* New York: John Day.

Way, P. (1977). *The Encyclopedia of Espionage: Codes and Cyphers.* London: Danbury.

Wendt, L. (1979). *Chicago Tribune: The Rise of a Great American Newspaper.* Chicago: Rand McNally.

Wendt, L., and H. Kogan (1953). *Big Bill of Chicago.* Indianapolis: Bobbs-Merrill.

White, G. E. (1976). *The American Judicial Tradition: Profiles of Leading American Judges.* New York: Oxford University Press.

White, L. D. (1931). *Chicago Police Problems.* Chicago: University of Chicago Press.

White, W. A. (1938). *A Puritan in Babylon: The Story of Calvin Coolidge.* New York: Macmillan.

Wigdor, D. (1974). *Roscoe Pound.* Westport: Greenwood.

Wilbur, R. L. (1960). *Memoirs of Ray Lyman Wilbur* (ed. Eugene Robinson and Paul C. Edwards). Stanford: Stanford University Press.

Wilson, F. J., and B. Day (1965). *Special Agent: A Quarter Century with the Treasury Department and the Secret Service.* New York: Holt, Rinehart & Winston.

Wilson, J. H. (1975). *Herbert Hoover: Forgotten Progressive.* Boston: Little, Brown.

Wooddy, C. H. (1934). *The Growth of the Federal Government 1915–1932.* New York: McGraw-Hill.

Woodiwiss, M. (1988). *Crime, Crusades and Corruption: Prohibition in the United States, 1900–1987.* New York: Barnes & Noble.

Woods, A. (1918). *Crime Prevention.* Princeton: Princeton University Press.

——. (1919). *Policeman and Public.* New Haven: Yale University Press.
——. (1931). *Dangerous Drugs: The World Fight against Illicit Trade in Narcotics.* New Haven: Yale University Press.
Wright, T. (1966). *Rape in Paradise.* New York: Tower.
Zangrando, R. L. (1980). *The NAACP Crusade against Lynching.* Philadelphia: Temple University Press.
Zieger, R. H. (1969). *Republicans and Labor, 1919–1929.* Lexington: University of Kentucky Press.

ARTICLES

Arnold, P. E. "Herbert Hoover and the Continuity of American Public Policy." *Public Policy* 20 (Fall 1972): 525–544.
——. "The 'Great Engineer' as Administrator: Herbert Hoover and Modern Bureaucracy." *Review of Politics* 42 (July 1980): 329–348.
Arnold, T. W. "Law Enforcement—An Attempt at Social Dissection." *Yale Law Journal* 42 (November 1932): 1–24.
Bain, D. H. "The Man Who Made the Yanquis Go Home." *American Heritage* 36 (May 1985): 50–61.
Banton, J. H. "The Third Degree." *St. John's Law Review* 7 (December 1932): 60–66.
Barnes, H. E. "Scientific Treatment of Crime." *Current History* 27 (December 1927): 309–314.
Bates, S. "Criminal Records and Statistics." *Journal of Criminal Law, Criminology and Police Science* 19 (May 1928): 8–14.
——. "Scientific Penology." *Prison Journal* 10 (January 1930): 1–2.
——. "A Program of Protective Penology." *Prison Journal* 10 (October 1930): 16–18.
——. "The Status of Federal Probation." *National Probation Association Proceedings* 24 (1930): 137–139.
——. "Modern Trends in the Development of Federal and State Correctional Programs." *American Prison Association Proceedings* 60 (1930): 377–391.
——. "Probation in the United States Courts." *National Probation Association Proceedings* 25 (1931): 69–73.
Bauman, M. K. "Prohibition and Politics: Warren Candler and Al Smith's 1928 Campaign." *Mississippi Quarterly* 31 (1977–78): 109–118.
Berkowitz, E. G., and K. McQuiad. "Bureaucrats as 'Social Engineers': Federal Welfare Programs in Herbert Hoover's America." *American Journal of Economics and Sociology* 39 (1980): 321–335.
Beyle, H. C., and S. Parratt. "Measuring the Severity of the Third Degree." *Journal of Criminal Law and Criminology* 23 (July-August 1933): 485–503.
Binford, J. F. "Cook County Roadhouses." *Journal of Social Hygiene* 16 (May 1930): 357–364.
——. "May We Present the Road House?" *Welfare Magazine* (July 1927): 5–6, 11.
——. "Police and Women Offenders." *Policewoman's International Bulletin* 3 (November 1927): 2–3.

Bishop, R. L. "Bruce Barton—Presidential Stage Manager." *Journalism Quarterly* 43 (1966): 85–89.

Black, F. R. "The Expansion of Criminal Equity under Prohibition." *Wisconsin Law Review* 5 (April 1930): 412–425.

Brearley, H. C. "The Negro and Homocide." *Social Forces* 9 (December 1930): 247–253.

Bruce, A. A. "The New Era and the Law." *Bar Briefs* (State Bar Association of North Dakota) 8 (December 1931): 57–66.

———. "One Hundred Years of Criminological Development in Illinois." *Journal of Criminal Law and Criminology* 24 (May-June 1933): 11–49.

Burnham, J. C. "New Perspectives on the Prohibition 'Experiment' in the 1920's." *Journal of Social History* 2 (1968): 51–83.

Calder, J. D. "Presidents and Crime Control: Kennedy, Johnson and Nixon and the Influences of Ideology." *Presidential Studies Quarterly* 12 (Fall 1982): 574–589.

———. "Industrial Guards in the Nineteenth and Early Twentieth Centuries: The Mean Years." *Journal of Security Administration* 8 (December 1985): 11–22.

———. "Al Capone and the Internal Revenue Service: State-sanctioned Criminology of Organized Crime." *Crime, Law and Social Change* 17 (April 1992): 1–23.

Capeci, D. J. "Al Capone: Symbol of a Ballyhoo Society." *Journal of Ethnic Studies* 2 (1975): 33–46.

Cantor, N. "Crime and the Negro." *Journal of Negro History* 16 (January 1931): 61–66.

Cardozo, B. "A Ministry of Justice." *Harvard Law Review* 35 (December 1921): 113–126.

Cass, E. R. "National Crime Commission Conference." *Journal of Criminal Law and Criminology* 18 (February 1928): 497–513.

Caton, C. B. "Effect of National Prohibition on State Criminal Jurisdiction." *Cornell Law Quarterly* 14 (June 1929): 492–496.

Chamberlin, H. B. "Some Observations Concerning Organized Crime." *Journal of Criminal Law and Criminology* 22 (January 1932): 652–670.

Clark, C. E. "Present Status of Judicial Statistics." *American Judicature Society Journal* 14 (October 1930): 84–88.

Coates, A. "Criminal Law and Criminology." *North Carolina Law Review* 7 (December 1928–29): 150–155.

Conboy, M. "Organized Crime as a Business and Its Bearing upon the Administration of Criminal Law." *New York University Law Review* 7 (December 1929): 339–351.

Cuff, R. D. "Herbert Hoover, the Ideology of Voluntarism and War Organization during the Great War." *Journal of American History* 64 (1977): 358–372.

Davis, J. S. "Herbert Hoover, 1874–1964: Another Appraisal." *South Atlantic Quarterly* 68 (1969): 295–318.

Day, D. S. "Herbert Hoover and Racial Politics: The DePriest Incident." *Journal of Negro History* 65 (1980): 6–17.

Degler, C. N. "The Ordeal of Herbert Hoover." *Yale Review* 52 (June 1963): 563–583.

Dyer, L. C., and G. C. Jones. "Constitutionality of Federal Anti-Lynching Bill." *St. Louis Law Review* 13 (May 1928): 186–199.

Eagle, C. W. "Urban-Rural Conflict in the 1920's: A Historical Assessment." *Historian* 49 (November 1986): 26–48.

Eggeman, R. F. "Federal Court Interventions in Trials of Prohibition Officers." *Notre Dame Lawyer* 5 (April 1930): 400–403.

Ernst, M. L. "Report on Crime and the Foreign Born." *American Bar Association Journal* 18 (January 1932): 869–870.

"Federal Intervention Against Racketeering." *Columbia Law Review* 32 (January 1932): 100–104.

Finnegan, R. J. "Chicago Not a Breeder of Crime." *Illinois Medical Journal* 52 (August 1927): 152–157.

Forrester, J. J. "Ten Years of Prohibition." *Current History* 33 (March 1931): 807–813.

Garcia, G. F. "Herbert Hoover and the Issue of Race." *Annals of Iowa* 44 (Winter 1979): 507–515.

———. "Black Disaffection from the Presidency of Herbert Hoover, 1928–1932." *Annals of Iowa* 45 (Fall 1980): 14–23.

Garland, D. "British Criminology Before 1935." *British Journal of Criminology* 28 (Spring 1988): 1–18.

Gault, R. "A Progressive Police System in Berkeley, California." *Journal of Criminal Law and Criminology* 9 (November 1918): 319–322.

Giglio, J. N. "Voluntarism and Public Policy between World War I and the New Deal: Herbert Hoover and the American Child Health Association." *Presidential Studies Quarterly* 13 (Spring 1983): 430–452.

Glad, P. W. "Progressives and the Business Culture of the 1920's." *Journal of American History* 53 (1966): 75–89.

Glueck, S. "Principles of a Rational Penal Code." *Harvard Law Review* 41 (February 1928): 453–482.

———. "Predictability in the Administration of Justice." *Harvard Law Review* 42 (January 1929): 297–329.

Graham-Mulhall, S. "Drug Addiction and Crime." *Annals of the American Academy of Political and Social Science* 214 (May 1926): 162–165.

Hacker, E. "Criminality and Immigration." *Journal of Criminal Law and Criminology* 20 (November 1929): 428–438.

Hall, J. "Social Science As an Aid to Administration of the Criminal Law." *Dakota Law Review* 3 (April 1931): 285–298.

———. "Law As a Social Discipline." *Bar Briefs* (State Bar Association of North Dakota) 9 (December 1932): 92–110.

Haller, M. H. "Urban Crime and Criminal Justice: The Chicago Case." *Journal of American History* 57 (December 1970): 619–635.

———. "Organized Crime in Urban Society: Chicago in the Twentieth Century." *Journal of Social History* 5 (1971–72): 210–234.

Hamilton, D. E. "Herbert Hoover and the Great Drought of 1930." *Journal of American History* 68 (1982): 850–875.

Hawley, E. W. "Herbert Hoover, the Commerce Secretariat, and the Vision of an 'Associative State,' 1921–1928." *Journal of American History* 61 (June 1974): 116–140.

Hazard, H. "Women Prisoners: The United States Government Undertakes a New Project." *Howard Journal* 2 (June 1929): 298–301.

Hershberger, G. "The Development of the Federal Prison System." *Federal Probation* 43 (December 1979): 13–23.

Hoover, J. E. "The Benefits to be Derived through Cooperation with the Bureau of Investigation of the United States Department of Justice." *International Association of Chiefs of Police Proceedings* 36 (1929): 73–79.

———. "National Division of Identification and Information." *American Journal of Police Science* 2 (May 1931): 241–251.

———. "Police Problems." *St. John's Law Review* 7 (December 1932): 46–59.

Hughes, C. E. "Progress in Administration of Justice." *New York State Bar Association Proceedings* 52 (1929): 545–553.

Hurley, J. D. "The Narcotic Problem: Federal Control." *Cornell Law Quarterly* 13 (June 1928): 627–630.

Irvine, F. "Third Degree and the Privilege against Self-Incrimination." *Cornell Law Quarterly* 13 (February 1928): 211–218.

Johnson, G. E. Q. "Unified Law Enforcement: The Factor of Coordination in Crime Suppression." *Police '13-13'* 5 (January 1931): 7, 27.

———. (Remarks to State Bar Association Concerning Crime and Administration of Justice.) *Bar Briefs* (State Bar Association of North Dakota) 9 (December 1932): 144–151.

———. "Investigation and Detection of Crime." *Indiana Law Journal* 10 (January 1935): 234–244.

Johnson, J. P. "Herbert Hoover and David Copperfield: A Tale of Two Childhoods." *Journal of Psychohistory* 7 (1980): 467–475.

———. "Herbert Hoover: The Orphan As Children's Friend." *Prologue* 12 (1980): 193–206.

Jones, B. C. "Nullification and Prohibition, 1920–1933." *Social Science Quarterly* 44 (March 1964): 389–398.

Kaiser, F. M. "Origins of Secret Service Protection of the President: Personal, Interagency, and Institutional Conflict," *Presidential Studies Quarterly* 18 (Winter 1988): 101–128.

Kane, F. F. "The Challenge of the Wickersham Deportations Report." *Journal of Criminal Law and Criminology* 23 (November-December 1932): 575–613.

Karl, B. D. "Presidential Planning and Social Science Research: Mr. Hoover's Experts." *Perspectives in American History* 3 (1969): 347–409.

Kauper, P. G. "Judicial Examination of the Accused—A Remedy for the Third Degree." *Michigan Law Review* 30 (June 1932): 1224–1255.

Kehl, J. A. "Defender of the Faith: Orphan Annie and the Conservative Tradition." *South Atlantic Quarterly* 59 (1960): 192–203.

Kelsey, C. "Immigration and Crime." *Annals of the American Academy of Political and Social Science* 214 (May 1926): 165–174.

Killigrew, J. W. "The Army and the Bonus Incident." *Military Affairs* 26 (Summer 1962): 21–33.

Kollock, W. "The Story of a Friendship: Mark Sullivan and Herbert Hoover." *Pacific History Review* 18 (1974): 31–48.

Knodt, Ellen A. "The American Criminal: The Quintessential Self-Made Man." *Journal of American Culture* 2 (1979): 30–41.

Lambert, R. "Hoover and the Red Cross in the Arkansas Drought of 1930." *Arkansas Historical Quarterly* 29 (1970): 3–19.

Langeluttig, A. "Federal Police." *Annals of the American Academy of Political and Social Science* 235 (November 1929): 41–54.

Landesco, J. "Gang Life and Organized Crime in Chicago." *American Bar Association Report* 55 (1930): 579–593.

———. "Prohibition and Crime." *Annals of the American Academy of Political and Social Science* 163 (September 1932): 120–129.

———. "Chicago's Criminal Underworld of the 80's and 90's." *Journal of Criminal Law and Criminology* 25 (March-April 1935): 928–940.

———. "The Woman and the Underworld." *Journal of Criminal Law and Criminology* 26 (March 1936): 901–912.

Lashly, A. V. "The Illinois Crime Survey." *Journal of Criminal Law and Criminology* 20 (February 1930): 588–605.

Lawes, L. E. "Dealing with Criminals." *North American Review* 225 (March 1928): 321–330.

Lee, D. D. "The Politics of Less: The Trials of Herbert Hoover and Jimmy Carter." *Presidential Studies Quarterly* 13 (Spring 1983): 305–312.

———. "Herbert Hoover and the Development of Commercial Aviation, 1921–1926." *Business History Review* 58 (1984): 78–102.

Lehr, M. A. "The Law of Searches and Seizures Incident to the Enforcement of Amendment 18 to the United States Constitution." *Tennessee Law Review* 7 (February 1929): 84–106.

Lembke, F. T. "Law Enforcement." *Bar Briefs* (State Bar Association of North Dakota) 5 (March 1929): 211–212.

Lindsey, E. "Legislation on Crime in Twenty-Five Years." *Journal of Criminal Law and Criminology* 24 (May-June 1933): 109–117.

Link, A. S. "What Happened to the Progressive Movement in the 1920's?" *American Historical Review* 64 (July 1959): 833–851.

Liss, J., and S. Schlossman. "The Contours of Crime Prevention in August Vollmer's Berkeley." *Research in Law, Deviance and Social Control* 6 (1984): 79–107.

Lodge, A. "What Al Capone Started." *Journal of Accountancy* 32 (November 1985): 32.

Loesch, F. J. "The Criminal and His Allies." *Nebraska Law Bulletin* 9 (July 1930): 88–96.

Lowden, F. O. "Criminal Statistics and Identification of Criminals." *Journal of Criminal Law and Criminology* 19 (May 1928): 36–48.

MacCormick, A. H. "Rehabilitation through Books." *Journal of Adult Education* 3 (October 1931): 433–437.

———. "The Selection and Training of Institution Personnel." *American*

Prison Association Proceedings 63 (1933): 237–238.

Maddox, R. J. "Rum, Romanticism, and Tammany Hall." *American History Illustrated* 3 (1968): 20–27.

Maxwell, R. S. "The Progressive Bridge: Reform Sentiment in the United States between the New Freedom and the New Deal." *Indiana Magazine of History* 63 (June 1967): 83–102.

McCaffrey, G. H. "The Police and the Administration of Justice." *Annals of the American Academy of Political and Social Science* 52 (March 1914): 56–60.

McCarthy, G. M. "Smith vs. Hoover: The Politics of Race in West Tennessee." *Phylon* 39 (1978): 154–168.

McGuire, O. R. "The Crusading Spirit—Mabel Walker Willebrandt." *Case & Comment* 32 (June-August 1926): 73–74, 96.

McNulty, W. J. "Drug Smuggling from Canada." *Current History Magazine* (October 1924): 93–95.

Mead, B. "Progress and Results of the Federal Census of Prisoners in the United States." *American Prison Association Proceedings* 54 (1929): 168–176.

Merriam, C. E. "The Police, Crime and Politics." *Annals of the American Academy of Political and Social Science* 235 (November 1929): 115–120.

Miller, J. "Public Opinion and Crime." *South Atlantic Quarterly* 30 (April 1931): 141–154.

Mitchell, J. G. "Said Chicago's Al Capone: 'I Give the Public What the Public Wants. . . .'" *American Heritage* 30 (1979): 82–93.

Mitchell, W. D. "Appointment of Federal Judges." *Minnesota Law Review* 16 (December 1931): 105–117.

Mohler, H. C. "Convict Labor Policies." *Journal of Criminal Law and Criminology* 15 (February 1925): 530–597.

Moley, R. "Politics and Crime." *Annals of the American Academy of Political and Social Science* 214 (May 1926): 78–84.

———. "Some Tendencies in Criminal Law Administration." *Political Science Quarterly* 42 (December 1927): 497–523.

———. "The Collection of Criminal Statistics in the United States." *Michigan Law Review* 26 (May 1928): 747–762.

———. "Crime As a Profession." *Current History* 30 (September 1929): 999–1006.

Monkkonen, E. H. "Systematic Criminal Justice History: Some Suggestions." *Journal of Interdisciplinary History* 9 (Winter 1979): 451–464.

———. "The Organized Response to Crime in Nineteenth- and Twentieth-Century America." *Journal of Interdisciplinary History* 14 (Summer 1983): 113–128.

Moore, J. R. "The United States Probation System." *Journal of Criminal Law and Criminology* 23 (November-December 1932): 638–648.

Morse, W. L. "Hoover Crime Commission." *Oregon Law Review* 9 (December 1929): 56.

———. "The Social Scientist and the Criminal Law." *Commonwealth Review* 12 (March 1930): 3–10.

Morse, W. L., and R. Moley. "Crime Commissions As Aids in the Legal-Social

Field." *Annals of the American Academy of Political and Social Science* 145 (September 1929): 68–79.

Morse, W. L., and R. H. Beattie. "Survey of the Administration of Justice in Oregon." *Commonwealth Review* 12 (January 1931): 329–372.

Munro, D. G. "The American Withdrawal from Haiti, 1929-1934." Hispanic *American Historical Review* 49 (1969): 1–26.

Munroe, W. B. "Campaign in Retrospect." *Yale Review* 28 (December 1928): 246–261.

Murray, L. L. "Andrew W. Mellon, the Reluctant Candidate." *Pennsylvania Magazine of History and Biography* 97 (1973): 511–531.

Murray, V. "The Relation of Prostitution to Economic Conditions." *Journal of Social Hygiene* 18 (June 1932): 314–321.

Nash, G. H. "The Social Philosophy of Herbert Hoover." *Annals of Iowa* 45 (1980): 478–496.

Nickel, S. "The Real Elliot Ness." *American History Illustrated* 22 (October 1987): 42ff.

Noggle, B. "The Twenties: A New Historiographical Frontier." *Journal of American History* 53 (September 1966): 299–314.

Ogburn, W. F., and N. S. Talbot. "A Measurement of the Factors in the Presidential Election of 1928." *Social Forces* 8 (December 1929): 175–183.

Ogden, J. M. "Attitude of the Indiana Bar Towards the Crime Situation." *Indiana Law Journal* 6 (October 1930): 3–15.

Olson, J. S. "Herbert Hoover and 'War' on the Depression." *Palimpsest* 54 (1973): 26–31.

———. "The Philosophy of Herbert Hoover: A Contemporary Perspective." *Annals of Iowa* 43 (1976): 181–191.

Olssen, E. "The Progressive Group in Congress, 1922-1929." *Historian* 42 (February 1980): 244–261.

O'Reilly, K. "Herbert Hoover and the FBI." *Annals of Iowa* 47 (1983): 46–63.

Page, J. A. "Organized Crime and Suggested Remedies." *Missouri Bar Journal* 1 (May 1930): 5.

Peterson, V. W. "Chicago: Shades of Capone." *Annals of the American Academy of Political and Social Science* 347 (1963): 30–39.

Pfiffner, J. M. "Activities and Results of Crime Surveys." *American Political Science Review* 23 (November 1929): 930–955.

Pigeon, H. D. "Woman's Era in the Police Department." *Annals of the American Academy of Political and Social Science* 143 (May 1929): 249–254.

Pound, R. "The Causes of Popular Dissatisfaction with the Administration of Justice." *American Bar Association Report* 29 (1906): 395–417.

———. "What Can Law Schools Do for Criminal Justice?" *Iowa Law Review* 12 (February 1927): 105–113.

Pusey, M. J. "The Nomination of Charles Evans Hughes as Chief Justice." *Supreme Court Historical Society Yearbook* (1982): 95–99.

Ratcliffe, S. K. "Triumph of Herbert Hoover." *Contemporary Review* 134 (December 1928): 689–697.

Rinn, F. J. "President Hoover's Bad Press." *San Jose Studies* 1 (1975): 32–44.

Robbins, W. G. "Herbert Hoover's Indian Reformers under Attack: The Failures of Administrative Reform." *Mid-America* 63 (1981): 157–170.

Robinson, L. N. "History of Criminal Statistics, 1908–1933." *Journal of Criminal Law and Criminology* 24 (May-June 1933): 125–139.

Roosevelt, F. D. "States Should Solve Crime Problems." *New York State Bar Association Bulletin* (October 1929): 333–338.

Rosenberry, M. B. "Upholding the Law and Administering Justice." *Wisconsin Law Review* 4 (July 1927): 209–216.

Rusnak, R. J. "Andrew W. Mellon: Reluctant Kingmaker." *Presidential Studies Quarterly* 13 (Spring 1983): 269–278.

Schade, T. "Prison Officer Training in the United States: The Legacy of Jessie O. Stutsman." *Federal Probation* 50 (December 1986): 40–46.

Schofield, K. "The Public Image of Herbert Hoover in the 1928 Campaign." *Mid-America* 51 (1969): 278–293.

Sears, K. C. "Appointment of Federal District Judges." *Illinois Law Review* 25 (May 1930): 54–75.

Sellin, T. "The Negro Criminal." *Annals of the American Academy of Political and Social Science* 140 (November 1928): 52–64.

———. "The Basis of a Crime Index." *Journal of Criminal Law and Criminology* 22 (September 1931): 326–356.

Shalloo, J. P. "The Private Police of Pennsylvania." *Annals of the American Academy of Political and Social Science* 235 (November, 1929): 55–62.

Sherman, J. S., J. Christensen, and J. Henderson. "Reorganized Crime: The Creation of the Uniform Crime Reports." *Research in Law, Deviance and Social Control* 4 (1982): 3–52.

Smith, B. "Municipal Police Administration." *Annals of the American Academy of Political and Social Science* 235 (November 1929): 1–27.

Stutsman, J. O. "A Uniform, a Club and a Gun; Or a Profession." *Prison Journal* 11 (1931): 4–11.

———. "The Prison Staff." *Annals of the American Academy of Political and Social Science* 157 (September 1931): 62–71.

Sullivan, E. D. "I Know You Al." *North American Review* 228 (September 1929): 257–264.

Sutherland, E. H. "Murder and the Death Penalty." *Journal of Criminal Law and Criminology* 15 (1925): 522–529.

———. "Crime and the Conflict Process." *Journal of Juvenile Research* 13 (January 1929): 38–48.

———. "The Person Versus the Act in Criminology." *Cornell Law Quarterly* 14 (February 1929): 159–167.

———. "The Prison as a Criminological Laboratory." *Annals of the American Academy of Political and Social Science* 157 (September 1931): 1–6.

———. "Social Process in Behavior Problems." *Publications of the American Sociological Society* 26 (1932): 55–61.

Swanson, J. A. "Progress in Administration of Criminal Law." *Illinois State Bar Association Proceedings* (1931): 308–318.

Tarter, B. "'All Men Are Equal Before Fishes': Herbert Hoover's Camp on the Rapidan." *Virginia Cavalcade* 30 (1981): 156–165.

Van Waters, M. "The Socialization of Juvenile Court Procedure." *Journal of Criminal Law and Criminology* 13 (May 1922): 64–69.

Vivian, J. F., and J. H. Vivian. "The Bonus March of 1932: The Role of General George Van Horn Moseley." *Wisconsin Magazine of History* 51 (1967): 26–36.

Vollmer, A. "The Prevention and Detection of Crime as Viewed by a Police Officer." *Annals of the American Academy of Political and Social Science* 214 (May 1926): 148–153.

——. "Police Organization and Administration." *Public Management* 10 (March 1928): 140–152.

——. "Coordinated Effort to Prevent Crime." *Journal of Criminal Law and Criminology* 19 (August 1928): 196–210.

——. "Police Progress in Practice and Theory." *American City* 43 (September 1930): 111–112.

——. "Police Progress in the Past Twenty-Five Years." *Journal of Criminal Law and Criminology* 24 (May-June 1933): 161–175.

Warner, S. B. "Crimes Known to the Police—An Index of Crime?" *Harvard Law Review* 45 (December 1931): 307–317.

——. "A Note on 'Crimes Known to the Police.'" *Harvard Law Review* 45 (January 1932): 533–534.

Warren, E. "Scope and Functions of State Bureau of Criminal Identification." *Peace Officers Association of California Proceedings* 9 (1929): 65–69.

Warren, F. H. "Crime—A Complex or a Process." *Notre Dame Lawyer* 4 (December 1928): 147–157.

Watson, R. L., Jr. "The Defeat of Judge Parker: A Study of Pressure Groups in Politics." *Mississippi Valley Historical Review* 50 (September 1963): 213–234.

Whitin, E. S. "A Plan for the Interstate Sale of Prison Products." *Annals of the American Academy of Political and Social Science* 214 (May 1926): 260–264.

Wickersham, G. W. "Shortcomings of the Administration of Justice—Causes and Remedies." *New York State Bar Association Bulletin* 2 (May 1930): 294–299.

——. "The Program of the Commission on Law Observance and Enforcement." *American Bar Association Journal* 16 (October 1930): 654–661.

——. "Prevention and Punishment of Crime: The Practice and the Theory." *American Prison Association Proceedings* 60 (1930): 110–117.

Wilcox, C. E. "Parole: Principles and Practice." *Journal of Criminal Law and Criminology* 20 (November 1929): 345–354.

Wilkerson, J. H. "The Challenge to the Courts." *United States Law Review* 66 (December 1932): 650–658.

Willebrandt, M. W. "The National Prohibition Act in Its Relation to Section 3450 P.S." *Case & Comment* 34 (1928): 3–10.

——. "Federal and State Control of Air Carriers by Certificates of Convenience and Necessity." *Journal of Air Law* 3 (April 1932): 159–166.

Willig, S. "Violation of Eighteenth Amendment and the Volstead Act as Elements of Crime in New York." *Cornell Law Quarterly* 12 (June 1927): 509–513.

Willing, J. K. "The Profession of Bootlegging." *Annals of the American Academy of Political and Social Science* 214 (May 1926): 40–48.

Wilson, J. R. M. "The Quaker and the Sword: Herbert Hoover's Relations with the Military." *Military Affairs* 38 (1974): 41–47.

Wilson, S. B. "The Crime Situation." *Minnesota Law Review* 12 (1927): 54–66.

Witmer, H. E. "The Development of Parole in the United States." *Social Forces* 4 (December 1925): 318–325.

Wolfe, S. M. "Is the Criminal Wholly to Blame?" *South Atlantic Quarterly* 31 (January 1932): 4–14.

Wood, A. E. "Program for Criminological Research." *American Journal of Sociology* 33 (November 1927): 431–443.

———. "Crime and Penology." *American Journal of Sociology* 36 (May 1931): 1017–1029.

Yankwich, L. R. "Some of the Social Phases of the Administration of Justice." *Southern California Law Review* 5 (February 1932): 189–208.

Youngquist, G. A. "Crime Prevention and Law Enforcement." *Bar Briefs* (State Bar Association of North Dakota) 6 (December 1929): 94–105.

Ziegler, R. H. "Labor, Progressivism, and Herbert Hoover in the 1920's." *Wisconsin Magazine of History* 58 (1975): 196–208.

Index

ABOUT THE AUTHOR

JAMES D. CALDER is Associate Professor of Criminal Justice in the Division of Social and Policy Sciences, The University of Texas at San Antonio. He has published extensively in the *Presidential Studies Quarterly, Crime, Law and Social Change,* and other scholarly journals.